TOWARDS A GODLESS DOMINION

MCGILL-QUEEN'S STUDIES IN THE HISTORY OF RELIGION
Volumes in this series have been supported by the Jackman Foundation of Toronto.

SERIES ONE   G.A. RAWLYK, EDITOR

1 Small Differences
Irish Catholics and Irish Protestants,
1815–1922
An International Perspective
Donald Harman Akenson

2 Two Worlds
The Protestant Culture of
Nineteenth-Century Ontario
William Westfall

3 An Evangelical Mind
Nathanael Burwash and the
Methodist Tradition in Canada,
1839–1918
Marguerite Van Die

4 The Dévotes
Women and Church in
Seventeenth-Century France
Elizabeth Rapley

5 The Evangelical Century
College and Creed in English Canada
from the Great Revival to the Great
Depression
Michael Gauvreau

6 The German Peasants' War and
Anabaptist Community of Goods
James M. Stayer

7 A World Mission
Canadian Protestantism and the Quest
for a New International Order,
1918–1939
Robert Wright

8 Serving the Present Age
Revivalism, Progressivism, and
the Methodist Tradition in Canada
Phyllis D. Airhart

9 A Sensitive Independence
Canadian Methodist Women
Missionaries in Canada and the Orient,
1881–1925
Rosemary R. Gagan

10 God's Peoples
Covenant and Land in South
Africa, Israel, and Ulster
Donald Harman Akenson

11 Creed and Culture
The Place of English-Speaking Catholics
in Canadian Society, 1750–1930
Edited by Terrence Murphy
and Gerald Stortz

12 Piety and Nationalism
Lay Voluntary Associations and
the Creation of an Irish-Catholic
Community in Toronto, 1850–1895
Brian P. Clarke

13 Amazing Grace
Studies in Evangelicalism in Australia,
Britain, Canada, and the United States
Edited by George Rawlyk
and Mark A. Noll

14 Children of Peace
W. John McIntyre

15 A Solitary Pillar
Montreal's Anglican Church
and the Quiet Revolution
Joan Marshall

16 Padres in No Man's Land
Canadian Chaplains and the Great War
Duff Crerar

17 Christian Ethics and Political Economy
in North America
A Critical Analysis
P. Travis Kroeker

18 Pilgrims in Lotus Land
Conservative Protestantism
in British Columbia,
1917–1981
Robert K. Burkinshaw

19 Through Sunshine and Shadow
The Woman's Christian
Temperance Union, Evangelicalism,
and Reform in Ontario,
1874–1930
Sharon Cook

20 Church, College, and Clergy
A History of Theological
Education at Knox College,
Toronto, 1844–1994
Brian J. Fraser

21 The Lord's Dominion
   The History of Canadian Methodism
   Neil Semple

22 A Full-Orbed Christianity
   The Protestant Churches and Social
   Welfare in Canada, 1900–1940
   Nancy Christie and Michael Gauvreau

23 Evangelism and Apostasy
   The Evolution and Impact
   of Evangelicals in Modern Mexico
   Kurt Bowen

24 The Chignecto Covenanters
   A Regional History of Reformed
   Presbyterianism in New Brunswick
   and Nova Scotia, 1827–1905
   Eldon Hay

25 Methodists and Women's
   Education in Ontario, 1836–1925
   Johanne Selles

26 Puritanism and Historical
   Controversy
   William Lamont

SERIES TWO   IN MEMORY OF GEORGE RAWLYK
DONALD HARMAN AKENSON, EDITOR

1 Marguerite Bourgeoys and Montreal,
  1640–1665
  Patricia Simpson

2 Aspects of the Canadian
  Evangelical Experience
  Edited by G.A. Rawlyk

3 Infinity, Faith, and Time
  Christian Humanism and
  Renaissance Literature
  John Spencer Hill

4 The Contribution of Presbyterianism
  to the Maritime Provinces of Canada
  *Edited by Charles H.H. Scobie
  and G.A. Rawlyk*

5 Labour, Love, and Prayer
  Female Piety in Ulster
  Religious Literature,
  1850–1914
  Andrea Ebel Brozyna

6 The Waning of the Green
  Catholics, the Irish, and Identity
  in Toronto, 1887–1922
  Mark G. McGowan

7 Religion and Nationality
  in Western Ukraine
  The Greek Catholic Church
  and the Ruthenian National
  Movement in Galicia,
  1867–1900
  John-Paul Himka

8 Good Citizens
  British Missionaries and
  Imperial States, 1870–1918
  *James G. Greenlee and
  Charles M. Johnston*

9 The Theology of the Oral Torah
  Revealing the Justice of God
  Jacob Neusner

10 Gentle Eminence
   A Life of Cardinal Flahiff
   P. Wallace Platt

11 Culture, Religion, and Demographic
   Behaviour
   Catholics and Lutherans in Alsace,
   1750–1870
   Kevin McQuillan

12 Between Damnation and Starvation
   Priests and Merchants
   in Newfoundland Politics,
   1745–1855
   John P. Greene

13 Martin Luther, German Saviour
   German Evangelical Theological
   Factions and the Interpretation
   of Luther, 1917–1933
   James M. Stayer

14 Modernity and the Dilemma
   of North American Anglican
   Identities, 1880–1950
   William H. Katerberg

15 The Methodist Church on
   the Prairies, 1896–1914
   George Emery

16 Christian Attitudes towards
   the State of Israel
   Paul Charles Merkley

17 A Social History of the Cloister
   Daily Life in the Teaching
   Monasteries of the Old Regime
   Elizabeth Rapley

18 Households of Faith
Family, Gender, and Community
in Canada, 1760–1969
Edited by Nancy Christie

19 Blood Ground
Colonialism, Missions, and
the Contest for Christianity
in the Cape Colony
and Britain, 1799–1853
Elizabeth Elbourne

20 A History of Canadian Catholics
Gallicanism, Romanism, and
Canadianism
Terence J. Fay

21 The View from Rome
Archbishop Stagni's 1915 Reports
on the Ontario Bilingual
Schools Question
*Edited and translated by
John Zucchi*

22 The Founding Moment
Church, Society, and the
Construction of Trinity College
William Westfall

23 The Holocaust, Israel, and
Canadian Protestant Churches
Haim Genizi

24 Governing Charities
Church and State in Toronto's
Catholic Archdiocese, 1850–1950
Paula Maurutto

25 Anglicans and the Atlantic World
High Churchmen, Evangelicals,
and the Quebec Connection
Richard W. Vaudry

26 Evangelicals and the
Continental Divide
The Conservative Protestant
Subculture in Canada and
the United States
Sam Reimer

27 Christians in a Secular World
The Canadian Experience
Kurt Bowen

28 Anatomy of a Seance
A History of Spirit
Communication
in Central Canada
Stan McMullin

29 With Skilful Hand
The Story of King David
David T. Barnard

30 Faithful Intellect
Samuel S. Nelles and
Victoria University
Neil Semple

31 W. Stanford Reid
An Evangelical Calvinist
in the Academy
Donald MacLeod

32 A Long Eclipse
The Liberal Protestant
Establishment and the Canadian
University, 1920–1970
Catherine Gidney

33 Forkhill Protestants and Forkhill
Catholics, 1787–1858
Kyla Madden

34 For Canada's Sake
Public Religion, Centennial
Celebrations, and the Re-making
of Canada in the 1960s
Gary R. Miedema

35 Revival in the City
The Impact of American
Evangelists in Canada, 1884–1914
Eric R. Crouse

36 The Lord for the Body
Religion, Medicine,
and Protestant Faith Healing
in Canada, 1880–1930
James Opp

37 Six Hundred Years of Reform
Bishops and the French Church,
1190–1789
*J. Michael Hayden and
Malcolm R. Greenshields*

38 The Missionary Oblate Sisters
Vision and Mission
Rosa Bruno-Jofré

39 Religion, Family, and Community
in Victorian Canada
The Colbys of Carrollcroft
Marguerite Van Die

40 Michael Power
The Struggle to Build the Catholic
Church on the Canadian Frontier
Mark G. McGowan

41 The Catholic Origins of Quebec's
   Quiet Revolution, 1931–1970
   Michael Gauvreau

42 Marguerite Bourgeoys and the
   Congregation of Notre Dame,
   1665–1700
   Patricia Simpson

43 To Heal a Fractured World
   The Ethics of Responsibility
   Jonathan Sacks

44 Revivalists
   Marketing the Gospel in
   English Canada, 1884–1957
   Kevin Kee

45 The Churches and Social Order
   in Nineteenth- and Twentieth-
   Century Canada
   *Edited by Michael Gauvreau
   and Ollivier Hubert*

46 Political Ecumenism
   Catholics, Jews, and Protestants in
   De Gaulle's Free France, 1940–1945
   Geoffrey Adams

47 From Quaker to Upper Canadian
   Faith and Community among
   Yonge Street Friends, 1801–1850
   Robynne Rogers Healey

48 The Congrégation de Notre-Dame,
   Superiors, and the Paradox of Power,
   1693–1796
   Colleen Gray

49 Canadian Pentecostalism
   Transition and Transformation
   Edited by Michael Wilkinson

50 A War with a Silver Lining
   Canadian Protestant Churches
   and the South African War,
   1899–1902
   Gordon L. Heath

51 In the Aftermath of Catastrophe
   Founding Judaism, 70 to 640
   Jacob Neusner

52 Imagining Holiness
   Classic Hasidic Tales in
   Modern Times
   Justin Jaron Lewis

53 Shouting, Embracing,
   and Dancing with Ecstasy
   The Growth of Methodism
   in Newfoundland, 1774–1874
   Calvin Hollett

54 Into Deep Waters
   Evangelical Spirituality and
   Maritime Calvinist Baptist
   Ministers, 1790–1855
   Daniel C. Goodwin

55 Vanguard of the New Age
   The Toronto Theosophical
   Society, 1891–1945
   Gillian McCann

56 A Commerce of Taste
   Church Architecture
   in Canada, 1867–1914
   Barry Magrill

57 The Big Picture
   The Antigonish Movement
   of Eastern Nova Scotia
   Santo Dodaro and Leonard Pluta

58 My Heart's Best Wishes for You
   A Biography of Archbishop
   John Walsh
   John P. Comiskey

59 The Covenanters in Canada
   Reformed Presbyterianism
   from 1820 to 2012
   Eldon Hay

60 The Guardianship of Best Interests
   Institutional Care for the Children
   of the Poor in Halifax, 1850–1960
   Renée N. Lafferty

61 In Defence of the Faith
   Joaquim Marques de Araújo,
   a Brazilian Comissário in the
   Age of Inquisitional Decline
   James E. Wadsworth

62 Contesting the Moral High Ground
   Popular Moralists in
   Mid-Twentieth-Century Britain
   Paul T. Phillips

63 The Catholicisms of Coutances
   Varieties of Religion in Early
   Modern France, 1350–1789
   J. Michael Hayden

64 After Evangelicalism
　The Sixties and the United
　Church of Canada
　Kevin N. Flatt

65 The Return of Ancestral Gods
　Modern Ukrainian Paganism
　as an Alternative Vision
　for a Nation
　Mariya Lesiv

66 Transatlantic Methodists
　British Wesleyanism and
　the Formation of an Evangelical
　Culture in Nineteenth-Century
　Ontario and Quebec
　Todd Webb

67 A Church with the Soul of a Nation
　Making and Remaking the United
　Church of Canada
　Phyllis D. Airhart

68 Fighting over God
　A Legal and Political History
　of Religious Freedom in Canada
　Janet Epp Buckingham

69 From India to Israel
　Identity, Immigration, and the Struggle
　for Religious Equality
　Joseph Hodes

70 Becoming Holy in Early Canada
　Timothy G. Pearson

71 The Cistercian Arts
　From the 12th to the 21st Century
　*Edited by Terryl N. Kinder
　and Roberto Cassanelli*

72 The Canny Scot Archbishop James
　Morrison of Antigonish
　Peter Ludlow

73 Religion and Greater Ireland
　Christianity and Irish Global
　Networks, 1750–1950
　*Edited by Colin Barr and
　Hilary M. Carey*

74 The Invisible Irish
　Finding Protestants in the Nineteenth-
　Century Migrations to America
　Rankin Sherling

75 Beating against the Wind
　Popular Opposition to Bishop Feild
　and Tractarianism in Newfoundland
　and Labrador, 1844–1876
　Calvin Hollett

76 The Body or the Soul?
　Religion and Culture in a Quebec
　Parish, 1736–1901
　Frank A. Abbott

77 Saving Germany
　North American Protestants
　and Christian Mission to West
　Germany, 1945–1974
　James C. Enns

78 The Imperial Irish
　Canada's Irish Catholics Fight
　the Great War, 1914–1918
　Mark G. McGowan

79 Into Silence and Servitude
　How American Girls Became Nuns,
　1945–1965
　Brian Titley

80 Boundless Dominion
　Providence, Politics, and the Early
　Canadian Presbyterian Worldview
　Denis McKim

81 Faithful Encounters
　Authorities and American
　Missionaries in the Ottoman Empire
　Emrah Şahin

82 Beyond the Noise of Solemn
　Assemblies
　The Protestant Ethic and the Quest
　for Social Justice in Canada
　Richard Allen

83 Not Quite Us
　Anti-Catholic Thought in English
　Canada since 1900
　Kevin P. Anderson

84 Scandal in the Parish
　Priests and Parishioners Behaving
　Badly in Eighteenth-Century France
　Karen E. Carter

85 Ordinary Saints
　Women, Work, and Faith
　in Newfoundland
　Bonnie Morgan

86 Patriot and Priest
　Jean-Baptiste Volfius and
　the Constitutional Church
　in the Côte-d'Or
　Annette Chapman-Adisho

87 A.B. Simpson and the Making
　of Modern Evangelicalism
　Daryn Henry

88 The Uncomfortable Pew
   Christianity and the New Left
   in Toronto
   Bruce Douville

89 Berruyer's Bible
   Public Opinion and the Politics of
   Enlightenment Catholicism in France
   Daniel J. Watkins

90 Communities of the Soul
   A Short History of Religion
   in Puerto Rico
   José E. Igartua

91 Callings and Consequences
   The Making of Catholic Vocational
   Culture in Early Modern France
   Christopher J. Lane

92 Religion, Ethnonationalism,
   and Antisemitism in the Era
   of the Two World Wars
   *Edited by Kevin P. Spicer
   and Rebecca Carter-Chand*

93 Water from Dragon's Well
   The History of a Korean-Canadian
   Church Relationship
   David Kim-Cragg

94 Protestant Liberty
   Religion and the Making of
   Canadian Liberalism, 1828–78
   James M. Forbes

95 To Make a Village Soviet
   Jehovah's Witnesses and the
   Transformation of a Postwar
   Ukrainian Borderland
   Emily B. Baran

96 Disciples of Antigonish
   Catholics in Nova Scotia,
   1880–1960
   Peter Ludlow

97 A Black American Missionary
   in Canada
   The Life and Letters of Lewis
   Champion Chambers
   Edited by Hilary Bates Neary

98 A People's Reformation
   Building the English Church
   in the Elizabethan Parish
   Lucy Moffat Kaufman

99 Towards a Godless Dominion
   Unbelief in Interwar Canada
   Elliot Hanowski

Towards a Godless Dominion

Unbelief in Interwar Canada

ELLIOT HANOWSKI

McGill-Queen's University Press
Montreal & Kingston · London · Chicago

© McGill-Queen's University Press 2023

ISBN 978-0-2280-1882-7 (cloth)
ISBN 978-0-2280-1883-4 (paper)
ISBN 978-0-2280-1956-5 (ePDF)
ISBN 978-0-2280-1957-2 (ePUB)

Legal deposit fourth quarter 2023
Bibliothèque nationale du Québec

Printed in Canada on acid-free paper that is 100% ancient forest free (100% post-consumer recycled), processed chlorine free

This book has been published with the help of a grant from the Canadian Federation for the Humanities and Social Sciences, through the Awards to Scholarly Publications Program, using funds provided by the Social Sciences and Humanities Research Council of Canada.

We acknowledge the support of the Canada Council for the Arts.

Nous remercions le Conseil des arts du Canada de son soutien.

Library and Archives Canada Cataloguing in Publication

Title: Towards a godless dominion: unbelief in interwar Canada / Elliot Hanowski.

Names: Hanowski, Elliot, author.

Series: McGill-Queen's studies in the history of religion. Series two; 99.

Description: Series statement: McGill-Queen's studies in the history of religion. Series two; 99 | Includes bibliographical references and index.

Identifiers: Canadiana (print) 20230222331 | Canadiana (ebook) 20230222382 | ISBN 9780228018827 (cloth) | ISBN 9780228018834 (paper) | ISBN 9780228019572 (ePUB) | ISBN 9780228019565 (ePDF)

Subjects: LCSH: Irreligion—Canada—History—20th century. | LCSH: Religious tolerance—Canada—History—20th century. | LCSH: Christianity and atheism—History—20th century. | LCSH: Atheists—Canada—History—20th century. | LCSH: Religion and politics—Canada—History—20th century.

Classification: LCC BL2530.C3 H36 2023 | DDC 200.971—dc23

This book was typeset by Marquis Interscript in 10.5/13 Sabon.

Contents

Figures xiii

Acknowledgments and Dedication xv

Abbreviations xvii

1 Introduction 3

2 Canada's Professional Atheist: Marshall Gauvin in Winnipeg, 1926–1940 37

3 The Winnipeg Rationalist Society 74

4 The Sterry Trial and the Debate over Blasphemy 97

5 Unbelief in Toronto the Good 123

6 "Je suis un athée fieffé": Militant Unbelief in Interwar Montreal 167

7 Unbelief on the Coasts 199

8 Conclusion 220

Notes 227

Bibliography 303

Index 325

Figures

2.1 Marshall Gauvin, early 1920s, University of Manitoba Archives and Special Collections, Marshall Gauvin fonds, PC 36, Box 1, Folder 7, Item 8   41

2.2 Marshall Gauvin, c. 1930s, University of Manitoba Archives and Special Collections, Marshall Gauvin fonds, PC 36, Box 1, Folder 3, Item 3   45

3.1 Birth year of Winnipeg Rationalist Society supporters, with data derived from Marshall Gauvin fonds, censuses, and army attestation papers   79

3.2 Urban ethnicity in Manitoba, 1931, with data derived from *Seventh Census of Canada, 1931,* vol. 2, *Population by Areas* (Ottawa: J.O. Patenaude, King's Printer, 1933), 500–3   83

3.3 Ethnicity of Winnipeg Rationalist Society supporters, with data derived from Marshall Gauvin fonds and censuses   83

3.4 Religious denominations of Winnipeg Rationalist supporters, with data derived from Marshall Gauvin fonds, censuses, and army attestation papers   87

3.5 Employment of male supporters of Winnipeg Rationalist Society, with data derived from Marshall Gauvin fonds and censuses   89

4.1 Ernest V. Sterry, 1927, from *Toronto Star,* 15 January 1927   101

4.2 E. Lionel Cross, 1930, from *Toronto Star,* 24 March 1930, 3   103

4.3 Courtroom sketch of Sterry and Cross, 1927, from *Toronto Star*, 25 January 1927, section 2, 1   108
5.1 William Styles and Bertram Leavens, 1927, from *Toronto Star*, 20 January 1927, 17   128
6.1 Albert Saint-Martin, 1905, from *Le Passe-Temps*, 1905, and accessed through Wikimedia Commons   174
7.1 William J. Curry, 1925, from *Canadian Labor Advocate*, 16 October 1925, 1   205

Acknowledgments and Dedication

Without the support, assistance, and encouragement of many more people than I can mention here, this book would not have been possible. Historical scholarship, although at times solitary, is ultimately a collective effort (though all errors and omissions are my own!). I would like to express my gratitude to the following people.

My MA and PhD supervisor, Ian McKay, who first interested me in the topic of Canadian unbelief and suggested I look at the Gauvin collection. I benefitted enormously from his counsel and kind encouragement, and his intellectual rigour and tireless work ethic offered much inspiration.

Three other members of my committee: Marguerite Van Die, for encouraging me to pursue the study of religious history, and offering rigorous criticism and generous support; Peter Campbell, for reading early drafts and providing helpful feedback; and Lynne Marks, for likewise commenting on early drafts and allowing me to read her own work-in-progress on unbelief in British Columbia.

A scholar whom I've never met in person: Susan Lewthwaite. When she learned of my interest in this area she generously shared with me the results of her research on the Rationalist Society of Canada. She also read drafts of the Toronto chapters and offered helpful comments and encouragement.

Two of my professors at the University of Winnipeg who helped lay the groundwork for this project: Nolan Reilly introduced me to the fascinating history of the Canadian left, and Garin Burbank supported my interest in the history of religion. Both acted as mentors and encouraged me to pursue graduate studies (while also warning me of pitfalls).

My fellow graduate students at Queen's who helped me through the PhD program, especially Patrick Corbeil, Lorne Beswick, and Christine Elie. Patrick, a fellow scholar of unbelief, enthusiastically discussed this history and theory with me over dinners and drinks, as well as during squash matches and board games. Lorne's friendship and unfailing humour helped minimize the sanity damage caused by grad school. Christine, who was also researching Albert Saint-Martin, urged me include a chapter on Montreal, shared her own findings, and kindly helped me tidy up my French translations.

My friend Chris Douglas, for reading a draft and offering helpful feedback from an educated layperson's perspective.

My fellow members of the International Society for Historians of Atheism, Secularism, and Humanism, who offered a supportive community for learning, discussion, and debate on unbelief, especially Nathan Alexander, Elizabeth Lutgendorff, Anton Jansson, and Tina Block.

Kyla Madden and the other editors at McGill-Queen's University Press, whose patient guidance and assistance made this publication possible. As well, I'd like to thank the anonymous reviewers enlisted by MQUP, who each read two drafts of the manuscript and offered valuable suggestions.

Many helpful librarians and archivists at Queen's University, the University of Manitoba, the University of Winnipeg, the University of Victoria, the United Church of Canada Archives in Toronto, Library and Archives Canada, the Archives of Manitoba, the Archives of Ontario, the Nova Scotia Archives, and Bibliothèque et Archives nationales du Québec.

The organizations that asked me to present on this topic over the years, particularly the atheist and humanist groups that are today's descendants of the groups I researched. Being able to talk about these ideas with people outside the academy helped me clarify my thoughts and see the subject with fresh eyes.

Jo Ozubko and Rick Petit for all their support, particularly with travel expenses, and Rob Person and Treena Klagenberg, for providing me with writing space in Winnipeg for over a year.

Most of all I want to express my love and gratitude to Melly Ozubko, my wife, who not only read many drafts and offered valuable feedback but gave unflagging love and support at every step of the process. This book is dedicated to her.

Abbreviations

4A (or AAAA)	American Association for the Advancement of Atheism
ACJC	Association catholique de la Jeunesse canadienne-française
AH	Association humanitaire
CCC	Canadian Christian Crusade (Against Atheism)
CCF	Co-operative Commonwealth Federation
CEF	Canadian Expeditionary Force
CLDL	Canadian Labour Defence League
CLP	Canadian Labor Party
CPC	Communist Party of Canada
CPR	Canadian Pacific Railway
CSS	Canadian Secular Society
ESP	École sociale populaire
IODE	Imperial Order of the Daughters of the Empire
JOC	Jeunesse ouvrière catholique
LAC	Library and Archives Canada
MP	Member of Parliament
MPP	Member of Provincial Parliament
NSS	National Secular Society
OBU	One Big Union
UO	Université ouvrière
RAF	Royal Air Force
RCMP	Royal Canadian Mounted Police
RSC	Rationalist Society of Canada
TLC	Trades and Labour Council
WPC	Workers' Party of Canada

TOWARDS A GODLESS DOMINION

1

Introduction

In the early twenty-first century, atheism became a hot topic. So-called New Atheists, reacting against fundamentalist extremism and the continued vigour of religious politics in some parts of the world, were popularizing an especially irreverent and aggressive criticism of religion. Belief, they claimed, was a delusion; they urged a campaign of secular enlightenment.

But a backward look into recent history shows that, although their social context has greatly changed over the last century, such attitudes are not new. A reader of Toronto's *Christian Inquirer* in 1926, for instance, would have encountered the following: "This touchy Jehovah whom the deluded superstitionists claim to be the Creator of the whole universe, makes one feel utter contempt for the preachers and unfeigned pity for the mental state of those who can retain a serious countenance as they peruse the stories of His peculiar whims, freaks and fancies, and His frenzied megalomaniac boastings."[1] This provocation would not have seemed unusual coming from a twenty-first-century New Atheist writer such as Richard Dawkins or Christopher Hitchens. But in 1927, rather than being offered a publishing deal as they were, the author of these words was convicted of the crime of blasphemous libel. He was sentenced to sixty days on a jail farm, and an order was issued for his deportation from Canada.

Even in the 1920s, however, such rhetoric was not universally unpopular in Canada. In 1929 a debate between a fundamentalist and an atheist living in Winnipeg drew an impassioned audience that numbered over three thousand. A reporter compared the mood at the event to that of a hockey game, and at the end the atheist was overwhelmingly voted the winner.[2] In Montreal, meanwhile, a radical group offered free weekly lectures, many of them vehemently anti-religious. One attendee recalled: "When you went up the stairs to the hall, you had to pass a huge picture of Jesus Christ with a knife in his hand dripping from the blood of the worker he was stabbing. And thousands of French-Canadian workers tipped their hats to that picture."[3] Despite stiff official opposition, hostility to Christianity was evident in a number of different spaces in the interwar period. It was played out in lecture halls, newspaper letter columns, the streets and parks of major cities, books written by disillusioned veterans, and elsewhere.

These challenges to the dominant religion of the day in Canada between 1920 and 1940 are the subject of this study. It examines the organized activities of anti-religious skeptics as well as contemporary reactions to those activities. The book focuses primarily on groups in Winnipeg, Toronto, and Montreal that promoted a strictly secular view of life, and considers the religious contexts in which such groups operated.

Why look at this subject now? The high profile of irreligion in the twenty-first century has led a variety of scholars to turn their attention to its intellectual origins and social context.[4] Recent New Atheist campaigns were possible because religion had already lost a great deal of its former strength in many Western countries. In 2019 over a quarter of all Canadian citizens reported that they had no religious affiliation.[5] This did not mean that they were all rigorous, thoroughgoing skeptics, but the fact that they felt free to reject religious labels speaks to the weakened social presence of organized religion. This reality raises questions about the past. What are the roots of contemporary unbelief in Canada? What were the consequences of being an open unbeliever a century ago? What was the experience of those who were non-religious in a devout society? What issues or causes motivated unbelievers? What was their class, their gender, their ethnicity? Did they pursue a political agenda? These are the sorts of questions I explore in the course of the chapters that follow.

HISTORICAL ROOTS AND THEORETICAL FRAMEWORKS

Opposition to religion has its own historical tradition, which dates back further than Canada's existence as a nation. Thus, to understand Canadian unbelief we need to begin outside its borders. Also, to avoid confusion, we need at the outset to define our terms and theoretical framework. The tradition of modern irreligion we will be examining emerged in the eighteenth century out of the radical wing of the European Enlightenment. Promoted to popular audiences by writers such as Voltaire and Thomas Paine, this tradition spread throughout the Western world over the next three centuries. Its adherents argued that Christianity was irrational, immoral, and oppressive, that reason and science would free humanity from such superstition, and that a secular society would usher in a golden age of progress and justice.

The names given to this tradition over the past few centuries were various: deism, atheism, agnosticism, infidelity, secularism, rationalism, humanism, and freethought. Some distinctions can be briefly drawn among these different terms, although observers and participants often used them interchangeably. "Deists" (including Voltaire and Paine) believed in a Supreme Being but rejected miracles and revealed religion as baseless supersitition. "Atheism," disbelief in a god or gods, originated as an accusation used by believers against one another, but was eventually reappropriated and adopted by unbelievers. The term "agnostic," coined by Thomas Henry Huxley in 1869, suggested that true knowledge of religious or metaphysical matters was impossible for human beings. To be a secularist or a freethinker spoke to one's attitude to the socio-cultural reality of religion. Such people were not always strict atheists (some were deists) but they were strongly opposed to established churches, creeds, and religious tests, and struggled to reduce the influence of religion on society.

"Secularism" was primarily a British term, while skeptics in America usually referred to themselves as freethinkers. "Rationalism," as the name implies, tended to have a more intellectual focus, emphasizing the triumph of reason and verifiable ideas over superstition and blind faith. "Humanism" placed its emphasis on what religious skeptics *did* believe in, namely, humanity's life, thought, and well-being, and the term began to be used in the 1930s in the sense of "secular humanism." Atheism, or a less confrontational agnosticism, was of course the popular intellectual position for most of the people belonging to these movements, but not for all.[6]

In this study I use "unbelief" and "unbelievers" as umbrella terms for the variety of labels mentioned above. The term "unbelief" offers the benefit of not having been monopolized by any particular group, and for this reason it has gradually been adopted by scholars in this field.[7] Unfortunately it emphasizes what such people did *not* do – that is, hold religious beliefs. As we shall see, some unbelievers did define themselves in negative terms; but to avoid such connotations of the word "unbelief," I refer to unbelievers wherever possible by the labels they themselves used: as rationalists, humanists, or secularists, for instance.

With that in mind, let me say at the outset that there is no single "unbelief," no universal secularity to which the deconverted naturally return or in which the unevangelized naturally dwell. The thoughts and actions of historical unbelievers bear resemblances to those of modern secularists, but they were not "ahead of their time."[8] Every form of unbelief or heterodoxy is a product of its own time and place, belonging to its own local intellectual traditions and social contexts. This perspective applies equally to unbelief in twentieth-century Canada. People's quarrels with religion were invariably shaped by the language they spoke, the region they lived in, and the latest news from the United States and Europe. The challenge is to describe irreligion both in terms of its traditions and lineage and also in terms of its unique historical moment.

Further in this vein, this study draws on the approach laid out in Laura Schwartz's work on nineteenth-century British secularist women, *Infidel Feminism*. Schwartz acknowledges that the attitudes of the women she researched were profoundly shaped by their (typically evangelical) Christian origins. Secularism always existed in tension, dialogue, and conflict with contemporary religion. At the same time, Schwartz seeks to avoid collapsing secularism into a simple epiphenomenon of Christian society. The movement had its own internal logic. It grew mainly from Christian roots, yes, but it developed into something new. Schwartz argues against the "subtraction" metaphor, which sees secularity simply as the natural result when layers of religion are stripped away from humanity. Scholars need to "leave behind a definition that treats secularity as a mental stance that is free from or untainted by religion and look instead at what positively constitutes a stance of 'irreligion' or self-proclaimed Secularism."[9]

Similarly, I suggest that rationalists, humanists, and anticlerical activists in Canada were engaged in a constructive project: they were trying to build something new. They were not just Christians who had lost their way, but neither had they simply shed their illusions and returned to some generic, default state of secularity. They were attempting to advance a certain view of the world, one profoundly shaped by their own time and place, to be sure, but which looked forward to new human possibilities. Their stories deserve to be told.

That said, I do not want to simply add unbelievers to the historiography of Canadian religion by treating them as just one more religious minority. Learning about unbelief should also tell us something about the broader outlines of belief, its power, and its limitations. It is for this reason that the following study devotes space to the religious contexts in which Canadian irreligion existed.

To speak of secularists or secularism is, however, not the same thing as speaking about secularization. The latter concept usually relates to broad social forces and society as a whole. The growth of religious indifference is a separate story from that of unbelief; the unbelievers I discuss were by no means indifferent about religion. This study does not enter directly into the extremely complex debates surrounding secularization theory. By unearthing the lives of Canadians who dreamt of and worked for a secular world, however, I do aspire to shed a little more light on these broader questions.

Clearly a post-Christian life was possible for some members of Canadian society. At the same time, the fact that they had to struggle demonstrates the continuing power and relevance of religion in Canada; in the backlash that many unbelievers faced, we find evidence of the resilience of the religious frameworks they confronted. Thus the following study assumes roughly the picture of gradual secularization that British historian Hugh McLeod has sketched out.[10] McLeod acknowledges the position of scholars like Callum Brown, who contend that the 1960s marked a radical disjuncture in the religious world of most Western countries. Nevertheless, McLeod also points to a long and slow weakening of Christianity's public and cultural presence, as unbelief slowly became more acceptable for various segments of society, before becoming a possibility for the majority in the 1960s. "New ways of living" blossomed in that decade, but the preconditions had been slowly evolving for more than a century.

When explaining secularization, McLeod also uses the concept of "Christendom," an idea that is helpful in understanding the Canadian story. He defines Christendom as "a society where there were close ties between the leaders of the church and those in positions of secular power, where the laws purported to be based on Christian principles, and where, apart from certain clearly defined outsider communities, every member of the society was assumed to be Christian."[11] The decline of Christendom has been a gradual process, which McLeod breaks down into four stages: first, Christian states began to tolerate various forms of Christianity; second, anti-Christian ideas were openly published; third, church and state were formally separated; and finally the ties between church and society slowly unravelled.[12] How does this progression relate to unbelief in interwar Canada? The reaction of state authorities to unbelief in Toronto and Montreal in the interwar years shows that many Canadians still felt it was their duty to defend Christendom from anti-Christian ideas. The sociologist of religion Kurt Bowen argues that it was only after the Second World War that churches in English-speaking Canada began to see the Canadian state as an independent entity that needed to follow its own secular agenda; in Quebec that shift took place later, during the Quiet Revolution of the 1960s.[13]

In the interwar period, although the state was not formally attached to any particular church, it defended Canada as a Christian nation. McLeod's suggestion that several Christendoms survived well into the twentieth century helps us make sense of the behaviour of political elites in Toronto, Ottawa, and Montreal. He singles out Quebec as a particularly clear example of one such mini-Christendom.[14] Leaders in Ontario and Quebec both used the same laws to suppress anti-Christian arguments, but each jurisdiction clearly had its own ideas of what this meant. The priority in Quebec was to defend francophone Roman Catholicism, while elite Torontonians were more likely to work for the preservation of a society structured around evangelical Protestantism. Politicians in Ottawa had to negotiate between competing Christendoms, but they were committed to the overarching framework of a Christian Canada.

While atheism was indeed possible for some Canadians prior to the 1960s, it was very much in a minority position until the late twentieth century. Only in 1971 did the non-religious become a significant presence in the national census. In that year 929,580 Canadians said they belonged to no religion, and even then they made up just 4 per cent of the entire population.[15] For most of the nineteenth and twentieth centuries, Canada was, outwardly at least, a Christian nation. Indeed, the American historian Mark Noll has argued that, for much of its history, it was more religious than the United States by a number of measures. But after the 1960s these roles were reversed.[16] As we see in later chapters, some interwar Canadians considered atheism to be a foreign threat creeping into a devout country from the United States and Britain. While it is true that transnational connections with these countries were vital to secular movements in Canada, Canadians developed homegrown varieties of unbelief as well, although the question of their originality is a thorny one.

SECULARISM AND FREETHOUGHT IN THE ANGLO-AMERICAN WORLD

Unbelief among anglophones in interwar Canada emerged from British, American, and Canadian roots.[17] British secularism had grown in the nineteenth century out of working-class movements inspired by the radical wing of the Enlightenment as popularized by revolutionary pamphleteers like Thomas Paine. As its name suggests, secularism was more than an intellectual dissent against religion; it advocated for a secular society, free from religious tests and the established church. Its ideas were propagated primarily by lectures and debates that offered both education and entertainment mainly to working-class audiences. Between events the life of the movement was sustained by small local secularist societies, which typically had attached reading rooms. Many committed secularists were artisans who sought mutual aid and self-improvement through education. A number of political strands could be found among them, from socialism with its cooperative ethic to liberal individualism focused on freedom of conscience.[18]

The movement's most prominent spokespersons, George Holyoake and Charles Bradlaugh, disagreed bitterly over the role that secularism should play in British society. Holyoake strove to make unbelief a respectable option for Britons, a position that led him to make alliances with the reigning powers of the day. In his view, secularists could work with progressive Christians to help change society. Bradlaugh and his followers, on the other hand, took a more militant stance: there could be no cooperation in politics between believers and unbelievers because their metaphysics and ethics were worlds apart.

The majority of secularists were skilled or semi-skilled male workers, independent craftsmen and artisans as well as small business owners.[19] For these working-class secularists, criticism of religion was "part of a general attack on corrupt authority."[20] Towards the end of the nineteenth century, British secularism evolved into rationalism, whose practitioners were somewhat more interested in intellectual enlightenment than in social change. Rationalists, active into the twentieth century, promoted a scientific critique of outmoded patterns of thought and a thorough-going humanist worldview. Both secularism and rationalism offered ordinary people an avenue to identify themselves with the advances of science and scholarship, and "the self-educated artisan was of great social importance as the main interpreter of ideas to others of his class."[21] They also shared a sense of moral indignation; religious beliefs were not only mistaken but offensive. By the standards of Enlightenment or Victorian morality, many tenets of the Bible and Christianity came to be regarded as morally objectionable.[22]

American freethought, although sharing its lineage with British traditions of secularism and rationalism, demonstrated its own unique emphases. American freethinkers esteemed Thomas Paine just as highly as the English rationalists did, but they added homegrown American heroes such as Robert G. Ingersoll, "The Great Agnostic." Because there was no established church in nineteenth-century United States, unbelievers fought somewhat different battles than their counterparts in Great Britain, striving instead to defend the country's initial separation of church and state from religious interference.[23] The period between 1875 and 1914 in America was a "golden age" for freethinkers, a time when they were able to spread their message far and wide using lectures and pamphlets. Most support for freethought came from male Anglo-Americans in the North and West United States.[24]

The American freethought tradition was politically diverse. While many freethinkers identified with the Progressive movement, some used Social Darwinist ideas to justify conservatism.[25] Many socialists were atheists or agnostics, but the American freethought movement as a whole retained some distance from socialism, with some freethinkers even accusing it of being a surrogate religion.[26] In the new media environment that arrived with radio towards the turn of the twentieth century, freethinkers struggled to get their message out. Radio began to displace the lecture as a popular form of communication and entertainment, and was "far less open than the old speakers' platforms to unconventional ideas about religion."[27]

As noted, unbelief was especially popular in both the United States and the United Kingdom from about 1870 to 1914. During this same period, the traditions described above were also active in Ontario, anglophone Quebec, and British Columbia. While the Great War seems to have marked a downturn in the fortunes of rationalism and freethought, the interwar period saw a revival of organized unbelief, which in Canada was most active between roughly 1925 and 1940. Similar trends can be seen in the United States; the American Freethinkers' League and the American Association for the Advancement of Atheism were both formed in 1925. Interestingly, although in a very different social context, that year also marked the formation of Russia's League of the Militant Godless.[28] The spread of a transnational communist movement in the 1920s meant that Soviet anti-religious campaigns intensified local debates about unbelief in countries around the world.

CANADIAN DOUBT: SECULARIZATION AND SECULARISM

Before discussing the local and provincial roots of unbelief, let us first consider the broader context of Canadian culture as a whole. What were some of the influences that may have led Canadians to question or abandon their religion at the time of our study? What was the relationship between religious skepticism and political radicalism? And what was the broader social response to such skepticism, including the response of the state? The contextual framework sketched here will help us understand the more specific case studies in the chapters that follow.

Popular unbelief in Canada has received little scholarly attention. I suspect that one reason Canadian historians have not looked for unbelief in the interwar period in particular is that they have viewed that time as either too religious or too secular, depending on their assumptions. If secularization was well advanced by the 1920s and '30s, open unbelief would be unremarkable; or, as long as Canada remained religious, unbelief would not exist or would be so marginal as to be insignificant. Instead, Canadian historians have generally concerned themselves with secularization on a wider scale, asking questions such as: How and when did churches lose societal influence? When did Christianity's prominence diminish from being the dominant national faith to being simply a personal and private choice? These questions are often framed in terms of broad sociological shifts and institutional change. Another aspect of secularization historiography has been intellectual history, the study of how heterodox or secularizing ideas were received by nineteenth-century academics and clergy.[29]

By the late nineteenth century, Canadian society had become relatively open to rationalism. This burgeoning openness was due in part to the gradual filtering through society of Darwinian thought and the growing influence of "higher biblical criticism," the application of critical historical tools to scripture. These new ideas did not provoke a large-scale loss of faith, however. As A.B. McKillop and others have shown, different sectors of Canadian Protestantism found ways to incorporate, minimize, or ignore the new ideas.[30] And with the First Vatican Council in 1868, the Catholic Church had entered a militant phase and simply condemned much modern thought outright, a stance it would maintain until the Second Vatican Council almost a century later.[31] Many ordinary Canadians were at least curious about claims that traditional Christianity was being called into question by new science and scholarship. This curiosity opened further opportunities for unbelieving activists to popularize their pamphlets and lectures.

Unbelief among the working classes was often seen as a greater danger than the musings of academics because it threatened the social order underpinned by Christianity. In Canada the influential nineteenth-century intellectual Goldwin Smith in particular was concerned about what would happen if the influence of Christianity were to wane. Though he was himself a freethinker, Smith was offended and dismayed by aggressive popular atheism, singling out a pamphlet entitled "The Comic Life of Christ" as an especially crude example. Irreverence of that sort, he argued, was to be blamed on intellectuals who had left ordinary people "in quiet possession of traditional beliefs." What would happen if the lower classes, having no guidance from subtle and moderate thinkers, suddenly became aware of startling modern ideas? They would be shocked into simplistic unbelief: "Mechanics read and think; the result of their being left to their own reading and thinking is the 'Comic Life of Christ.'" More seriously, the foundations of morality would crumble, and society would fall apart.[32] Militant unbelievers threatened to hasten this process.

Concerns about irreverence among the working classes were related to concerns about working-class political radicalism. While many pre-war radicals and socialists remained Christians, a vocal minority denounced religion entirely. For some, such as Socialist Party of Canada organizers W.A. Pritchard and J.H. Burroughs, for instance, socialism was necessarily atheistic. Their views of course played into contemporary conservative stereotypes about "godless leftists." It is difficult to distinguish intellectual tendencies among the early socialists, especially on the question of religion. Such thinkers and activists drew from an eclectic brew of influences that included Thomas Paine and Karl Marx. In this time period the question, "Is one a socialist freethinker or a freethinking socialist?" was not an easy one to answer. The two traditions had been connected in various ways since Robert Owen's utopian socialist movement of the early nineteenth century.

Similarly, many socialists in Canada saw no contradiction between attacking religion, campaigning politically, and organizing workers; these activities were equally important. Militant rejection of religion was especially pronounced in the Socialist Party of Canada, and frequently proclaimed in socialist journals like *Cotton's Weekly*, *Red Flag*, and the *Western Clarion*. Over a century later the anger displayed by these activists still burns brightly in their words: "Who but an abject ignorant slave of the belly-crawling type would in these days pray to an idol of imaginary form 'for thine is the kingdom, the power and the glory, for ever and ever[?]'" asked one. They considered religion an unmanly, degrading, ignorant, superstitious, but above all exploitative cover for the depredations of capitalists.[33] As we shall see in succeeding chapters, some interwar unbelievers like W.J. Curry, Marshall Gauvin, Albert Saint-Martin, and the leaders of the One Big Union cut their teeth among pre-war radical movements. They carried these eclectic influences with them into later decades.

THE GREAT WAR

Historians have long debated the cultural consequences of the Great War. What role did its memory play in interwar unbelief? One major school of thought, centred around Paul Fussell's classic *The Great War and Modern Memory*, sees the war as unleashing the disenchantment of the modern age. Traumatized by the vast machine of industrialized warfare, most veterans returned home deeply skeptical of authority figures and official narratives. Fussell does not address religion in any detail, but the implications of his argument are clear: the chaos of war exposed a world devoid of divine meaning.[34]

The historian Jonathan Vance takes issue with Fussell's interpretation in *Death So Noble*, his examination of Canada's memory of the Great War. Pointing out that Fussell rests his argument mainly on the work of elite writers and thinkers, Vance turns instead to newspapers, war memorials, lesser novels, and patriotic memoirs, and finds that many (perhaps most) ordinary Canadians could not accept a cynical, modernist critique. To say that the war had been futile and meaningless was to disparage the sacrifices made by veterans and their families, and this was intolerable. Thus, Vance argues, Canadians constructed a myth to justify the war, whereby noble soldiers fighting to defend Christianity and civilization had laid down their lives in willing sacrifice, like Christ himself.[35]

When it comes to the question of religious doubt, the two positions are not as far apart as they might appear. Vance acknowledges that many Canadian soldiers came to view "the entire edifice of organized religion more sceptically after four years of war." While some veterans may have found the language of soldier-as-Christ deeply satisfying, this view did not necessarily entail respect for organized churches or reverence for a providential God.[36] The stress and horror of war also led many men to discard the norms of Christian propriety in everyday life.[37] Vance notes too that, upon returning to Canada, a significant proportion of Methodist chaplains and probationers cut their ties to the church. Duff Crerar's study of Canadian chaplains in the Great War, *Padres in No Man's Land*, confirms a similar pattern for seminary students of all denominations who served overseas. He mentions as an example the fact that most of the students from Queen's Theological College who enlisted chose not to return to their studies after the war.[38] The Methodist leader S.D. Chown said: "In many minds the war shook with the violence of a moral and intellectual earthquake the foundations of Christian faith. It shattered many structures of belief in which devout people found refuge from the storms of life."[39]

Crerar surveyed other scholars' research on the British and Australian armies and found that only a small minority of enlisted men, perhaps as few as 10 per cent, were strongly devout Christians. A great many more, perhaps even a majority, were hostile to religion and to the chaplains, while the remainder were lukewarm or ambivalent in their feelings.[40] From his own research, Crerar estimates similar proportions among Canadians: a small contingent of faithful Christians, a large number of "sceptics and cynics," and a third group, the largest, which was "uncommitted and disillusioned but not entirely irreligious." Crerar mentions the memoir of Thomas Dinesen, an unbelieving Dane who enlisted to fight alongside the Canadians. Dinesen found that many of the soldiers with whom he spoke were skeptical of organized religion but also refused to accept his brand of hard-edged atheism.[41]

Army chaplains were aware of this widespread dearth of religious sentiment. The historian David Marshall summarizes the findings of a Baptist chaplain who interviewed a number of soldiers on their return to Canada: "Few of the soldiers expressed belief in any particular creed, and they did not express their religious beliefs in biblical language. Moreover, many claimed to hold no religion." The chaplain attempted to put a positive spin on the situation by claiming that the soldiers nevertheless displayed Christian character through their actions. A fellow Baptist took issue with this interpretation, arguing that the chaplain was moving the goal posts. The men in question were "unbelievers," not Christians in disguise.[42] Apathy and sheer ignorance were also problems the churches encountered among soldiers. Presbyterian chaplains who were surveyed near war's end complained that the men exhibited "an amazing ignorance of the Bible" and the Christian creeds. These clergymen had to confront the fact that, even before the war, many Canadian men had had only a vague and shallow relationship with the churches.[43]

Crerar expresses the view that novels and memoirs of the interwar period overstate how cynical and disillusioned soldiers were about religion. He suggests, rather, that it was in the 1920s and '30s, as Canadian veterans grappled with a harsh economic situation and a difficult transition back to civilian life, that their mood soured. They could not help but notice that the Kingdom of God on Earth preached by optimistic chaplains had failed to materialize, and they began to wonder if their sacrifices had really been worthwhile. Crerar suggests that during the war itself soldiers were somewhat more idealistic than they later recalled being.[44]

It is true that there is little evidence of unbelief arising directly from the war years. Expressions of atheistic angst in letters, for example, would neither have encouraged family members at home nor made it past the censors.[45] Canadians were frequently told, after all, that they were fighting a crusade for the survival of Christianity itself.[46] For the purposes of this study, however, irreverence on the part of Canadian veterans in the interwar period is worth noting. Even if they came late to their doubts, the fact that they began expressing them in the 1920s tells us something about the mood of the time.

We find such skepticism in the work of a few Canadian authors who were themselves combat veterans. Peregrine Acland had fought and been badly wounded at the Battle of the Somme. In his semi-autobiographical novel *All Else Is Folly*, published in 1929, the main character finds himself alone with a kindly Anglican priest who invites him to take Communion with him: "Falcon was embarrassed. He had been brought up a sound Anglican, but he had long since lost his belief in orthodox Christianity. He had, now, no religion ... except a love for his fellow man. And his being here, as a soldier, was the absolute negation of *that*. He couldn't, however, explain all these things to the Canon."[47] For Acland, war destroyed not only faith but whatever secularized ethics remained in its wake.

The canon in Acland's novel is likely a fictionalized version of Canon Frederick George Scott, who earned a good reputation among Canadian soldiers for his tireless efforts on behalf of the enlisted men. James H. Pedley's 1927 memoir, *Only This*, mentions Scott directly with great respect. But he makes it clear that in his opinion Scott was an exception when it came to chaplains. Before Pedley met him he assumed the man was simply another "highly successful fakir," a term used contemptuously. Pedley's feelings went beyond a general anticlericalism, extending, as with Acland, to theology itself. Later in the book, Pedley mulls over one of the horrible injustices of war and asks: "Is there a God? ... Must this kind of rough-and-ready justice be ascribed to all-seeing Deity, or to sportive chance? Who will dare to say?"[48]

Canadian veteran George Godwin's autobiographical 1930 war novel *Why Stay We Here?* concludes with an affirmation of the notion of soldier-as-Christ and holds out hope for an eventual resurrection. The body of the book conveys a much more skeptical tone, however. As the main character, Stephen, and his comrade Piers wander over a battlefield where "sixty thousand Frenchmen" were killed earlier in the war, they reflect bitterly on faith. Piers concludes: "Well, personally, I've given up speculating about that sort of thing. I don't know, and I don't much care whether there's a God or no. This place is enough evidence that He returns the compliment. If He exists at all, then He must be an impersonal God who doesn't care a hoot about mankind." Stephen concurs: "Exactly what I feel lately."[49]

The best-known novel about the Canadian Expeditionary Force (CEF) is Charles Yale Harrison's *Generals Die in Bed*, first serialized in 1928 and then published in book form in 1930. Harrison served in the CEF from 1916 to 1918. Of Jewish descent, he seems to have already been an unbeliever before the war. He was born in Philadelphia and spent much of his life in the United States, so his work may not be entirely representative of the disenchanted Canadian. He was, however, observant of his Canadian comrades, and the book illustrates the critique of religion that was common in anti-war literature of the period.

Generals Die in Bed opens with a scene of new recruits returning to their Montreal barracks after visiting assorted brothels. Anderson, a middle-aged Methodist lay preacher from northern Ontario, sits on a bunk reading his Bible. He attempts to tell the younger men about the sinfulness of their actions but is shouted down. "Shut up, sky pilot!" yells one drunken teenager. The narrator's own attitude to Anderson is not clear at first. As the book progresses, however, we see that Anderson represents something larger than himself: the old-fashioned effort to justify the war in terms of Victorian evangelical piety. The character also tries to predict the war's end using chronological calculations drawn from biblical prophecy. In response, his younger comrades heap mockery and abuse on him. When Anderson tells the young men they should not curse, the narrator muses bitterly:

> To think we could propitiate a senseless god by abstaining from cursing! What god is there as mighty as the fury of a bombardment? ... How will we ever be able to go back to peaceful ways and hear pallid preachers whimper of their puny little gods who can only torment sinners with sulphur, we who have seen a hell that no god, however cruel, would fashion for his most deadly enemies? Yes, all of us have prayed during the manic frenzy of a bombardment. Who can live through the terror-laden minutes of drumfire and not feel his reason slipping, his manhood dissolving?[50]

The book's predominant view is that religion is for irrational women and feminized men who have lost their wits. Harrison goes on to condemn the religiosity of those supporting the war in Canada: "Back home they are praying too – praying for victory – and that means we must lie here and rot and tremble forever."[51]

Generals Die in Bed and *All Else Is Folly* are often cited as the most original and realistic of Canada's Great War novels, alongside a third text, *God's Sparrows*.[52] Written by Philip Child and published in 1937, the book was based on Child's own experience of the war. The protagonist, Dan Thatcher, is a relatively steady sort who maintains his faith throughout the novel, but much of the text's emotional energy centres on two other characters, the mystic Dolughoff and Dan's philosophical cousin Quentin. Dolughoff is convinced that he has a message from God that will bring an end to the war. Overcome by the horror of battle, he runs out into no-man's-land and in God's name orders both sides to stop. When they ignore him and continue to slaughter one another, Dolughoff shoots himself in the head, terrified of what the "indifferent and empty" sky implies.[53] Quentin, on the other hand, is a sensitive character who doubts that he has a soul or that any providential God is watching. In one extended sequence Dan dreams of a dead Quentin wandering a bureaucratic, mechanized afterlife in search of a "Commander-in-Chief" whom he never finds.[54]

It seems unlikely that these veteran authors who expressed doubt or unbelief were simply offering a cynical audience a position they did not personally hold. It is not hard to imagine that other CEF soldiers suffered a personal crisis like that of the Victoria Cross recipient Cyril Martin, a Baptist who began to doubt God's goodness while serving in France. Seeing children with missing limbs deeply disturbed him. It "really got to me," he later recalled. "I thought, if God is all-powerful, why doesn't he stop this war? And it was quite a while afterwards before I got [my faith] back." Martin returned to Christian belief by reinterpreting the war as a sin, a revolt against God's will.[55] Others never did regain their faith. As one Canadian Anglican recalled about his grandfather, who had fought in the Great War: "I don't think he ever got over what happened to him in the war. He used to say that the church told him God wanted him to go to war. What he saw in the war made him believe there was no God. He never wanted to be a hypocrite – so he never went back inside a church." The veteran in question was the son of Anglican priest and had previously been very active in the church, but after his loss of faith he would not even attend the weddings of his children and grandchildren. As his grandson put it, "He wasn't willing to pretend something that wasn't real for him anymore."[56]

THE INTERWAR RELIGIOUS CONTEXT

Many returned soldiers had reasons to disbelieve religious claims and to reject the teachings of the churches. What was the mood among other members of the population in the interwar years? When surveyed, most Canadians claimed to be religious believers; a majority of the 8.8 million respondents in the 1921 census said they belonged to one of the major Christian denominations. The largest group were Roman Catholics, with 3.4 million adherents reporting (39 per cent of the population). The other denominations represented – those with more than a million self-professed adherents – were the Presbyterians (16 per cent of the population), the Anglicans (16 per cent), and the Methodists (13 per cent). There were also about 420,000 Baptists (5 per cent of the population), and almost 300,000 Lutherans (3 per cent). The largest non-Christian religion was Judaism, with about 125,000 adherents (1.5 per cent). Of the remaining 650,000 Canadians, approximately 500,000 (6 per cent of the population) said they belonged to smaller Christian churches or sects. About

47,000 said they belonged to Indigenous traditions (called "Pagans" by the census) or to world traditions such as Buddhism, Confucianism, Shintoism, or Islam. Overall, 96 per cent of all responding Canadians said they were Christians of one variety or another.[57]

The most significant religious shift of the interwar period in Canada occurred in 1925, when the Methodist Church, the Congregational Union of Canada, and about 70 per cent of the Presbyterian Church in Canada came together to form the United Church of Canada. In the 1931 census, which surveyed some 10.4 million Canadians, the new United Church was the second largest denomination, with 2 million adherents (19 per cent of the population), second only to the Roman Catholic Church's 4.3 million (41 per cent). There were 1.6 million Anglicans (15 per cent) and about 870,000 Presbyterians (8 per cent); the numbers of Baptists and Lutherans were now more comparable (4 per cent of the population for each), and Judaism continued to be the largest non-Christian religion (still at 1.5 per cent). Some smaller conservative churches and sects saw significant growth, boosted by the fundamentalist movement and disaffection with the United Church, but they remained a relatively tiny percentage of the whole. Overall, the pattern of religious affiliation had changed little since 1921, with Catholicism the largest denomination, followed by a few large Protestant churches with a major national presence, and then a host of smaller churches and sects. In terms of raw numbers, Christianity was hegemonic, while Jews and adherents of other world religions were still marginal.[58]

National church attendance statistics for the interwar period are hard to come by, but a Gallup poll in 1945 found that roughly 65 per cent of Canadians claimed to have attended a religious service in the three weeks following Easter Sunday. Quebec was the most religiously active province, with about 90 per cent of respondents claiming recent attendance at church. While not offering details, the pollsters noted that western Canadians were less likely to be in church than those from the east. In fact, in some western provinces, more people stayed away than attended church.[59] As we shall see in chapter 7, British Columbia most closely fits this description of the unchurched west, with Christianity having a weaker presence there than in any other province.

In terms of numbers alone, self-proclaimed unbelievers were a negligible presence in interwar Canada. According to the 1921 census, there were just 594 agnostics, 1,041 atheists, and 1,126 freethinkers in the entire nation. A few other responses related to religious identity also suggest unbelief: 76 said they were communists, 18 liberals, 34 materialists, 29 "philosophers," 56 rationalists, and 50 socialists. In addition, 21,739 people reported "no religion." (The latter number was actually a drop of about five thousand from the previous census in 1911.) There was a stark divide between the sexes. A total of 452 agnostics were men, as opposed to 142 women. For atheists, these categories were 787 and 254, respectively; and for freethinkers, 770 to 356. Even those with no religion were similarly divided, with 15,647 men and only 6,092 women.[60]

Obviously not everyone who reported "no religion" was a strict atheist or agnostic. As the number of Canadian religious "nones" have grown in recent decades, scholars have discovered a complex and sometimes contradictory reality behind that category.[61] Even in the interwar period that answer was given for a variety of reasons. It provides us, however, with a rough approximation of those who were willing to distance themselves from religion in general. This is particularly important because the following censuses, 1931 and 1941, did not report in as much detail as 1921; "no religion" was the only relevant category available. In 1931 the number of those with no religion declined slightly, to 21,071. And in 1941 it fell still further, to 19,161. (It was only in 1951 that the figure rose again, to almost 60,000 respondents.) In terms of the total population of Canada (which was 8.8 million in 1921, growing to 11.5 million in 1941), these were tiny minorities. Even if some unbelievers wound up being counted in other categories such as "not stated" or "other," they still barely registered.[62]

There are, however, reasons to doubt that this picture is entirely accurate. Unbelievers who answered honestly may not have had their answers recorded correctly (as we shall see in chapter 3). Between 1931 and 1981 the religious categories that were available on the census were quite limited.[63] In 1951 a rationalist in Regina complained:

> When the census taker came around [my] wife was out and
> I answered the questions. She asked wife's religion and I replied
> Lutheran and that son was on his own but was a member of
> the United Church. Then [she] asked me mine and I told her
> I had no creeds but it could be defined as Rationalist or Science
> Research and Reason. Well, said she, there is no place for such
> answers. Well, said I, is it possible the government would ask
> us questions and deny us the right to answer them? They are
> not endeavouring to make a nation of hypocrites are they?[64]

Furthermore, it is well established that many Canadians will lie about their religious attitudes or behaviour when surveyed. This is most notable when they are asked about church attendance, which is generally over-reported.[65] For various reasons, including moral respectability, many people feel the need to assert a strong religious identity where one does not exist. In the early twentieth century, census enumerators were drawn from local neighbourhoods, and responses were given verbally, so one's answers could easily become common knowledge. There is little doubt that appearing outwardly irreligious had more serious social consequences in the interwar period than it would today, so people hesitated to say they had no religion.[66] In my third chapter I present evidence that significant numbers of Winnipeggers identified themselves as religious on the census and then joined a rationalist organization that was profoundly hostile to religion.

While unbelief and religious indifference were likely more widespread than the censuses suggest, their practitioners still formed a minority. Nevertheless, unbelievers occupied a curiously large space in the popular imagination. They represented a certain social option about which many people thought or spoke, without themselves pursuing it. Religious conservatives saw them as a major threat to society – pride and selfishness run amok. Some Christians believed religious skepticism was fostered directly by the devil. Even moderate or liberal Christians viewed unbelief with suspicion; to them it represented untrammelled human reason taken to its logical conclusion; science without spirit; the end result of a reckless modernity which had intelligence but not wisdom. Unbelievers served as a cautionary tale.

THE ROARING TWENTIES?

The decade of the 1920s in Canada was, as it was elsewhere, multifaceted. After the postwar recession, certain areas of the country, especially big cities and central Canada, experienced prosperity. At the same time rural areas, the Maritimes, and much of the west continued to struggle through harsh economic conditions. On the cultural front, some contemporary observers saw a wave of change, even of chaos. They fretted about moral decay, decrying hip flasks, jazz orchestras, flappers, and "petting."[67] Clergymen worried that Canadians were being seduced by a new consumerist culture of automobiles and radios, to the detriment of religion and national pride.[68] In Quebec the Catholic Church also battled movies and popular newspapers.[69] Much concern was directed towards the young, that new generation which, in the words of F. Scott Fitzgerald, grew up "to find all Gods dead, all wars fought, all faiths in man shaken."[70] The historian Fraser Sutherland writes that a "debunking spirit prevailed" in Canada after the Great War: "After the war's carnage, and the horrendous influenza epidemic that followed it, human beings had quite enough reminders of death to do them for some time. They wanted to live, and part of living was to reject the past. All the old institutions and ideas of status, the ideal of chivalry itself, were eminently mockable."[71]

Some contemporary observers contended that irreverence and materialism were American vices, not Canadian. Defensive sermons and editorials insisting that Canada's youth were in fact morally sound were not uncommon. It can be argued that the vehemence of these anti-modern jeremiads was a testimony to the resilience of Victorian values and mores in the country. For example, the introduction of the Ku Klux Klan to Saskatchewan in the 1920s as a political force opposing non-British immigrants spoke both of resistance to the changes brought by immigration and modern life, and of the continuing strength of the traditional British Protestant identity.[72] Paul Rutherford's description of the decade captures these conflicting impressions:

> The Canada of the 1920s seemed a land of contrasts. On
> the one hand, an observer might emphasize the consumer
> boom, the hedonistic mood, the fascination with professional
> sports, the decline of partisanship, the American style of life.
> On the other hand, this same observer could find the persistence
> of the Victorian imprint, the vigour of limited identities,
> the survival of a puritanical zeal, the health of amateur sports,
> a deep loyalty to British ways and the British connection in
> English Canada or a great respect for Catholic dogma and
> the Catholic Church in French Canada. The "modern" had
> not yet overtaken the "traditional."[73]

These contrasts extended also to Canada's moral and religious life. Canada remained a Christian nation in which the clergy held a respected position, and religious messages were broadcast from pulpits, newspaper columns, and radio shows. Nevertheless, some historians have stressed the uncertainty brought by the 1920s. A.B. McKillop senses a certain lack of conviction, even a quiet desperation, among the country's theologians and religious instructors: "The will to believe existed as it had before the war. Yet post-war popular judgments on theological matters often lacked the ring of conviction. As often as not they testified instead to a new mood of pessimism in the English-Canadian churches."[74]

Robert Wright finds mainline Protestant clergymen worrying about disillusionment among the young and the spread of irreligion and outright atheism. Anxieties about religious fragmentation and sectarianism developed as well, as independent fundamentalists, pentecostals, spiritualists, theosophists, British Israelites, and other small groups saw their numbers grow in the interwar period.[75] Wright notes further that "the clergy's complicity in wartime propaganda was also seen by many Protestant students in Canada to have represented 'the practical failure of Christianity.'" Some students "lashed out as well against the churches' apparent acquiescence in an exploitative social system, their refusal to come to terms with modern intellectual and scientific advances, and their seemingly incessant theological squabbling."[76]

VARIETIES OF UNBELIEF

McKillop and Wright focused on Protestantism. The rationalist and secularist tradition in English-speaking Canada was in some ways an anti-Protestant movement and, like Protestantism, it emphasized abstract beliefs. But those opposed to religion in other cultures sometimes displayed their non-conformity in different ways. For French-Canadian ex-Catholics this stance could involve shunning baptism, confirmation, and the last rites, sacraments that retained considerable social power even for those who were not orthodox believers.

Traditional practical markers of religious commitment were particularly noticeable among Canadian Jews; observance of the Sabbath and maintenance of a kosher diet were just as important to Jewish identity as formal belief and synagogue attendance. By measuring these practices among Toronto Jews in the interwar period, historian Stephen Speisman found signs of religious decline in the 1920s: the city's Jews became less likely to associate with a synagogue; fewer kept the Sabbath or observed the ban on working on other holy days; some turned to secular courts rather than to rabbis to resolve disputes with other Jews; the Yiddish language was emphasized over Hebrew.[77]

On the question of declining Sabbath observance, Speisman noted a few important factors: straightforward economic pressure and competition for jobs in non-Jewish firms; a gradual move towards socio-cultural integration on the part of second-generation immigrants; and "increased numbers of Jewish secularists." He gives the following explanation: "These had been present in Europe, but social pressure had forced them either to keep their religious violations secret or branded them outcasts. Moreover, in any particular *shtetl*, they had been relatively few. The persecution of social radicals in the late nineteenth and early twentieth century, however, forced thousands of them to emigrate and in North America, while still a minority, they organized far more openly. More important, centralized religious authority was no longer present to make them pariahs. Consequently, they were able by example to exert considerable influence."[78] Many secularized Jews put their energies into progressive and radical political movements, which provided new subcultures and a new approach to ethical imperatives.[79]

Thus, we have evidence that different ethnic and religious communities felt the influence of unbelievers, and that they expressed that influence in various ways. Most of the unbelievers discussed in this book were of white British or French-Canadian descent and were reacting against Protestant or Catholic Christianity. Other communities, particularly Jews, Eastern Europeans, and Black Canadians, are also represented. It is important to recognize the diversity of Canadian unbelief, not only to put the majority in its proper context but also to encourage future research.

Of course, the category of "unbelief" has conceptual limitations in this regard. For example, in this time period many First Nations people were also struggling against the hegemony of Christianity. In J.R. Miller's history of the residential schools, *Shingwauk's Vision*, we learn of Indigenous youth who were resisting the Christian education imposed on them by church and state. Sometimes they literally fought with missionaries who were attempting to take them to school. Others mocked Christian rituals in their own languages, or stole communion wine, or wrestled abusive nuns into submission. Some ran away from school or burned down church-owned buildings. Does this qualify as unbelief? It could be viewed in that light; but it is perhaps more fruitful to understand it as a form of resistance for self-preservation and the protection of First Nations culture. Miller notes that one of the victories of First Nations people in their struggle against cultural colonization was the continuation of forbidden spiritual traditions like the Sun Dance or potlatch.[80] As we shall see, some interwar rationalists and secularists were quick to equate Christianity with the "superstitious rituals" of "savages," a position that implicitly denigrated both European religion and the spiritual traditions of Indigenous peoples. Even if some white Canadian unbelievers had a more nuanced view of non-European cultures, those we discuss seem to have paid scant attention to First Nations communities.[81]

THE "MONKEY TRIAL"

The interwar period witnessed a number of events that came to symbolize clashes between belief and unbelief in Canada; two in particular became touchstones for the decades of this study. The first was the famous Scopes trial in Dayton, Tennessee; the other was the secret formation of Canada's Communist Party in a barn near Guelph, Ontario.

In the summer of 1925, a young man named John T. Scopes was prosecuted for teaching evolution in the state of Tennessee. The trial itself would be enlarged and embroidered upon in ensuing decades until it became, in popular memory, an epic confrontation between science and religion.[82] But even at the time it provoked much public interest and was popularly nicknamed "the monkey trial." The groups involved – civil liberties advocates, fundamentalists, and the Dayton town fathers – had expressly designed it to be a media circus.[83] They succeeded wonderfully. Reporters flocked to the scene and sent in breathless dispatches that became front-page headlines. The confrontation – between William Jennings Bryan, champion of the fundamentalists, and the agnostic lawyer Clarence Darrow – made for great drama.[84] The fact that Bryan died a few days after the trial only added to the excitement. Fundamentalists considered the trial a legal and spiritual victory; Scopes was found guilty, and Bryan's death made him a martyr. Unbelievers also benefited from the publicity garnered by the skeptical Darrow; it is no coincidence that 1925 also saw the formation of new atheist organizations such as the American Association for the Advancement of Atheism in the immediate aftermath of the trial.[85]

Contemporary Canadian reaction to the trial has been unearthed by Edward G. Betts, whose thesis, "The Argument of the Century," examined Ontario newspaper coverage of the proceedings and Bryan's death.[86] Betts found that some papers, particularly those affiliated with the Liberal Party, made a great deal of the trial, devoting front-page headlines to it. Others were more reserved and disdainful, but virtually no one ignored it altogether. A few papers, notably Toronto's *Globe* and the *Ottawa Journal*, sided with Bryan and the fundamentalist cause. Most commentators, however, were appalled by what they saw as the disruptive and extremist nature of the fundamentalists. This is not to say that Ontario papers favoured Darrow's sardonic agnosticism. As the *Toronto Star* put it: "Both sides to the Dayton debate were unfortunate in their champions: evolution because Darrow is an agnostic, and fundamentalism because Bryan, pious and sincere as he was, took a more extreme position than has been adopted by any great nation-wide church assembly."[87] Editorials stressed that Canadians valued moderation, order, tolerance, and stability. Much was said of Canadian and British superiority over the rowdy and demagogic Americans.[88] A number of papers were clearly pro-evolution, but they all took pains to editorialize about how true science harmonized with true religion. In their view, hope for human progress lay in combining traditional faith with modern science and technology. A Christian moderation – what Betts, quoting Michael Gauvreau, calls the "progressive-orthodox" or "conservative-progressive" position – ruled the day.[89]

Indeed, Canadian churches mostly avoided the sharp divisions that formed between fundamentalists and modernists in the interwar United States. Peace was maintained, but it could be a delicate peace. Betts points out that Canadian church newspapers were cautious, saying very little about the trial. The Anglican *Canadian Churchman* and the United Church's *New Outlook* both called for tolerance but otherwise did not commit themselves; there was doubtless concern about taking sides and inflaming the differences within Canada's Protestant churches.[90] As we see in the chapters that follow, however, not everybody was satisfied with the middle way. Enthusiastic crowds in Winnipeg attended debates on evolution, pitting fundamentalists against unbelievers; Toronto reporters declared a local blasphemy trial to be Canada's answer to the monkey trial. The modernist-fundamentalist controversy created rifts in the evangelical consensus that had governed Protestantism for decades. Even if Canadian churches did not fall to pieces like some of their American counterparts, the cracks created space for unbelievers to make their voices heard.

GODLESS COMMUNISTS?

The secret formation of Canada's Communist Party in Guelph, the second touchstone event related to irreligion in the interwar decades, took place in 1921. In the interwar years communism and atheism would come to be closely identified in the public mind, an association that continued until at least the 1980s. The Communist Party of Canada's relationship to religion and unbelief was to be a complex and shifting one.

A sense of that complexity can be gleaned from an anecdote related by veteran Tom McEwen, a member of the Canadian Communist Party. In his memoirs he revealed that the "most embarrassing experience of [his] lifetime" involved a debate about atheism. A blacksmith by trade, McEwen in 1922–24 belonged to the Saskatoon branch of the Workers' Party of Canada (WPC), a front for the Communist Party, which was illegal at the time. One of his comrades was a German-Canadian carpenter named Franski, "who thought the main business of the WPC branch was to follow the Ingersoll-McCabe god-blasting trail." Through their mutual involvement in the Trades and Labor Council (TLC), Franski came into conflict with J.A. Donnell, a United Church minister.[91] The carpenter and the minister agreed to debate the question "[Does] the Bible serve any useful purpose?" before a large audience.

As McEwen later recalled, "Franski had secured a large family Bible, and with his 'strong points' marked out with long flowing strips of ribbon like a hula skirt, he mounted the rostrum." The carpenter's English was not very good, however, so he asked McEwen to read out the biblical passages for him to elaborate on. The blacksmith reluctantly agreed: "Franski had selected a large number of what he thought were the most salacious paragraphs from various books of the Old Testament (out of context, of course), which I had to read and upon which Franski would offer rather crude comment. When I got to the prophecy in Deuteronomy (23:1) which reads, 'He that is wounded in the stones or hath his privy member cut off, shall not enter into the congregation of the Lord,' the audience roared — and the women folk more so when Franski got going with his intriguing elaboration."[92] At this, McEwen decided he'd had enough of reading for the night and surrendered the Bible to his comrade. After Franski and Donnell had delivered their presentations, the TLC audience unanimously declared the clergyman the winner. The local WPC told Franski to leave them out of any future debates, counselling him to "learn the difference between a philosophical atheist and one who doesn't know what he is trying to talk about."[93]

This was not simply a matter of embarrassment over a crude debater. The incident illustrates an ongoing disagreement among communists about how to approach religion. Some remained attached to the "god-blasting" style of open confrontation along rationalist lines which had been prominent among an earlier generation of socialists. Others believed their first priority was to organize workers, not debate metaphysics with them; religious beliefs would presumably fade away on their own once material conditions changed. As McEwen pragmatically put it: "Communism may be atheist in its objective outlook because Communism is the essence of all the sciences applied to the material well-being of mankind, but Communism cannot 'win friends and influence people' by ignorantly trampling upon the religious beliefs and ideals of others."[94]

Was a restrained, nonconfrontational atheism the "true" communist position? The question was never entirely settled. In 1923 the Communist International had declared that Communist Party members should be atheists, and that anti-religious propaganda should be disseminated; at the same time, care should be taken not to alienate religious workers.[95] The Canadian Communist Party maintained an independence from the dictates of the Comintern, and its overall attitude to religion was tactical and pragmatic, following the need of the moment. Attacking religion could be helpful in opening working-class minds to scientific materialism, but it could also be a hindrance. Whatever position was taken could be justified by appeals to different parts of the Marxist canon or to various aspects of the Soviet experience.[96] That is to say, if Franski had been more popular and successful, he might have been embraced by his comrades in the WPC. They could have cited Comintern statements, anti-religious campaigns in Soviet Russia, or Marx's critique of religion. But Franski's offensiveness turned away workers, so the leadership counselled him to be a more sensitive "philosophical" atheist instead.

DANGEROUS WORDS

Like unbelievers more generally, communists were a small minority in Canada, even though they occupied a large space in public consciousness. But what was going on in mainstream culture? We have seen how some veterans expressed religious skepticism through memoirs and novels. Was this attitude of cynicism common in Canadian literature? On the contrary, the historian John Herd Thompson detects a "buoyant" attitude among Canadian interwar writers: "Canadian intellectuals escaped the disillusionment that in the wake of the war drowned their counterparts in Britain; few of them displayed the bitter cynicism that drove America's 'lost generation' to refuge in Greenwich Village or into exile in Paris."[97] And it is true that, aside from its presence in war novels, little explicit irreligion appears in Canadian literature of the time.

Politically radical writers were often not religious believers, but in the interwar period their works either ignored religion altogether or borrowed biblical symbols to protest modern injustice.[98] Works of experimental, avant-garde Canadian authors in the interwar period did challenge Christian orthodoxy; rather than promote a rationalist or atheist worldview, however, they encouraged a kind of cosmic consciousness inspired by mystics like Richard Maurice Bucke or Walt Whitman.[99] A few tried to move their fellow Canadians away from Christian patterns of thought; Bertram Brooker's 1927 poem "The Destroyer," for instance, proclaimed:

we are the only creators there are
there is no creator
there is no creation
except our own creation.[100]

But even Brooker's musings were couched in mystical language that engaged with Christianity using its own symbols. Such writers attempted to subsume Christianity into an ecumenical vision of cosmic evolution with a theosophical or pantheist flavour.

If we consider the reading population as a whole, however, we must remember this: few Canadians actually read Canadian authors. Not counting textbooks, more than three-quarters of the books sold in Canada were imported, mainly from the United States and Great Britain.[101] Publishing Canadian fiction or poetry was not a profitable enterprise; publishers had to subsidize such books with income from textbooks and other educational materials.[102] Magazines were slightly more sustainable, but American publications dominated the market. In 1924, six out of every seven magazines read in Canada came from the United States. Between 1931 and 1938, Canadians captured a greater share of the market, but American periodicals were still ubiquitous.[103]

Strong doses of religious skepticism were evident in the literature – primarily American or British – that Canadians were reading. *Elmer Gantry,* Sinclair Lewis's savage parody of American evangelicalism, for instance, was the best-selling book in the United States in 1927. (Lewis made no secret of his disdain for religion and once famously dared God to strike him dead.[104]) *Gantry* was well reviewed in Toronto's *Canadian Forum,* but it was not only big-city critics who were reading such material.[105] A survey of books checked out of a rural library in 1930s PEI found that Lewis's satires were highly popular with local readers. American and British publications were also in the majority there, and readers paid little attention to a book's country of origin.[106] *Elmer Gantry* was not unique; 1927 was a particularly notable year for irreligious books. It also marked the publication of Bertrand Russell's *Why I Am Not a Christian* and Freud's *The Future of an Illusion*, which would become classics of religious skepticism.[107] Two other works sparked controversy that year by firmly rejecting Christian sexual morality: Dora Russell's *The Right to Be Happy* and Judge Ben Lindsay's *The Companionate Marriage.*[108]

Material of that nature was also found in the periodical press. From 1924 to 1933, the militant American atheist H.L. Mencken vented a steady stream of sarcasm and disdain towards religion in his *American Mercury*, which featured many of the era's most celebrated writers. And in December 1926 the American writer Carl Van Doren's influential essay "Why I Am an Unbeliever" appeared in the highly respectable *Forum*.[109] Ernest Hemingway, meanwhile, expressed his bleak view of life and religion in stories like "A Clean Well-Lighted Place" (1933), with its despairing parodic prayer that begins, "Our nada who art in nada, nada be thy name."[110] Some of the irreverent new modernist literature was deemed too offensive for Canadians. James Joyce's *Ulysses* was banned from the country from 1923 until 1949, although likely more for its sexual content than for its assertion that God was "a shout in the street."[111]

Unbelief was not limited to "high" culture; it was also found in American pulp magazines like *Argosy* or *True Detective Mysteries.* Moralists naturally worried about the effect of lurid "true crime" stories on young people, but such magazines also contained more philosophical challenges to religious belief. Some of the most evocative pulp stories came from Howard Philips Lovecraft, a Rhode Island writer whose work gradually acquired an enormous influence over Anglo-American horror fiction. Many of Lovecraft's tales relied for their effect on existential dread about the place of humanity in the universe, as revealed by modern science. His characters discover that they live in a vast and ancient cosmos that is profoundly indifferent towards life on Earth; the only "gods" that exist are hideous alien beings that either ignore or despise humanity. One recurring theme evoked contemporary anxieties about evolution.[112] A protagonist would go insane after discovering that his ancestors were not human; in one story, they were apes, and in another, hybrid fish-people.[113]

In sum, a good deal of skeptical material was available to reading Canadians at the time. It would have been relatively easy to encounter the idea that, in the words of a song from the 1935 opera *Porgy and Bess*, "The things that you're liable to read in the Bible – it ain't necessarily so."[114] Of course, many Canadians remained averse to such ideas. They sought to defend the Christian nature of their country, which was sometimes seen as being under threat from outsiders, not least its irreverent neighbours to the south.

LEGAL RECOURSE

One of the tools through which Christian Canada retained its formal hegemony was the law against blasphemous libel: Section 198 of the Criminal Code. Based on similar laws in the British legal tradition, the law in the interwar period read as follows: "198. Every one is guilty of an indictable offence and liable to one year's imprisonment who publishes any blasphemous libel. 2. Whether any particular published matter is a blasphemous libel or not is a question of fact: Provided that no one is guilty of a blasphemous libel for expressing in good faith and in decent language, or attempting to establish by arguments used in good faith and conveyed in decent language, any opinion whatever upon any religious subject."[115]

Essentially, the law forbade public attacks on religious topics which were intended to insult or hurt the feelings of religious people. While it was not always strictly enforced, the mere fact that the law existed certainly inhibited the spread of anti-religious ideas throughout the interwar period. In 1921, for instance, Matteo Campanile, an Italian immigrant to Toronto, was charged with blasphemous libel. He had posted a sign in his store window that read, "Free-thinkers' book – knocks religion higher than a kite – shows that Jesus is not your saviour." Inspector McKinley of the Toronto morality squad inspected the book (a volume of Robert Ingersoll's writings) and decided it was not itself objectionable under the law. The public display of the sign, however, was definitely deemed offensive. Campanile seems to have been let off with a warning, but the sign was taken down.[116] Six years later, when Toronto rationalist Ernest V. Sterry put out a skeptical newspaper, the law was invoked with more serious results. His case, discussed in detail in chapter 4, indicates that Christian Canada could at that time be quite severe about suppressing those who criticized it.

While the law of blasphemous libel prohibited certain types of communication within Canada, a different mechanism was employed to keep dangerous ideas from entering the country. The Department of National Revenue controlled the flow of books and magazines from abroad. Explicitly anti-religious publications were considered libellous and injurious to Canada's moral fabric. As with seditious and pornographic material, therefore, they could be stopped at the border.[117] But there was no systematic policy for doing so. Typically, an outraged Canadian from an advocacy group such as the National Council of Women or the Imperial Order of the Daughters of the Empire, would contact the federal government and demand that a certain publication be forbidden.[118] The complaint would be passed on to the Department of National Revenue, whose "Examiner of Publications," if he took the complaint seriously, would send a memo out to customs inspectors. A centralized list of prohibited books and journals was maintained by the department but it was kept secret from the public.[119] In 1938 the Examiner of Publications received roughly 1,400 letters from customs collectors and members of the public and, of the 800 books and periodicals sent for his inspection, 56 titles were added to the prohibited list (39 magazines and 17 books).[120]

Although these prohibitions limited the contact between Canadian unbelievers and their counterparts in other countries, they did not prevent it altogether. The variable accessibility of the *Truth Seeker*, the leading rationalist periodical in the United States, is a good example. As of 1895 it was banned from entering Canada.[121] Enforcement was spotty, however, and over time the prohibition lapsed. Canadian subscribers could access the magazine unhindered until 1926, when the acting deputy minister of customs and excise instructed customs inspectors to once again ban the *Truth Seeker*, alongside books entitled *The Tyranny of God* and *Convent Cruelties*.[122] A decade later, in January 1938, the magazine was again permitted to enter Canada. In that month the minister of national revenue, James Ilsley, had given a speech praising tolerance and freedom, including "freedom of conscience and religious belief even for those whose religion or lack of religion you disapprove." The editors of the *Truth Seeker* immediately sent him a letter requesting that he live up to his ideals by removing their magazine from the prohibited list. The few Canadian subscribers who had found ways to circumvent the ban also sent the authorities "courteous, well-worded" letters that seem to have contributed to its removal.[123]

The Quebec Catholic newspaper *L'Illustration nouvelle* immediately attacked the decision. In an editorial entitled, in translation, "Ottawa Decrees 'Liberty for Atheism,'" the paper denounced the "forces of evil" that had broken "an interdiction of forty years." The *Truth Seeker* replied contemptuously, "Quebec is the cancer of Canada." Invoking the entanglement of the Catholic Church with the government, its editor complained that "medieval Catholicism rules that unfortunate province." Fortunately for freethinkers, he concluded, the federal government was more enlightened.[124]

Was it? On 7 June 1938 Ernest Lapointe, Mackenzie King's minister of justice, sent the prime minister a heated message. "I desire to protest against this decision having been reached, which I believe to be wrong as a matter of principle as well as one of politics," he objected. "Surely, blaspheming is a crime in Canada, as well as immorality or indecent matters. I cannot hold myself responsible for this decision which I think is fundamentally wrong."[125] Three weeks later Lapointe objected again. His mail was now "flooded with protests" against the *Truth Seeker*, he said, reminding King of "the importance this question [might] take in the Province of Quebec."[126] The prime minister turned the question over to James Ilsley, who retorted that if the Ministry of Justice found the material to constitute blasphemous libel, then his Department of National Revenue could ban it. Ilsley went on to note, almost apologetically, that only fifty-five copies of each issue of the *Truth Seeker* were routinely sent to Canada; nor was it banned "by any of the States of the Union or by any other country in the world."[127]

If this was Ilsley's half-hearted way of standing up for the "freedom of conscience" he had earlier praised, it was not effective. By September 1938 the federal government had once again placed the magazine on the prohibited list. The *Truth Seeker* broke the news to its readers with the title "Catholic Intolerance Rules Canadians." The editor had surmised, correctly, that Catholic objections had been pivotal: "The Catholic Church is the enemy," he seethed. "It is an international conspiracy against reason and liberty."[128]

Without resorting to conspiracy theories, it is clear that government policy was genuinely hostile to expressions of unbelief in the interwar period. Liberal principles of freedom of speech were decidedly limited when it came to arguments that threatened the religion of the majority. Of course, federal restrictions specifically targeted popular expressions of unbelief; academics and prominent writers were not persecuted for their skeptical ideas. This distinction was justified in terms of privileging polite and respectful speech over vulgar and offensive diatribes; as we see in the coming chapters, there was clearly a class dimension to prohibitions against expressions of unbelief.

This short survey has touched on the numerous influences that led Canadians to question or reject religious belief in the interwar years – the trauma of war, the growth of radical politics, debates over evolution, and access to irreverent literature. Canada was still, however, officially a Christian nation and, in different ways across the nation, government policy reflected that reality.

OUTLINE OF THE BOOK

The following chapter, our second, outlines the career of Winnipeg-based rationalist Marshall Gauvin, who from 1926 to 1940 made his living by delivering weekly lectures, most often on anti-religious topics. Why start with Winnipeg? Gauvin's story and that of his society are uniquely well preserved, thanks to the donation of his extensive papers to the University of Manitoba Archives after his death. We look first at Gauvin's day-to-day practice as a spokesperson for rationalism, and then at his clashes with fundamentalist, moderate, and radical Christians. His engagement with Winnipeg's left is considered, from his short-lived alliance with the Marxists of the One Big Union (OBU), to his involvement with Popular Front causes and his complex relationship with communism in the mid- to late 1930s.

Our third chapter delves more deeply into Canadian social history by examining the ordinary people who supported Gauvin's Winnipeg Rationalist Society. A comparison of membership lists with census data, army records, and other sources allows us to learn about the racial, ethnic, gender, and class makeup of this community of unbelievers. Working-class English and Scottish immigrants dominated the group, but a variety of other identities were also present.

Toronto is the setting for chapter 4, in which we recount the trial of Ernest V. Sterry, charged with blasphemous libel in 1927. Turning from Sterry's background to press coverage of the prosecution, we discover that, with Canada still considering itself a Christian nation, public expressions of unbelief generated serious opposition. Chapter 5 looks at Sterry's context by exploring the activities of his colleagues in the Rationalist Society of Canada. These rationalists were forceful in bringing their message to the public, and authorities in "Toronto the Good" tried to silence them during the free-speech battles of the early Depression. Like Gauvin, Toronto's rationalists had a complex relationship with the local left, although the actors involved were more diverse. The chapter compares the Rationalist Society with a group formed specifically to combat unbelief, the Canadian Christian Crusade Against Atheism, which had the backing of many reform-minded evangelicals among the city's elite. While most of the Rationalist Society's records have been lost, advertisements and public announcements give us some sense of the group's activities. The greatest amount of detail comes, however, from court documents and news reports of their conflicts with the authorities.

Shifting our focus to Quebec, chapter 6 explores the activities of the Université ouvrière and the Association humanitaire, Montreal organizations formed by the independent communist Albert Saint-Martin and his followers. While these groups were more explicitly political than their counterparts in Winnipeg or Toronto, they also directed their energies to attacking religion, specifically the Catholic Church. Saint-Martin encouraged working-class Quebeckers to study politics, science, and history in order to liberate themselves from oppression. But it was his anti-religious work that the state chose to punish him for, using the law of blasphemous libel, and his organizations faced harsh retaliation through both official and unofficial channels. Saint-Martin's conflicts with state authorities, the Catholic Church, and his rivals in the Communist Party left the sources that made this chapter possible.

Chapter 7 delves into interwar religious controversies in British Columbia and Nova Scotia in order to catch a glimpse of unbelievers in these coastal provinces. A comparison between the two reminds us that the religious and social context in which unbelief operated varied widely across the country. Their respective conflicts saw Christians accusing one another of being closet atheists and gave unbelievers an opportunity to promote their criticism of Christianity. Census data and the events surrounding a debate about faith healing show that interwar British Columbia was unusually open to unbelief compared with the rest of Canada. In Nova Scotia by contrast, a conflict surrounding the teaching of evolution suggests that the province was much less welcoming to unbelievers, and that criticism of Christianity was more limited and restrained.

Unbelievers were always a minority in Canada in the interwar years, but they had an outsized place in the public imagination. Their experiences shed light on the religious and political contexts of their society. Studying their little-known lives opens a window not only on Canada's past but on its present as well.

2

Canada's Professional Atheist

Marshall Gauvin in Winnipeg, 1926–1940

He was an apostle of reason as well as an enemy of cant and hypocrisy.

A.B. McKillop[1]

The chill in the air that Sunday evening in February of 1929 did not discourage the crowds from flocking to downtown Winnipeg to hear a debate between the atheist and the fundamentalist. People said it would be Winnipeg's answer to the infamous Scopes trial, when the populist champion William Jennings Bryan had battled the pugnacious agnostic Clarence Darrow. The Walker Theatre filled to bursting with over three thousand people, and "hundreds more almost fought to gain admittance." When police tried to remove the people crowding the aisles, they found themselves "subjected to impertinence." Those who could not be accommodated at the Walker – over a thousand Winnipeggers – were eventually moved to the nearby Garrick Theatre, where they listened in over a telephone hook-up. The keen excitement of the crowd, particularly when the notorious atheist Marshall Gauvin rose to speak, was likened by a reporter to that of an intense hockey game. Gauvin's oratory power, and the bombast displayed by the poorly prepared fundamentalist John Sturk, heightened the tension.

The reporter James H. Gray described the proceedings: "Mr. Sturk entered with his Bible under his arm. Then came Gauvin followed by two assistants bearing a heavy oaken table. They set the table down, departed and returned immediately, staggering beneath arm-crushing burdens of books. They came and went, came and went, until the table was piled high with weighty tomes. Poor Mr. Sturk! The sight of so much reading matter stacked in one place completely unnerved him."[2]

Gauvin declared, "No human being knows more about God than a mosquito I swatted last summer." His theatrics continued: "I come to tell you that the religion Mr. Sturk represents is not true. I say that none of you is going to the hell in which he believes."[3] When the dust settled, the audience in both theatres voted overwhelmingly for Gauvin. The battle captured the attention of the city and, not surprisingly, put some of Winnipeg's churches on the defensive.[4]

Gauvin was a professional atheist, a self-educated Canadian rationalist who worked as a lecturer in Winnipeg between 1926, when he first came to the city, and 1940, when he retired from public speaking. His career opens a valuable window onto popular unbelief in Canada, as well as a new perspective on dramatic episodes in Winnipeg's religious life in the 1920s and '30s, when fundamentalism and modernism were both on the rise. I suggest that in the relatively new city of Winnipeg rationalism became a viable alternative belief system that largely avoided persecution, even while mainstream society remained strongly Christian.

Aside from being a freethinker, Gauvin sometimes called himself a socialist, in the sense of advocating economic democracy. To him social egalitarianism was a natural fit with a rationalism that sought to bring democratic debate and rational argument to the hierarchical and irrational realm of religion. Gauvin's career proceeded in the border areas between liberalism and socialism, and he alternately used the language of each. Throughout the interwar period, he encountered tension and conflict as he sought alliances and tried to work out what godless politics might look like. It is my contention that it was the strain of these contradictions that caused Gauvin's career eventually to fall apart.

MARSHALL J. GAUVIN

Gauvin was born in 1881 into a working-class Acadian family in Dover, New Brunswick. He spoke both French and English, though his later life was predominantly anglophone. His father was a Baptist and his mother a Catholic, so he was raised in a household where religious differences were inescapable. As a teenager he worked briefly at the *Moncton Daily Times* and was then trained in his father's profession of carpentry. Gauvin also came under the influence of a charismatic local Baptist minister and in 1899 he was baptized. Later that year he travelled to Boston to stay with two older siblings, both of whom had, unbeknownst to him, given up on Christianity and become freethinkers. Under their influence he began to investigate contradictions he had previously noticed in the Bible. Gauvin read works by the famed American agnostic Robert Ingersoll and attended lectures at the Paine Memorial Building, Boston's centre of freethought. Deeply impressed by Ingersoll and the new intellectual vistas that were opened before him, Gauvin rejected religion and was converted to the cause of rationalism. He began to study the Bible critically, eventually memorizing large passages from it. He also became a voracious reader of books on science, philosophy, economics, and a range of other topics.

What was the content of Gauvin's rationalism? He was an atheist who saw the Bible as a collection of legends and lies. He believed that all religions, and especially Christianity, were founded on error and perpetuated through ignorance. Religion was more than an innocent mistake, however; it was a malevolent plot by priestly classes to consolidate their control over ordinary people. The lies and superstitions of religion were profoundly immoral and thus degrading to human nature. Fortunately, in his view, over the last few centuries science and secular scholarship had begun to enlighten humanity. The problem was that educated elites often kept these new concepts from the masses, and it was thus the mission of the rationalist to spread ideas and liberate minds. Gauvin was in ethics a utilitarian and in metaphysics a materialist. He was, however, more a polemicist than a philosopher and tended to draw on philosophical positions pragmatically rather than systematically. For example, as we see later in the chapter, he rejected the idea that people possessed free will; humanity was shaped by its biology and its environment. He also believed, on the other hand, that education could enlighten people and reshape their environment, and that humans were thus free to make up their own minds. As a rationalist he was not interested in resolving the potential contradictions between these positions, but turned rather to the practical issues at hand.

Gauvin was still working as a carpenter when he started giving public speeches on freethought in 1907, and in 1909 began contributing to the *Truth Seeker*, the pre-eminent North American rationalist magazine. He also became interested in socialism and proclaimed economic democracy alongside his anti-religious message. In 1912 Gauvin began a full-time career as a freethought lecturer. After a short stay in Toronto he obtained positions with American rationalist societies in Indianapolis, Pittsburgh, and then Minneapolis. In early 1926, while still living in Minneapolis, he came into contact with a group of working-class Marxists in Winnipeg. They belonged to the One Big Union (OBU), a militant labour organization that had grown out of the Winnipeg General Strike of 1919. The union published its own newspaper, the *OBU Bulletin*, and sponsored radical speakers for a lecture series entitled the OBU Forum. Recent talks on evolution and religion by well-known British rationalist Joseph McCabe had proved so popular that another religious skeptic seemed a good choice as a speaker. So Gauvin was invited to Winnipeg by the union's central figure, R.B. Russell, to speak under the auspices of the forum. He arrived in March 1926, and his appearances at the Pantages Playhouse Theatre drew large and enthusiastic crowds.[5] After his last talk Gauvin asked for a show of hands to determine who would be interested in supporting a full-time rationalist lecturer in Winnipeg. Satisfied with the positive response, he returned in October with his wife, Bertha, and daughter, Madeleine, to take up permanent residence in the city and to organize the Winnipeg Rationalist Society.

Winnipeg was sufficiently tolerant of religious diversity to allow Gauvin to make a career there, and yet it was also conservative enough that his attacks on religion seemed novel and provocative to many people. Looking back at the city during that period, James Gray wrote that Winnipeg had "sheltered and nurtured Marshall J. Gauvin, Canada's only professional atheist," but that Gauvin only contributed to an existing diversity of ideas: "Winnipeg had always been a city in ferment with the ideas wayfaring strangers dropped off, from the single tax to British Israelism. In so cosmopolitan a community, everybody belonged to some minority and the differences in both thought-processes and conviction made Winnipeg's minorities volubly aggressive."[6] Indeed, Gauvin would become a fixture of Winnipeg's public life for the next fourteen years, a capable and contentious spokesperson for its unbelieving minority.

This will not be an account of Gauvin's entire life, as he was unusually long-lived (1881–1978), and our focus is Canada in the interwar period. Nor will it be an in-depth investigation of his beliefs as a rationalist, since Gauvin was not a particularly original thinker. His role was that of a debater, educator, and popularizer. We shall thus look mainly at his activities as a lecturer and leader in Winnipeg, from his arrival from Minneapolis in 1926 until his retirement from full-time lecturing in 1940.

Figure 2.1 Marshall Gauvin, early 1920s

THE RATIONALIST TRADITION

The brand of rationalism that Gauvin brought to Canada descended from the long-established Anglo-American tradition described in the introduction. A visitor to Gauvin's house in 1969 noted large portraits of Charles Bradlaugh and Robert Ingersoll, respectively leading figures of British and American freethought.[7] Gauvin's trajectory fits with larger patterns of British, American, and Canadian secularism, rationalism, and freethought: an early religious commitment giving way to unbelief, working-class autodidactism, political awakening, commitment to science, and moral outrage. His practice as a lecturer and debater also aligned with longstanding rationalist conventions. Gauvin's conversion to freethought and his decision to become a lecturer took place in the "Golden Age" of freethought before 1914. During the Great War, Anglo-American freethought seems to have entered a quiet period. Gauvin's ambitions in the United States would at times suffer from apathy and dissension among freethinkers who, as one might expect, were not known for their uniformity or willingness to follow leaders. In 1933 the writer and critic George Seibel, one of Gauvin's friends from Pittsburgh, half-humorously lamented the weakening of the organized rationalist tradition: "The current lack of interest has come to such a point that the vast majority of unbelievers will not even attend meetings. When Marshall J. Gauvin, the best rationalist lecturer of the present day, now head of a society in Winnipeg, appeared at Indianapolis and Pittsburgh, scores of professed freethinkers declined to support his movement. 'I don't want to hear him kill God every Sunday,' said one. 'The funeral was over long ago.'"[8]

Despite the challenges he had faced in the United States, Gauvin managed to attract sizable audiences in Winnipeg for fourteen years.[9] How did he draw them in? His most popular stock in trade was condemnation of religious superstition. And he actively sought out conflict by challenging clergymen to debates. He was a showman as well, with considerable theatrical flair. "In addition to his oratorical style," wrote Gray, "Gauvin was a natural born-mimic" who delighted in mocking travelling revivalists. "His imitations of their eye-rolling, arm-throwing styles rocked the theatres with laughter."[10]

During Gauvin's first five years in Winnipeg, advertisements for his lectures were carried in the city newspapers' crowded "church pages" on Saturdays, alongside announcements of the next day's sermons and services.[11] Thus, the advertisement of a preacher's upcoming topic might be accompanied by an ad from the rationalist, explaining that he was going to demolish that preacher's sermon from the previous week. He attended numerous church services to take notes and had agents who knew shorthand do the same so that he could rebut sermons point by point.

Gauvin also acted as the local debunker, attacking pseudoscientific ideas such as phrenology. An entrepreneurial guru whom Gauvin tackled was Orlando Miller, who promoted a combination of popular psychology, faith healing, and "visualization," that is, causing reality to change by thinking positively. Gauvin also took aim at "new religious movements" led by charismatic figures. One such opponent was the mystic teacher Eugene Fersen, who claimed to be an exiled Russian baron and the nephew of Leo Tolstoy. Fersen styled himself "Svetozar, the Lightbearer." In 1930 Gauvin debated him before an audience of 1,600 people and, according to all three judges and two-thirds of the audience, emerged the victor.[12]

Where did he get his ideas? Gauvin loved books. They had been his university, and they, along with magazines, were his means of keeping abreast of useful developments in rationalism, science, politics, and biblical studies. In one lecture he explained: "The men who have done mighty things in the world have not done them because they were educated in colleges. The great have been great because they were great naturally and because they fed their greatness from the wellsprings of the world's thought as it is found in books."[13] Visitors to Gauvin's home commented that it was overflowing with volumes on every topic imaginable.[14] His lectures were frequently extended reviews or summaries of books he had read; they profoundly shaped his discourse and his understanding of the world. It should also be remembered that, as a professional speaker, Gauvin was dependent on financial contributions from his listeners. Some variations in emphasis – or outright contradictions – that one finds between certain of his lectures reflect his need to cater to the current interests and tastes of his audiences. Religious controversy seems never to have gone out of style. As Gray commented in 1935, although Gauvin "puts on such a superlative performance in his jousts with priestcraft, his audience refuses to support him if he lapses into secular subjects. Even before the breadlines, socialism, communism and C.C.F.-ites carried off too many of his followers[,] he had difficulty in making ends meet when he turned from Yahweh to science."[15]

Gauvin did want to promote the constructive or positive side of his message. He sought to discuss what an enlightened, secular humanity was doing and could yet do to make the world a better place. In 1934 he changed the name of his society from Rationalist to Humanist, partly in response to the perception that "rationalist" was old-fashioned, but also to emphasize the positive side of his own beliefs. The word "humanism" has a long and complex history, but its identification with a secular view of life is relatively recent.[16] It was beginning to come into use among English-speaking unbelievers during the 1930s, a trend with which Gauvin was no doubt familiar.

The first impulse towards "humanism" as a label came from an American intellectual movement based largely on progressive Unitarianism. In its sense of "secular, human-centred religion" the term dated back to at least 1908, but it was only in the late 1920s that it gained wider currency. In 1927 a Humanist Fellowship was formed in Chicago by Unitarian seminarians and professors, and in 1928 they began publishing *The New Humanist* magazine. The following year Unitarian minister Charles Frances Potter founded the First Humanist Society of New York, which came to have luminaries like Julian Huxley, Albert Einstein, and John Dewey on its advisory board. It was Potter who helped orchestrate the publication of the first Humanist Manifesto, espousing a secular, human-centred view of life, in 1933.[17] (In 1938 he wrote a friendly letter to Gauvin on Humanist Society letterhead, referring to past acquaintance and enquiring about the Winnipeg society's activities.[18]) Unitarians like Potter tended to define "humanism" as a religious alternative to worldviews based on the supernatural, while rationalists and secularists adopted the term as a fresh way to describe their own movements. The rising popularity of this concept in the interwar period did not go unnoticed by Canadian theologians, who debated what tack the churches should take in response.[19]

Despite Gauvin's interest in demonstrating what secular people could or should believe in, he had trouble attracting audiences for such themes and, as it turned out, created serious controversy by addressing topics on which he was not an expert. As Gray implied, Gauvin had been forced to cut short lecture series on "Economics" and "Psychology" partly because of a lack of interest, and partly because his somewhat liberal view of economics did not always align with the views of the many socialist members of his audience. Attacks on Christianity and the Bible therefore remained his bread and butter. In order to dethrone Christianity, the dominant Canadian faith, Gauvin would on occasion speak on other world religions like Islam or Buddhism. While he believed that all religions were ultimately misguided, he would at times say positive things about such non-Christian faiths, to combat the notion that Christianity was somehow superior.[20]

In many ways Gauvin acted as a minister would with a congregation. On occasion his talks were even preceded by an organ recital. More generally, Gauvin spoke every Sunday (except in summer), passed a collection plate, delivered funeral addresses (albeit secular ones), wrote

Figure 2.2 Marshall Gauvin, c. 1930s

letters of recommendation, and served as a patron for rationalists who needed help.[21] In early 1929, for instance, Gauvin intervened with the authorities on behalf of a woman who regularly attended his lectures. Her husband, W.A. Craig, was a bank employee who found himself in straitened circumstances. He had stolen a large sum of money but then, according to Gauvin, returned it of his own accord. Some 1,200 Winnipeggers (both members of Gauvin's Rationalist Society and sympathizers) passed a resolution urging clemency for Craig, and Gauvin corresponded with various government officials on the man's behalf. Not forgetting his *raison d'être*, he took the opportunity to accuse the churches of remaining silent on the case.[22]

FREETHOUGHT *VERSUS* FUNDAMENTALISM

It was Gauvin's skill in rhetorical combat that had helped bring him to Winnipeg in the first place. In the 1920s he had been invited to debate William Bell Riley, the celebrated American evangelist who was the founder of the World Christian Fundamentals Association. The advertisement in the OBU *Bulletin* that announced his invitation had spoken highly of his qualifications: "Recommended by [British rationalist lecturer and ex-monk] Joseph McCabe as the most capable man in America to meet Dr. Riley, the Fundamentalist Leader. Dr. Riley has been invited to meet Gauvin on the above dates in Winnipeg in debate, in acceptance of his challenge made in the daily Press when Joseph McCabe was leaving Winnipeg."[23]

Why did this challenge matter? Contrary to popular myth, fundamentalists, who had been defended by the late William Jennings Bryan in the 1925 Scopes affair, did not slink away into ignominious obscurity or political apathy after the trial. In fact, they were intensely active in the late 1920s. Popular attitudes as to which side had come out on top in the media circus generated by the Scopes case were at first divided; but by the end of the 1920s fundamentalist leaders generally recognized that they had lost the battle for public opinion and control of the major Protestant denominations. Thus, in the 1930s and '40s they renewed their determination to found or expand organizations such as nondenominational churches, Bible colleges, revival circuits, laymen's associations, and radio ministries to protect and propagate their version of Christianity.[24] (D. Bruce Hindmarsh, for one, has demonstrated that Winnipeg was an important hub in this transnational fundamentalist network.[25]) Secular socialists associated with the Winnipeg OBU were keenly aware of these developments – and concerned about them – and their *Bulletin* regularly reported fundamentalist campaigns against evolution. OBU sponsorship of rationalist lecturers may be seen as a counterattack.

Riley was trying, with some measure of success, to take up Bryan's mantle as national spokesperson for American fundamentalists. A skilled orator, he had confronted a number of scientists in public debates on evolution and usually won audience approval. He linked his opposition to modern science and modernist theology with support for conservative politics; in the 1930s he would become an outspoken anti-communist and antisemite.[26] In 1922 the Twin City Rationalist Society, based in Minneapolis and led at that time by

Gauvin, had attacked Riley's anti-evolutionary stance and adopted a resolution "defending the teaching of evolution and condemning church interference in education."[27] The OBU had tried to draft Gauvin to debate Riley, according to McCabe's suggestion. This had proven fruitless; the fundamentalist giant refused, considering Gauvin an inferior opponent to the well-known McCabe.[28] Riley would go on to speak at Winnipeg's Elim Chapel on a number of occasions, but Gauvin had to content himself with taking potshots at him from afar.[29]

A few years later, however, Gauvin was able to confront a different fundamentalist adversary – activist John N. Sturk, secretary of the local Fundamentalist Association of Church Laity. This organization was chiefly concerned with battling modernists in the United Church of Canada, but it did not take Gauvin's provocations lightly either. In January 1929 Sturk lashed out, couching his attack on the rationalist in political terms: "Our objection to Mr. Gauvin is entirely on patriotic grounds. He belittles the Bible, scorns God and teaches ... that man is an ascendant animal. Such doctrines destroy the homes of our land, knock the props from beneath our civilization and undermine our moral foundation."[30] Sturk then sent a hostile letter challenging Gauvin to a debate on creationism *versus* evolution. After some discussion of terms the two settled on a date – 24 February 1929.[31] As we have recounted, that highly dramatic debate attracted a crowd numbering in the thousands, and those in attendance on that frigid Winnipeg evening overwhelmingly voted Gauvin the winner.

On 2 March Sturk fought back. He wrote to the *Free Press* defending his performance. He claimed that Gauvin's followers had rushed the doors to pack both theatres, and grumbled that even "the Archangel Gabriel could not have secured a decision from these audiences." The problem, he argued, was political subversion: "When I announced the National Anthem at the close of the meeting, there were barely enough loyal citizens present to enable us to carry the tune. Almost the entire audience gave it the 'horse-laugh.' Over 3000 agnostics and bolshevists were opposed to me on Sunday night."[32] On 6 March Sturk rallied his followers by holding another meeting at the Walker Theatre. There, he attempted to re-argue the debate, answering points made by the rationalist. Disbelief had serious political consequences, he claimed, pointing to the terrors of the French and Russian revolutions and the role that "Atheistical and Modernistic

Germany" played in the Great War. At the end of Sturk's monologue the audience this time voted *him* "the winner." Gauvin was present and tried to interrupt, backed by some of his followers; but when Sturk reminded him that he had earlier refused an invitation to speak, he gave up.[33]

Not long after that debate, Winnipeg's fundamentalists received reinforcements. One was David Eugene Olson, an enterprising American evangelist who had in 1913 founded a Bible college in Minneapolis and claimed expertise in a number of fields.[34] When he visited Winnipeg in April 1929, he delivered lectures on immigration, billing himself as "organizer and director of the Americanization movement inspired by high officials of the United States to eradicate atheism, anarchy and Communism" among new immigrants to that country.[35] Olson had clashed with Gauvin before, in Minneapolis: they had twice debated the Bible in 1921.[36] Now he challenged Gauvin to a rematch in Winnipeg.[37] The rationalist declined, stating that previous experiences had satisfied him that Olson was an "utterly untruthful" person. In the end the two contented themselves with blasting away at one another from their respective strongholds. Olson tried to wrest the mantle of scientific authority from Gauvin by styling himself as an "inventor, scientist, geologist, mineralogist, paleontologist and biologist, Master of Science." He delivered fiery sermons at various local churches, reassuring his audiences that biblical literalism was being verified by science.[38] Like Sturk, Olson mixed fundamentalist religion with conservative politics, railing against both atheists and "bolshevists." Gauvin, meanwhile, added rebuttals of specific arguments by the evangelist to his regular weekly lectures, as well as attacks on Olson's credentials and activities as an oil promoter.[39]

In 1930 Gauvin would go on to debate another fundamentalist, a clergyman and seminary professor from Pittsburgh named R.J.G. McKnight. The turnout was roughly the same as that for the Sturk debate: over four thousand people crowded into the Olympic Rink in Winnipeg's North End. The clash was front-page news but proved less exciting than Gauvin's battle with Sturk; the audience was well behaved, and McKnight a rather staid opponent, merely reading from a prepared lecture.[40] The appointed judges could not agree on a winner and so the event was declared a draw. This would be Gauvin's last public debate with a fundamentalist in Winnipeg. The movement as a whole was beginning its long turn inward.

RADICAL CHRISTIANS AND MODERNISTS

Not all the Christians Gauvin encountered were as theologically or politically conservative as the fundamentalists. Some, like labour leader William Ivens, a major figure in the 1919 General Strike, combined radical politics with their Christian ideals. In the midst of the strike, Ivens had organized the Labor Church as a radical Christian alternative to conservative or apolitical mainstream churches. The Labor Church flourished briefly, setting up a number of branches around the province, but gradually declined through the 1920s. When Gauvin arrived in Winnipeg, it was entering its final years, although small notices of its services would still appear in the pages of the *OBU Bulletin* near announcements of his lectures.

Did Gauvin ever visit a Labor Church gathering? Contemporary evidence is lacking. Former OBU leader R.B. Russell, in a 1961 interview, recalled both Gauvin and McCabe attending the Labor Church as "frequent visitors." He believed that their rationalist views became prominent within the organization and helped hasten its demise as a religious movement.[41] It does seem plausible that Gauvin would have taken advantage of an opportunity to speak under the church's auspices and to assail whatever religiosity it retained. When asked in 1973, however, Gauvin stated that he had never attended the Labor Church.[42] Nor do his papers contain any reference to it. Whether Gauvin visited it or not, the ideas he championed may well have worked to undermine Ivens's project, as Russell suggested. It seems that in the mid-1920s Gauvin's Rationalist Society became a popular working-class alternative to mainstream Christianity in Winnipeg, a niche that the Labor Church had previously aspired to fill.

Gauvin challenged radical Christianity more directly in 1938, when he responded to an address by J.S. Woodsworth. The former clergyman and then-leader of the democratic socialist Co-operative Commonwealth Federation (CCF) had appeared at Winnipeg's Unitarian Church to speak on the question "Is Christianity Practicable?"[43] Woodsworth thought that Christianity, as an ethical creed, was indeed practicable, albeit difficult, and that it presented a radical challenge to the unjust structures of society.[44] Gauvin, who attended the lecture, professed admiration for Woodsworth and caustically noted that a great many churches were not open to his progressive message. Gauvin had his objections, however, to Woodsworth's claims for Christianity. Even if the religion could be reduced to a system of ethics, which the rationalist doubted, Jesus' moral teachings were totally inadequate for a complex, competitive society. By blessing the "meek" and "poor in spirit," Gauvin declared, the Sermon on the Mount glorified inferiority, timidity, and stupidity. "Any wise father would be pained to discover that his son was inclined to be meek and would advise him to cultivate the habit of trying to hold his own in the world," he scoffed. Gauvin also rejected Woodsworth's pacifism, asserting that war was sometimes unavoidable and that nations must always be ready to defend themselves. To Woodsworth's condemnation of imperialism as a "sickening story of grasping on the part of all nations," Gauvin countered that imperialism was responsible for much good and that "the evils ... connected with it [were] largely due to its abuse." Imperial projects had built up whole nations and civilizations, he insisted.[45] Woodsworth's anti-imperialist politics were too radical for the rationalist.

Apart from this rebuke, Gauvin seems to have spent little time attacking radicals like Woodsworth or Ivens. His more usual targets were mainstream Protestant clergymen who were neither very conservative nor particularly radical. Alhough he obviously enjoyed combatting fundamentalists, he most frequently spoke out against liberal modernists, typically United Church ministers, who accepted most of the claims of higher biblical criticism and the natural sciences, including evolutionary theory, and believed the Bible needed to be reinterpreted in the light of modern knowledge. To them, Christianity was not a static body of dogma, but a progressive revelation of new insights as humanity became more enlightened. Downplaying doctrine, modernists emphasized Christianity as an ethical system relevant to the modern world, even though they did not necessarily espouse the social gospel or progressive politics.

Gauvin believed that the apparent moderation and flexibility of modernists was a greater threat than the rigidity of fundamentalists; they fooled people by obscuring the stark choices that had to be made between faith and reason, tradition and modernity, religion and science. Gauvin also saw these ministers as closet atheists who refused to admit the truth because they wished to maintain their comfortable lives. He assailed them for reinterpreting the historic creeds, on the one hand, and for preaching a thinly disguised secular humanism on the other. This stance frequently put him in the odd position of claiming to define what "real" Christianity was and was not.[46] Gauvin seems to have had little concern for such contradictions; for him, "real" Christianity was the irrational Biblical literalism he had rebelled against as a teenager.[47] Accordingly, he had no patience for allegories or fine theological distinctions. When the Church of England began officially to adopt some modernist ideas on biblical interpretation, he scoffed: "Our Anglican thinkers tell us that the physical features of the Ascension story are to be 'interpreted symbolically.' Your grandmother's knitting is to be interpreted symbolically! The language means what it says or it means nothing."[48] Ironically, in this Gauvin agreed with the fundamentalists: theology was prose, not poetry.

Gauvin was also deeply skeptical of the churches' social message, which he saw as insincere, hypocritical, and self-interested. In 1937 he delivered a provocative lecture on "Jesus Christ the Communist." Gauvin's most commonly expressed position on Christ was that he was a complete fabrication, a myth.[49] In this case, however, the rationalist suspended his disbelief and extrapolated from the figure described in the synoptic gospels. On that basis, Gauvin argued, Jesus was a thorough-going social reformer.[50] He was a large-hearted radical egalitarian who would sweep away existing hierarchies and demand justice for all. He stood as a stark challenge to wealthy churches, whether fundamentalist or modernist. "What are the churches going to do with this human Christ, the Communist Agitator?" Gauvin thundered. "How are they going to interpret to the world the message of the man whose mission was to transform the whole world order with a view to the establishment of a co-operative commonwealth?"[51] When so inclined, the rationalist was as capable of summoning up the radical elements of the Bible as any exponent of the social gospel or liberation theology. Nevertheless, Gauvin's Jesus (if he existed at all) was only human. As historian Ian McKay put it in his description of earlier Canadian socialists, this sweeping vision of a radical democracy meant that even Jesus "would have to agree that he was just one participant in a democratic public sphere in which he enjoyed only rational and political, not magical or supernatural, rights to free expression."[52]

Gauvin's first rationalist lecture, in 1907, and the one he chose as his first in Winnipeg in 1926, was "An Appeal for Truth in Religious Teaching." He charged that mainstream clergy, trained in higher criticism, were aware of the myths and contradictions of the Bible but deliberately hid them from the masses.[53] McKay describes the spirit of this critique as "the pursuit within the sphere of religion of the democratic impulse that socialists wanted to root in politics, economics, and social life."[54] There are echoes here of the radical Protestant criticism of Catholicism (or any established church) for being an unjust hierarchy that reserved access to the sacred to experts and mediators. In Gauvin's opinion, the clergy could no longer remain above the fray of honest questioning and debate; the realm of the sacred had ceased to be a kingdom and become a democracy. His choice of lectures and his daily practice expressed this view. Church ministers who used their pulpits to deliver opinions on science or critiques of the unfaithful would find their remarks recorded, analyzed, and then answered point for point by an articulate, confident, and committed atheist.

The liberal clergy did not allow Gauvin's levelling mission to go unchallenged. Near the end of 1930 the *Free Press* and the *Winnipeg Tribune* suddenly informed him that they would no longer carry advertisements for his lectures on the church page; such ads would be placed on the theatre page. A delegation of clergy, led by United Church ministers, had demanded the change. They were tired of Gauvin's tirades and argued that, since the Rationalist Society was not a church, it should not be allowed to advertise on the church page. The newspaper editors had acquiesced. Gauvin immediately began lobbying to have this decision reversed. He haunted the papers' editorial offices, fired off letters and phone calls to ministers, and gave a number of lectures on the topic, with titles such as "The Clergy of the United Church Against Marshall J. Gauvin – The Modernists Declare War on Rationalism."[55]

One editor asked Gauvin why he was fussing over something so unimportant; nobody cared about the church page, he said, except a bunch of old ladies.[56] Gauvin saw his banishment from the page very differently – as a symbolic attempt to keep the realm of religion separate from the realm of democratic debate and rational argument. In a lecture he declared: "The action of the clergy of the United Church shows that they are unwilling to play the game according to the rules. Instead of answering me they seek to suppress me; they go as far as they dare in this direction by having my advertisement removed from the page to which people look for announcements of Sunday meetings."[57] Gauvin's esteem for the printed word likely intensified his outrage over the incident; to him, texts, even the daily newspapers, carried some authority. He did care about the church page. Religion was malign, but it mattered. In his attempts to rectify the situation he repeatedly argued that because rationalism was concerned with truth, it too was religious. It was in fact a higher and purer form of religion than Christianity, and as such it belonged on the church page.[58]

Through dogged detective work Gauvin discovered that most of Winnipeg's clergy knew nothing about the matter. Eventually he learned the names of the delegates who had visited the newspapers; two United Church ministers in particular had orchestrated the change. These two denied their role and, as a series of hostile letters and phone calls transcribed by Gauvin attest, spread the blame for as long as they could.[59] But at last the truth came out. They were Frederick William Kerr and John Sutherland Bonnell, pastors of two of the city's largest and most popular churches, Knox United and Westminster.

Kerr had previously been condemned by local fundamentalists for his advocacy of modernism. During the furor over evolution provoked by McCabe and Gauvin in 1926, Kerr had preached to an overflowing audience a sermon urging an open mind towards science.[60] Bonnell likewise sought to convince his congregation that science was "The Ally of Religion."[61] The two were not especially radical politically, but Bonnell occasionally discomfited his listeners with sermons such as "If Jesus Returned Today" on the hard-heartedness and injustice of Christian Canada.[62] Because of their popularity, their pronouncements on science, their moderate social views, and their attacks on atheism, Gauvin had frequently given talks debunking their sermons. In 1929, for instance, he gave one of his lectures the provocative title, "But, Prof. Kerr, if God Does Not Control the Forces of Nature, What Does He Do? How Does He Care for Human Beings?"[63] He argued that modernism was merely a dishonest front, a temporary waystation between genuine, fundamentalist Christianity and the truth of secular rationalism. "I am a Rationalist," he declared. "I stand on the hill, watching the upward struggle of the devotees of 'modern religious movements' hampered as they are by creeds that are 'antediluvian' and 'indefensible.'"[64] In 1930, when Bonnell delivered a series of sermons against unbelief, including one called "The Nemesis of Atheism," Gauvin counter-attacked with "Is There a Nemesis of Atheism?"[65] He strenuously objected to Bonnell's efforts to reconcile science with religion, especially when the minister quoted contemporary scientists.[66]

Their visit to the newspapers shows that Kerr and Bonnell were clearly aware of and irritated by Gauvin's attacks. It also demonstrates the social standing that clergy enjoyed at the time; despite Gauvin's efforts, and retractions by the two other ministers who had accompanied Kerr and Bonnell, rationalist advertisements were not allowed back on the church pages. But if the plan was to silence Gauvin, it backfired. He redoubled his attacks on the modernists. He studied his adversaries, collecting newspaper clippings, church bulletins, and sermon transcripts.[67] He wrote, published, and distributed a pamphlet entitled "An Open Letter to Prof. F.W. Kerr, Minister of Knox Church, Winnipeg, Manitoba."[68] Soon afterward, in 1932, Kerr left Winnipeg to take up a pulpit elsewhere. Gauvin kept hammering away at Bonnell; beginning in January 1933, he gave a series of five lectures all aimed at sermons Bonnell had preached. For example, the minister had claimed that Western women owed their emancipation to Christianity; the rationalist fought back with "Woman's Victory over the Church," arguing that women's liberation had come *in spite of* Christianity.[69]

Despite Gauvin's contempt for Bonnell, the two made peace briefly in 1934 in an incident that is revealing of the political climate of the time. In a letter dated 7 February 1934, Gauvin graciously thanked Bonnell for "the good gift you brought me last week." The gift was a book published that very year, *Russia To-Day: What Can We Learn from It?* by Sherwood Eddy, a Christian socialist and former missionary and administrator of the YMCA. A frequent visitor to Soviet Russia, Eddy believed the country had valuable lessons for the rest of the world, although he was also critical of its disregard for civil and religious liberty. He argued that capitalism was doomed and that the way forward was some blend of socialist economic justice and Anglo-American democracy.[70] Gauvin pronounced himself "greatly impressed" with the book and assured Bonnell that he would draw on it for his upcoming lecture series, "The World Revolution on its Way." "It matters little what name we give to our social philosophy, or whether we name it at all," he continued. "What matters is that the machinery of production can and so must serve the essential needs of all mankind. This is the vision for the realization of which in practice Sherwood Eddy is battling so bravely and so splendidly." Remarkably, Gauvin went on to compliment Bonnell for a recent evening sermon he had attended at Westminster. In concluding, he thanked Bonnell again and added: "Let me say that I shall be glad to spend an hour with you sometime to compare notes involving matters on which we agree and some on which we do not."[71]

It would seem that a shared love of books or, more important, a shared interest in socialist ideas, might overcome old animosities. Widespread questioning of capitalism provoked by the Great Depression may also have helped create a rapprochement. The ceasefire did not last long, however. Bonnell moved to New York in 1935 to take over the prestigious pulpit of Fifth Avenue Presbyterian Church. Before the minister left Winnipeg, Gauvin delivered one last broadside. Entitled "A Humanist Looks at Dr. Bonnell and That Call to Fifth Ave. Church," the fourteen-page lecture lambasted the clergy as glorified entertainers and salesmen, and savaged Bonnell as a "cynical, determined, persistent deceiver," dwelling especially on his role in having Gauvin's announcements removed from the church pages.[72]

The rationalist outlasted Bonnell and Kerr in Winnipeg, and for the rest of his career kept up his critique of modernist clergymen.[73] Throughout the interwar period, however, he was never able to match the social standing, popular appeal, or wealth of his opponents. The church-page controversy illustrates that mass media favoured some messages over others, a bias that became even more obvious with the advent of new technology. Bonnell had a weekly radio broadcast on Winnipeg's CKY. Fundamentalists also had radio ministries. Gauvin had only his own voice.[74] As Susan Jacoby has noted for the United States, the gradual eclipse of in-person lecturing by radio would have serious consequences for the more earthbound rationalism.[75]

Perhaps just as important to understanding Gauvin's limited success is that his attacks generally assumed that what mattered most to churchgoers was the formal, intellectual content of the sermons they sat through.[76] He had little appreciation for the emotional appeal of religious communities. The liturgy, the music, art, and architecture, the poetry of theology, the power of myth, the archetypal narratives found in scripture – that is, the overall aesthetic of Christianity that drew people into churches – was to him only empty theatre. A sense of fellowship with Christians both near and far, and the obligations people felt to the long traditions of their ancestors – for Gauvin these were nothing but fond imaginings, outdated relics that could – and should – be exchanged for a far more expansive secular brotherhood encompassing all humanity.[77]

RATIONALISM ON THE LEFT

The brotherhood Gauvin promoted could not avoid sectarianism; political and philosophical differences among unbelievers were not easily overcome. As we saw in chapter 1, some socialists followed Marx in considering religion a secondary phenomenon that would fade away when material conditions improved. At the same time, many rationalists, even those sympathetic to socialism, argued with evangelistic fervour that people's minds needed to be changed by teaching them enlightened beliefs. Gauvin in the interwar period was in the latter camp. In one early lecture he declared: "The business of socialism is not to oppose religion, but to strive for improvement in the industrial world, and in this the Christian and the Freethinker can and do work side by side ... no changes that can take place in the industrial world will suffice to destroy superstition and clothe man with the full power of his rational faculties. That is the work of Freethought. Freethought is the only force that can illumine the dark recesses of superstition with the light of reason."[78] Socialism, he believed, would not cause religion to disappear but rather: "when the Christian gets rid of his religious nonsense, he will turn his attention to the improvement of life in this world."[79] Some socialists saw this view as naïve, while some freethinkers distrusted the more doctrinaire and utopian versions of socialism. Many were liberal individualists, wary of any movement that made far-reaching claims on its adherents.

It was perhaps for such reasons that Gauvin maintained his political independence from organizations and parties other than his society. During his career as a lecturer, however, he did see himself as part of the left and would refer to himself as a socialist. In 1935 he declared: "In the year 1910 I delivered in Commercial Hall, in Boston, a lecture entitled 'Socialism: The Destiny of Democracy.' Never since that time have I wavered in my belief that the goal of progress would be the establishment of some form of Socialist society."[80] Gauvin usually defined "socialism" broadly, as a project that built upon and expanded the essential virtues of liberal democracy rather than replacing them.[81]

Naturally, as the purveyor of an unpopular minority viewpoint, and in keeping with the rationalist tradition, Gauvin was outspoken in his defence of civil and religious liberty.[82] In this he was consistent. Although he had often predicted the benefits that would flow from the end of religion, he took the side of dissenting Christians in their struggle against the Nazis in Germany. "Christianity is being destroyed in Germany," he said, "but we cannot look forward to wholesome results from the stupid racialism which is taking its place."[83] In his opposition to antisemitism, whether it originated with Henry Ford or the forged *Protocols of the Elders of Zion*, Gauvin was also consistent.[84] He took note of the Nazis' treatment of the Jews early on, and his society joined many other Manitobans in condemning German persecution of Jews in April 1933.[85]

Gauvin was, though, affected by North American racist attitudes common in his day. He expressed white supremacist prejudices about the intellectual inferiority of African Americans and the virtues of the Ku Klux Klan's first incarnation during the post–Civil War Reconstruction era, asserting that it was "an innocent affair" because it "served to protect the white man from the black menace in the South." When the Klan appeared on the Canadian prairies, however, he vociferously opposed it. He condemned the contemporary Klan in the harshest of terms and challenged its Canadian organizer, Daniel Carlyle Grant, to a debate in 1928.[86]

One of Gauvin's most consistent allies in local politics was the controversial independent socialist judge Lewis St. George Stubbs. Stubbs was himself a rationalist – a "belligerent agnostic" – who had attended some of Gauvin's lectures and acted as chair for his debate with the fundamentalist professor R.J.G. McKnight. In 1932 and '33 Stubbs was the subject of a Royal Commission of Inquiry for leftist political utterances against the rich and powerful that he had delivered in the courtroom. During this inquiry Gauvin served as the chair of Stubbs's (ultimately unsuccessful) defence committee. The issue, which at bottom seems to have been about a public feud that Stubbs had initiated with the provincial attorney-general, led to his removal from the bench. Stubbs nevertheless went on to become a successful provincial politician, and he and Gauvin continued to work together in left-wing causes such as gathering support for Spain's democratically elected Republicans during the Spanish Civil War.[87]

GAUVIN, R.B. RUSSELL, AND THE OBU

It is significant that it was militant socialists – the radical One Big Union – who had first invited Gauvin to Winnipeg, and that Gauvin's first lectures, like those of Joseph McCabe, took place under the auspices of the ongoing OBU Forum. In March 1926 R.B. Russell reported to the OBU leadership that he had been in contact with "Mr. Gauvin of the Rationalistic Society in Minneapolis," and suggested that he be invited to appear at the forum.[88] McCabe's recent popularity had helped inform Russell's choice, as did the idea that Gauvin could potentially fill in for McCabe in a dramatic debate with fundamentalist leader William Riley. Gauvin's lectures were promoted on the front page of three consecutive *Bulletins* and were followed up by highly positive reviews summarizing what he had said.[89]

Even before the arrival of McCabe or Gauvin, there had clearly been a lot of enthusiasm in the OBU for an anti-religious message. Significantly, Russell had long since rejected the Presbyterianism of his youth. As historian Peter Campbell writes: "Although respectful of his wife's religious beliefs, Russell himself stopped going to church at some point in 1912 or 1913. His move away from the church is evidenced by the fact that the first Russell child, Margaret, was baptized, while the second, a son, David, was not."[90] Attacks on Christianity as well as news stories showing religion in a negative light were common in the pages of the *Bulletin*. Announcements of Gauvin's first few visits, for example, appeared alongside detailed coverage of the ongoing Anthony Bimba case. (Bimba was a Lithuanian-American communist who in 1926 was tried on charges of blasphemy and sedition in the state of Massachusetts for publicly saying God did not exist.[91]) In another issue an article criticized religion on five counts: that it was, broadly speaking, "fictitious, childish, anti-scientific, murderous and reform[ist]," the last charge being the gravest insult of all in the Marxist vocabulary of the OBU. Socialism, the writer asserted, was "the very opposite," because it was "scientific."[92]

In the pages of the *Bulletin*, the defence of science was also considered essential to the war against capitalism. An article entitled "The Master-Class Viewpoint of Evolution: A Sore Point with the Bosses," for instance, highlighted the opposition of Manitoba's provincial Conservative Party to teaching evolution in the schools, which it linked to the shared interests of churchmen and capitalists.[93] The *Bulletin* regularly published McCabe's columns on evolution, religion, and history.[94] While it was not always stated explicitly, the socialists of the OBU seem to have regarded evolution with a sense of proprietary defensiveness. Although the visions of cosmic evolution common among early Canadian socialists between 1890 and 1920 were slowly fading in the 1920s and '30s, there seems to have been a residual feeling that biological evolution somehow underwrote social evolution, which in turn implied the inevitable triumph of socialism.[95] To demonstrate biological evolution was to prove social evolution; an attack on one was an attack on both. More generally, evolutionary thought and a greater scientific understanding of deep time relativized and undercut any claims that existing social structures were natural or unchanging. Thus, socialists in the OBU provided an eager audience for McCabe and Gauvin to prove the reality of evolution over and over again.[96] In 1928 the *Bulletin* proudly announced that after McCabe had lectured in Winnipeg, its city libraries were overwhelmed with requests for books on evolution.[97]

In the relationship between socialism and secularism, however, tensions and contradictions sometimes turned fractious. To begin with, militant atheism in the Winnipeg OBU could hamper union efforts elsewhere to organize workers for whom religion was important. Russell's long-time secretary, Mary Jordan, described in her memoir of his work the effect of anti-religious rhetoric on OBU activities in Quebec. When McCabe visited Winnipeg, she wrote, the "*OBU Bulletin* began reprinting his lectures on evolution, headlining them in glaring black letters about Religions vs. Atheistic Principles. Nothing else could have so hindered organizers of the OBU from making progress in Montreal." Although rank-and-file workers had favoured OBU policies, the Catholic confessional unions were able to present themselves as defenders of the faith and argue that the OBU was creating religious dissension. Organizers in Quebec "threw up their hands at each issue of the *OBU Bulletin*. They were through." Jordan cited Gauvin as one of the rationalist speakers subsequently sponsored by the union in Winnipeg. She felt that Russell was not entirely aware of the effect that anti-religious argument had on efforts in Quebec but noted that the union's constitution was eventually changed to forbid "discussion of religion on the floor of the Labour Council."[98]

Jordan's account is corroborated by OBU records, though some events may have taken place later than she remembered. The minutes of the union's joint executive board meeting for 2 April 1927 refer to "questions raised by some of the organizers in Montreal, re. the religious attacks in the *O.B.U. Bulletin*, stating that the information gathered was that it was detrimental to the activities of the organization."[99] The matter was investigated and discussed at a later meeting, but the officials present seem to have been somewhat puzzled by the claim and thus dropped the issue.[100] At a meeting in October of the same year, however, it was resolved that the *Bulletin* "eliminate as much as possible religious discussion."[101] In December 1927 union officials deemed their efforts in Montreal to have been a failure and withdrew their organizers.[102] The situation in that city was complex, but Jordan was correct in recalling that the *Bulletin*'s anti-religious stance in those years sometimes hurt the union's cause.

Gauvin's relationship with the OBU began to fall apart around the same time the union's mission to Montreal did. This had less to do with his anti-religious message, however, than with his beliefs about economics. A few months into his second season of lectures (1927–28), he gave a talk entitled "Labor's Reward: A Message of Hope for All Workers." He predicted great improvements in machinery and production that would enable goods to be manufactured in large quantities. The resulting economies of scale would mean that companies would reap large profits, enabling them to pay high wages. In order to open up markets for their products, employers would have to pay workers well, and workplace councils would enable employees to deal collectively with employers. The end result would be prosperity and greatly reduced work weeks for all.[103] Gauvin's idealistic vision was decidedly not that of the Marxist OBU, which considered fierce struggle between owners and workers to be inevitable.[104]

The ensuing controversy between the rationalist and his socialist allies is illuminating; its details highlight some of the deep disagreements among different varieties of Canadian unbelievers. Soon after Gauvin's lecture on economics, the OBU *Bulletin* featured a letter to the editor from a writer identified as "D. McA." He opened by establishing his long-time status as an atheist but then criticized the rationalist's lecture for being no better than empty metaphysics. His main accusation was that Gauvin had said "there should be no such thing as a class struggle."[105] In the *Bulletin*'s next issue, Gauvin retorted that he had been misrepresented; what he had said was that "there is no necessary war between Capital and Labour." He challenged "D. McA." to disprove this statement, but not simply by "mentioning the name of Marx, as though that name had in it some divine magic." He went on to accuse the letter writer of merely substituting Marx for God. Gauvin denied that there were only two main classes in society and that it was in the best interests of them both to wage war on each other. Furthermore, he argued that his opponent's viewpoint grossly underestimated the power of religion. The rationalist project of enlightening the people was still a vital one, regardless of what economic determinists thought.[106]

Around the time of this first exchange, OBU insiders began to express discomfort with Gauvin's seeming betrayal of the workers' cause. At a meeting of the OBU Central Labour Council, it was revealed that he would not sell OBU literature at his meetings because the manager of the theatre at which he spoke would not permit it. Nor would he hold his fundraising drives at the OBU Hall, because he felt this would alienate half his audience. One comrade replied in disgust that this was a poor excuse because, when Gauvin had recently asked his audience where they had heard of his meetings, the "overwhelming majority" had cited the *Bulletin*. Another speaker added that he was "more convinced than ever that Gauvin was doing the labor movement harm instead of good."[107]

Meanwhile Gauvin's rebuttal in the *Bulletin* did nothing to settle the matter. The next issue of the paper featured two lengthy columns attacking him. The first, "The Shoemaker to His Last," accused him of provoking a hornet's nest of controversy among workers; the general consensus on the workshop floor, it pronounced, was that he did not know what he was talking about and was overstepping the bounds of his competence. It went on to deliver an extensive lesson in the labour theory of value and the history of classes.[108] The second column was an editorial conveying the official opinion of the *Bulletin*. It expressed some surprise that an enlightened man such as Gauvin should fall into the trap of believing in free will. Under capitalism people were shaped and forced into certain class roles, regardless of their intentions. "While capitalism endures," the editorial asserted, "there will be two classes: one owning because they cannot do otherwise, and the other working, because the economic system condemns them to that task."[109]

Gauvin responded again the following week in a politely worded letter. He insisted that he did not believe in free will. He argued, however, that human beings acted in accordance with their "consciousness" and it was possible for education to shape that consciousness. Furthermore, harmonious dealings were in the best interest of both capital and labour, and the sooner they realized this, the better off both would be. He listed a number of contemporary international examples of cooperation between employers and employees that suggested a brighter world was on its way.[110] A few days later, at a meeting of the Central Labour Council, a member suggested that the union should try to arrange a public debate with Gauvin on economic questions, but this idea was shunted off to the appropriate committee.[111]

The next week, in response to that letter, a *Bulletin* editorial argued that his idea depended on there being some sort of absolute standard of justice on which both classes could agree. In reality, both felt their respective causes were just. Morality and truth were relative to one's economic standing. Gauvin, said the editor, was avoiding "the actual realities of life," and in so doing aligned himself "with those who would cover up the exploitation of one class by the other."[112] As if to issue a final riposte, Gauvin wrote a brief letter to the *Bulletin*. Since he had been told to keep his replies to under 400 words, he began, he would be unable to continue the controversy. He objected, however, to the accusation that he sided with the exploiters: "If labor has a better friend than I am – a man who works harder during more hours a day, seven days a week, to bring sound information to the worker – I should be delighted to see him." He was working, he wrote, for "the coming of the day when there will be no exploitation of labor."[113]

Three weeks later, in a column entitled "The Irrational Rationalist," the *Bulletin* published a fierce attack on Gauvin's motives. Its author, Eric Brooks, portrayed Gauvin as a charlatan who had climbed to fame on the shoulders of Winnipeg's workers and then betrayed them by preaching capitalist propaganda in his lectures. This was doubtless because his audience had changed from a "more or less radical type to a petty bourgeois and more conservative type," Brooks suggested. Gauvin, he said, was merely a puppet of economic determinism, in which he refused to believe. From the rationalist's evasive public utterances and his repetition of capitalist apologetics, Brooks declared under the sub-title "Karl Marx and Gauvin Have Never Met," it was clear that Gauvin had never once studied Marx's work; "as Gauvin is to a fundamentalist on the science of evolution, so is Karl Marx to Gauvin on the science of economics."[114]

Gauvin wrote back angrily in the following week's *Bulletin*. He rejected Brooks's accusations and took particular offence at the statement that he had climbed into the limelight on the shoulders of the OBU. In fact, he went on: "Six months after addressing the O.B.U. Forum, when my audiences were upward of a thousand, I returned to Winnipeg, and in response to advertisements in the two daily papers and in the "*Bulletin*," my first audience at the Metropolitan numbered only about three hundred. For several weeks I ran my lectures at a financial loss owing to the smallness of the audiences. If Mr. Brooks thinks this is climbing into the limelight on the shoulders of the O.B.U., he is welcome to his judgment."[115] Tellingly, however, Gauvin's response said little about his knowledge of economics in general, or Marxism more specifically. There is little evidence that he was familiar with Marx's writings; Brooks may well have been correct on this point.

After this the controversy had died down, at least in public, Gauvin continued to advertise in the *Bulletin*. But nothing had really been settled, and less than a year later, the conflict broke out again. On 10 January 1929 a new broadside, "Morality of Social Evolution: A Reply to Mr. Gauvin at the Garrick," authored by a Frank Roberts, appeared in the paper. Its objections, just like those debated a year earlier, constituted an all-encompassing critique of the rationalist project. Taking aim at Gauvin's latest lecture, Roberts wrote that the rationalist indulged "in the act of chasing God out of the universe one week" and then smuggling him in "through the back door the next, all trimmed up in the fantastic garb of Modern Science." Rationalism, he charged sarcastically, was just as apathetic socially as traditional Christianity: "Resignation is the chief virtue ... There is a golden age just fifty years away for the faithful, a higher form of morality is to come about by rationalist inquiry; all you have to do is seek the truth, denounce the church and wait for something to turn up." Rationalists, he further argued, laid the blame for all the world's troubles at the door of the church, but this was a waste of time: "Our problem is an economic problem, not a religious one ... the church is only the effect, not the cause." Knowledge and science were useful, but not the panaceas Gauvin preached, because they could just as easily oppress the working class as elevate them.[116]

Gauvin retorted that Roberts had misrepresented a lecture in which he had employed a utilitarian standard of morality aligned with those of philosophers like Herbert Spencer and J.S. Mill, which were not based on transcendent values. Religion was no mere side effect of capitalism but played an active and malicious role in society. Throughout history, "the church denounced and prohibited secular studies, banned science, strangled intellectual liberty, murdered thinkers and did her best to destroy the intellectual light of the world." In closing, Gauvin rejected Roberts's wider claim that everything, and especially intellectual questions, could be understood in terms of economics. After all, he asked, if the problem were an economic one, why did so few people show an interest in economics while so many went to church?[117]

And so it went. The two blasted away at each other in ever-longer columns. Roberts labelled Gauvin a naïve utopian socialist who ignored hard realities and dispensed "foolish sentimental soporific platitudes" derived from "romancing troubadours" like H.G. Wells.[118] Gauvin shot back that there had been socialists before Marx, and that Marxist theory had long since been superseded; no living scientific economist accepted that there was one over-arching class struggle going on in the world, and to imagine that an all-out class war would result in peaceful change was foolishness. "I have no love for dictatorships of any kind. And I am satisfied that a dictatorship of the 'proletariat' would be about the worst thing that could happen to the workers," Gauvin wrote. A better world was possible through progressive, directed change. If Roberts wanted to call that prospect utopian, so be it.[119]

After this exchange, the *Bulletin* published several letters and a column criticizing Gauvin's remarks about economics, militarism, and scientific progress.[120] Roberts also struck back with a lengthy article entitled "Mr. Gauvin Repudiates the Class Struggle."[121] The *Bulletin*'s new editor, Charles Lestor, wrote a column stressing how insignificant both religion and rationalism were to the OBU mission. He referred indirectly to Gauvin's just-concluded debate with Sturk, saying that he personally was uninterested in topics religious or atheistic. What really mattered, Lestor argued, was organizing workers and engaging in class struggle. Apart from those concerns, "it doesn't matter what religion a man believes in; he is O.K. from our standpoint if he remains true to the interests of his class." This was in fact a significant change of tone for Lestor, who, in his early columns had fiercely attacked religion on both rationalist and Marxist grounds. When McCabe visited Winnipeg in 1928, Lestor had praised the brilliance and nobility of his intellect, cheering on his work of clearing away the "discarded fables" of religion.[122]

Gauvin responded with one final rebuke – "Dr. Gauvin Still Repudiates the Class Struggle."[123] He rejected his critics' materialist interpretation of history, their understanding of the origins of the Great War, and their Marxist belief that workers' conditions were deteriorating. No modern thinkers took Marx seriously, he claimed; Marx was only historically important as an agitator. The capitalism that he had described was passing away, and a new form was replacing it. Ordinary people were now becoming stockholders of the companies they worked for and realizing that they held common interests with "the leaders of modern industry." No large-scale class struggle was in sight, and it was now the British Labour Party that pointed the way forward by espousing the interests of the whole nation, not just of one class. In conclusion, he reminded his opponents of words that McCabe had once spoken before a Winnipeg audience: "Marxism is dead."[124]

In the same issue, a bewildered reader wrote in to ask Roberts, Gauvin, and the other correspondents what on earth all the fuss was about. Why could Gauvin and the *Bulletin* not just go about their respective good works without assailing each other? Furthermore, he asked, since there was no difference between the teachings of Gauvin and McCabe, "why do you fellows put your arm around McCabe and stick a knife into Gauvin with the other hand? Would it be possible that you are jealous of Mr. Gauvin being able to interest man, woman and child with his eloquent reasoning?"[125] It was too late for reconciliation, however. "Dr. Gauvin Still Repudiates the Class Struggle" was Gauvin's final contribution to the *Bulletin*. Roberts fought back with "Mr. Gauvin Answered", the following week, and two weeks later an unsigned editorial entitled "Marx and His Critics" rebutted Gauvin's claim that Marxism was dead. Gauvin himself remained silent.

Silence seems to have been his choice. At a meeting of the Central Labour Council on 21 March 1929, "Comrade Ashton of the C.P.R. Unit" suggested that, "because of Gauvin's persistent evading of the issues raised his articles should be cut out of the *Bulletin* entirely."[126] Lestor expressed the opinion that "the controversy between Gauvin and Roberts had done good as it had created interest." It was later suggested that a public debate be arranged. But it was not to be. "Comrade Mace ... reported he had talked with Gauvin re[garding] a debate with either Lestor or Russell, and while he was not unwilling to debate yet he felt it could not be made to pay; in other words, he felt there would not be enough interest shown in it."[127] Nevertheless, it was decided that a formal letter should be written to Gauvin, inviting him to participate in a debate on "the Class Struggle." He seems to have turned the offer down.[128] His advertisements kept appearing in the *Bulletin*, but only until the end of that lecture season in June 1929. He never advertised in the *Bulletin* again; this may have been one reason that he would later prove so sensitive about his ads being reclassified by the *Free Press* and the *Tribune*.

The only correspondence with the OBU leader that was found among Gauvin's papers indicates that Gauvin and Russell did not entirely lose contact after the conflict played out in the pages of the

Bulletin. It also provides a window onto the day-to-day life of Gauvin's Rationalist Society. In October 1931 Russell wrote to Gauvin for help in raising funds for a "Comrade Bain," whose wife had died and whose family was in financial distress. Two months later he wrote to Gauvin again, asking for the subscription lists he had provided as well as any donations received. Gauvin wrote back to say that no money had been raised: the members of the society had very little to spare, and when he had approached the Rationalist Women's Club he found that what funds they had were dedicated to putting on a Christmas party for the members' children.[129] Further, some of the women were reluctant to help because they knew Bain had a part-time job and this meant he was already better off than many others. On top of all this, Gauvin sheepishly admitted that he had thrown away the lists.

The fact that the rationalist women knew about Bain's personal situation indicates that there was still some overlap between the OBU constituency and that of the Rationalist Society. But the fact that formal letters were written and that the mix-up happened in the first place would suggest that the two groups were no longer close. Gauvin's comments to Russell also give us a sense of the troubles he faced during the Depression: "It has been more than a little difficult to raise enough money from the audiences this season to keep the work going, so many of our people being out of work or otherwise economically handicapped."[130]

After its altercation with Gauvin, the *Bulletin* did not immediately stop printing anti-religious articles, but such material soon became less prominent. In its remaining years, the paper sent the occasional barb in Gauvin's direction, delivered usually by Lestor. When Gauvin debated McKnight, Lestor sardonically remarked that "the audience who decided by a two-thirds majority that belief in a deity was not necessary or feasible finished the proceedings by one and all singing enthusiastically 'God Save the King' so everything ended harmoniously." Elsewhere in the column Lestor stressed the irrelevance of religious debate: "The law of Historical Materialism enables us to understand what lies at the basis of religion and the man who studies history and religion from the standpoint of Scientific Socialism will eventually look upon the God-killer as he looks upon the parson; there's little difference between the two."[131] In 1933 Lestor reiterated that he did not care whether his socialist comrades were believers. Those who lined up "unequivocally" in favour of the new social order were friends of the workers, whether they were religious or not.

Moreover, he added: "It has been my experience that professional atheists are not all socialists by a long shot, and some of them have even less knowledge of economics than those who hold religious views." His target was clearly Gauvin.[132]

GAUVIN AND THE COMMUNIST PARTY

Gauvin's relationship with communism was even more complex.[133] In 1917 he had initially been enthusiastic about the possibilities of the Russian Revolution, but as he learned more about the turmoil and violence taking place in Russia, he condemned the brutal tactics of the Bolsheviks.[134] Notes he made in 1923 on an article entitled "Russia's Departure from State Socialism" reveal that he watched the Soviet experiment closely.[135] In a 1930 lecture on "Russia in Revolution," he spoke out against political repression, collectivization, and famine in that country. At the same time, he praised the treatment of Russian workers and the regime's attitude towards women's sexual freedom. In sum, though, when he asked, "Has the gain been worth the cost?" he responded, "I think not." Some form of revolution had been inevitable, and Russia could not return to tsarist times, but Gauvin believed the country would have been far better off if it had adopted a parliamentary model.[136]

As of 1934 or 1935, he had come to view Soviet communism in a more favourable light.[137] This change was in part a reaction to the crisis of the Great Depression, the rise of fascist powers, and the leading role of the Communist Party of Canada in challenging the government and organizing the unemployed. In this it was likely connected with the overtures that Communist Party members made to other leftists during the Popular Front period, which in Canada officially began in 1935.[138] (The Popular Front was a strategy on the part of communists to defend liberal democracy from fascism by cooperating with allies, first on the left and eventually in the political centre.) In March 1935 Gauvin compared the Canadian government's treatment of Communist Party leader Tim Buck to Galileo's persecution at the hands of the Inquisition – a significant comparison in a tradition for which Galileo was the pre-eminent secular martyr. In that fiery lecture Gauvin went on to present a systematic defence of the communists' right to pursue revolution against the war-mongering dictatorship of capital. But here again he defined the left very broadly: "The Communists are Socialists, the C.C.Fers are Socialists, and the members of the I.L.P. [Independent Labour Party] are Socialists. That is to say, in ultimate aim and ideal all these parties are agreed." Gauvin had not suddenly converted to Marxist theory; he was still a skeptic. He was by no means a member of the Communist Party, and in 1935 he would again publicly criticize Stalin's ruthless dictatorship.[139]

What appreciation Gauvin held for the Communist Party no doubt came about also thanks to his side-by-side work with communists in Popular Front campaigns. In 1935, after the RCMP and local police had brought the On-to-Ottawa Trek of the unemployed to a bloody end in the Regina Riot, Gauvin went to Regina with other members of a Winnipeg committee formed to support the trekkers. The committee included James Litterick, provincial secretary of the Communist Party of Manitoba; Independent Labor Party MLA Fred Lawrence; and socialist feminist Beatrice Brigden.[140] Gauvin addressed a crowd of more than three thousand people at a heated protest meeting in Regina on 5 July 1935, blaming the federal government and the police for the riot. "Are you people going to continue paying a high wage to a body of men who can become assassins of your life as well as your liberty?" he demanded. He condemned Prime Minister Mackenzie King in particular: "The crime is that of the moral bully who sits in Ottawa and his henchmen!" he bellowed.[141]

On 18 September 1936 Gauvin chaired a meeting of the local branch of the League Against War and Fascism, and complimented the speakers "on their talents and courage."[142] He was also active in the Committee to Aid Spanish Democracy, speaking at its events and helping to bring representatives of Spain's left-leaning Republican government to Winnipeg.[143] When the communist Norman Bethune came to the city in 1937 to raise support for the beleaguered Republicans, Gauvin helped arrange a mass meeting and gave the overflowing audience a brief history of the Spanish Civil War before introducing the famous doctor.[144]

Between 1936 and 1939 Gauvin's enthusiasm for the Soviet experiment grew even further. In those years he gave lectures calling for a "Five Year Plan for Canada" and praising the "New Russian Constitution." He delivered a lengthy series of speeches on the theme of "The Communist Challenge to the Churches." His talk on "How the Russians Like Living in Russia" declared that the Russians liked it very well. Gauvin even gave a special Christmas Day lecture entitled "Russia: Humanity's Living Christ," which re-appropriated religious language to proclaim the new gospel of Soviet Russia: "Mankind will be saved not in another world but in this. They will be saved not by a Christ who is dead but by the saving efforts of living men and women. Russia points to the way of humanity's social salvation. Hail, then, to Russia, Humanity's living Christ!"[145]

This effusive admiration for communism was destined to be short-lived. Towards the end of 1939, when the Soviets signed a non-aggression pact with Nazi Germany Gauvin's hopes for communism were irrevocably dashed. He was stunned by the Soviets' apparent betrayal of the struggle against fascism. When he began his final lecture season in September 1939, he did not immediately address the issue, speaking instead against Nazi Germany's aggressive actions. But later in the season he gave a lecture criticizing Russia's attack on Finland.[146]

There were other signs, too, of Gauvin's change in attitude. On 17 December 1939 he participated in a memorial for the then-recently deceased Norman Bethune. Everything seemed to be going smoothly at the event until the prominent communist William Kardash bluntly reminded all present that Bethune had been a communist and that "it takes a Communist to do what Bethune did." This gruff assertion of the superiority of communism was received poorly by some in the crowd. Professor W.F. Osborne of the University of Manitoba responded that the meeting was not about communism but rather about Bethune's good deeds. Then, to the obvious enjoyment of the RCMP informant in the audience, the final speaker rose: "Marshall J. Gauvin condemned Stalin and warned the worshiping enthusiasts of diabolic diplomacy not to be quite so sure of themselves. As the Communist Party had been chiefly responsible for the meeting and most of the audience were Party sympathizers, the remarks of Prof. Osborne and Marshall Gauvin were received with bad grace."[147] Less than a month later, on 14 January 1940, having prepared extensively, Gauvin delivered his formal statement on the Soviets, one of the most important lectures of his life. It was called "Just What Has Happened in Russia?" This was followed by five other lectures with such titles as "Russia in Chains" and "Stalin's Massacre of the Innocents."

The deletions and additions scribbled on Gauvin's typewritten lecture notes reveal just how difficult and controversial he found the topic. His original notes for "Just What Has Happened in Russia?" acknowledge his about-face: "I know that some will say that I have changed my attitude regarding Russia. Some are greatly displeased because of what I have said regarding Russia's part in the war." Gauvin then reviewed his early denunciations, in the 1920s, of "the terrors and the bloodshed" of the Russian Revolution. But then, he said, when Russian communism appeared to enter a constructive new phase, he felt it would be pointless to dwell on past problems: "So I praised the new developments. And it may well be that I saw more in those developments than actually was there. But if I was fooled to a degree, millions of other progressive thinkers who cherished only the best wishes for Russia were likewise fooled."[148]

His illusions were shattered, Gauvin confessed, by "the greatest surprise of the modern world – the Russo-German non-aggression pact that led to the war ... Treason more foul is not recorded in the annals of the world." It pained him, he said, to speak of these matters but it needed to be done to set the record straight. "There are some among us whose sympathies are strongly against Great Britain because they think that Russia is fighting the cause of the common people; they need to be disillusioned by being told the truth about Russia." In addition, Gauvin wished to disabuse those who still thought there was anything admirable in the Russia economic system. "I speak as one who believes ardently in the coming of economic democracy," he maintained. Nevertheless, "this beneficent development, which civilization demands" could not come through violence and bloodshed. In final comments to those accusing him of inconsistency, he openly acknowledged his error: "My attitude towards Russia has changed ... because Russia has changed. I am speaking now not of the Russia that talked in favour of peace and democracy in 1938, but of the Russia that had destroyed peace and is fighting democracy in 1940."[149] In a later lecture he admitted that he had been misled to some extent by his reliance on books: "How far the [Soviet] government carried its oppression and repression, I did not know, and I am satisfied that none of the writers whose books I read knew."[150]

There can be little doubt that these pronouncements alienated elements of Gauvin's society, particularly after the rationalist had been so lavish in his praise of Soviet communism. When A.B. McKillop asked him in 1969 whether his lectures had become less popular because he began to speak increasingly against communism, Gauvin replied unequivocally, "Oh, yes, certainly, I lost a great deal of support."[151] That loss related to his political views contributed to ending Gauvin's career as a professional atheist. The 1939–40 lecture season was his last. The problem was not only the message but also the medium. Late in life Gauvin recalled: "The age of the lecturer was passing when I entered it. The movies, the cars, radio and television have made it impossible for public speakers to attract the audiences of the old days." He comforted himself with the observation that even if "all wheels" rolled away from lecture halls, the same held true for churches.[152]

Furthermore, in his conversation with McKillop, Gauvin conceded that "even before I gave those lectures [on Russia] I could see that interest was waning somewhat because we were in a depression and many people simply could not afford to put even a nickel on the collection plate."[153] Dependent as he was on the donations of his audience, few of whom were wealthy, there can be little doubt of the problems the Depression caused him. Nevertheless, it is significant that Gauvin had managed to survive the harsh 1930s and yet ended his career immediately after repudiating communism.

In the 1950s Gauvin turned his skills against the cause he had previously embraced. For example, in an article entitled "The Challenge of Communism," he wrote: "Like a snowball rolling down a slope, the Communist menace grows. Everywhere its agents are at work stimulating unrest, inciting to violence, cultivating hatred of established institutions."[154] This sort of paranoid rhetoric appeared whenever Gauvin wrote about communism after 1940. Just as he had earlier declared economic democracy the inevitable destiny of humanity, in his later years Gauvin would frequently proclaim capitalism to be natural: "It is basic in human nature. You cannot get away from it. Man is made that way," he told McKillop in 1969. Gauvin asserted that the underlying fact of human history was that "the upper classes pulled the working class up by the scruff of the neck and the heels and tried to make something of him."[155] He had by then abandoned his egalitarianism along with his hopes for socialism.

RETIREMENT

In 1940 when Gauvin retired from lecturing, he was fifty-nine. He returned to manual work, this time for a local company producing planes for the war effort. He would later travel to New York City in search of a new career. After the war he sought to become head of the National Liberal League, an organization for American freethinkers, but fell victim to in-fighting and was eventually obliged to return to Winnipeg. For the rest of his life Gauvin continued writing pieces for the venerable freethought magazine *The Truth Seeker*.

Unfortunately, Charles Lee Smith, the editor from 1937 to 1964, and his successor, James Hervey Johnson, were fanatical racists and anti-semites who turned the journal into a vehicle for those views, thereby alienating much of the readership.[156] Although Gauvin remonstrated with Smith in private letters, he kept on contributing articles to the magazine.[157] Perhaps he hoped to be a moderating force, but over time he became the sole representative of traditional freethought in its pages.

Gauvin's career as a lecturer in Winnipeg is instructive for a number of reasons. Although North American rationalism in the interwar period lacked the vigour that propelled it in the late nineteenth century, Gauvin was able to attract sizable audiences. They supported him for fourteen years. Even though fundamentalism had many adherents in Winnipeg and the mainstream churches were well attended, Gauvin's entire career indicates that a significant minority of people, and in particular working-class people, questioned or rejected Christianity. The popular enthusiasm for Gauvin's confrontations over evolution demonstrates that the topic could still cause great excitement. Furthermore, a reading of his lectures reveals the vitality of the rationalist tradition, despite some setbacks and changes in emphasis. Robert Ingersoll would have recognized Gauvin's underlying message as his own, just as Gauvin would have recognized many of the polemics of the "New Atheists" who emerged in the early twenty-first century.[158]

The rhetoric of fundamentalists like Riley, Sturk, and Olson shows the close connections between conservative Christianity and conservative politics. It was a common tactic to paint leftists as being godless and immoral, but the attack clearly worked the other way as well. Atheists could be written off as "bolshevists," regardless of their actual politics. Furthermore, the public's interest in clashes between fundamentalism and modernism on questions like evolution provided an opening for those who, like Gauvin, rejected religion altogether. Meanwhile, the machinations of the ministers Bonnell and Kerr during the church-page affair illustrate the type of strategy that leading liberal clergymen were willing to deploy to maintain their prerogatives. A word from an authority figure into the right ear could be more effective than a dozen passionately argued lectures. Influence over the media could ensure that unorthodox messages were marginalized. That being said, in contrast to his counterparts in Toronto or Montreal, Gauvin faced no official persecution.

Gauvin's presence in the Winnipeg left illustrates the broader tensions between freethinkers, who were dedicated to saving humanity by rationally enlightening it, and secular socialists, who looked forward to revolutionary material change. Both saw themselves as scientific and scorned the other as naïve. Of course, we must be careful not to draw these distinctions too sharply: Gauvin, though no Marxist, often drew on the language of socialism; the OBU published a good deal of anti-religious material, and sponsored speakers such as McCabe and Gauvin. But when attacks on religion cost support and Gauvin challenged Marxism, the union was quick to change its tune. Russell and Lestor began to insist that religion did not really matter in the final analysis. Socialists could be Christians or atheists, as long as they organized to fight capitalism: their metaphysical beliefs would inevitably be refashioned as material conditions changed. Meanwhile, Gauvin's rationalism came down on the side of correct belief. An enlightened labourer, regardless of his economic position, would be much better off than one who remained a slave to superstition. Furthermore, education could lead to positive change in the world of work; class struggle was not inevitable. Thus, Gauvin's blend of progressive liberalism and idealist socialism clashed with the more militant Marxism of the OBU and ended the hitherto unproblematic alliance that had existed between the Rationalist Society and the One Big Union.

During the dark days of the Depression, with fascism on the rise, Gauvin began to see the Communist Party as a powerful ally in building a just, peaceful, and secular society. He remained at arm's length from the party but cooperated in causes that it backed. He also spoke enthusiastically about the Soviet experiment. Nevertheless, his liberal commitments made him deeply critical of Bolshevik violence and Stalinist repression. The Soviet Union's about-face and surprise pact with Hitler shocked and dismayed him. His bitterness towards communism after 1940 was that of the betrayed lover, even after the Soviet Union again became an ally against fascism in 1941. Gauvin's conversion to a fervent anti-communist stance would demonstrate the truth of Lestor's contention that "professional atheists are not all socialists by a long shot."[159] Nevertheless, it seems that many members of his audience remained attached to socialist ideals, a fact that contributed to ending his career.

But just who were the people who attended Gauvin's lectures? What did his constituency of unbelievers in Winnipeg look like? These are the questions we explore in the coming chapter.

3

The Winnipeg Rationalist Society

It has for the most part been difficult to learn much about ordinary unbelievers through historical research. Like most people, they left little by way of detailed written material about their lives. Moreover, unbelievers held unpopular opinions, which often encouraged them to remain silent and led others to disparage or ignore them. Thus, the records of the Winnipeg Rationalist Society preserved by Marshall Gauvin offer us a unique opportunity to study the social makeup of unbelief in Canada in the interwar years. As we shall see, the Rationalist Society was made up primarily of working-class British immigrants, although it contained a cross-section of other ethnicities and classes. The majority of its supporters were male, but women were a surprisingly substantial presence, given the gendered masculine nature of unbelief in these years.

To appreciate the context in which the society operated, we can look to contemporary government sources. The 1921 census reported that Manitoba was home to 52 agnostics, 113 atheists, 79 freethinkers, and 1,491 people with "no religion." Out of a population of 610,118, this meant that a small proportion (about 0.28 per cent) of Manitobans were willing to identify themselves as unbelievers.[1] In 1931 the categories were not as detailed, but 2,629 Manitobans in a population of 700,139 (0.37 per cent) said they had no religion.[2] As we shall see, some of those unbelievers associated themselves with the Winnipeg Rationalist Society, whereas others did not.

Observations by Gauvin and his contemporaries give us a partial view of of the society. To begin with, Gauvin only moved to Winnipeg because his talks at the One Big Union (OBU) Forum received a warm welcome from city residents. It seems likely, therefore, that the core of the society's membership, at least in the early years, was made up of workers who had heard of him through union events. Sometime in the latter half of 1927 Gauvin asked his audience where they had first learned of his lectures, and an "overwhelming majority" indicated that it had been in the pages of the *Bulletin*.[3]

In December 1927, however, an OBU official reported that Gauvin had refused to hold his fundraising whist drives at the OBU Hall, for fear of driving away part of his audience.[4] In 1928 and '29 the rationalist was several times accused by union spokesmen of catering to the "bourgeois" elements in his audience. One such accusation came from union member Eric Brooks, who in 1928 wrote an article in the *Bulletin* claiming that Gauvin had bowed to the forces of "economic determinism" by distancing himself from the OBU and injecting pro-capitalist economics into his lectures: "Today the class-conscious workers are only a small minority of his audience. It is the petty bourgeois upon whom he depends to swell the collection plate."[5] As discussed in the previous chapter, this rift meant that Gauvin's advertisements had by 1930 vanished from the pages of the *Bulletin*, though a civil exchange of letters with R.B. Russell in December 1931 suggested the divorce was not absolute. That exchange, regarding donations for the widower "Comrade Bain," indicated that some of Gauvin's "congregants" were also still involved with the social world of the union.[6]

In 1935 the journalist James Gray asked: "Why is [Gauvin's] small congregation so preponderantly middle-aged, working class, poverty stricken? Where are all the Liberals and the liberals whose cause he pleads and the labour leaders, and the radical pedagogues, and the University student body? And where, oh where, are the editors of liberal newspapers? There are the people who should support his work and we wonder at their continued absence."[7] Gray would later describe himself as "a communicant of Marshall Gauvin's," so his comments here were based on first-hand observation.[8] This description, which puts greater emphasis on who *wasn't* at Gauvin's meetings than on who was, does not fit neatly with Eric Brooks's view of the society. Brooks felt that the petty bourgeoisie were dominating the group, while Gray's lament was that liberal-minded middle-class people and educated professionals were not attending.

Gauvin was himself asked in 1969 about the composition of his Winnipeg audiences. "Oh," he replied, "they would be largely working people, of course, but that, too, means more or less – some of them would be intelligent people; some of them readers and some of them people who liked to talk of their views and, of course, some of them just plain working people."[9] This description is no doubt accurate as far as it goes, but it still leaves much to the imagination. To sum up these disparate observations: some of those attending Gauvin's meetings had connections with the radicals of the OBU; they were mainly of the petty bourgeoisie; they were poor, working-class, middle-aged, and largely uneducated; they were mainly working people but a mixture of intelligent autodidacts and those who were less well informed. These impressions say nothing about other factors, like gender or ethnicity.

There is, however, another source of information on the ordinary rationalists and humanists who came to lectures and supported the Rationalist Society. The Gauvin archival collection contains a number of membership and mailing lists. Other information about supporters can be gleaned from Gauvin's correspondence.[10] Of course these data are incomplete and occasionally garbled. Over the fourteen years of his lecturing career in Winnipeg, Gauvin experimented with different methods of raising money that included selling memberships and tickets that gave the bearer preferred seating privileges. He also seems to have kept track of those who bought neither but who donated or at least expressed interest. One set of ticket and membership lists comes from the 1929–31 lecture seasons, and another set includes dates from 1933 to 1935. Although the mailing lists are undated they clearly come from different periods. A number of names appear in more than one list and in the correspondence; others appear only once.

Using this information, I constructed a database that contains 1,018 names, beginning with Mrs M.H. Abremovitch and ending with Mrs J. Zeemel.[11] I then cross-referenced it with a number of contemporary sources. Chief among these were the three censuses closest in time that were available in manuscript form: the 1921 general census and the 1916 and 1926 special Prairie Provinces censuses. I also consulted the records of the Canadian Expeditionary Force from the First World War,[12] and was able to match Gauvin's lists to the census and/or military records for 385 people, or about 38 per cent of the total list.[13] Despite the intervening years, a significant number of the names and home addresses Gauvin had recorded matched those in government sources exactly. Details regarding family members or type of employment from Gauvin's records helped determine positive matches for others. The information provided by these 385 matches was supplemented by other sources such as naturalization records, the 1932 Henderson directory for Winnipeg, and information from the *Manitoba* (later *Winnipeg*) *Free Press*.[14]

Before analyzing these data, we should note that the people associated with Gauvin's society were by no means the only unbelievers present in Winnipeg at the time. This becomes clear upon examining the 1916 and 1921 censuses, which tracked religion. People willing to reveal their unbelief to a census enumerator (typically someone recruited from their neighbourhood) can be considered fairly committed in their heterodoxy. Thomas and Kate Laycock, farmers in rural Manitoba, for instance, are listed along with their five children as "religion 'none.'" Herman and Anna Anderson, immigrants from Denmark living in Selkirk, Manitoba, called themselves "freethinkers." Frederick Burland, a farm labourer, told the enumerator that his religious denomination was "socialist," while Ernest McBain rejected the Christian Science beliefs of his family by saying "none." None of these people show up in Gauvin's records, and there are others like them in the census.[15] Gauvin's records do not constitute the whole picture, but they can give us a useful snapshot of unbelievers in Manitoba.

GENDER OF RATIONALIST SOCIETY SUPPORTERS

Out of the entire rationalist database of 1,018 names, 501 are male (49 per cent), 314 (31 per cent) are female, and 203 (20 per cent) cannot be identified either way.[16] If we remove the "unknowns" from the list, males make up roughly 60 per cent of the gendered names, and females the remaining 40 per cent.[17] Since there is no way to ascertain the sex of the names of unknown gender, all we can say for certain is that women made up somewhere from 30 per cent to 40 per cent of Gauvin's supporters, with the total number of men ranging from 60 per cent to 70 per cent. We may recall from the second chapter that the 1921 census indicated the gender of those who identified as atheists, agnostics, and so forth. In that categorization, 24 per cent of atheists and agnostics were female, as were 32 per cent of freethinkers. Among those with "no religion," 28 per cent were female.[18] Women may thus have been proportionally somewhat overrepresented in the Winnipeg Rationalist Society.

Did the women listed actually come to lectures, or did men just provide their wives' names out of some sense of propriety? Many women in the database do appear alongside their husbands, but not all do. For example, the women of the Mains family (Bessie, Esther, Fannie, and Jessie) are listed as dues-paying members of Gauvin's society, without any male relatives. Margaret and Donald Barrie are both listed as members; according to the census, she was the head of the household and he was her youngest son. The enumerator listed Margaret as married, but we find no mention of Mr Barrie.

Indeed, at least 120 female names appear in Gauvin's records without husbands being listed. This comprises about 40 per cent of the total number of women; the true number is likely higher, since some uncertain cases have been counted as being part of a married couple. Some of these women and girls are listed alongside their parents or children. Others appear alone but gave their husband's name, like Mrs George Patton. Still others simply gave their own names, like Fannie Wortman or Miss Elizabeth Dyck. We cannot assume that wives listed with their husbands were necessarily less committed to the cause of rationalism. Sam and Hilda Dunnett, who lived in Transcona, a small town just east of Winnipeg proper, were both members of the society. It was beneath her name (as Mrs S. Dunnett) that Gauvin wrote: "She is a leading spirit among the members from Transcona, and could … take charge of the matter [there]."[19]

A GREYING MEMBERSHIP?

Was James Gray right to call Gauvin's congregants "middle-aged" in 1935? In that year, at least, it appears he was. Birth years have been found for 395 Gauvin supporters. Two-thirds of those, a surprising 66 per cent, were between the ages of forty and sixty in 1935; 23 per cent were aged thirty-nine or younger; the youngest was nineteen. The remaining 12 per cent were sixty or older; the oldest people in the sample would have been seventy-nine years old in 1935. Viewing this data visually in figure 3.1, we can see the clear predominance of middle-aged adults.

A few cautions are in order. It is clear that this sample skews slightly towards greater age, because the most recent available records date from 1914 to 1926.[20] Further, there is some evidence to suggest that at least some teenagers attended Gauvin's lectures, as a few names on the wider list appear to fit a parent-child relationship. Bessie, Esther,

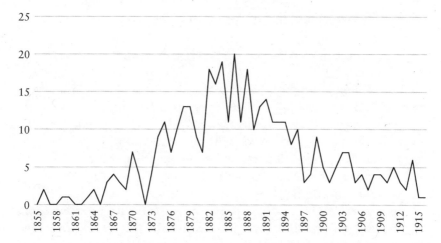

Figure 3.1 Year of birth of Winnipeg Rationalist Society supporters

Fannie, and Jessie, mentioned above, were likely a mother and her daughters.[21] If we choose to examine the society's demographics from an earlier point in its existence – 1928, for example – we find many of its supporters in their mid-thirties.

Despite these caveats, it seems that a majority of the members and supporters of the society were indeed middle-aged and older. Even if the sample omits younger members, the concentration of those born between 1875 and 1895 is quite striking. Why might this be so? First, let us remember that Gauvin was himself born in 1881 and turned fifty-four in 1935; the age and outlook of the lecturer no doubt had an influence on the makeup of his audience. On a more prosaic level, younger parents may have been too busy to attend or unwilling to bring their children. Correspondence from December 1931 does mention that the Women's Club was putting on "a Christmas party for the benefit of the children of members and friends of the Society."[22] Nevertheless it is difficult to imagine young children sitting through Gauvin's lectures, and I have discovered no mention of their presence there.[23] Gauvin's files contain a number of funeral addresses that he gave in Winnipeg but there was apparently no secular equivalent for baptizing or christening children.[24] Another reason may have been that lecturing was seen as a somewhat old-fashioned pastime. The new popular culture of movies, radio, and automobiles was certainly more attractive to young people than sitting through a lecture, much less one delivered weekly by the same middle-aged man.

COUNTRY OF ORIGIN AND ETHNICITY

Using government records and a few other sources, I was able to find the ethnicity and immigration status of 385 of Gauvin's supporters; both the military and the census takers asked people where they were born. Of that number, 130 people (34 per cent) were born in Canada (many had come to Manitoba from other provinces, especially Ontario and Nova Scotia). But the majority of our total sample (255, or 66 per cent) were immigrants to Canada: 31 per cent were born in England and Wales, 12 per cent in Scotland, and 4 per cent in Ireland. Thus 140 (47 per cent) of the sample group were born in the British Isles.

The next largest country of origin was Russia, with 26 immigrants (7 per cent), almost all of Jewish or German descent, as we see below. The United States followed, with 17 people (4 per cent). Another 26 people (7 per cent) came from other European countries, and the remaining five people in the identified sample came from other British colonies.[25]

In the context of the settlement of Manitoba, the predominance of immigrants is not surprising. The province's population increased almost tenfold between 1881 and 1921, leaping from 62,260 to 610,118 as white settlers surged onto the Prairies.[26] Winnipeg's population grew at twice that rate in the same period (from 7,985 to 179,087).[27] Is it thus safe to assume that Gauvin's supporters, even those born in Canada, were all of settler stock? The same sample of people has been organized by ethnicity, on the basis of their answers in the 1916, 1921, and 1926 censuses to the question of their "racial or tribal origin." Of the sample group, 171 (44 per cent) were of English descent, 85 (22 per cent) Scottish, 38 (10 per cent) Irish, and 3 (1 per cent) Welsh. Those percentages of the total indicate that almost 78 per cent of this group were of Anglo-Celtic descent. What of the other 22 per cent? The largest non-British group were Jews, with 29 (7.5 per cent) people, most of whom originated in Russia but were recorded as Jewish, Hebrew, or Yiddish. Of the remainder, 11 (3 per cent) were German, 10 (3 per cent) were of Icelandic background, and 7 (2 per cent) were Dutch. Among the remaining twenty-three rationalist congregants, there were small numbers of other European ethnicities and four Americans.[28]

Groups that were not represented deserve mention as well. The sample was exclusively white (to the extent that Jews and Eastern and Southern Europeans were considered "white" at the time). Judging by the census data, there were no First Nations people, and none of Winnipeg's Black Canadians were included.[29] Nor were any East or South Asian Canadians, though some Chinese immigrants living in Winnipeg appeared in the censuses with their religion listed as "none." Of course, we do not know for certain that such groups were entirely absent from the broader list, or that no person of colour ever attended Gauvin's lectures or debates. But there is no evidence that they did. As noted in the previous chapter, Gauvin spoke out against the contemporary Ku Klux Klan, but repeated racist tropes about the original Klan serving as a bulwark against "the black menace" in the South. In theory, he was usually opposed to racism, or "racialism," but still held that Black people were generally less intelligent than whites. The underlying attitude would not have encouraged the attendance of African Canadians nor, one presumes, of any other people of colour.[30]

Gauvin was more vocal and consistent in condemning antisemitism. This attitude may have encouraged Jews who were more secular in outlook to attend and support his lectures in an era when antisemitism was widespread. Jews make up 8 per cent of the sample, and a look at the broader list reveals a number of other surnames that were very likely Jewish.[31] Adding people from the sample to other probable candidates, I found at least sixty names that are definitely or likely Jewish in origin, such as Hy Lepkin, Aaron Gurvitch, and Eva Arenowsky. This group amounts to about 7 per cent of the entire list. As Gray noted in his histories of the interwar Prairies, some Jews in Winnipeg changed their names to avoid prejudicial treatment, and there are likely other people on the broader list who had done just that.[32] Therefore a Jewish presence of roughly 7–8 per cent overall seems probable, and is consistent with the statistics of religious affiliation discussed below.

How does the ethnic makeup of the Rationalist Society and its sympathizers compare with that of its social context? The large majority were from Winnipeg and its surrounding towns. Statistics for the city alone would be incomplete; but figures for all the urban areas of Manitoba in 1931 are as follows.[33] People of Anglo-Celtic descent constituted about 61 per cent of Manitoba's urban population (those of English descent made up 29 per cent, Scots 19 per cent, and Irish 12.5 per cent). Ukrainians represented over 7 per cent, Jews (or "Hebrews") about 6 per cent. The other major groups were Poles (5.5 per cent), Germans (5 per cent), and French (4.5 per cent). The diverse remainder comprised 11.5 per cent of the population. It is striking that those of English descent are significantly overrepresented among the sample of rationalists. Scottish, Jewish, and Icelandic people are also slightly overrepresented. On the other hand, the Irish, Ukrainians, Poles, Germans, and French are underrepresented among Gauvin's supporters. Why might this be?

As the rationalist sample is rather small, some distortion is to be expected. The difference in date may also have been a factor; while Gauvin's lists come mainly from the 1930s, the government sources used to determine ethnicity are somewhat earlier. Specifically, this helps explain the underrepresentation of Germans among the ranks of the rationalists. Given the immense hostility to Germans during the Great War (when some of the government records were generated), some people of this ethnicity may not have been willing to identify themselves as such.

English and Scottish men seem to have predominated in the One Big Union and the radical (and mostly skilled) workers who read the *OBU Bulletin*. Within its pages one finds much nostalgia for British football and frequent references to Britain as "The Old Country." This connection might help explain the overrepresentation of these groups. The skeptical, Unitarian intellectual tradition among Icelanders, and the sizable community of secular Jewish leftists in Winnipeg, helps explain why both of these ethnicities would have been more attracted to unbelief than others. Meanwhile, groups for whom a tradition of minority nationalism or ethnic pride was usually bound up with Catholicism – French-Canadians and some of the Irish – may have been less open to rationalism. As we shall see, people with Catholic backgrounds made up only 6 per cent of the sample. Of course, linguistic considerations may also have been a factor in determining who attended and who did not. While Gauvin seems to have retained some grasp of French, he never lectured in that language. European immigrants whose grasp of English was tenuous would likely have stayed away.

RELIGIOUS DENOMINATIONS

Why would skeptics and unbelievers have a religious affiliation? As odd as it may seem, 94 per cent of people in the sample group did acknowledge a religious denomination to the 1921 census enumerators or on their attestation papers. (Of course, this was five to twelve years before Gauvin first arrived in Winnipeg in 1926. The 1926 special

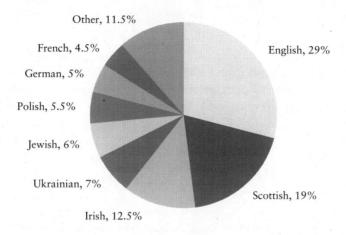

Figure 3.2 Urban Ethnicity in Manitoba, 1931

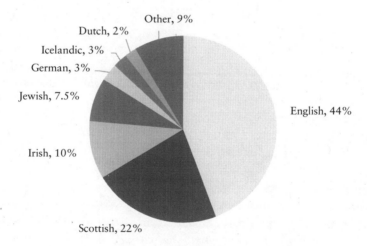

Figure 3.3 Ethnicity of Winnipeg Rationalist Society supporters

census did not ask about religion.) Some may have considered themselves observant Christians or Jews at that time. There are also reasons that those who were skeptical or apathetic towards religion would not have identified themselves as such to the state. To begin with, unbelief does not appear to have been an option on attestation papers. The military's administrators were not interested in the personal beliefs of their recruits, but rather in allocating chaplains and providing for appropriate burial arrangements. In regard to the census, the enumerators were likely to speak only to one household member and record whatever answers that person gave, a procedure that may have silenced unbelievers who lived with religious housemates. Considerations of respectability and peer pressure may also have played a role in responses. Identifying oneself as an unbeliever in the midst of the Great War, often propagandized as a crusade for Christianity and civilization, would have required a great deal of conviction. And lastly, doubters may have lacked a vocabulary for identifying themselves until a group of like-minded individuals coalesced in the city.

That being said, seventeen people (6 per cent) in the sample did identify themselves as unbelievers, or at least religiously unaffiliated, in the 1916 and 1921 censuses. Their responses indicate that committed unbelief predated Gauvin's arrival in the city, and thus deserve a closer look. Some unbelievers were isolated within their own families. David Barry was an Irish-born Canadian Pacific Railway (CPR) foreman who called himself a Freethinker, although his wife, Louise, identified as a Methodist.[34] Similarly, Henry David Cleal, who had arrived from England in 1913, called himself a Freethinker, while his children were brought up as Methodists. Another divided family was the Williamses. The father, James R. Williams, a railway worker, told the enumerator in 1916 that he was an agnostic. His wife and three sons were listed as Methodists, but the middle son, Harold (only five when the census was taken), would later join his father on Gauvin's lists.

Also caught between rationalism and Methodism was Ruth Birchard. She was only two years old in 1916 when her family (her parents and younger brother, along with Ruth) had their religion listed as "None." In 1921, when she was seven, the Birchards told the enumerator they were Methodists. Regardless, Ruth later bought tickets to Gauvin's lectures and also wrote him a note (in French) thanking him for a favour he had done for her. Other people moved in a more straightforward fashion from belief to unbelief. The Kaulback family, James (a railway conductor), Mary, and their son Aldrich, called themselves Presbyterians in 1916, but agnostics in 1921. They all became paying members of the Rationalist Society. A fellow member, Mary Van Leuven, an American widow, had claimed to be a Presbyterian in 1911, but by 1916 her religion was listed as "N.A."

Lynne Marks, in her study of unbelief in British Columbia, has noted the high correlation between single men, particularly those living in rooming or boarding houses, and declarations of atheism. This pattern also pertains in Winnipeg.[35] William B. Brown, an unmarried boarder, was a twenty-seven-year-old immigrant who had come from England in 1910. He was listed as a civil servant who worked at city hall, and his religion was recorded as "None." Also of interest is the fact that the "roomer" listed immediately before Brown was Arthur Mercer, who would later be a member of Gauvin's society, a reliable donor and a three-time correspondent. Doubtless the two had remained in touch in the ensuing years. In the 1916 census, however, Mercer was listed as a Congregationalist. Another single male roomer who gave "none" as his religion was Ernest Crook, an auto salesman who appears in the 1921 census. On his earlier army attestation papers, Crook had called himself a Methodist. His experience of the war may have led him to lose his faith. Perhaps another influence was his roommate, Sidney Chatfield, who also reported having no religion (Chatfield does not appear on any of Gauvin's lists). The same pattern applies to John Hughson, an American-born railway clerk who in 1916 was a single boarder whose chosen religion was "none." Hughson lived with fellow American Harry Miller, who was a "none" and who, like Chatfield, does not appear in Gauvin's records. Men's degree of religious commitment was frequently tied to their marital status and to the company they kept.

Married life did not necessarily imply religiosity, however. An English bricklayer named William H. Downes (39), his wife, Mary (36), and their children Kenneth (5) and Winona (4) were listed as "Agnostic" in the 1916 census; the first three would later be counted among the members of Gauvin's society.[36] Another unbelieving family, the Hulls, had a harder time registering their protest against religion. John T. Hull would become one of Gauvin's supporters in the 1930s. In 1916 the Hull family was living in Saskatoon, where the forty-one-year-old John T. Sr, an English immigrant, worked as a journalist. John T. Jr was only seven. It is unclear which John T. ended up on Gauvin's list. On the census the entire family (both parents and all six children) were listed as rationalists. At some later date, however, the enumerator or some other editor scribbled a large "Anglican" across the column of carefully written "rationalists." Someone had decided that rationalism was not an acceptable label, and that the Hulls should more appropriately be considered lapsed members of England's state church.

Even from this small sample a few patterns emerge. One is that is that unbelief, like religion, ran in families. Harold S. Williams, Ruth Birchard, and possibly John T. Hull Jr, followed in the footsteps of unbelieving parents, while the Kaulbacks, the Hulls, and the Downeses all came from households in which unbelief was the norm. Lynne Marks's point about unbelief among single male roomers is borne out by William Brown, Ernest Crook, and John Hughson. Finally, the fact that four of these unbelievers worked for railroad companies is not coincidental; as we shall see below, a significant percentage of Gauvin's supporters were employed on the railways.

What of the majority who did give a religious denomination? No fewer than 91 (30 per cent), said they were Anglicans, while 71 (23 per cent) responded that they were Presbyterians. Together these two denominations made up a substantial proportion (53 per cent) of the total. The next largest group was Methodists, at 12 per cent (37), followed by Jews and Catholics each at 6 per cent (19), and Lutherans at 5 per cent (14). Unitarians made up 3 per cent of the sample (8), while a handful of other Protestants (Congregationalists, Baptists, Pentecostals, and others) amounted to 8 per cent of the total (20 people in all). Five (2 per cent) told the census-takers they were members of the Labor Church, the working-class alternative to mainstream Christianity that grew out of the Winnipeg General Strike.[37]

The data also show signs of apathy towards religious labels. For example, two men who had cited one religion to enumerators later gave a different one to military authorities. Many others cited one religion in 1916 and a different one in 1921. No doubt some were moving from church to church, in the so-called Circulation of the Saints, but it is equally likely that some respondents just did not care much about their denominational identity. A few people gave vague answers, like "Non-Conformist," or simply "Protestant." The Lemon family, Ada and her husband, John W., for instance, told the enumerator in 1916 that they were "Undenominational" but both later became members of the Rationalist Society. "Undenominational" was a term sometimes used by fundamentalists to indicate their rejection of mainstream churches, but in this case it likely reflected disillusion with organized religion in general.[38]

Why would Anglicans and Presbyterians be so heavily represented in the sample?[39] One answer is that, as we have seen, the Rationalist Society was dominated by English and Scottish immigrants, who were most likely to be affiliated with those churches. But this common

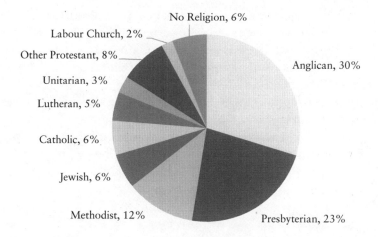

Figure 3.4 Religious denominations of Winnipeg Rationalist Society supporters

observation – that religious affiliation is often as much about national or ethnic identity as it is about belief – can be viewed in a more critical light.[40] Most of Gauvin's supporters had emigrated from countries where one belonged to a national church by default. Even in Canada, Anglicanism, Presbyterianism, and to a lesser extent Methodism, had served as quasi-establishment bodies, at least for English speakers.[41] In the Canadian or British context it was relatively easy to hold a mainly ethnic affiliation with the Anglican or Presbyterian Church, in comparison to a group like the Baptists. The same correlation between ethnicity and religion largely holds true for the Lutherans (Germans, Scandinavians) and Catholics (Irish, French) on the list. This is not to say that some of Winnipeg's rationalists and humanists did not previously identify sincerely with the religious doctrines of these churches, but that as a whole they tended to identify with religious traditions that had low requirements for membership and a high degree of ethnic/family-based commitment. Nor is it surprising that Anglicans are so highly represented; they were the Protestant denomination with the lowest rates of regular church attendance.[42] In the case of John T. Hull and his family, mentioned above, the enumerator seems to have decided that rationalists of English descent were merely lapsed Anglicans.

The proportion of Jews in the sample, 6 per cent, is consistent with the percentage counted as ethnic Jews, 7 per cent. In the portions of the 1916 and 1921 censuses that I have studied, Jews were always marked as both religiously and ethnically Jewish (or Hebrew or

Yiddish). There was no category for "secular Jew." Meanwhile, the presence of Unitarians reminds us of the currents of skepticism running through that tradition. There is evidence in Gauvin's correspondence to suggest that he was a supporter of Winnipeg's Unitarian Church late in his life.[43]

Supporters were not the only people who attended Gauvin's lectures and debates, of course. Correspondence and letters to the editor reveal that Christians came to listen, often with the intent of trying to stump or debunk Gauvin.[44] As James Gray recalled, "Gauvin customarily spoke for an hour, caught his breath while the collection plate was passed, and then answered questions for another hour. It was during the question period that the believers sought to confound Gauvin by quoting the scriptures in rebuttal of his theses." But this "was a fatal mistake," thanks to Gauvin's prodigious memory, broad familiarity with biblical scholarship, and quick wit. "Against Gauvin, the Christadelphians, Mormons, Baptists, and Plymouth Brethren were massively undergunned," Gray recalled. Such opponents eventually grew frustrated and stopped coming at all.[45]

PROFESSION AND EMPLOYMENT

Was Gauvin's congregation largely poor and working-class, or was it dominated by "the petty bourgeois," as OBU writer Eric Brooks termed them? There seems to be support for both views. Employment information was found for 285 Rationalist Society supporters. Most of this information dates from the 1914–21 period, athough some of it comes from Gauvin's lists, and some from obituaries and other later descriptions.

A total of 214 of those listed (72 per cent of the sample) were male. Of these, 111 (52 per cent of all men) did work that can be considered "blue-collar": they were carpenters, prospectors, riveters, locomotive engineers, teamsters, milkmen, mail carriers, and the like. A further 44 (21 per cent) performed clerical duties or similar work. This category includes clerks, bookkeepers, telegraph operators, insurance agents, and low-level civil servants. Meanwhile, 31 (15 per cent) were business owners, and for most this meant small business: peddlers, a few barbers and café owners, merchants who sold fruit or fur, a self-employed painter, and a bicycle shop owner. One man, "Professor" Peter R. Scott, owned a dance academy. About 20 (9 per cent) could be considered white-collar professionals: medical practitioners, a few

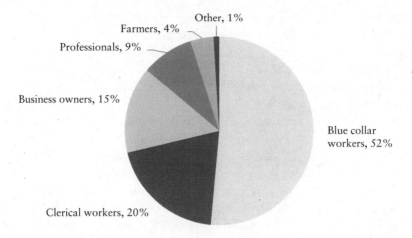

Figure 3.5 Employment of male supporters of Winnipeg Rationalist Society

managers, two journalists, two lawyers, and a judge.[46] Only eight men (4 per cent) were farmers or farm labourers.

Railway work appears very frequently as a source of employment for the men. A total of 59 men (28 per cent of 214) were employed by railway companies. When wives, children and a few other family members are factored in, we find that those dependent on railway work amount to 87 persons (or 29 per cent of the wider sample of 300 people). The types of railway jobs included were diverse: engineers, conductors, labourers, clerks, boilermakers, ironworkers, and firemen, among others. One man, Raymond Sellar, worked as a caterer for the CPR shops and lived on site with his wife.

Was there something about working on the rails that inclined people to religious skepticism?[47] Did this triumph of human ingenuity speak to the irrelevance of God? Humanity's growing control of its own destiny through science and technology was in fact a key component of rationalist thought. In this case, however, economic and sociological patterns are a more direct cause. Many Winnipeggers worked for rail companies because the city was the major land transport hub for Western Canada. Rail workers also represent the early core of supporters that had learned of the Rationalist Society's meetings through the *OBU Bulletin*. By the time of the Great War, skilled railway workers had become central to labour radicalism in Winnipeg.[48] R.B. Russell, the OBU's chief organizer, had come into labour activism as a machinist from a railway shop.[49] The OBU had limited success in formally recruiting rail workers, but they remained important players in labour politics in the city. Russell and the *Bulletin* thus frequently appealed to men in the "running trades."[50] Gauvin had also been a carpenter in a railway shop in Moncton for thirteen years before starting to lecture full-time, and this may have inspired some sense of camaraderie.[51]

What of the women on the list? Employment information was found for 71 adult women. No fewer than 53 of them (75 per cent) were housewives or widows who did not work outside the home. The remaining 17 (25 per cent) were engaged in paid employment. Three were teachers: Beulah Strachan, Mrs M. Melanson, and Winnifred D. Boughton. The latter, in fact, was also the principal of the rural school where she taught.[52] Rose Bogoch was listed as a housewife in 1916 but as an office worker on her 1934 naturalization papers. Edna Olive Gillingham, the daughter of a railroad foreman, was only a child in 1916, but went on to a long career as a secretary at the Royal Bank of Canada.[53] Several women worked as cleaners or domestic servants. Jean Mallon worked as a domestic, while her husband, William, was a gardener for the same employer; the two went on to own the Bird's Eye Café together. In 1929 Jean Pazareno moved out to Saskatchewan and attempted to open her own beauty salon, but this enterprise failed.[54]

Some of Gauvin's supporters did manage to create successful business enterprises, even in the midst of the Depression. Nathan Portnoy, who appears on one of Gauvin's mailing lists, was a Russian Jewish entrepreneur. After serving in the Canadian Expeditionary Force, he founded a dry-cleaning company, Perth's, which came to dominate the Winnipeg market for those services throughout the twentieth century.[55] Norman Gooch was a correspondent and financial supporter of Gauvin's. Born in Manitoba to English parents, he founded a popular bicycle shop in 1927 which continued to be run by his family into the twenty-first century. The most successful businessman to appear on Gauvin's lists was Max Freed, who eventually owned a diverse set of companies and became a major figure in the city's horse-racing culture.[56] Like these three, most of the business owners on the list seem to have been men of British or Jewish descent.

These proportions are not dramatically different from those found among nineteenth-century British unbelievers. The historian Susan Budd found that 40 per cent of the secularists she studied were semi-skilled or unskilled workers, 20 per cent were skilled or craft workers,

20 per cent were white-collar workers, and 15 per cent were small business owners, which left 3 per cent as rural workers and 2 per cent as professionals. Edward Royle, meanwhile, found a smaller percentage of semi-skilled workers and a higher rate of small business ownership. These percentages generally accord with my findings for the Winnipeg rationalists, although I have not distinguished between semi-skilled and skilled workers. Given the heavy concentration of men in the running trades, however, I suspect the Winnipeg group was generally more highly skilled than the British norm.[57]

One other detail derived from the profession sample was the number of veterans it included. Out of 214, some 64 (30 per cent) were veterans of the Great War. The great majority had enlisted of their own accord, sometimes right when they turned seventeen or eighteen, although a few were drafted in 1918. A handful served as officers. Charles Butler Hallwood enlisted in September 1914 as a private and was eventually promoted to lieutenant, even serving as acting captain for a time. During the war he was both bayoneted and shot but the wounds were apparently minor. Stanley Gordon Fogg enlisted in December 1914 and by war's end was a sergeant in an artillery brigade, having received several shrapnel wounds and earned a Distinguished Conduct Medal. Those who served in the CEF were mostly of British stock, and in fact many had been born in Britain.[58] Did their experience of war have any connection with their later unbelief? The question is intriguing, but detailed evidence is lacking. As noted in the first chapter, many Canadian veterans did become disillusioned with organized religion. It seems likely that some members of the Winnipeg Rationalist Society shared that experience.

POLITICAL VIEWS

In the previous chapter we discussed Gauvin's position on the left, his falling-out with the OBU, and the loss of support he experienced when he denounced Soviet Communism in 1939. Given the content of his lectures it appears that the political leanings of his followers were largely left of centre, ranging from progressive liberals to labourites, democratic socialists, and Marxist militants.

A few political activists, some well known to historians and others not, appear among Gauvin's supporters. We have previously discussed Gauvin's involvement with the outspoken leftist judge and later Member of Parliament Lewis Stubbs. Another prominent activist was

Frederick J. Dixon, the one-time labour leader known for his role in Winnipeg's General Strike.[59] In late December 1928 Dixon stepped in as a replacement lecturer when Gauvin was ill. He spoke on "Tolstoy's view of the land question and regarding war and peace."[60]

Other politically active rationalists did not achieve the same fame (or notoriety) as Stubbs or Dixon. One was Stephen Sawula, a lawyer and socialist activist of Ukrainian descent, who was both a member of the society and a significant donor.[61] Nils-Erik Johnson, a Swedish immigrant who wrote to Gauvin asking for help in spreading the rationalist message among Manitoba's Swedish-Canadians, advocated for the rights of the unemployed during the Depression.[62] Dr Robert John Yeo, a dentist and member of the society, held various positions in the Co-operative Commonwealth Federation (CCF) in the late 1930s.[63] Max Tessler, who appeared on one of Gauvin's mailing lists, was a Jewish Marxist who had been active in the Socialist Party of Canada, the Tailors' Union, and the Winnipeg Trades and Labour Council.[64] Finally, Mrs Frances Chrispin, Mrs Delia Jones, and Mrs Jessie McLennan were part of Lewis Stubbs's election committee when he successfully ran for parliament in 1936.[65] Political awareness seems to have been fairly high among Gauvin's supporters, although few of them ran for office or became famous.

SUMMING UP

What were the benefits to all these people of their attendance at the Rationalist Society lectures? The condemnation of religion, the more scathing the better, seems to have always been the biggest draw. Attacks on superstition and religious hypocrisy were always well attended, while lectures on other topics were less popular. As Gauvin said years later, many of his supporters were "inclined to believe that the old story was not quite sound and they liked to hear a man talking about the various phases of it."[66]

Gauvin himself usually stressed the educational quality of his work, and supportive correspondents often complimented him on spreading reason and enlightenment. The rationalist's mission was of course part of a longer tradition. Writing of nineteenth-century Britain, Edward Royle observed that "the informal education provided by Mechanics' Institutes, secularist schools and the like meant a great deal to intelligent working men whose natural abilities were not matched to their opportunities."[67] It is likely that at least some of Gauvin's

British working-class supporters were familiar with this tradition of popular and autodidact education and saw the Winnipeg Rationalist Society as an extension of it.

Gauvin also attracted audiences with his consummate skill as an orator. A letter of New Year's congratulations to the Gauvin family from a Mr and Mrs Scott concluded by saying, "There are two men in the world whom we greatly admire, and love to listen to, they are Sir John Martin Harvey + Marshall Gauvin."[68] Sir John Martin-Harvey was an English actor who was popular in Canada thanks to frequent North American tours. There was certainly entertainment value in attending Gauvin's lectures. We have already noted the rationalist's skill in mimicry and the sometimes comedic nature of his presentations. At the very least, they gave people who were not interested in religion or the male culture of heavy drinking something to do on Sunday afternoons.[69] And finally, the lectures were free. You did not have to contribute if you were short on funds, an attractive feature, especially during the Great Depression.

Gauvin's correspondence contains hints of the social life of the Rationalist Society. A few passing mentions are made of a Rationalist Women's Club and its secretary, a Mrs Clouter, though little detailed information survives. One person wrote anonymously to Gauvin complaining about how unfriendly his wife, Bertha, had been when greeted recently. In this case, at least, Bertha seems to have been put into the unenviable social position of being a preacher's wife, or rather the secular equivalent. We read of other small frictions as well. After Gauvin introduced a premium seating arrangement to raise money, there were conflicts over who got to sit where and for how much.[70] Of course, small antagonisms can be found in any organization. But what, we must ask, was it that accounted for the Winnipeg society's remarkable staying power? It may have been the largest single group of its type in Canadian history, and it endured throughout the harsh environment of the Depression.

Credit must be given to Gauvin's remarkable talent as a publicist, orator, and organizer. He used the experience he had gained from years of lecturing in Minneapolis, Pittsburgh, and elsewhere to good effect. He tapped into an existing community in the One Big Union and the radicals who associated with it or were sympathetic to it. What's more, to the chagrin of OBU officials, the Rationalist Society was not identified simply with one section of the left. As we have seen from the statistics, it was a coalition of different communities; the British blue-collar workers at its core were joined by secular Jews, Icelandic ex-Unitarians, long-time rationalists, and other groups. And, important especially for the times, it managed to appeal to a significant number of women.

In the Anglo-American context, women have historically been a definite minority among secularists, and a decided majority among churchgoers.[71] Women did challenge Christian orthodoxy in this era, but rather than become secularists they were far more likely to turn to new religious movements like spiritualism, Christian Science, Theosophy, or Pentecostalism.[72] Callum Brown's influential *The Death of Christian Britain* reshaped the field of secularization theory by arguing that, since about 1800, British Christianity had depended for its survival on women.[73] By linking religiosity tightly with a discourse of female domesticity and respectability, Christianity became an integral part of society, even for non-churchgoers. In this view, the rapid secularization of Britain starting in the 1960s was due to women finally rejecting this Christian discourse as well as removing themselves from the churches. In a more recent study, Brown has argued that this shift was even more rapid in Canada.[74] Churchgoing and Christian identification remained higher here through the 1950s than in the USA or Britain, but as of the 1960s it plunged more precipitously than in any other country save the Netherlands.

Thus, it is not surprising to find that men dominated the Winnipeg Rationalist/Humanist Society. It is interesting, however, that women, a significant number of them not socially attached to men, still made up between 30 and 40 per cent of Gauvin's supporters. Why might this be so? It might have to do with the way his society tapped into existing "alternative" communities, mentioned above, of which women were already an integral part. The fact that Winnipeg was still in many ways a new and cosmopolitan city with a plethora of unusual subcultures, as James Gray observed, may also have been a factor; perhaps the pressure for women to conform to Christian respectability was not as strong in such a diverse setting.[75] Another explanation might be that the society modelled itself as a secular alternative to churchgoing. It was different, yes, but not outlandishly so. Meetings occurred every Sunday and were advertised on the church page. The same older male authority figure spoke at every meeting, and the event was sometimes preceded by an organ recital.[76] Nor did the meetings take place in an exclusively male setting. The venue was not the OBU Hall, an Oddfellows' Hall, or some other male refuge, but a mainstream theatre.[77] Gauvin's strong emphasis on rationalism being more moral than religion, and his frequent invocation of Ingersoll's high standards of domesticity, would have also helped establish the Rationalist Society as a respectable place. No doubt some women did not care about this type of respectability, and Gauvin's fundamentalist opponents were not won over. But it is possible that enough women found these markers attractive to make a difference in the overall gender ratio.

There are also hints that Gauvin actively tried to involve women to some degree, although he definitely remained in charge. Bertha Gauvin, his wife, seems to have been a frequent presence and played a social role. The Women's Club Christmas party and its gatherings (typically hosted by Mrs Gauvin, although the secretary was Mrs Clouter) have been mentioned, as have Mrs Hilda Dunnett of Transcona and Gauvin's note that she might "take charge" of some business of the Rationalist Society in that area. Gauvin also occasionally spoke on "the woman question" and insisted that Christianity had always historically oppressed women.[78]

What, then, is our overall picture of the members and supporters of the Winnipeg Rationalist Society in the interwar years of our study? They were probably all white, and there were typically more men present than women, though women made up a significant minority. Most could safely be called "working class" but they were generally skilled workers, many in the "running trades." Like most of Winnipeg's residents, a majority had immigrated from Europe or eastern Canada in the previous twenty to forty years. Most came from religious backgrounds, chiefly from mainstream Protestant denominations, although the extent of their prior commitment is open to question. In the early years of the society, most of its adherents were in their thirties, forties, and fifties; as the group's later years approached, so did theirs. Many came out of a self-consciously radical working-class tradition, but the society was not monolithic in this regard. As mentioned, it represented a coalition of people from various backgrounds: lapsed Anglicans and Presbyterians associated with secular Jews, ex-Unitarians, and former Labour Church members; railway workers rubbed shoulders with small business owners and clerical workers; and Britons attended meetings alongside a wide variety of continental Europeans and a few Americans. The unifying attraction was the popular education, enlightenment and entertainment offered by Marshall Gauvin and his interpretation of the rationalist tradition.

One detail is easy to overlook by its very absence: Winnipeg's rationalists do not seem to have faced much opposition for their beliefs. There was a social cost to the rejection of Christianity, and clergymen denounced unbelief from the pulpit, but there is no record indicating that local unbelievers faced organized persecution. This was in fact remarkable, as we see in turning our attention to Toronto and Montreal, where conflict over unbelief was more intense. One of the most dramatic manifestations of this conflict, a trial for blasphemous libel, took place in Toronto in 1927. It is the subject of our next chapter.

4

The Sterry Trial and the Debate over Blasphemy

The accused man sat quietly and showed no emotion as the charges against him were read out.[1] A bespectacled, formally dressed British Canadian, he did not appear to be particularly dangerous, but many Torontonians considered him a menace to God, to the nation, and to public morality. He was a "mongrel cur," said one prominent clergyman, and his office should be disinfected as the Augean stables had been.[2] His "scandalous, impious, blasphemous and profane" writings aimed a "death blow" at the Canadian state.[3] For these reasons he became the first person in English Canada to be tried for the crime of blasphemous libel.[4]

Why such vituperation? How had it come to this? Late in 1926 Ernest Victor Sterry had found himself out of work. At loose ends, he decided to write and publish a newspaper to spread rationalist ideas among his fellow Torontonians. He gave it a slightly misleading title: *The Christian Inquirer: A Publication Directed to Furthering the Modernist Movement*.[5] The first number was alliteratively described as "A Pithy, Popular Presentation of Profound Problems Perplexing the People." Sterry intended to follow it up with more issues, but that was not to be.[6] The purpose of the paper, he wrote, was to further the populist mission of rationalist education: "to provide in the cheapest form the reviews and arguments and demonstrable facts usually kept more or less concealed from the mass of the people by the aristocracy of intellect."[7]

The eight pages of the *Inquirer* featured more than thirty short entries on a variety of topics. Sterry managed to include a broad array of classic rationalist arguments, most of which are still employed by skeptics and atheists today. These ranged from a rehearsal of the moral defects of the Bible and the improbability of immortality, to the problem of evil and the cruel wastefulness of nature: "O! The myriads that have been chased for dear life tormented by frantic fear, only to fall and be overtaken by ravenous, flesh-eating animals," read one dramatic entry entitled "Endless Destruction of Life."[8] "Will you face a bitter truth or hug a fond delusion?" the rationalist asked his readers. Sterry pointed to scriptural contradictions and the doubts of modern clergymen to call into question the veracity of the Bible. Certain sections of the *Inquirer*, like Sterry's condemnation of the "cold, dull shadow" cast over the Canadian people by "The Curse of Puritanism," were aimed directly at the sensibilities of Toronto's Protestants.[9] The paper promised that its next issue would discuss the insights of skeptical Canadian luminaries such as Sir William Osler and Professor Goldwin Smith.[10] Like many other self-taught rationalists, Sterry wished to communicate the obscure but explosive truths of modern science, philosophy, and biblical criticism to ordinary people who might not otherwise hear of them.

One passage in particular would come back to haunt Sterry. Under the title "The Jewish God," he wrote:

> The God of the Bible is depicted as one who walked in the Garden of Eden, talked with a woman, cursed a snake, sewed skins together for clothes, preferred the savoury smell of roast cutlets to the odors of boiled cabbage, who sat in a burning bush or popped out from behind the rocks, this irate Old Party who thunders imprecations from the mountain or mutters and grouches in the tabernacle, and whom Moses finds so hard to tame, who in his paroxysms of rage has massacred hundreds of thousands of his own Chosen People, and would often have slaughtered the whole lot if cunning old Moses hadn't kept reminding him of "What will the Egyptians say about it?" This touchy Jehovah whom the deluded superstitionists claim to be the Creator of the whole universe, makes one feel utter contempt for the preachers and unfeigned pity for the mental state of those who can retain a serious countenance as they peruse the stories of His peculiar whims, freaks and fancies, and His frenzied megalomaniac boastings.[11]

The passage was not the only one in the *Inquirer* that mocked the Bible and those who held it sacred; but it was a particularly vivid and sarcastic piece of writing. And most significantly, it was aimed directly at God.

Sterry began distributing the first issue of his paper free of charge that December, in time for Christmas. He made a point of giving copies to members of Toronto's elite in person. He wandered the halls of the provincial parliament and handed copies directly to G. Howard Ferguson (the premier), W.H. Price (the attorney-general), and Charles McRea (the minister of mines.) He visited the office of crown attorney Eric Armour to give him a copy, and left papers at every other office he could. Sterry also visited Toronto's city hall and delivered copies personally to each of its various departments. He then distributed the paper to students at McMaster University, a Baptist institution then in Toronto. He later estimated that he had given out at least five hundred copies of the *Inquirer*. He asked each person he met while distributing the paper to read and critique it. While everyone seemed friendly enough, he was disappointed by the lack of thoughtful responses.[12]

There were only two advertisments in the first issue of the *Inquirer*, both from fellow unbelievers and members of the local rationalist organization. These were A. Newton, who offered "general house repairs," and Ethelbert Lionel Cross, a barrister.[13] It was in fact fortunate that Sterry knew a lawyer. On 10 January 1927 he was visited at his office by three police officers and arrested. Accompanied by Cross (whose office was in the same building), he was taken to Inspector McKinney of the Morality Department and charged with blasphemous libel. The indictment read, in part, "Ernest Victor Sterry did, contrary to law, publish certain blasphemous, indecent and profane libel of and concerning the Holy Scriptures and Christian religion."[14] The charges went on to cite the "touchy Jehovah" passage from the *Christian Inquirer* (quoted above) as a prime example of Sterry's blasphemy. His writings, the indictment concluded, were "to the high displeasure of Almighty God and to the great scandal and reproach of the Christian religion."[15]

The prosecution of Sterry has been discussed in two separate articles, by Susan Lewthwaite and Jeremy Patrick. Lewthwaite's coverage is in the context of an article on E. Lionel Cross, Sterry's lawyer; Patrick's account is part of an examination of blasphemy law in Canada as well as judicial and public attitudes to the crime of blasphemy.[16] My account draws mainly on primary sources to examine Sterry's place in the social history of Canadian unbelief in an attempt to establish the significance of his prosecution in the context of interwar Ontario. I argue that Sterry was prosecuted not just because of his irreverence but also because he was a working-class man who was trying to spread anti-religious ideas in a popular manner to a general audience. He threatened the moral order, which is to say, the conservative Christian hegemony that still governed Toronto, Ontario, and indeed Canada as a whole. While many Canadian liberals were uneasy with his prosecution, conservatives were insistent that he had to be punished as an example to others who would challenge that order. When Sterry's allies on the left tried to abolish the law of blasphemous libel, they found themselves shouted down by a political elite who believed that Canada must remain an explicitly Christian state.

Sterry's arrest aroused a good deal of public attention. It received prominent coverage in the *Globe* and the *Star*, and was mentioned in Ottawa and Winnipeg newspapers.[17] International interest was aroused as well; over the next few days *The Times* of London reported on the case, as did the *New York Times*, the *Chicago Tribune*, and the *Los Angeles Times*.[18] The latter put the story on the first page, while the *Tribune* reprinted the entire "God of the Jews" passage in order to illustrate the nature of Sterry's offense. *Time* magazine likewise gave its readers a sample of the *Christian Inquirer*.[19] Smaller papers across the United States also began reporting the case over the next two weeks, and many included a picture of the alleged culprit.[20]

ORIGINS OF A BLASPHEMER

Ernest Sterry had become infamous overnight. But who was he? The fifty-five-year-old rationalist was born in Lowestoft, a port town on the east coast of England, in 1872. His father (John Steward Sterry, 1834–1908) was a wealthy coal merchant, ship-owner, and Swedenborgian deacon. His mother (Ellen Calver Butcher, 1838–1899) was an avid amateur botanist and a committed atheist who had developed her views under the influence of the lectures and writings of Annie Besant, Herbert Spencer, and Charles Bradlaugh. Sterry recalled: "She would travel long distances to hear any of these famous thinkers although in my case she used to smile at me when I was a little boy and say that 'mother love was greater than the Darwinian theory.'" Religion and "social questions" were frequently discussed at their house. Sterry recalled his father as being a "hard-headed business man" who "used to think the rest of us were trying to show off our knowledge of these things." Considering that the elder Sterry was a member of a tiny mystical sect and was married to an atheist, however, it seems that he was comfortable with a certain degree of heterodoxy.[21]

The Sterry Trial and the Debate over Blasphemy

Figure 4.1 Ernest V. Sterry, 1927

Sterry attended a Baptist school in England and then for a time a Catholic school in Belgium (although according to later court documents, his studies were only at an "elementary" level, not a "superior" one).[22] He got involved with the Unitarian church at Great Yarmouth, serving as its secretary. He also was an early subscriber to Britain's Rationalist Press Committee in the 1890s. Desiring to see the world and to spread the rationalist message, he travelled to New Zealand, intending to "convert" the Maoris. But "after living among them for two years they converted me," he later recalled, "for I found I could leave my door unlocked, and no one would attempt to steal anything."[23] Around this time his father disowned him for his rationalist and socialist views. At some point Sterry had married an English woman, Ellen Maude Farrar, but she refused to move to Auckland to be with him.[24]

After experiencing the relative cultural freedom of the colonies, Sterry no longer wished to live in England. The couple compromised by moving to Toronto in 1909 with their two daughters.[25] Sterry held a number of different jobs, from working for a printer to real estate to construction, but for the most part did not prosper. He had previously come to the attention of the police "as a result of his street-corner orations," as the *Globe* reported, "he being one of the speechmakers who draw crowds to evening gatherings on James Street."[26] Sterry later explained that he was not a regular outdoor orator but that in the summer of 1926 he had spoken several times on that street (in front of City Hall).[27] That same year, Sterry became one of the founders of a local organization for skeptics and unbelievers, the Rationalist Society of Canada (RSC).[28] (I examine the RSC in greater detail in the following chapter.)

Although Sterry may have been a socialist in his youth, by the time of his arrest he claimed he was not. In response to some newspaper reports that had called him a communist he insisted: "The Rationalist Society is not interested in political affairs as a body. There may be one or two who have some leaning in that direction but the larger element are either Conservative or Liberal in their politics. Personally, I have always been a Conservative. So far as Communism is concerned we have always held that rationalist thought should take up all our efforts."[29] It is reasonable to wonder if Sterry was being entirely honest about his politics now that he was defending himself in the press. But in his public rationalist activities he seems to have stuck to traditional anti-religious topics and avoided political discussion.

Sterry's lawyer, E. Lionel Cross, also an unbeliever, was a fellow member of the RSC. His background was rather unusual for a Torontonian of the time. Born in 1890 in San Fernando, Trinidad, Cross was a Black man who had worked as a journalist in New York and Halifax. He had served as a sergeant in the Canadian Expeditionary Force's Second Construction Battalion. After the Great War he studied law at Dalhousie University and was called to the bar in Nova Scotia in 1923. He then moved to Toronto, studied law at Osgoode Hall, and in 1924 became the first Black lawyer to open a law practice in the city. He was certainly a novelty in the city, and virtually every newspaper article that mentioned him included descriptors such as "coloured" or "Negro." Questioned by the *Toronto Star* about his support for the rationalists, Cross commented, "I am a colored man, but I can truthfully say that I prefer the slavery of the body to the slavery of the mind and, if I had to make a choice, I would go back to the slavery of the body." This philosophical commitment led him to deliver a number of lectures at RSC meetings.[30]

Figure 4.2 E. Lionel Cross, 1930

TRIAL PREPARATIONS

Soon after charging Sterry with blasphemous libel, Toronto police discovered an outstanding complaint against him that had been on their books since 1924. A Chinese man named Joseph Ying alleged that he had given Sterry $200 as part of a deal to construct a laundry building and that the Briton had then disappeared with the money. Sterry claimed to be the victim of a third party, a contractor who had taken the money in question and then moved to Chicago. The case was tried within two weeks; despite Cross's best efforts in his defence, Sterry was convicted and sentenced to four months in prison with an additional "indeterminate" sentence of six months.[31] An appeal was swiftly quashed.[32] Thus, as the blasphemy trial progressed, Sterry was already behind bars, a detail that caused some problems for the RSC in terms of public perception. Several ads appealing for donations to his defence featured the statement: "We Are Defending the Principle — not the Man."[33]

The defence of freedom of speech as a principle attracted a mysterious group of potential benefactors. On 14 January the *Evening Telegram* reported that "a sympathetic source" had offered Sterry the services of "one of the most eminent criminal advocates in this province." Cross's insistence on acting as senior counsel had, however, scuttled the deal.[34] The next day Cross told the *Star* he wished to set the record straight. Certain local parties had indeed approached Sterry. They had told him that "they did not approve of his views yet they were wholly out of sympathy with what they regarded as a form of persecution and ... were prepared to finance his defense." They also offered legal counsel who would "collaborate" with Cross. But Cross felt that this collaboration amounted to a takeover of the case by others, which would have put him in the position of betraying the cause.[35]

Just who were these potential benefactors? Neither Cross nor the Toronto newspapers specified. An article in the *Winnipeg Tribune* of 13 January, however, may shed light on the question. Entitled "Communists to Fight for Free Speech," it reported that "the Communist Party of Canada is prepared to assist Victor Sterry ... although it has no interest directly or indirectly in the Rationalist movement." John MacDonald, party secretary, stated: "We are ready to take part in a fight for free speech and a free press if the police press the charge."[36] Thus it is possible that it was the Communist Party that had offered assistance and been rebuffed by Cross. It is also possible that the sympathetic group represented other religious minorities such as Unitarians or Jews, or that they were liberal-minded Christians who disliked the blasphemy law. In any case, Cross seems to have felt that their lawyer would have misrepresented Sterry's position, while he as a fellow rationalist could handle the case more appropriately.

There were also rumours of help from further afield. On 12 January, the *Evening Telegram* suggested that a coalition of Chicago freethinkers had discussed enlisting Clarence Darrow in Sterry's defence.[37] The next day Cross told the *Star* that he had received a telegram from New York offering $10,000 and Darrow's assistance.[38] Ten days later William Styles of the RSC was asked if the famous American was coming. He responded that "the story was largely a newspaper concoction," continuing, "if Darrow does come, he will come as junior counsel to our own Lionel Cross." But he added that it was a possibility, since there was an organization in the United States that had paid Darrow's expenses when he fought similar cases across

North America. (This was likely a reference to the American Civil Liberties Union.)[39] It is hard to imagine the limelight-loving Darrow playing the role of junior counsel, however. Unsurprisingly, a few days before the trial Cross told the press that the famed lawyer would be "unable to attend the proceedings on account of illness."[40]

This setback may not have been unexpected, but it was still unfortunate for Sterry and his fellow rationalists. They needed all the help they could get; a lot was riding on the case. Col. W.W. Denison, solicitor to Ontario's Department of the Provincial Secretary, had within hours of Sterry's initial arrest stated that if the rationalist was found guilty, the government should cancel the Rationalist Society's charter. He believed that, by "propagating atheism," the society had "exceeded the powers granted them." Clubs and societies that had been found to promote gambling had had their charters revoked, Denison explained; similarly, organizations that broke the law by blaspheming should be disbanded. He stated that he would personally recommend such a move to Provincial Secretary Lincoln Goldie, should Sterry be convicted.[41]

In Canada's Criminal Code, blasphemous libel, the offense with which Sterry had been charged, did not apply to all attacks on Christianity or disbelief in God. Its precise stipulation was that: "no one is guilty of a blasphemous libel for expressing in good faith and in decent language, or attempting to establish by arguments used in good faith and conveyed in decent language, any opinion whatever upon any religious subject."[42] The problem was not with the opinion but with the libelous way it was expressed. In a lengthy discussion of the law, the *Evening Telegram* explained to its readers that "It is the choice of language that is involved in Mr. Sterry's case ... Vulgar or profane language can transform a legitimate philosophical argument into a blasphemous libel."[43] If Sterry's rhetoric outraged the religious feelings of Christian Canadians, he was guilty. There was little doubt that he had written most of the content of the *Christian Inquirer*, and no question that he had personally distributed it. Thus the case quickly came down to the highly subjective issue of whether the Christians of Toronto should feel offended by his words. The outcome of the case would depend upon the attitude of those tasked with defining what was offensive: the jury and the judicial authorities.

Early indications were not promising. Crown attorney Eric Armour, who had initiated Sterry's prosecution, promptly showed a copy of the offending material to Inspector McKinney of the

Morality Department; he agreed that it was blasphemous.[44] Subsequently authorities always stressed the gravity of the offense in their public statements. Magistrate R.J. Browne, when committing Sterry to jury trial, called the *Inquirer* article not only blasphemous but also "a most indecent and offensive attack on Christianity and the scriptures, couched in the most scurrilous and opprobrious language." It was clearly Sterry's intention, he said, to "asperse and vilify Almighty God, in composing and publishing these scandalous, impious, blasphemous and profane libels of God."[45] When a date for the case was initially listed, the presiding judge, Emerson Coatsworth, emphasized its importance, explaining to reporters that blasphemy consisted of an "indecent or offensive" attack on God or the scriptures, "attacks which are calculated to enrage the feelings of the community."[46]

Behind the scenes, matters were not as clear-cut. Only two days after Sterry was charged, W.H. Price, Ontario's attorney general, received a letter condemning the case. It was from a retired minister, one J.C. Hodgins, a man Price considered a "very high type" who had "done a great deal of speechmaking throughout the Province." Perturbed by the minister's letter, Price asked his deputy why charges had been laid in this case "more than in many others that seem just as bad." The deputy in turn asked Armour, the crown attorney, for a report, particularly on "whether the defendant was warned to discontinue and if not, why this was not done." Armour downplayed his own involvement and commented that it was true that editors who published objectionable material were usually given a warning first. "This publication, however," he added, "is not a newspaper or a periodical but a propagandist sheet ... I have no doubts about getting a conviction but as a charge of theft has also been laid against the above, if he is sent to jail on that charge, the libel charge could be dropped. The local religious organizations here have been raising much ado about the publication in question, and it perhaps would be better to go on to a finish now [that] a prosecution has been commenced." Furthermore, he commented, "I do not think this charge should ever have been laid and would suggest that after a true bill is found by the Grand Jury a Stay of Proceedings be entered." Price responded, "I am not sure that I would have entered this case at the beginning. Now that it has been entered I rather think it would be inadvisable to have it withdrawn."[47] Price kept his reservations mostly quiet and allowed the case to continue.

There were, however, people willing to take the rationalist's side publicly. The *Toronto Star* provided a sympathetic platform for Sterry and Cross to put forward their views, though the paper never editorialized directly on the case. Support was to be found among the clergy as well. Not long after Sterry's arrest, Rabbi Ferdinand Isserman of Holy Blossom Synagogue agreed to speak at a rally in his support. Although the rabbi had to cancel at the last minute for family health reasons, he wrote a lengthy two-part article for the *Canadian Jewish Review* entitled "A Religious Teacher's View of Blasphemy."[48] In the first half Isserman blended rabbinical commentary with a higher-critical interpretation of Jewish religious history, and examined changing conceptions of God and offenses against God. Isserman's statement that "the war-God of Israel, called by some the cruel Jehovah" had been abandoned in favour of a more merciful deity was, in essence if not in tone, reminiscent of Sterry's "touchy Jehovah" critique.[49] In the second half of the article, published the following week, Isserman wrote that, while he believed a liberal religious outlook was superior to the rationalist view, he knew that unbelievers could be decent and sincere people. Their questions and challenges should be dealt with honestly and charitably, rather than punitively. "Religion does not need courts to defend it," Isserman argued. In fact, he concluded, the violence and oppression meted out by supposed defenders of religion were more blasphemous in the eyes of God than verbal insults.[50]

THE TRIAL AND ITS AFTERMATH

Sterry's case was finally heard on 14 March, before a court "jammed to the doors" with spectators.[51] The only witnesses called were Sterry and McKinney, the police inspector who had initially charged him. The prosecutor was E.J. Murphy. Lionel Cross was assisted in the defence by a junior lawyer named Nathan Waldo.[52] From the outset the defence strove to change the focus of the trial and to question the legal framework being constructed around Sterry. They challenged the "archaic and obsolete" language of the indictment and argued that it did not clearly define the meaning of blasphemous libel. Cross pointed to the difficulty in determining intent from the language Sterry's paper had employed; the use of provocative language did not necessarily imply a desire to outrage the people of Toronto. Cross also brought up prominent thinkers who had said very similar things about

Figure 4.3 Courtroom sketch of Sterry and Cross, 1927

God or the Bible and had faced no legal consequences. He further asked if any of the Torontonians who had supposedly been offended by the paper would be brought in to testify.[53]

All these approaches were quickly shut down by the judge or the prosecutor, who insisted that Cross's objections were irrelevant or off-topic. The language used by the court and by Sterry clearly meant what it said, they argued, and the only point of the trial was for the jury to decide if the *Inquirer* offended them or not. Frustrated and hemmed in by "common sense" interpretations hostile to his case – and likely sensing that he was in an unwinnable situation – Cross retorted, "I will go to others higher than this court. Perhaps your honor will be a little more charitable to me then." Judge Coatsworth "vehemently objected."[54] The prosecution, meanwhile, focusing on the passage of the *Inquirer* quoted above, pointed to Sterry's characterization of God as "this irate Old Party" and "this touchy Jehovah" as clear evidence of blasphemous intent. The statement that God preferred roast cutlets to boiled cabbage was also cited as highly objectionable, despite Sterry's plea that he had simply been referring to the story of Cain and Abel. The prosecutor and police witness both raised the spectre of the *Inquirer* getting into the hands of children, which the rationalist denied was his intent.[55]

If Sterry had hoped for a dramatic, Scopes-style showdown between reason and religion, he was disappointed. He seems to have been eager to have such a public platform for his views. He read certain excerpts from his newspaper to the courtroom "in a dramatic manner," concluding the quotations by shouting, "It is upon this that I base my defence!" He addressed the jury at some length, but unfortunately "the rest of the crowded court room were unable to hear his excited harangue." After being asked a question about his view of God, he began to again address the jury on the topic. At this point he was chastised by Judge Coatsworth: "Don't make a speech!" Sterry went on to claim that his use of the phrase "deluded superstitionists" did not apply to all Christians but specifically to fundamentalist "hardshelled Baptists" and the like. Here Cross warned him not to mention specific creeds.[56]

When arrested, Sterry had insisted to Police Inspector McKinney: "It's not your God, but the God of the Jews, I was speaking of."[57] That question became central to the trial. Sterry argued that the point of his oft-cited article was that the easily outraged God of the Old Testament, who acted in cruel and petulant ways unworthy of a human being, was not the same as the God of the New Testament, or as the passionless "supreme intelligence" in which most modern people believed.[58] The authorities would have none of this. McKinney stated that he had told Sterry: "I knew but only one God. I thought we all believed in the one God. I was taught that as a child." Waldo for the defence asked him if Christians believed in Jehovah, and McKinney agreed that they did. Waldo then asked him if he believed in the Trinity, but to this question Murphy, for the prosecution, objected.[59] For the authorities there was only one God (the Christian one) who ruled over Jews, Christians, and Canada's civil religion alike.[60]

In his concluding address Murphy told the jury that their duty was to convict, because Sterry's crime posed a mortal threat to Canada. "Were the crown to tolerate and permit such a wicked and profane libel of God to go unnoticed it would deal a death blow to the state and would blot out all that relates to God and is sacred to a Christian people," he warned, closely echoing a sermon given by the Presbyterian minister L.H. Gibson some three months earlier.[61] (Gibson had been attacking the Rationalist Society of Canada, the organization that

Sterry had helped found.) Murphy went on to repeat another line, virtually word for word, from Gibson's condemnation: "I do not believe in restricting free speech, but when it descends to indecency and vulgarity and attacks the very foundation of the nation as in this case, it is a different matter."[62] With "crafty sneers" and "polished sarcasm," Sterry had maliciously endeavoured to defeat justice, to "mislead the ignorant and unwary," said the prosecutor.[63] Murphy ended by warning the jury they needed to defend the gospels on which they had been sworn in; if they did not, the entire legal system would become senseless.[64]

After this it was time for Judge Coatsworth to instruct the members of the jury before they retired to make their decision. He explained the concepts of reasonable doubt and blasphemous libel, and then proceeded to give the jurors what can only be described as a sermon. "Probably nothing is more sacred to us than our religion. We have ever been taught to reverence the name of God," he began. He laid out the basic doctrines of Christianity, stopping just short of reciting the Apostles' Creed, and peppered his talk with Biblical quotations. God was important to Canadians, he asserted, because "we regard him as the supreme Ruler of the Universe. Also as our Maker and Creator through whom alone we believe we live, move and have our being." He informed the jurors that taking God's name in vain was a sin and explained that: "Our conception of God is so much a part of every life that it is an integral part of our national life. So much is this the case that we are prepared to say that love [of] God and trust in Him are the very foundation of our nation's greatness." The Bible, he went on, was "the basis of every good law in our country." Thus, Sterry's offense struck not only at the sacred doctrines of Christianity but at the very foundations of the nation. He reiterated the claim that Sterry had intended "to have copies distributed among school children." Coatsworth concluded by telling the jurors it was their duty to decide if Sterry's arguments had crossed the bounds of acceptable discourse, and then sent them off to deliberate.

Cross seemed slightly stunned by this effusion of piety; it was one thing for the prosecutor to quote from a sermon, but for the judge to give one was something else entirely. The lawyer told Coatsworth that he had "a few observations in regard to [his] charge to the jury." He asked the judge to call the jurors back and clarify that their own feelings were not enough; they also needed to decide if Sterry's *intent* had been to "arouse the outraged feelings of the community." In this the judge obliged him.[65] After only twenty-five minutes, however, the jury was back again, and informed the court that they found Sterry guilty.[66] Despite the fact that the courtroom was filled to capacity, there was "no demonstration of any kind when the verdict was announced." Sterry displayed no signs of emotion besides a brief nod in the direction of his lawyer.[67]

His sentencing was left for the following day. It seems that even in defeat Sterry was famous, or infamous; crowds thronged the corridors outside the court room, eagerly waiting to be admitted. When the doors finally opened, a reporter noted that "the crowd pouring in comprised many Jews."[68] When the proceedings began, Cross asked the judge for a suspended sentence, and Waldo suggested that Sterry would prefer deportation over further jail time. Since the rationalist was "55 years of age, and no longer a young man," he continued, "any sentence in jail will not alter his opinions." Thus, "the ends of justice might be met without a jail sentence" and, since Sterry was originally from England, "there might be an order for deportation to England. I don't think the accused will mind that." One observer noted, however, that when deportation was mentioned, "Sterry actually winced." Ultimately the judge sentenced the rationalist to sixty days on a jail farm, to be served consecutively with his sentence for theft. On top of this there would be an order for Sterry's deportation.[69] The Toronto police's Morality Department began deportation proceedings the next day. Inspector McKinney acknowledged that Sterry would not normally be eligible for deportation, since the rationalist had lived in Canada for seventeen years but stated that his department would seek a special dispensation from the governor-general.[70]

The guilty verdict was widely reported, even more so than Sterry's initial arrest.[71] The *Ottawa Citizen* and the *Ottawa Journal* both made it a front-page headline. The *Journal* later editorialized that the case was "unpleasantly reminiscent of medieval fanaticism, of the stake and the torture chamber."[72] The *Citizen* labelled those who wished to abolish blasphemy laws "extremists," but in an editorial asserted that "most persons felt uneasy" about the prosecution and argued that it was not the place of the courts to interpret religious doctrine.[73] The *Manitoba Free Press* was uncomfortable with the decision: "If the country accepts the doctrine that a man can be put in jail on account of his opinions and the form in which he expresses them, it may be accepting that comes pretty close to subversion of one of the fundamental principles of our traditional liberty."[74] The *Vancouver*

Sun was blunter: "We do not want this country to become a refuge for licentious religious spouters. But neither do we want it to become a country of closed minds and enforced bigotry."[75] The *Common Round*, a Vancouver magazine edited by veteran columnist James Butterfield, said that blasphemers were best left alone in obscurity; prosecution only spread their views further.[76] Sterry's conviction was also the topic of a lecture entitled "God, the Bible, and Blasphemy," delivered by Marshall Gauvin before the Winnipeg Rationalist Society. As would be expected, Gauvin defended Sterry's statements and condemned the blasphemy law as a monstrous relic of less enlightened times. He predicted that before very long it would be swept away by the forces of progress.[77]

Americans were also paying attention. Newspapers from across the United States reported on the verdict, including the *Washington Post*, the *New York Times*, the *Los Angeles Times*, the *Hartford Courant*, the *Christian Science Monitor*, the *Chicago Tribune*, the *Boston Globe*, and the *Atlanta Constitution*. In a piece entitled "Jehovah, Jupiter, Baal," *Time* magazine suggested Sterry was found guilty because his "Jewish god" defence did not convince the "devout men" of the jury.[78] Major news outlets tended not to editorialize on the case, however. Arthur Brisbane, an editor whose columns were widely syndicated in rural papers, did remark that, if Sterry was guilty, "the punishment is deserved, [for] you have no more right to hurt the religious feeling of others than you have to hurt their bodies."[79] Brisbane went on to state that "no outstanding agnostic" had ever been happy and that the wise course for those who doubted the beliefs of their countrymen was to keep silent about it.[80] A few days later the American *Literary Digest* commented: "The case attracts no little attention this side of the border, where the Scopes case is still fresh in memory." It quoted editorials from the *Pittsburgh Gazette-Times*, the *Hartford Times*, and the *Omaha Bee*. These tended to be supportive of the prosecution, with one writer wishing that the United States would deal with its own blasphemers in the same way.[81]

Other American publications viewed Sterry's conviction differently. Excerpts from the *Louisville Times*, the *Peoria Transcript*, the *Rock Island Argus*, the *Fort Worth Star-Telegram*, the *Indianapolis News*, the *New Orleans Item*, the *Brooklyn Daily Eagle*, and the *Omaha World-Herald* were printed in the *Toronto Star*.[82] While few of the articles cited were sympathetic to Sterry, most suggested that the verdict was unnecessary. The *Louisville Times* of Kentucky pointed out that libel typically involved "substantial injury," which seemed to imply that Sterry had somehow hurt God – a ridiculous notion; if anything, Sterry should have been found guilty of disorderly conduct. The *Peoria Transcript* and the *Rock Island Argus* both agreed that the case did little but bring unnecessary attention to a minor figure, whose coarse words should have been left in obscurity. This was the general attitude of the papers cited by the *Star*: blasphemy was no laughing matter, but it was better left to wither under "silent contempt" than made a spectacle of through the courts. In response to that piece, a letter writer calling himself "Canadian" invoked the image of the irreligious American. That the American writers were dismissive of the prosecution was "a sure sign that their faith is feeble and their sense of reverence greatly impaired."[83]

The *Literary Digest*'s observation about the influence of "the Scopes case" on the Sterry coverage was insightful. Many journalists and commentators drew the comparison, and it is possible that Sterry would have gone unnoticed outside of Toronto had it not been for that earlier trial.[84] The reading public of 1920s North America seems to have been keen to hear about clashes between religious tradition and modern skepticism. Intriguingly, not long after the Scopes trial, one Canadian writer had raised the possibility that the same thing could happen in Ontario. In a *Saturday Night* magazine published in February 1926, Grace H. Hunter examined "The Legal Status of Christianity in Ontario: Court Decisions that Remind One of Tennessee and the Scopes Trial." Hunter did not specifically address blasphemous libel, but she discussed previous cases involving local freethinkers in which the Christian religion was found to be part of the common law of the province. She suggested that theological Modernists could, after uttering their opinions, find themselves in trouble with the courts. The piece also took note of Lord's Day laws, which forced a certain conception of Christian propriety on society. Hunter pointed out the haphazard, often class-based way these were applied, commenting wryly, "Sometimes it seems that what is merely choleric in the Colonel is blasphemous in the private." Her discussion implied that it was only a matter of time before a resident of Ontario fell afoul of Christianity's legal protections.[85]

Soon after Sterry's conviction made Hunter's prediction a reality, prominent figures spoke out against the law of blasphemous libel. Rabbi Isserman, in a sermon to his congregation, compared Sterry's trial to that of Scopes, called the blasphemy law anachronistic, and said, "anaemic indeed is the religion that needs law to protect it."[86] About two weeks after the trial J.S. Woodsworth, at the time an Independent Labour MP, introduced a bill in Parliament calling for the repeal of the Criminal Code's law against blasphemous libel.[87] In England, George Lansbury, a veteran Labour MP, introduced a new bill proposing the abolition of prosecutions for "blasphemy, schism, heresy, or atheism." Canadian observers claimed that Lansbury's initiative was inspired by Sterry.[88] Around the same time the *Toronto Star* published a lengthy review of *Elmer Gantry*, Sinclair Lewis's new satire on American Christianity, which detailed the book's many skeptical and cynical passages. Entitled "'Elmer Gantry' Constitutes a Problem for the Police," the article drew numerous parallels with the Sterry case and asked scornfully if Toronto authorities were going to seek to punish Lewis or ban his book.[89]

In Toronto, Baptist minister W.A. Cameron condemned the prosecution and promoted the separation of church and state, arguing that their intertwining resulted in either an "enslaved state" or an "enslaved church."[90] The famous anarchist Emma Goldman, then resident in the city, excoriated liberal-minded Torontonians in a *Toronto Star* article for failing to speak out or contribute to Sterry's defence. "Why didn't he say that before the trial?" she said of Cameron. Goldman argued that a sufficiently loud public outcry would have prevented Sterry's conviction, which she referred to as a "shooting in a cellar." And, referring back to the Scopes trial, she reasoned that in the face of international derision Toronto would have been unwilling to "become a laughingstock like Dayton." "Important persons," including "Rebecca West, Lady Rhondda, Philip Snowden, Ramsay MacDonald," not to mention George Bernard Shaw and Theodore Dreiser, could have been enlisted to speak on behalf of Sterry. Besides, she added, the statements for which Sterry was prosecuted were mild in comparison to writings by more famous figures like D.H. Lawrence or Anatole France. She pointed out that the wealthy and powerful could get away with heterodox ideas much more easily than the poor and obscure; unbelievers needed to enlist influential friends if they wished to hold the forces of intolerance at bay.[91]

The next day a response to Goldman from Lionel Cross appeared in the *Star*. He pointed out that the Rationalist Society of Canada, composed of Torontonians, had in fact been supporting Sterry all throughout the case. (Indeed, his bail of one thousand dollars was provided by local rationalist Aaron Newton.)[92] Nevertheless, Cross admitted that despite "a general appeal to more than 350 various [Canadian] organizations, from coast to coast ... all the support received was a lot of sympathy – which, of course, does not fight battles in the courts."[93] Cross hadn't ended his fight, however. He had been sincere in his statement about "going to others higher." As he worked on Sterry's appeal, the RSC began raising money to finance it.[94]

The appeal was heard on 4 May, with Cross and Waldo representing Sterry in the second appellate division of Ontario's Supreme Court. Unfortunately for the rationalist, the five judges who heard the appeal were no more sympathetic than Coatsworth had been.[95] Cross raised the point that Woodsworth in Canada and Lansbury in Great Britain were trying to do away with blasphemy laws. The judges responded that this was no concern of theirs, and besides, English law was different from that of Canada. When Cross tried to argue that a charge of blasphemy was an archaic relic of the past, he was told that history was irrelevant and that he should "get down to brass tacks." Cross went on to argue that the law was unclear, that Sterry had not intended offense, and that his writing was merely a retelling of biblical stories. The judges responded that the language was clearly offensive and that no other jury would have found to the contrary. Nor were they interested in the fact that other, more prominent authors had used similar language. Justice Orde stressed that Canada was "a country which had been based on religion." When Cross took issue with this argument, Chief Justice Latchford told him to get to the point; if the lawyer did not stop "wandering around in the wilderness," he would stop listening. Cross moved on to criticize the way Coatsworth had charged the jury; Orde responded that the judge had acted "quite properly." In less than an hour, the judges had dismissed all of Cross's arguments and upheld Sterry's conviction.[96]

After the appeal failed, F.J. Moore, contributing to the *Canadian Forum*, called for the abolition of the blasphemy law. He argued that "public good sense and taste" should be enough to deal with offensive remarks. Bringing blasphemy to trial would only broadcast it further, and people were liable to "hate more intensely the religion that strikes back with the arm of the law." He suggested that in Sterry's case a narrow, fundamentalist view of the Bible had "exercised a considerable influence even on the lawyers and judiciary" and probably on some members of the jury, too. He also invoked the Scopes trial, cautioning that this conviction brought Canada "perilously near to Tennessee, from which state may God defend us!"[97]

In September 1927 the *Star* reported that Cross and some other rationalists had been to visit Sterry in the Ontario Reformatory in Guelph. They found him in good health. Cross expected that his client would have to serve out the rest of his sentence and would be released sometime in November.[98] Despite all the talk of deportation, Sterry returned to Toronto when his sentence was up. It seems that his seventeen years in Canada did afford him some protection.

THE PARLIAMENTARY DEBATE ON BLASPHEMY

Although Sterry soon returned to relative obscurity, the issues raised by his trial did not. J.S. Woodsworth's bill to remove blasphemous libel from the Criminal Code continued to make its way through Parliament. As a former clergyman who had wrestled with religious doubt for much of his career in the church, Woodsworth was well aware of the issues involved.[99] In addition, he himself had been charged with seditious libel some nine years before, because of his vocal support for the Winnipeg General Strike. The charges had been dropped in part because, to the government's embarrassment, two of the passages considered seditious proved to be quotations from the Bible.[100] For these reasons Woodsworth was uniquely positioned to advocate for freedom of speech in religious matters. The MP assembled a file of documents related to the case, including a copy of the *Christian Inquirer*, Rabbi Isserman's articles on blasphemy, and a chart listing British legal precedents. His notes suggest that he examined Lansbury's proposed bill for inspiration. He took particular note of Judge Coatsworth's instructions to the jury. After copying down Coatsworth's assertion, "We look upon the Bible as the basis of every good law in our country," Woodsworth jotted, "In light of recent controversy, which Bible?" He then wrote down a list of religious groups whose beliefs seemed blasphemous to each other. Among others it included "Jews vs. Christians," "Modernists vs. Fundamentalists," and "Protestants vs. Catholics."[101]

Woodsworth's bill reached second reading in Parliament on 10 February 1928, almost a year after Sterry was found guilty. The government at the time was a Liberal minority under Mackenzie King. Challenged by Ernest Lapointe (the minister of justice and King's lieutenant in Quebec) to justify his proposed amendment, Woodsworth laid out his case. He argued that the law was antiquated and had been applied in a prejudiced manner by Judge Coatsworth. The judge had claimed to be defending the Bible and the feelings of religious Canadians. But which Bible was he talking about? Nor did all religious Canadians agree with the judge. Woodsworth noted that he had received "a great many" communications from "clergymen of various denominations" who felt that the law of blasphemous libel was unjust. He made special mention of Rabbi Isserman and presented a favourable summary of the rabbi's articles on blasphemy. Woodsworth went on to point out that the Criminal Code did not clearly define blasphemy, and because of this many groups were liable to consider each other guilty of that crime.[102] He reminded his colleagues that the Thirty-Nine Articles of the Church of England called the Roman Catholic Mass a "blasphemous fable." Furthermore, both Socrates and Jesus had been accused of blasphemy by their contemporaries.[103]

The member for Winnipeg Centre continued by calling the law "a menace to the free expression of religious opinion." He acknowledged that it did contain a safeguard stipulating that arguments made in "good faith" and "decent language" were exempt from prosecution. But given this, why was Sterry found guilty? "The article in question," Woodsworth concluded, "is no more extreme than many articles which are written, in perhaps less popular language, in the theological journals of a great many bodies that are carrying on religious work here in Canada. This man Sterry may have been infelicitous in his way of expressing himself, but ... it is dangerous to leave on the statute books a law which may be invoked against an individual for expressing himself along religious lines."[104] In Woodsworth's view, the law was too open to subjective interpretation, and could be aimed at anyone with an unpopular opinion on religion. The Sterry case showed that regardless of how they expressed themselves, members of the heterodox minority were vulnerable to unfair prosecution by the majority.

Lapointe responded by highlighting a fatal flaw in Woodsworth's proposed legislation. He explained that removing the provision from the Criminal Code would not in fact prevent people like Sterry from being prosecuted. Offenses not covered explicitly by the Criminal Code were dealt with using common law precedents instead; and the punishments for blasphemy under that regime would be considerably harsher.[105] The minister also pointed out that both England and the United States had similar laws; why should Canada do away with its version of the legislation? "I do not think we should be so anxious to protect people who really want to offend what is the religious feeling of the people of Canada. This is a Christian country." Lapointe hastened to add that he was an advocate for freedom of speech, but that if two courts had ruled against Sterry, then justice had most likely been done.[106]

At this point George R. Geary, Conservative MP for Toronto South, rose to speak.[107] He noted that he so seldom agreed fully with Lapointe that it gave him "a great deal of pleasure" to do so in this instance. There was "no limit to free speech" or discussion of religion anywhere in Canada, he insisted "so long as it is properly done." But if someone insisted on being as outrageously offensive as Sterry had been, it was just as well that Canada had a law to punish him. He doubted very much that Woodsworth would want to read Sterry's article or "to associate himself with the statements made in it." Geary's argument was more about defending propriety than it was about upholding piety. This focus helps explain the lengthy wrangling that ensued when Woodsworth responded that he would be happy to read the article aloud. In this debate, which took up as much time as had the discussion of the bill itself, Woodsworth's ally was Thomas W. Bird (formerly a United Church minister), who belonged to the Progressive Party.[108] His opponents were Geary and R.B. Bennett, leader of the Official Opposition (and future prime minister).

Bird announced that, in order to protect Woodsworth "from any unjust reflection," he would undertake to read out Sterry's article. According to the *Globe*, this move "shocked the Commons."[109] Bennett rose to object to the Speaker. Certain rules governed the language that could be used in Parliament. Could material that had been judged blasphemous by the courts be read aloud there? The Speaker of the House at the time was Rodolphe Lemieux, Liberal member for Gaspé. He replied that he had no way of knowing without having read the article himself. While the courts had declared it blasphemous, Parliament was itself the highest tribunal in Canada, and could thus make its own decisions. Bennett pointed out that the word "damn" was considered unparliamentary in Great Britain, and that blasphemous language was similar. The Speaker asked Bennett to come up with a more official authority; in the meantime he asked Bird to give him the passage from the *Christian Inquirer* so that he could read it for himself.[110]

The debate continued along these lines for some time while the Speaker read. When the prime minister was asked his opinion of the subject, King said simply, "I have every confidence in the judgment of Mr. Speaker on a matter of this kind."[111] Lemieux finally announced that Bird could read the article aloud if he so wished: "although to me personally it is highly objectionable, yet this is the temple of freedom of speech." More than that, "it is the temple of freedom of thought." Thus, the Speaker concluded, "I think I should give the broadest freedom possible to any member who brings before the house a subject of the nature of that now in question." But Bird had had enough and conceded to the majority: "Out of deference to what seems to be the view of a large section of the house, I have no intention now of reading the article." He would instead try to summarize it.[112]

Even this concession did not end the sparring between Bennett and Lemieux. The latter brought up Charles Bradlaugh, the British atheist MP who had (eventually, after much legal wrangling) been permitted to take his seat without swearing an oath. The Speaker continued: "To-day in England free-thinkers as well as believers can take their seat and declare what they believe in." Bennett objected that the Bradlaugh case was not at all analogous. The two were still disagreeing when, irritated, Bird broke in to ask if he would now be permitted to finish what he had begun to say.[113]

Calling it "a burlesque on the story of creation," Bird proceeded to deliver a summary of Sterry's article. He argued that a similarly skeptical view of that story had become common among scholars of religion. All the rationalist had done was to imitate "his betters," but had expressed himself in a more colloquial manner. Then, employing considerable irony himself, Bird went on to play up the class dimension of Sterry's plight and the self-importance of "Toronto the Good": "This unfortunate man happily does not belong to the elite; he is apparently some rough-mannered, long-haired individual who jumps on a soap box somewhere in the holy city of Toronto, which stands four-square against the waves of heterodoxy sweeping over the country, a city hallowed by its staunch support of all that is orthodox and traditional both in fiscal theory and in biblical belief." Bird may have misrepresented Sterry's physical appearance but he was correct about the rationalist's social status. He also accurately described the Christian conservatism that was so dominant in Toronto, especially among the city's elite.[114]

Despite Woodsworth's efforts, the bill was voted down with "a roar of almost angry disapproval."[115] Bearing out Bird's characterization of Toronto, the *Globe* enthusiastically backed the decision, which would no doubt "have the hearty approval of the vast majority." The

British Empire was the freest in the world, the paper proclaimed, but "these virtues were not won for the British people by atheists and agnostics of the Sterry order." Nor did such freedoms really apply to such people. Freedom of speech and thought were "rooted, grounded and built up on the integrity of the Divine Word and reverence for Almighty God." Permitting God to be mocked would strike a blow at the stability of the Empire which could not be tolerated. And if Bird was right that such sentiments were commonly uttered in theological colleges, then the laity should wake up and "demand a housecleaning of the institutions their money goes to support."[116] The *Montreal Gazette* agreed that Woodsworth had been wrong to challenge the existing law. In response to his argument that the law did not clearly define blasphemy, it pointed to the members of the jury in Sterry's trial. They had no trouble in identifying blasphemy when they saw it, and "it is reasonable to assume that a dozen men, taken from various walks of life and sworn to give an honest verdict, are not likely to act upon an illiberal view in this very liberal age." The paper went on to praise Coatsworth's charge to the jury, noting with approval that it was based on the assumption that Canada was still a Christian country, and that "there are still some things that a majority of the people hold sacred."[117]

The *Globe* and the *Gazette* may have been right about widespread support for the law against blasphemous libel; it remained entrenched in the Criminal Code until 2018. But its penalties would be applied very selectively. A few months after Woodsworth attempted to abolish it, blasphemous libel made its way back into Toronto papers. On 17 April 1928, the *Star* reported on the case of Professor W.A. Irwin of the University of Toronto. A modernist biblical scholar, he had made the charge that the God of the early books of the Old Testament "was not only an unscrupulous liar himself as well as an encourager of liars," but was also guilty at times of "moral turpitude."[118] His comments provoked a minor uproar in the press. Rev. Stuart Parker, a local Presbyterian, shot back that Irwin's brusque dismissal of the scriptures lacked historical perspective and was "like cutting your grandfather's throat because he is old and doddering."[119] Several concerned Torontonians demanded that Irwin be fired and brought to trial for blasphemy. There was of course recent precedent, as W.G. MacKendrick wrote: "The arm of the law prosecuted a peddler of a rationalist paper for a much less offensive utterance: will that arm of the law be shortened because the offender in this case is a professor in our highest seat of education? I hope not."[120]

Unsurprisingly the arm of the law did prove rather short in this case. Irwin was never tried for blasphemous libel, even though he would go on to say other provocative things about the accuracy and moral qualities of the Bible. As Sterry's defenders had argued, it may indeed have been true that social standing determined who was deemed dangerous and thus persecuted, and who was judged eccentric and left alone.[121]

What became of Ernest Sterry? He continued to reside in Toronto. In October 1928 he chaired a meeting for the visiting British rationalist Joseph McCabe and in the following weeks he delivered a few lectures.[122] An odd article in the *Star* noted in January 1929 that Sterry had been laid off from his job with the Might City Directory Co. two months earlier, and that "since then [he had] been unable to get work, also being refused deportation." Had the rationalist given up on Canada? No matter what his attitude to the country, Sterry remained in Canada. In February 1929 he represented his fellow rationalists at a conference on free speech and in October 1932 he delivered a lecture to the RSC.[123] Throughout the 1930s Sterry worked as an art and stamp dealer.[124] None of this made him wealthy, however. By 1941, at age sixty-nine, he had again fallen on hard times and was receiving a shelter allowance from Toronto's welfare department.[125] After this he disappears from the city's newspapers.

SUMMING UP

What do the Sterry trial and its aftermath say about interwar Canada, or more specifically, about interwar Toronto? It seems clear that the rationalist ran afoul of an elite Toronto establishment that was, for the most part, self-consciously Christian and conservative. He might have remained in obscurity if he had contented himself with giving lectures or distributing papers among people of his own social stratum; the offense that got him noticed was handing the *Christian Inquirer* to authority figures in the halls of power. Once the case had been initiated and brought into the public eye, Sterry had to be punished; those same authority figures had to demonstrate that they would uphold the Christian social order, even though much of the liberal popular press was against the prosecution. His working-class status also made him an easier target for public discipline than a professor like Irwin.

The fact that most members of the Commons were unwilling to let any rationalist sentiments even be read aloud in Parliament also speaks to the intense stigma attached to unbelief, enforced by a shared sense of Christian propriety. The law was not simply a relic of earlier times; most parliamentarians believed that it remained valuable, and thus refused to repeal it. Canada remained wedded to the idea of Christendom, of political power being used to support a Christian social order.

But why did this all happen in Toronto in 1927? Why was the Christian social order challenged in the first place, and why did it need to defend itself so visibly? As it happens, the Sterry case was only one skirmish in a wider struggle over belief and unbelief in interwar Toronto. To address these questions we now examine the broader context of Sterry's trial, from his colleagues in the Rationalist Society of Canada to Christian authority figures like Judge Emerson Coatsworth.

5

Unbelief in Toronto the Good

As of the mid-1920s, rationalist speakers would regularly hold forth in parks and on street corners in downtown Toronto, sometimes gathering audiences of hundreds to listen to their fiery condemnations of Christianity. In the spring of 1929, the city police began dispersing the crowds by threat of force. The leaders of the local rationalist association were outraged, declaring in the press: "As citizens and taxpayers they expect to be protected by the police who are their servants and not their masters, and who are not the keepers of their conscience. In matters of fundamental rights and liberties, they will permit no one to abrogate."[1] Rationalist lawyer Lionel Cross demanded to know why these meetings were being broken up, even though participants were orderly and well behaved. The police inspector in charge of the downtown division told him frankly that rationalist views were offensive to many people and to the police, and that was reason enough. His men "were under no obligation to protect any speakers on the street but religious ones."[2]

As this anecdote shows, Ernest Sterry's conviction for blasphemous libel was only the beginning of a battle over unbelief in interwar Toronto. This chapter explores the story of that struggle in three sections: the first describes the local rationalist organization and its activities; the second looks at the conflicts that surrounded unbelief in the city; and the third examines Toronto's vigorous anti-atheist forces.

The Rationalist Society of Canada (RSC) was a more diverse group than the Winnipeg Rationalist Society, but both associations developed close connections with their local leftist organizations. As the suffering of the Great Depression persisted, the RSC grew more and more politically engaged. It became clear to its chief organizer that building a secularist world would require committing to radical social and economic change. Ultimately he turned his attention away from it in favour of working for the democratic socialist Co-operative Commonwealth Federation (CCF). The Rationalist Society represented a threat to the evangelical orthodoxy that ruled Toronto, and was attacked for it, particularly during the "free speech" struggles of 1928–33. This threat was also the provocation for a campaign against atheism by the aging evangelical reformers who wished to maintain "Toronto the Good" as a Christian citadel.

THE ROOTS OF UNBELIEF IN ONTARIO

Despite the fears that Sterry and other rationalists aroused, organized unbelief was nothing new in interwar Ontario. A Toronto Free-Thought Association was formed in 1873, and in 1881 it was renamed the Toronto Secular Society. These secularists organized lectures, a library, and a debating club. Evangelical Protestants had a strong influence on the city, and to counter it local freethinkers campaigned for the taxation of churches, the secularization of education, and an end to Lord's Day laws restricting Sunday activities.[3] In 1877 the Toronto group joined the broader Canadian Secular Union, which brought together anglophone freethinkers from Ontario and Quebec. The union's first president was Joseph Ick Evans, a labour activist. Thomas Philips Thompson, a highly popular socialist writer, was a prominent member of the Toronto secularists, along with other trade unionists, like Alfred F. Jury and J.I. Livingstone.[4]

America's "Great Agnostic," Robert Ingersoll, was brought to Toronto in 1880 to lecture under the auspices of the Freethought Association. He moved on from there to speak in Ottawa, Montreal, Belleville, and Napanee.[5] Other rationalist speakers were invited from the United States to deliver lectures and to engage in public debates with members of the clergy.[6] They had connections with the British secularist movement as well. In 1882 Canadian freethinkers invited Charles Watts, a prominent British lecturer, to come and live in Toronto. This he did the following year. A charismatic speaker and able writer, Watts became the leader of the secularist movement in Ontario, founding and editing the journal *Secular Thought*. After he returned to England in 1891, the magazine was taken over by James Spencer Ellis. It achieved a circulation of approximately 800 in 1899 but had ceased publication by 1911.[7] There does not seem to have been much organized activity from this generation of Ontario secularists after that date.[8] Unbelievers remained a small minority. The 1921 census recorded that there were 65 agnostics, 132 atheists, 180 freethinkers, and 3,231 people with no religion in Ontario, out of a population of 2.9 million – about 0.1 per cent of the total. In the 1931 census, 3,418 Ontarians reported having no religion, again about 0.1 per cent of the total population.[9]

THE RATIONALIST SOCIETY OF CANADA

In the autumn of 1925 a new group of Toronto unbelievers began to come together on an informal basis.[10] They decided to seek legal incorporation, and attempted to register with provincial authorities as "the Agnostic Society." Their application was rejected by the official responsible, who told them that "no such organization would be authorized by the Ontario Government." Sometime later their lawyer returned with a new name for the group, the Rationalist Society of Canada, and a "new set of aims and objects" describing what the group stood for:

1 [To] promote the study of Science and Philosophy as laid down for us by the Great Masters;
2 To find our place in, and our duty to, the great Body Social;
3 To promote to our fellows true morality as based on Natural Law; [and]
4 To produce Unity and Concord along sane and logical lines; to produce Happiness and Prosperity in this Great Canada of ours.[11]

In order to pursue these aims, the rationalists intended to lecture and to "publish, circulate, sell and dispose of literature." To support these activities the group would "receive and accept gifts and property."[12] This declaration proved acceptable to the authorities, even though "it was known that the parties [involved] were agnostics or atheists." Thus the RSC was incorporated on 11 May 1926.[13] The fact that the activities of this supposedly national society were restricted to Toronto doesn't seem to have bothered its officers, who made little effort to link up with rationalists in other provinces. There appears to have been no direct contact with Marshall Gauvin and his Winnipeg organization, for example.[14]

The Toronto *Globe* took notice of the RSC's formation about a month later, reporting that "a branch of the American Association for the Advancement of Atheism has been incorporated at Ottawa under the title of the Rationalist Society of Canada." The American association (popularly known as "The 4 AS" or "4A"), was founded in 1925 by Charles Lee Smith. It was not a large organization but it was very good at generating publicity through controversy. For example, it advocated the formation of atheist "Damned Souls" clubs among college students, and called for the national adoption of Blamesgiving, a counterpart to Thanksgiving.[15] When the RSC was created, a number of newspapers across Canada ran stories in which it was depicted as a local off-shoot of the 4A. The *Halifax Evening Mail*, for instance, quoted Freeman Hopwood, general secretary of the 4A, who stated: "The policy to be pursued by the Rationalist Society will be similar to our methods in this country. After all, the church is as much a menace in Canada as in the States ... Regular meetings are already being held in Toronto in the hall used by the Agnostic Society of Canada, the body from which the new organization has sprung." Hopwood also claimed that the 4A had turned its Canadian membership list over to William Styles of the Rationalist Society.[16] While there may have been some early contact between the 4A and the RSC, I found few signs of ongoing cooperation, and no evidence of the group's incorporation at the federal level.

The Toronto *Globe* was dismissive of the RSC's creation. "The fact is not worthy of more than a passing mention. Every once in a while and for limited periods English-speaking countries are afflicted with a revival of this folly. As it does not last long, it has no real influence on the public mind." Despite this assurance, the *Globe* went on to express concern that the Canadian rationalists, "destitute as they are alike in intelligence and feeling," would try to warp the minds of college youth.[17] Unbelievers did not really matter, but they might have a malign effect on the vulnerable. Lionel Cross, the group's lawyer, responded with a blistering counterattack and defence of his organization. "You are in error when you state that free thought is a sporadic movement which from time to time blossoms forth among the deluded," the attack concluded optimistically. "As man removes the cobweb from his eyes and learns to understand his relationship with nature and his fellows he forgets the gods and leaves them to their own devices. Never before has this movement been stronger than today. The free thought army marches merrily on."[18]

The RSC may not have had obvious connections with their forerunners in the city or with their counterparts across the country, but evidence suggests that the group did evolve from an earlier form. This prior activity was outdoor "soap-box" lectures in Toronto's streets and parks. References to these gatherings date back to May 1926, and it seems likely that these provided the context in which the group originally came together in 1925.[19] By the fall of 1926 the newly incorporated society had rented a hall and had begun advertising for regular indoor meetings. The founding members of the group, as listed on their application for incorporation, were "Bertram Elijah Leavens, cabinet maker; William Henry Styles, rigger; Elizabeth Hunting, married woman; Harry Stiner, salesman; and Ernest Victor Sterry, labourer." As noted above, the society's legal counsel, who prepared the application, was Lionel Cross, whom we met defending Sterry in the previous chapter; but the group's main officers were Styles, who served as president, and Leavens, the secretary-treasurer.

William Styles was a third-generation Canadian of Irish descent, whose parents, he said, had "carved out their own farm by their own toil in Northern Ontario." Styles claimed that the only school he had attended was "the school of human experience," which would suggest he was an autodidact like Gauvin and many other rationalists. According to army records, he was born in 1894.[20] By the time he was nineteen, in 1911, he was living with his mother in the Huron County area of Ontario and working in a foundry. On his army attestation form, filled out in 1916, he gave his profession as "farmer." As noted above, in 1926 his profession was listed as "rigger." Styles was married and had two daughters and two sons.[21] The RSC's secretary-treasurer, Bertram (Bert) Leavens, was born in Owen Sound, Ontario, in 1886, a fourth-generation Canadian. A cabinetmaker, he had lived and worked in a number of smaller centres such as Stratford and Kitchener before coming to Toronto. Among the earliest places he mentioned living in was the town of Wingham in Huron County, so it is possible he knew Styles there before coming to Toronto. Leavens had not always been a rationalist; he had at one point been a Sunday school superintendent, and still owned the Bible he had been given in those days.[22] He was also married, with two sons and one daughter. His wife would eventually act as an official of the RSC, and his eldest son, William John (Jack) Leavens, would one day follow his father's example by giving rationalist lectures before the RSC.[23] Over the next ten years Bert Leavens would prove to be the most active leader and organizer of the society.

Figure 5.1 William Styles and Bertram Leavens, 1927

Lecturing was the main means used by the Toronto rationalists to spread their message, along with the occasional debate against a religious opponent. When the weather got cold (usually October through April) they would lecture in meeting halls; when it was warm, they would lecture in the streets and parks. One observer claimed that these gatherings could attract up to a thousand people.[24] Indoor meetings were typically held on Sunday evenings. A period for questions and discussion was scheduled from 7:30 to 8:00, with the lecture following. The group's leaders, Leavens and Styles in particular, were the most frequent speakers. Unlike Marshall Gauvin, however, the Toronto rationalists were not lecturing for a living. They had day jobs that occupied much of their time. They dealt with this situation in two ways: they recycled lectures, giving them several times over the years; and they often brought in guest speakers. This was a major difference from Marshall Gauvin's practice; Gauvin only once invited a guest lecturer to speak, and then only because he was sick that week. The RSC, meanwhile, had at least forty different people speak under its auspices, not counting the numerous debates that they hosted.

In the society's early years most of its lectures were aimed at debunking religion, but a minority dealt with current issues and popular concerns. This pattern can be seen in the RSC's first advertised season in the autumn of 1926, which took place at the Photodrome Theatre opposite Toronto's City Hall. In the first three weeks of October, Styles answered the questions "Is Christianity a Failure?" and "Should Religion Be Taught in Schools?" and Leavens spoke on "Christianity and World Problems."[25] On 24 October, however, the rationalists heard from the prominent doctor and eugenicist Oswald C.J. Withrow, president of the Birth Control League of Ontario, presenting a talk on (as one would expect) birth control.[26]

Inviting Withrow to speak in the first month of the RSC's first indoor season (not to mention openly advertising his talk) was an early sign of the group's willingness to court controversy. It was at that time illegal to disseminate information on birth control in Canada.[27] The doctor no doubt kept his mention of technical details vague enough to avoid charges, but in 1926 the topic was still highly inflammatory. Indeed, within seven months of that lecture, he found himself imprisoned in Kingston Penitentiary. The doctor had been running a secret abortion clinic for upper-class patients. Early in 1927 one of his patients died after he operated, and for this he was tried and convicted of manslaughter. He would spend seven years in prison.[28]

Interspersed with talks by Leavens, Styles, and Cross in the autumn of 1926 were presentations by other visitors. The speaker who travelled furthest to be there was Franklin Steiner from Chicago, who spoke on "The Gospel of Rationalism." Steiner, who was the secretary of the American Rationalist Association, had encountered the previous generation of Toronto rationalists in 1895 when he had lectured in the city at the invitation of J.S. Ellis. When he visited the RSC in 1926 he was pleased to meet the Cunninghams, a freethinking couple who were "the sole survivors" of that earlier generation. In his article about the trip for the American *Truth Seeker* magazine, Steiner complimented both Styles and Leavens on their speaking ability. He also enjoyed the "intelligence and courage" of the Toronto rationalists and contrasted it with the intense religiosity and provincial nature of the city in which they lived.[29] The other speakers at the RSC that autumn were James Birks, who spoke on Biblical patriarchs, and Florence Custance, who gave a talk on "Secular Education." Birks was a Toronto ironworker who had witnessed the society's application for incorporation; Custance was a member of the Communist Party active in organizing female workers.[30]

The first half of the season seems to have been a success, sometimes attracting six hundred people to a single lecture.[31] On 9 January 1927, thanks to their "ever increasing audience," the RSC was obliged to move to a larger venue, the Victoria Theatre on Yonge St.[32] Unsurprisingly this success also gave rise to opposition. In a sermon delivered on that same evening, Rev. L.H. Gibson of Cooke's Presbyterian Church called the RSC's meetings "a menace to morality" and said they should be banned. "I do not believe in restricting free speech, but when it descends to indecency and vulgarity and attacks the very foundation of the nation as in this case, it is a different thing," he proclaimed.[33]

Only two days later the city's attention suddenly turned upon the fledgling society when Ernest Sterry was charged with blasphemous libel for distributing his *Christian Inquirer*. Officials of the RSC were drawn into a flurry of press interviews, public rallies, and letters to the editor. In taking up Sterry's case, Cross was particularly visible. The added attention was a mixed blessing. On the one hand it attracted opprobrium from the powerful; Rev. F.C. Ward-Whate, Anglican vicar of Toronto's St Alban's Cathedral, and a prominent Orangeman, climbed into the pulpit one Sunday to declare the rationalists a gang of "nameless, mongrel curs" who should be swiftly jailed and then deported.[34] At the same time, the society also gained supporters. Montgomery Brown, the notorious "Red Bishop" who had been tried and convicted of heresy by the Episcopal Church, came from Ohio to speak under RSC auspices on the topic "Heresy and Blasphemy."[35] Franklin Steiner again travelled from Chicago to show the support of American freethinkers. He spoke on "Blasphemy: Historically and Legally," and on "Bradlaugh," the famous British rationalist who had been prosecuted for his unbelief.[36] Specially themed lectures were hastily written and delivered by Styles and Leavens on topics like "The Debt Owed to the Martyrs of Freethought."[37]

After Sterry was convicted and public interest in his case waned, the RSC's lectures moved into a regular pattern that lasted until 1931. A bit of verse by Longfellow that accompanied one of the Society's ads in 1927 summed up its underlying philosophy during those years: "If half the power that's used to fill this world with terror, if half the power bestowed on camps and courts, were given to free the human mind from error, there'd be no use for navies, arsenals and forts."[38] This "error," in the view of rationalists, consisted primarily of religious and philosophical delusions, and thus most lectures focused on dispelling such false beliefs. Styles and Leavens presented most of the talks, although they sometimes ceded the stage to fellow rationalists like Lionel Cross. Typical anti-religious topics included: "The Five Gospels of Rationalism," "Great Infidels," "The Evolution of the Idea of God," "Religion and the Sex Question," and "The Conflict between Science & Religion."[39]

Leavens and Cross also engaged in debates, usually with Christian laymen on theological or biblical topics, but occasionally with other rationalists on philosophical questions.[40] After a few seasons Styles and Leavens began to rebut the claims of specific clergymen, as Gauvin was doing in Winnipeg.[41] In 1929 Styles attacked the "False Claims of the Canadian Christian Crusaders," a Toronto-based group with powerful backers which had recently formed to combat atheism across the country (the Crusaders will be discussed in more detail in the final section of this chapter).[42] Not every lecture had a specifically rationalist theme, however: in 1928 G.H. Walters of the Anti-Vaccination and Medical Liberty League of Canada spoke on "The Right to Keep Well."[43] In October 1930 Leavens spoke on "Crime and Present Conditions," which seems to have been a reference to the Great Depression.[44] He also debated Mr W.A. Gappee of London on the resolution "Industrial Organization and Political Action Will

Emancipate the Workers." (Gappee argued for the "Pros," while Leavens took the side of the "Cons.") Presumably the latter followed the same line of thought that Gauvin had pursued in his disputes with the OBU, when he held that only rationalist education would free workers from the mental shackles of superstition.[45]

The society sometimes experimented with different formats as well. In November 1927, for example, they added a weekly discussion group on Wednesdays "for members and friends."[46] These seem to have petered out after a month or so. In the autumn of 1929 they again made an effort to widen their appeal to the public by advertising a Friday night euchre party, two dances accompanied by a "good orchestra," and a renewal of the Wednesday night discussion groups.[47] A later ad promoted the "U-Need-A-Social-Club" on Tuesdays and Fridays.[48] The following spring the Society made an even greater effort to reach out to sympathizers through their ads. In one, the organizers asked the "Canadian Atheist Association, Toronto Secular Society and West Toronto Agnostic Society [to] please note" the upcoming lecture.[49] In another they announced that reserved seats would be held until 8 pm "for members of the American Association for the Advancement of Atheism and the Hamilton Rationalist Society."[50] Aside from the 4As, these other groups seem to have vanished without leaving other traces, so it is impossible to know much about their size or significance.

In the autumn of 1928 the RSC's cause received an outside boost in the person of British rationalist and former monk Joseph McCabe.[51] He was in the city in mid-October as part of a nation-wide lecture tour sponsored by the One Big Union.[52] Before he arrived he challenged Rev. J.G. Inkster, an outspoken local anti-evolutionist, to a debate. The *Star* made Inkster's refusal its front-page headline, thus giving McCabe some free publicity.[53] Ernest Sterry acted as chair for his first appearance, on Sunday, 14 October at Margaret Eaton Hall. McCabe's lecture on "The Martyrdom of Man" was subject to interruptions by impassioned opponents of evolution. Shouted arguments between them and McCabe's supporters during the post-lecture question period caused an uproar that Sterry was unable to quell. The hall was eventually cleared, but "the arguments continued outside on the street."[54] McCabe went on to lecture every night that week.

On the last day of McCabe's visit he debated the famous American fundamentalist William Bell Riley.[55] The resolution at stake was "Evolution is a Fake and should not be Taught in the Schools." A crowd of nearly two thousand people paid the fifty-cent admission fee to watch the clash at Massey Hall. Rev. Oswald J. Smith, one of Toronto's most prominent fundamentalists, was the chairman.[56] Robert E. Knowles, a *Star* reporter (and former Presbyterian minister) who had been at the Scopes trial, was scornful of the debate, calling it "a joke in Sunday clothes." He contrasted the greatness of Darrow and Bryan with the "panting, breathless, intense and vehement stabs and slings and arrows of the excited and indignant Dr. Riley, who seemed to be in a fever of wrath against everybody in general, and Prof. McCabe in particular." Riley's performance was heavy with outrage but light on reasoning, Knowles wrote: the minister's opening speech was "more like someone splashing round in a bathtub than anything else." The reporter was a little more sympathetic to McCabe but found his performance dry; his decision to participate in such a ridiculous performance was at best questionable, and at worst motivated by greed.[57] The *Globe*'s coverage was more favourable to Riley and noted that his witty barbs against evolutionary theory often drew laughter and applause.[58]

At the end of the debate three-quarters of the audience voted against evolution.[59] Knowles was not surprised, having observed that much of the audience was hostile to McCabe from the outset. A few years later his colleague Salem Bland, who was also present, wrote in the *Star*:

> It was pathetic to note that to the anti-evolutionists the debate was no mere trial of skill. They listened as the prisoner at the bar listens to the two lawyers who are contending whether he is to go to prison for a long term of years or leave the court a free man with no stain on his good name, and when the vote was taken and the majority voted against evolution the intense feeling burst out spontaneously into the doxology. I doubt if such a debate would have found such a close in any other great British city in the world.[60]

(In addition to being a writer for the *Star*, Bland was a modernist United Church minister who was active in left-wing causes, so his disapproval of the anti-evolutionists was not unexpected.) The *Star*'s sardonic reporting also earned the paper an angry letter from a local clergyman, Rev. J. MacIntosh. He attacked evolution as a "ridiculous and childish absurdity" and insisted that Riley had been a fine debater who had simply used humour more effectively than McCabe.[61]

Ernest Sterry apparently decided to take advantage of the interest generated by McCabe's visit to deliver lectures in the following weeks, independent of the rest of the RSC. The week after McCabe's debate with Riley, he took out an ad promoting his lecture on "EVOLUTION."[62] The next week it was "Either Christian religion or evolution is a fake. Which? Reply to Rev. Inkster."[63] The third week brought Sterry into direct competition with the rest of the RSC. He spoke about people who were "Good Natured Despite Their Christianity," while Leavens was presenting a "rational exposition" of the Ten Commandments elsewhere.[64] After this, however, Sterry's separate meetings stopped and the RSC continued its accustomed program.

In the fall of 1930 Toronto received a visit from another famous unbeliever, namely Clarence Darrow. In contrast with McCabe's visit in 1928, the local rationalists seem to have had no direct involvement in the event. It was presented by the Jewish Holy Blossom Forum, which brought Darrow and Rabbi Barnett Brickner of Cleveland from the United States to reprise a debate they had held before, in 1928.[65] In an article entitled "U.S. Atheist Scoffs at Sacred Teaching in City of Churches," the *Globe* described the sold-out event, which centred on the question "Is Man a Machine?" at Massey Hall on 20 November. "Toronto literally fought for seats ... People clamored at front and rear doors," while others "begged to have cards sent to Mr. Darrow who, they were sure, could get them in." The hall's seats and its stage were filled to capacity with some three thousand spectators, a greater turnout than McCabe and Riley had attracted.

With his well-known cutting wit, Darrow denied that human beings possessed a soul, arguing for a purely material understanding of life. Humanity, he claimed, had evolved from inanimate matter and remained completely controlled by the laws of physics. Rabbi Brickner, on the other hand, argued that new things could emerge in the course of evolution, and that the potential for a free and spiritual humanity had been placed by the Creator in the basic building blocks of matter. Salem Bland was in attendance and estimated that, judging by the patterns of applause, only "a few score" in attendance sided with Darrow. Bland felt that the rabbi had won the debate, but conceded that Darrow was a good man, calling him a Christian at heart if not in philosophy.[66] The editors of the *Globe* were not so forgiving and found it necessary to print three separate rebuttals of Darrow's atheistic views: on the letters page, the church editorial page, and the regular editorial page.[67] Rather more gently an editor at the *Star* picked up on Darrow's statement that he was "an imaginative sort of slob" and responded that "an imagination that cannot conceive of a soul or of immortality is not very much of an imagination at all."[68]

The debate did not overlap with the RSC's regular schedule, so it is probable that some of the rationalists were among that "few score" that cheered Darrow on. The event did not, however, have any direct effect on their own program. Virtually all lectures in that season (1930–31) were given by Leavens (who also participated in a debate) or Styles, with only two exceptions. A Professor Lamb spoke on "Health vs. Religion," and the socialist-feminist activist Rose Henderson appeared twice. Her first talk, on 16 November, discussed "Bernard Shaw, the Rationalist," and the second, on 29 March 1931, considered "Woman and War."[69] These would be Henderson's only appearances before the RSC, but her presence there foreshadowed the more explicitly political direction the society would take in following years.

THE RSC'S LEFT TURN

This change in direction was precipitated by the departure of William Styles in 1931. The ad for Styles's lecture on 12 April 1931, "Christianity and Slavery," announced: "This will be your last opportunity to hear Toronto's famous Atheist." It is unclear whether the rationalist was retiring from lecturing or moving away. If the latter, he did not go very far, because he appeared once more that year: on 5 December he spoke on "The Truth about Edison." But that would be his last appearance for at least three years. [70] In the RSC's 1931 official incorporation papers, he was replaced as president by Stanley Lloyd.[71]

The ensuing lecture season (1931–32) was almost non-existent, thanks in part to Styles's absence and in part to outside pressures (discussed below).[72] The RSC only advertised four events. After missing the entire month of October, Leavens presented "Is Atheism a Negative Philosophy: An Answer to Rabbi Issendrath" on November 1. That ad indicated that there would be "lectures every Sunday evening [at] 7:30," but if these occurred, they left no trace.[73] In addition to Styles's talk about Edison, the only other presentations were by Dr Robert G. Jackson, a "prominent authority on health," who spoke on the innocuous topics of keeping healthy and the importance of diet.[74]

That might have been the end of the organization. But it made a remarkable comeback under Leavens's sole leadership in the next season. On 23 October 1932 Leavens gave a talk entitled "Is Rationalism a Negative Philosophy?"[75] With the question phrased like that, there can be little doubt his answer was "no," and the topics presented in the following weeks and years suggest that the RSC was indeed consciously moving away from a mainly negative approach. From 1932 to 1936 secularists mingled with socialists, single-taxers, and the scientifically minded to discuss what an enlightened, post-religious world should look like. Leavens's new involvement with Toronto's left was not entirely new; there had been a few hints of his politics in earlier seasons. During the Sterry controversy, for instance, the *Star* reported on a talk in which Leavens argued that "democracy" had become a meaningless word. During the Great War men were told that they were fighting to "make the world fit for democracy," but the rationalist scoffed, "I say, make democracy fit for the world."[76] It is also possible that police persecution had radicalized Leavens. If rationalists were continually being lumped in with the left, perhaps they decided they should embrace that identity. A more pragmatic reason for the RSC's new outreach was the fact that Styles's departure left it in need of speakers to fill its schedule.

We can better understand the RSC's shift to broader social questions by considering a contemporary article from the British secularist Robert Arch entitled "The Old Rationalism and the New," published in the 1931 *Rationalist Annual*. Arch contended that the purely negative approach of critiquing religion was facing sharply diminishing returns: "Attention has drifted away from religious issues not only because these issues are less alive, but because others have taken their place – in particular, issues of economics, sex ethics, war and peace." Modern people, he wrote, were just not very interested in events that may or may not have happened in ancient times; they wanted to hear informed discussion of events taking place now. "If we are content to remain purveyors of accurate but academic information on biology and Biblical criticism, salutary as such work is in its way, we shall cut no ice with the average man or the average woman. The Churches will laugh at us as effete mid-Victorians, and we shall go to our graves unwept, unhonoured, and unsung." Rationalists should therefore address themselves "with determination to issues like divorce law reform, birth control, peace" and other more relevant topics.[77]

Arch's position was not new. The debate between unbelievers who wanted a "positive" program and those who focused on making a critical and "negative" case against religion was a recurrent one that recalled the great schism between the secularist George Holyoake and the militant atheist Charles Bradlaugh in the nineteenth century.[78] But the urge to rebrand and rejuvenate unbelief was growing again in the early 1930s, due in part to the effect of the Depression on public attitudes.[79]

With this new approach the diversity of the RSC's speakers was much wider than it had been, although most of the new batch were associated with leftist organizations and progressive causes. Guests ranged from Charles H. Ingersoll, vice-president of the Single Tax Club of New York, to Rev. A. George Hall, a prison reformer, to Sam Scarlett, infamous Communist organizer.[80] Each of these speakers only visited once, but others appeared on a regular basis. Two new mainstays of the RSC were Ernest Walker and Jean Laing. Walker was billed as a "World Traveller & Lecturer," but aside from that his origins and qualifications are unknown.[81] Regardless, over the next four years he would give nine lectures and participate in two debates and one symposium.[82] Jean Laing was a trade unionist and feminist (and a friend of Rose Henderson) who spoke frequently though not exclusively about women, in talks like "Woman's Contribution to the Evolution of the Race," "Holy Women of the Bible," and "The Martyrdom of Woman."[83] When Walker asked that perennial rationalist question, "Why Are Women Religious?" he was soon followed by Laing's "Women in Religion and Economics," which was likely a response or rebuttal.[84] Laing gave seven lectures in total between 1932 and 1936.

Laing did more than speak; she also served as an RSC director for at least a year, which suggests a significant degree of commitment to the rationalist cause.[85] Serving as director along with her was William D. Dennison. Dennison was at the time the principal of the Toronto School of Speech Correction, but he would go on to be a successful municipal and provincial politician and eventual mayor of the city.[86] He spoke to the RSC on topics including Robert G. Ingersoll and "Insects and Men: Instinct and Reason."[87] Dennison seems to have maintained his skeptical views throughout his life; when he first ran for mayor in 1966, the *Globe & Mail* noted that he was "a man who could never see the need for both a prayer and the national anthem at the same meeting."[88]

Both Laing and Dennison were affiliated with the CCF, which was formed in 1932. A number of political figures who appeared before the RSC were also associated with the fledgling democratic socialist party. These included activists Thomas Cruden, Dr Luke Teskey, and Arthur H. Williams.[89] Leavens himself would pursue political office as a CCF candidate beginning in 1935. This association between the rationalists and the new party did not go unnoticed. A letter from a Pat Kennedy, published in the *Globe* of 2 May 1935, denounced the CCF for a host of reasons, one of which included rationalism. In a list of nine groups that he claimed made up the CCF, Kennedy included "the Rationalist Society (atheists)." He accused the rationalists, alongside others, of being "'baby reds' (semi-Stalinites), who are petted, mothered, blessed and cajoled by the international Red octopus, communism."[90]

Kennedy may have wildly overestimated the actual connection between rationalism and communism (and between the CCF and communism) but there was a grain of truth in what he wrote. Both current and ex-Communists appeared before the RSC in the 1932–36 period. As mentioned above, organizer Sam Scarlett came to speak on "Religion in Soviet Russia";[91] Edward Cecil-Smith, a writer and literary critic affiliated with the Communist Party of Canada (CPC), explained "The Role of Religion in China."[92] Scarlett and Cecil-Smith appeared in 1935 and 1936, respectively; their presence was probably part of the CPC's Popular Front strategy. The RSC also invited ex-Communists who had been expelled from the CPC in the 1929–30 period.[93] These included Jack MacDonald, former CPC chair, and William Moriarty, once a high-ranking Communist Party official. MacDonald addressed the connection between "Socialism and Religion," while Moriarty argued for "The Necessity of Socialism."[94] Toronto rationalists also heard from some of the city's independent leftists, typically union officials like John W. Bruce and Pat Sullivan. The former asked the philosophical question, "What Will We Do with Our Lives?"[95] At least one of the reformers who addressed the RSC in this period had come to activism as a result of his own personal suffering. On 29 October 1933, seven years after his first appearance before the rationalists, the birth control expert (and eugenicist) Oswald Withrow returned to speak about his experiences in the Kingston Penitentiary, and to present his new book on penal reform, *Shackling the Transgressor*.[96]

Of course, the Rationalist Society did not abandon anti-religious topics entirely. The above talks were interspersed with more traditional lectures, delivered mainly by Leavens. He routinely mounted attacks on perennial rationalist targets such as "The Absurdities of Christian Belief" and "Christian Intolerance."[97] He would also mix the traditional and the contemporary, with lectures like "Christianity and the Economic Crisis" and "Rationalism: Its Political Significance."[98] Some of the debates in which he participated also mixed anti-religious critique with modern concerns; for example, one resolved that "the practice of Christ's teachings would not tend to social or economic welfare."[99]

While many guests addressed political and economic topics, others kept their focus on religion and the rational approach to life.[100] Ernest Sterry, in his only advertised appearance with the RSC, brought forward his "Objections to the Christian Scheme of Salvation."[101] The society held a special tribute to the famous rationalist Robert G. Ingersoll. Four speakers, one of whom was William Dennison, praised "the man who drove from thoughtful minds the fear of Hell," and a free copy of Ingersoll's *Creed of Science* was given to every attendee.[102] One of only four women ever to appear before the RSC, Miss Margaret Lade of Melbourne, Australia, visited to speak on "New Values for Old."[103] Bert Leavens's son, William Jack Leavens, made his public debut with a short talk on "The Profits of a Religion."[104] Most strikingly, in 1934 William Styles returned from his three-year absence with the provocatively titled talk "Christ or Lenin, Which?"[105] Styles would remain a regular speaker for the rest of the RSC's life. He mainly addressed traditional rationalist topics such as "The Necessity of Atheism," but the wide-ranging schedule which had developed in his absence continued.[106]

The 1935–36 lecture season would prove to be the RSC's last advertised. Unusually, Leavens only spoke three times over the whole year. This was because he had begun to put his energy into leftist political activism. Already in 1933 we find Leavens at Toronto's May Day parade, organized by the local CCF, accompanied by Jean Laing, William Dennison and a large number of other leftists, including communists such as J.B. Salsberg and Sam Scarlett.[107] In 1935 Leavens ran for Parliament as the CCF candidate in the urban riding of Greenwood.[108] He came in third place with 4,813 votes, although this was only his first run for office. While Leavens was busy campaigning, Styles, Walker, Laing, and a few other new speakers took up the slack. Styles presented two lectures on Ingersoll and Thomas Paine, rationalism's biggest stars. He also rebutted a sermon by the social gospel stalwart Salem Bland, who had proclaimed "Atheism

Not to Be Feared."[109] Leavens finished the year off with "Blessed Are the Poor," the ad for which stated, "This will be the last indoor meeting of the season."[110]

The incorporation file for the Rationalist Society of Canada indicates that it was still in existence in January 1938, at least legally.[111] But though the rationalists continued with outdoor gatherings, March 1936 is when their advertising ends.[112] The most likely reason is that Leavens had decided to prioritize his political work over his rationalist activities. He had always been the mainstay of the RSC, delivering at least 82 lectures and partaking in 12 debates. Styles, meanwhile, gave 47 lectures but never participated in a debate. While he had been away it was Leavens who had built a network of connections, mostly with people on the left, to keep the society supplied with lecturers. Given that Styles's material usually eschewed politics and focused on traditional rationalist topics, it is possible that he was not entirely comfortable with the activists or the topics his friend had brought on board. Thus, the RSC that Leavens made and sustained fell apart when he turned his attention elsewhere.

After coming in third as the CCF provincial candidate for the Woodbine district in 1937, Leavens ran federally in Greenwood in 1940, coming in third again (this time with 3,430 votes). In 1940 he took on the duties of general secretary to the Ontario section of the CCF, a role he held until 1948.[113] He also worked as the business manager for the party's provincial newspaper, *The New Commonwealth*.[114] Leavens ran again with the CCF in Woodbine in the 1943 provincial election and finally won. He lost that seat in 1945 but regained it in 1948 and served until 1951.[115] He died two years later, at the age of sixty-eight, on 22 December 1953.[116] William Styles, meanwhile, did not entirely give up lecturing. In November 1938 he spoke before a Workers' Forum organized by the League for a Revolutionary Workers' Party on "Religion as discussed by a rationalist."[117] Despite being the younger man, he outlived Leavens by less than two years, dying on 29 June 1955.[118]

Lionel Cross's absence from the RSC lecture schedule after 1929 may be explained in part by his involvement in a high-profile case in 1930. As Constance Backhouse has detailed in her book *Colour-Coded*, Cross was a central part of an interracial alliance which in that year successfully pressured the Ontario judicial authorities to prosecute members of the Ku Klux Klan after they had publicly threatened and harassed a man in the town of Oakville.[119] Cross continued working as a lawyer until January 1937, when he was disbarred for "conduct unbecoming a barrister and solicitor in that he appropriated to his own use funds belonging to a client."[120] The details of what happened are unclear, and both Backhouse and Lewthwaite suggest Cross's trouble with legal authorities may have been prompted or aggravated by his racialized status.[121] After his disbarment Cross disappears from Toronto's recorded history, so it's likely that he moved elsewhere.

PERSECUTION AND CONTROVERSY

A perusal of the RSC's lecture schedule demonstrates how active the society was in spreading its message but it fails to illustrate the influence of that message. Despite being a relatively small group, the rationalists provoked a surprising amount of outrage and opposition. The Sterry case was only the beginning of the RSC's trouble with the authorities. These centred on the group's right to hold meetings outside lecture halls and turned into a major struggle for freedom of speech and freedom of assembly.

Not long after Sterry was released, Brigadier-General Denis C. Draper was appointed chief constable of Toronto.[122] He was brought into the position thanks to the influence of the septuagenarian police commissioners (and judges) Emerson Coatsworth and Frederick Morson. Deeply conservative, he was not only a veteran but also a devout Anglican and a Tory of United Empire Loyalist stock. He admired the way American police authorities were cracking down on their local communists and, with Coatsworth's outspoken backing he set about forming his own Red Squad. In the autumn of 1928 the Toronto Police Commission began its crackdown on radicals by banning public meetings in non-English languages and threatening to revoke the licenses of hall owners who hosted such gatherings. Communists defied these strictures and the police responded with beatings, tear gas, and arrests. As the Great Depression began swelling the ranks of the unemployed and the disaffected, the conflict escalated. There was chaos in the streets as police repeatedly beat protestors with fists, boots, batons, and rawhide whips. After more arrests, deportations, and endless court cases, all public meetings for which a license was not first obtained were eventually banned. The struggle led to the arrest and imprisonment in 1931 of key members of the communist leadership, the infamous "Eight Men" of the play *Eight Men Speak*.[123]

This story has been recounted by a number of historians, including Lita-Rose Betcherman, Ian Angus, and Michiel Horn.[124] They have argued, accurately enough, that communists were the main target of government repression because of their revolutionary political doctrines and the threat they posed to Canada's elites. What has been downplayed in their version of events is the fact that the struggle was not only political or economic but also cultural in nature. Groups besides the communists were targeted, including Toronto's rationalist community. An angry and paranoid rhetoric about atheist subversion became quite prominent in these years. This rhetoric was more than simply code for the economic fears of capitalist elites. Many Canadian Christians were, in fact, genuinely concerned that their religion was under threat. This is why they applauded the authorities' repression of outspoken atheism, regardless of its source.

Viewing the prosecution of Sterry as an early skirmish in Toronto's free speech struggle reframes the entire issue. The first chapter of Betcherman's *The Little Band* gestures in this direction by explaining the religious and cultural outlook of Toronto's elite and their defenders: conservative Protestant (usually evangelical in outlook), British or anglophile, Tory, staunchly imperialist, royalist, and pro-capitalist. Business owners, Conservative politicians, army officers, clergymen, the Orange Order, and the Imperial Order of the Daughters of the Empire were core components of this swath of Canadian society. A.E. Smith, the clergyman-turned-communist, bluntly described Toronto as "the citadel of reaction and religious Toryism," while J.S. Woodsworth called the city "smug," "intolerant," and "village-like."[125]

If, prompted in part by the Sterry trial, we view the Toronto free speech struggles not simply as another Red scare but more specifically as an attempt by the Anglo-Protestant elite to keep Toronto locked into late-nineteenth-century cultural patterns, we begin to see more clearly the reasons why rationalists and radical Christians were repressed alongside communists. One telltale connection is the presence of Emerson Coatsworth as the presiding judge in Sterry's trial. He was also the dominant voice on the Toronto Police Commission, and a key supporter of the Toronto-based Canadian Christian Crusade (CCC), an anti-atheist organization formed in 1929. We shall consider Coatsworth and the CCC in more detail in this chapter's final section. First we will examine the way rationalists were caught up in the struggle for Toronto streets.

On 5 May 1929, the police broke up a street meeting organized by the RSC. Cross, Styles, and Leavens promptly lodged a complaint with Chief Draper and the police commissioners. They asserted that police had orchestrated the situation "by aiding and abetting persons to create a disturbance at their meetings and then [intervening] under the guise of a 'breach of the peace being imminent' to justify their action." The RSC officials insisted that, "in matters of fundamental rights and liberties, they [would] permit no one to abrogate,"[126] and they would continue holding open air meetings, just as they had for "the past four years." They were aware, however, that Toronto's elite, despite their frequent praise for "British freedoms," did not believe that liberal principles protected radicals or blasphemers. On 4 August the *Star* published a letter from Cross spelling out this contradiction: "I have been trying to reconcile our ideas of British liberty with the attitude of the police in breaking up the meetings on the street of those with unconventional ideas, while religious gatherings are undisturbed." Cross was told by an inspector that both the public and his men found rationalist speeches objectionable, and that was reason enough. Admitting that appeals to the authorities had been a waste of time, Cross asked the readers of the *Star*: was it possible to "arouse an enlightened public sentiment to correct this?"[127]

On 13 August 1929, policemen forced a crowd out of Queen's Park, in an effort to forestall a communist meeting that had not even started. The violence meted out to communists and bystanders alike shocked many of those present and sparked a furor in the press.[128] While this incident has been discussed in the existing historiography of the "free speech struggle," another case only a few days later has been overlooked. On the following Sunday night (18 August), police ordered an "atheist" meeting of almost five hundred people near Massey Hall to disperse. This was almost certainly a gathering of the RSC. "The crowd took exception" to the interference of the police, and "as they walked slowly towards Yonge Street they jeered [at] the officers and called upon them to stop a religious meeting" being held on a nearby street corner.[129] Indeed, members of this "throng" themselves interrupted the religious gathering, which ended in disorder.

While this confrontation was not violent, the way it was reported in the next day's *Globe* reveals the extent to which Toronto's unbelievers were characterized as an existential threat to Canadian values, alongside communists and "foreigners." First of all, the paper argued that police action had been entirely justified because the rationalists had blocked the street. More significantly, however, its coverage of this story was surrounded on all sides by bold headlines warning Torontonians of the dire threat they faced from depraved agitators. The rhetorical question, "'Is It to Be Bolshevism or Constitutional Government?'" spanned the top of the page. Another headline trumpeted: "Communism Spells Murder, Pillage, Merciless Tyranny, Says Shields, and Would Eliminate Civilization." That lengthy article praised the eloquence and logic of a sermon by the fundamentalist Baptist minister T.T. Shields, who denounced atheism, communism, modernism, anarchy, and the *Toronto Star*. The adjacent piece interviewed four prominent Conservatives: Anglican canon H.J. Cody, war veteran and businessman J.J. Shanahan, politician Alfred Morine, and publisher S.B. Gundy. Not unexpectedly, all four praised the police and condemned leftists. "Exaggerated Stories on Reds, Distortion of Report Alleged," was the title of a nearby article about the police action in Queen's Park the week before. It reprinted a letter from someone who claimed to have been present and asserted that the police had had no choice but to break up the "sullen," "ugly" crowd, composed of threatening "foreigners" who would have become violent if given the opportunity; concerns over police brutality were simply the product of "scare headlines" and "gross misrepresentation" orchestrated by the *Star*. In the *Globe*'s coverage, the rationalists were merely one element of an ominous outside force that sought to overthrow "Toronto the Good."[130]

Rationalists, radicals, and their allies contested this view of events. On 2 October 1929 a heated meeting (which according to the mayor threatened to become "a regular donnybrook") was held at city hall to address concerns over the public exercise of free speech.[131] Chief Draper and Judge Coatsworth were present and subject to intense cross-examination by R.E. Knowles, Salem Bland, and others. Hard questions were aimed at Coatsworth in particular. After the judge explained that only seditious meetings were prohibited, an unnamed voice called out, "What about a man's religion?" Coatsworth replied, "I don't interfere with any man's religion," but he went on to caution that blasphemy would not be permitted either. One audience member pointedly asked him, "Aren't you connected with a religious organization?" (The judge was a prominent member of the United Church of Canada.) Coatsworth responded, "I've been connected with a religious organization all my life, but it interferes with none in their religion."[132]

William Styles attended that 1929 meeting as the RSC representative. He argued that his group had "inalienable rights" to hold meetings in public places, and that "any trouble in the parks has been caused by the police themselves." He complained about "a hysteria among certain people in the city that there is going to be a revolt." Styles said he had seen many socialist meetings and had never witnessed a riot; but "now every meeting is construed as being unlawful." He went on to declare that the rationalists would not "submit to a dictatorship," defiantly concluding, "I submit that the chief of police is the servant of this city and not a dictator."[133] When a Free Speech Conference was called for 12 October, the "Canadian Atheist Society" was listed among its supporters, alongside Bland, Knowles, and a number of communist-affiliated organizations.[134]

The conflict was played out well beyond the streets. Direct police pressure in 1929 led to theatre and hall owners reneging on their arrangements with communists and other leftist groups; it is possible the same thing happened to the rationalists. Early in the year, the RSC suddenly moved their meetings, going from the Victoria Theatre on 16 February to the Occident Hall a week later. After indoor lectures resumed in the fall, there were a number of other rapid venue changes: from the College Assembly Hall to the Brunswick Hall, and then, after a gap in the schedule, a move to Winchester Hall for the winter and spring of 1930. RSC officials never publicly addressed the changes but, given the timing, it is certainly conceivable that they were having trouble finding people who would rent them space.

A much bigger crisis was of course looming in 1929; in October the stock market crashed and the Great Depression began in earnest. The streets swelled with the unemployed and the disaffected, and the communists moved to organize them. These developments intensified the struggle over open-air meetings, but they also seem to have pushed battles over religion out of the limelight momentarily; the rationalists do not seem to have attracted much press attention in 1930. That would change early in 1931, when the *Globe* declared, "The eyes of atheism and the eyes of bolshevism in North America are fixed for the moment on Toronto."[135] This renewed burst of outrage was provoked by Emanuel Haldeman-Julius, luminary of the American freethought movement. His Kansas-based company, Haldeman-Julius Publications, was enormously prolific in its production of affordable books, pamphlets, and newspapers. His series of "Little Blue Books" would become particularly influential across North America. The publisher was himself a socialist and an atheist of Jewish descent who never shied away from controversy.[136] Upon hearing reports of the Toronto free speech battle, he decided to support local unbelievers and test the authorities by printing an "Atheist Special Edition" of his *American Freeman* newspaper and distributing "copies numbering in thousands" in the city.[137]

This provoked the ire of the *Globe,* which denounced not only Haldeman-Julius's atheism but also his support for "companionate marriage."[138] An editorial entitled "Keep This Trash Out" declared: "the atheist and the 'Red' have so much in common that it behooves Christian people to be on guard against their insidious style of propaganda. Their methods are so similar that general direction from Moscow is more than a suspicion."[139] The aim of both was the same: "the overthrow of established conditions that have been developed through the centuries." Something had to be done. Canadians could not reasonably be asked to tolerate "widespread circulation" of arguments in favour of companionate marriage and "blatant, scoffing atheism." Fortunately, something *could* be done: censorship. Crown attorney Eric Armour believed that the Atheist Special Edition of the *American Freeman* contained blasphemous libel and that anyone who distributed or kept it "would be subject to a criminal charge." Indeed, he believed many American publications should be barred from Canada. Chief Draper agreed that the *Freeman* should be kept from circulating by mail, and pronounced that if it were sold from the city's newsstands "police action" would be taken.[140]

Haldeman-Julius was not intimidated. He responded by sending a telegram to the *Globe* a few days later. It began: "Please announce in your columns that I am coming to your city for lecture in hall to be announced soon. Will explain to your people why I am an atheist and why atheism will make Toronto a more civilized city. Will defy your Chief Constable to stop my meeting. Will also print extra edition of *Freeman* for free circulation and will send friends of mine to every house in Toronto to deliver free copies of paper." The publisher also said he would attempt to bring Clarence Darrow with him because he anticipated trouble from Chief Draper, "who I understand is a tinpot tyrant and a small edition of Mussolini."[141] Haldeman-Julius then sent a message to Draper himself, asking if the chief would guarantee his safety at a Sunday afternoon meeting "explaining the philosophy of atheism and the falsity of Christianity and the corruption of the Catholic Church." He took pains to stress the fact that "this special campaign is not being financed by Moscow, but by myself personally as a great believer in free speech and free assembly."

Draper responded with a bland telegram stating: "the Police Department of Toronto impose[s] no restrictions on speech or orderly assembly, except those prescribed by law, and give[s] no guarantees of protection against unlawful acts." This only served to antagonize Haldeman-Julius further. He called Draper's reply "an amazing evasion" and insisted that "this bigot Draper and equally bigoted Toronto press must learn respect for free thought." The publisher argued that in Toronto "law and order" actually meant "disorder against all who disagree with priestcraft and official exponents of Fascism in a teapot." He concluded on an even more aggressive note: "Is Toronto afraid of ideas? I am not afraid to come to your mediaeval city and give forthright utterance to modern ideas. Does your small-town Mussolini intend to call out the army and navy to stop me?" It goes without saying that the *Globe* greatly disapproved of Haldeman-Julius's comments and once again called for his paper to be banned.[142] This in turn led American rationalists, no doubt inspired by Haldeman-Julius, to bombard the newspaper with hostile letters and atheistic literature extolling the virtues of free speech. Franklin Steiner, the Chicago-based rationalist who visited Toronto on occasion, was among those who added his voice of protest to the *Globe*.[143]

Haldeman-Julius seems to have changed his mind about visiting Toronto, but he did produce a special "Canadian Free Speech Edition" of the *American Freeman* for distribution in the city. In it he declared, "If there isn't free speech for an atheist in Toronto, then there is no free speech in Toronto." Since the man himself remained out of reach, the *Globe* decided to use Haldeman-Julius's example as a stick with which it could beat local free speech advocates. Earlier in the year sixty-eight professors from the University of Toronto had signed an open letter arguing that the actions of Draper and Coatsworth violated the British principle of freedom of speech. The *Globe*'s editorial writers claimed repeatedly (and without evidence) that Haldeman-Julius was allied with these professors and that militant atheism was the natural outcome of their line of thinking.[144]

One reason that the *Globe* took this approach was that it fit popular pre-existing narrative whereby orderly Christian Canada was threatened by irreverent and destructive outsiders. This narrative was extremely common when communists were being targeted, but it was invoked to explain and belittle the rationalists as well. The reader will recall Rev. F.C. Ward-Whate having employed the reliable rhetoric of outside agitators ("mongrel curs") during the Sterry case and calling for the rationalists to be immediately jailed and deported. At that time the *Evening Telegram* stressed the links between Canadian and American rationalists. In a breathless article entitled "U.S. Is Controlling Centre of Toronto's Rationalism," it warned that "organized atheism in this city is receiving support via the same channels as does Communism." As proof, the *Telegram* pointed to the RSC's friendly relationship with Franklin Steiner and his American Rationalist Association of Chicago, "whose horrible doctrines are a derivative of the black atheism of Moscow and Berlin."[145] In Ontario this type of anti-American imagery dated right back to the time of the United Empire Loyalists.[146]

Toronto's rationalists resented this line of attack and took pains to refute it. Cross "denied with considerable warmth" the claim that he had come from the United States. "I was born in the British West Indies, saw war service overseas and am now pleased to call myself a Canadian," he told a *Star* reporter.[147] When the Sterry incident began, Styles made a point of stating that the Rationalist Society stood for "the integrity of the British empire."[148] He and Leavens also strongly rejected the allegation that they were outsiders, insisting that they were, respectively, third- and fourth-generation Canadians. Styles derisively pointed out that it was Ward-Whate who was the immigrant.[149] The clergyman would probably have seen no shame in that: he was a Briton, and Toronto was a British city. It was Americans and "other" foreigners who were the problem.[150] We may, however, detect a certain irony in the fact that Canadian authorities wanted to eject Sterry from the body politic, even though he was a British citizen who had lived in Canada for seventeen years.[151] The quality of "Britishness" was claimed by both Toronto's elite and by the rationalists. It was frequently invoked by Toronto's elite as a marker of their authority, but they hastily distanced themselves from it when it became a limitation or a liability.

This backdrop helps explain why the intervention of American rationalists in 1931 was a mixed blessing for the RSC. It was around this time, beginning with the 1931–32 lecturing season, that the RSC virtually went dormant, with the departure of Styles and the withdrawal of most of its advertising. It seems likely that police harassment was taking its toll. It is also possible that Leavens purposely avoided advertising the meetings which did occur, to avoid official attention. But the hard times continued. In the summer of 1932 the *Star* reported that the Rationalist Society had been "banned from the streets entirely." The group organized a protest meeting at Winchester Hall on 26 June to denounce the police. The *Star* commented that corners normally occupied by groups like the rationalists, the Independent Labor Party, or the left-wing Fellowship for a Christian Social Order, were instead occupied by proselytizing religious groups.[152] On 10 July the rationalists attempted to hold meetings at two different locations but both gatherings were ordered to disperse. The authorities stated that "the police commission questioned the propriety of the organization" and stated that they would deliver a formal decision about it at their next meeting in September. Until then the RSC was forbidden from holding open-air gatherings.[153]

Strangely enough, given this situation, in late July or early August of 1932 a citizen approached Toronto mayor William James Stewart, to argue that atheists should not be permitted to preach their doctrines in public. The mayor responded by assuring citizens that he personally had no sympathy with atheists and that he believed that their public proselytizing was "offensive to the people of a God-fearing city." Nevertheless, he could not go beyond the limits of the law, and currently such speech was permitted. "So long as people expounding different doctrines on street corners are not responsible for traffic congestion and are not likely to create disorder, they are permitted to speak, according to a ruling of the Board of Police Commissioners," he pointed out.[154]

Despite this statement, it seems that the rationalists had been forced to hold their meetings indoors, at Windsor Hall, for much of the summer. They revealed in late August that police had for several weeks been interfering with even these (technically legal) gatherings, "by questioning members." An outdoor meeting on 28 August was also broken up. The RSC responded by seeking an injunction to prevent "the police commission, Mayor Stewart, Judge Parker, Judge Coatsworth, Chief Constable [Draper] and Inspector Douglas Marshall, or their servants or agents" from stopping open-air meetings.[155] It appears the rationalists were seeking not only an injunction but also damages. The case was halted on 23 October, when I.H. Hilliard, master of the supreme court at Osgoode Hall, ordered them to provide security for costs before the matter could proceed any further.[156] But the RSC did not have that sort of money on hand.

In the summer of 1933, rationalist meetings were again being dispersed by police. On 10 June a constable named Macauley told members of the society that "it was not permitted to hold meetings on the street." When they enquired as to the source of this statement, he claimed "the orders were issued by police headquarters."[157] Leavens and William Dennison asked the city's Board of Control to intervene, but the board simply forwarded the request to the police commission. A few weeks later the commission responded that the decision in question had been made by the inspector of the local police division, who had the proper authority to "take such action as he deemed advisable to maintain the peace and to keep the streets clear for traffic." Thus "in the interests of law and order and subject to the approval of the board, meetings of the Rationalist Society on the public streets would not be permitted in the No. 2 division."[158] The police commission had seemingly learned to deflect blame by passing discretionary authority over to the inspectors. The following year the rationalists again had their meetings broken up on at least one occasion. On 27 May 1934 Leavens was speaking at the corner of Albert and Yonge Streets when he was asked by a patrol sergeant to have the meeting "move on."[159]

These reported examples were doubtless not the only times the rationalists found themselves in this position, but such stories stop after 1934. Betcherman suggests that police repression in Toronto eased somewhat after 1933. As the Depression dragged on, the sympathies of the public had begun to shift away from the police. More specifically, Judge Coatsworth resigned from the police commission as of 31 December 1931, though he remained a police magistrate until 1934.[160] With his departure and that of Judge Morson, Draper could no longer count on the enthusiastic backing of the commission. This may explain why in the summer of 1933 the rationalists were told that responsibility for dispersed meetings rested not with the commissioners but with local inspectors. In September 1933, however, the commission ordered Draper to stop breaking up public meetings unless some law was being violated.[161] Of course, this order did not entirely prevent constables from asking rationalists to "move along" (as they did in 1934) if meetings could in any way be construed as disruptive.

ATHEISM ON CAMPUS

Unbelief was also seen as a threat in the halls of academe. We have already mentioned the letter in defence of free speech that sixty-eight University of Toronto professors sent the press on 15 January 1931. They faced an immediate wave of censure from the city's conservatives.[162] Many suggested that the professors were probably atheists and Red sympathizers. One letter-writer, E.B. McCullough, commented: "I would like to know if these professors are the ones to whom we are entrusting the education of our boys and girls. I think, without exception, they are evolutionists." On 31 January R.H. Knowles asked of the *Globe*: "Are the 68 professors who advocate free speech believers in Divine teaching, or are they atheist or agnostic in their views regarding religion? The parents and friends of the students of the university will surely be looking for a pronouncement as to whether certain members of the staff are either atheist or agnostic in their views." Other prominent figures such as clergymen and businessmen, and even the chancellor of the university, Sir William Mulock, intimated that the professors were communist sympathizers who should be deported.[163] The signatories avoided any official punishment thanks to Sir Robert Falconer, the university president, who believed British principles of free speech should protect them. Nevertheless, the university's board, led by chairman Henry J. Cody, passed a resolution officially disassociating the institution from the letter.[164]

The controversy had barely died down when Andrew Allan, editor of the University of Toronto's student newspaper (the *Varsity*) decided to stir it up again. The paper had previously clashed with the school's administration over issues of free speech, so there is little doubt that Allan intended to be as provocative as possible. To this end he wrote a pungent editorial which claimed that "the majority of graduates in Arts are practical atheists," and that this included "a large percentage of the students in theology." Undergraduates, particularly those in "philosophy, psychology, or the pure sciences," Allan wrote, proceeded from "a delicious feeling of naughtiness in the first stages of discovering that the Divinity was not all that one had been led to suppose" to a "condition of glassy sophistication" in which they proudly and defiantly stood apart from the "silly shopgirls and petrified crones who attend religious services."[165] In fact, Allan continued, most people in society lacked a truly personal, experiential belief in God. Thus "the divines who are most popular are those charming, engaging persons who read literary essays on Sunday and spend the week upholding the dignity of the church and trying to form a synthesis between St. Paul, Thomas Huxley, and Sir James Jeans."[166] The minority of university students who did attend church services were, he asserted, simply seeking an aesthetic thrill or trying to shore up their social status. People should be honest about their unbelief, Allan argued, rather than try to hide behind "bastard classifications" like "liberal believers" or "modernistic deists." Outright atheism was the "cleaner, healthier condition."[167]

As would be expected, controversy about the university roared back to life across the province, with newspapers in Chatham, Sault Ste Marie, St Thomas, Owen Sound, St Catharines, Stratford, Hamilton, Brantford, and of course Toronto weighing in. Some were inclined to see the *Varsity* editorial as the work of a few youthful skeptics who would eventually grow up and become good Christians. Others viewed the situation with alarm.[168] The *Brantford Expositor* noted that Allan was quite unrepentant and called for a thorough investigation. Toronto's *Evening Telegram* suggested that the province should cut off the university's funding and that parents should turn their children away from the institution.[169] Allan was fired as editor, the *Varsity* was suspended for the rest of the academic year, and the editorial was officially repudiated by the university's board.[170] Provincial politicians made the most of the scandal. Harry C. Nixon, leader of the "Progressive group," demanded "a full and sweeping investigation," and argued that until an investigation was held, the province should give "not one dollar" to the university's support.[171] He also suggested the attorney-general consider charging the author of the editorial with blasphemous libel.[172]

The *Globe*, true to form, proclaimed the atheism of undergraduates a threat to the nation. In a vehement rebuttal to Allan's suggestion that "practical atheism" was simply a common modern condition not restricted to universities, the *Globe* insisted that the content of higher education was itself a threat, proclaiming: "It takes but slight familiarity with the teachings rife today in most college and university classrooms, and in such subjects as Science and Medicine, to have convincing proof that instructors and professors are constantly going out of their way to throw doubt or ridicule upon the teachings of the Bible, with the result of shattered faith on the part of students." The writer decried the fact that no one was telling young people about atheism's tragic, life-destroying consequences, which he described in terms usually reserved for sexually transmitted diseases. The editorial concluded by gleefully citing Herbert Spencer's decline and death thirty years earlier as an example of the bad end to be expected by atheists.[173]

Despite the public backlash, the matter was largely left up to the student council, which was responsible for the content of the *Varsity*. Nor did everyone take the brouhaha so seriously. Not long after it broke out, the principal of Queen's University, W.H. Fyfe, in speaking to a gathering of Toronto alumni, concluded with the apparently tongue-in-cheek quip that "it probably would be wise to issue an order that no student must study atheism until after the grant had been received from the Government." The next speaker, Dr J.M. Young, hastened to add that the atheism scandal had been based on a misunderstanding. Most students were not atheists, he suggested, but simply had "doubt in their minds as to certain matters." As a matter of fact, Young continued, this was an encouraging sign that the university was teaching them critical thinking skills![174] Around the same time, Premier George Henry wrote privately to a clergyman who had inquired about the case to say, "I trust ... that the newspapers who have been seeking to fan the question will not be successful and that we have heard the last of the incident."[175] Indeed, the issue soon faded from public consciousness, although a general suspicion of universities as hotbeds of atheism and sedition remained alive among many conservative Canadians.[176]

One of these incidents, when considered in isolation, might be dismissed as an unfortunate aberration. Sterry? His was the only trial of its kind in English Canada, one that some officials hesitated to prosecute. And surely it was Sterry's boldness that provoked an otherwise tolerant judiciary. The struggles over free speech? The rationalists were simply collateral damage in a crackdown aimed at communists. The outrage over atheism at the University of Toronto was not dissimilar from moral panics about students today. Each situation could be downplayed and explained away. But considered together, they illustrate the paranoia prevalent among devout Torontonians in the interwar years. They also demonstrate the illiberal extremes to which many were prepared to go in defence of a Christian nation. Conservative believers would not, however, have seen any contradiction in this. In the arrangement known as Christendom, state power had been used to protect Christianity since Constantine. There may not have been an established church in Canada, but the Christian social order was still under official protection.

THE CANADIAN CHRISTIAN CRUSADERS

It is intriguing to note that interwar Toronto heard more about atheism from its religious opponents than from its secularist advocates. With the exception of the *Star*, the establishment newspapers (the *Globe*, the *Mail & Empire*, and the *Evening Telegram*) all made frequent reference to the encroaching menace of unbelief.[177] The context was often the Soviet Union, but just as often it was not. With its reputation as a righteous bastion of evangelical Christian orthodoxy to defend, Torontonians found the presence of local rationalists or visiting speakers like Joseph McCabe particularly troubling. The development of this Protestant dominance in nineteenth-century Ontario has been chronicled in studies like John Webster Grant's *A Profusion of Spires* and William Westfall's *Two Worlds*.[178]

Evangelical hegemony had been remarkably resilient, but by the interwar period there were signs that it was under stress. Anxiety about societal change was often expressed in conflicts over popular culture; in the words of one Baptist minister, Toronto's evangelicals were aware that they were "competing with the hip-flask and the jazz orchestra."[179] A 1928 editorial in the *Globe* warned that "a spirit of irreverence is abroad in the world, and it is a deadly thing"; it could be found everywhere, in "plays, pictures, books, magazines and current conversation." The writer cautioned that the irreligious might one day be struck dead where they stood.[180] But as we have seen above, evangelical opposition to modern irreverence could also adopt a political tone. In a 1931 article analyzing Toronto's free speech struggle, the *Canadian Forum* noted that "the [Toronto Police] Commission draws some considerable spiritual sustenance from religious orthodoxy."[181]

Their unbelieving opponents may have dismissed the orthodox as deluded superstitionists with a medieval mindset, or as pawns of the capitalist class, but we can seek a more nuanced view. Who were these people, how did they understand themselves, and why did they find the open atheism of a small minority so threatening? As noted above, contemporaries identified them as being Conservatives, imperialists, capitalists, and so forth, but this still leaves the picture somewhat vague. We have, however, a unique opportunity to focus in on a number of representative individuals, thanks to the existence of the Canadian Christian Crusade (CCC), a Toronto-based organization dedicated to fighting atheism.[182] It brought together leading citizens from various professions and Protestant denominations to defend the Christian nature of their city. Throughout the 1930s they kept up a steady campaign warning Torontonians against the dangers of unbelief.

The CCC was founded on 6 December 1928, in the home of a wealthy evangelical widow named Mrs R.J. Fleming. Anglican clergyman Canon Dyson Hague opened the meeting with a warning about "the tremendous danger faced in the propagation of communistic seed developing into a national disease." After this Mrs Maud Howe spoke at length. First she addressed the rapid spread of Communist groups aimed at indoctrinating young Canadians with "the spirit of Lenin." Then she drew attention to the activities of the American Junior Atheist League, displayed a blasphemous pamphlet circulating in the city, and condemned the parodies of familiar hymns that had been taught to "scores" of Toronto's children. Howe also made a point of mentioning Judge Coatsworth's support and read a letter from Mayor McBride "expressing interest in the movement." At this point a resolution was moved and seconded to authorize the new group to "fight against the evils of Bolshevism, communism and atheism in Canada." Howe was elected secretary and Henry O'Brien, King's Counsel, became treasurer. The executive was to consist of Howe, O'Brien, Mrs S.H. Blake, and Robert Richardson. After the vote, the latter told the Crusaders that "he had secured literature along communistic and atheistic lines from publishers in the United States. So objectionable was it that he declared he would not show it to a lady." He had sent the literature to Ottawa and claimed that the postmaster-general was looking into the matter.[183]

By mid-January the CCC had already taken concrete action by bringing in Mrs Elizabeth Knauss, an Iowan fundamentalist who was forthright in her opposition to communism.[184] She was to speak at four churches. Maud Howe, when interviewed about the event by the *Globe*, spoke of the "splendid support given the organization and the friendliness shown by Chief Constable Brig.-Gen. Draper."[185] Howe also provided an updated list of the group's officials and prominent supporters: "Henry O'Brien, K.C., Treasurer; Mrs. Maud Howe, Secretary; R.D. Richardson and Mrs. S.H. Blake, Advisory Council; Sir James Aikens of Winnipeg; W.H. Adamson of Toronto; Mrs. S.H. Blake, His Honor Judge Coatsworth, Rev. Canon Cody, Mrs. R.J. Fleming, J.J. Gartshore, Rev. Dr J.G. Inkster" and a few others.[186] Most of those listed were prominent members of Canadian society and were involved in evangelical causes. Capsule biographies of the most active and prominent members illustrate what an interdenominational group they were, how deeply they were involved in evangelistic outreach, and the extent to which they were simultaneously embedded in civic leadership. (Maud Howe is discussed in greater detail below.)

The group's treasurer, Henry O'Brien (1835–1931), was a retired lawyer, a veteran of the Fenian raids, a self-described "Old Tory," and an Anglican active in various evangelical causes, including the support of missions in China.[187] The *Globe* described him as "a vigorous exponent and defender of the great fundamental truths of Christianity," for whom "the Scriptures meant what they said."[188]

Robert Dennis Richardson (1854–1946), an Anglican, was a former businessman who was heavily involved with the Canadian branch of the Scripture Union, an interdenominational evangelical Christian ministry.[189] Mrs S.H. Blake (born Elizabeth Baird in 1877) was also a wealthy Anglican active in evangelical causes.[190] She was the widow (and former secretary) of Samuel Hume Blake (1835–1914), a prominent lawyer, judge, and uncompromising social reformer who had been highly influential in Ontario's evangelical Anglican circles.[191] Sir James Aikins (1851–1929), a millionaire investor, was a lawyer and the founder of the Manitoba Bar Association, who had been ninth lieutenant governor of Manitoba. He was a long-time Sunday school teacher for the Methodists and then the United Church, as well as a social reformer interested in education and temperance.[192]

Emerson Coatsworth (1854–1943) was not only a judge and a police commissioner but had served as a Member of Parliament and been the mayor of Toronto for two terms. He had for twenty years been a Methodist Sunday school superintendent, as well as acting as a church official. In 1931 the *Canadian Forum* noted that Coatsworth was "not without influence in the councils of the United Church of Canada."[193] He was a Mason, an Orangeman, and a "strong advocate" for temperance.[194] Canon Henry John Cody (1868–1951) was the rector of the country's largest Anglican Church, St Paul's Bloor Street, and the unofficial leader of evangelical Anglicans in Canada. He had previously served as an MPP and in 1932 would become president of the University of Toronto.[195] It was Cody who, as chair of the University of Toronto's board, would repudiate the *Varsity* newspaper for its editorial on atheism.

Mrs R.J. Fleming (born Lydia Jane Orford, 1863–1937) was very active in support of mission work. For many years she led the Canadian Auxiliary of the Zenana Bible and Medical Mission, which was aimed at helping women and children in India (which is where she eventually died).[196] She was the widow of Robert John Fleming (1854–1925), a Methodist temperance advocate who had been a popular politician and for a time Toronto's mayor.[197] Reverend John Gibson Inkster (1867–1946), a Presbyterian minister at Toronto's Knox Church, was active in support of missions as well as a frequent speaker on the North American Bible conference circuit.[198] Inkster was an outspoken anti-evolutionist and opponent of higher biblical criticism; as noted above, Joseph McCabe had in 1928 directly challenged him to a debate.[199] Canon Dyson Hague (1857–1935), who had opened the first meeting of the CCC, was a passionate defender of conservative evangelical Anglicanism. He served the Church of the Epiphany in Toronto and was a professor at Wycliffe College.[200]

We can see that the CCC was an ecumenical endeavour, in the sense that it brought evangelical Protestants together from a number of different denominations. In this it was like the YMCA or the Sudan Interior Mission or any of the extra-church bodies that evangelicals excelled at organizing. A more unusual detail of the CCC is the advanced age of its patrons and officials. Most did not survive the 1940s; four died in the 1930s. James Aikins did not even make it that far, dying only a few months after the group was formed. In 1929, the year the CCC became active, Coatsworth was 75, J.J. Gartshore was 79, and Henry O'Brien was 94.[201] The average age for those listed in the *Globe* article above was a little over 70.[202] In contrast, William Styles was 35 in 1929, Bert Leavens was 43, and Lionel Cross was 39. Ernest Sterry was a little older, at 57. It is clear that the clash between the CCC and the RSC was in part a generational one.

What is more, most of the aged Christian Crusaders had a long history of involvement with evangelical and civic causes. In a study entitled "Redeeming the City," historian Darren Dochuk explores the activities of Henry O'Brien, Samuel H. Blake, and their friend William Howland in late-nineteenth-century Toronto. He identifies them as conservative social reformers whose actions were motivated and shaped by their belief in premillennial evangelicalism. In this view the world was sinful and would be redeemed by Christ's literal second coming; evangelization and the conversion of individuals were thus their first priority. But this goal did not preclude other forms of social action, often carried out through voluntary evangelical organizations, or by holding political office. The presence of O'Brien and of Blake's widow in the CCC give us a sense for the group's conservative yet activist roots.[203]

The contrast between the working-class rationalists and the well-connected, generally wealthy Christian Crusaders is also striking. The objection could be raised that, by pointing to its powerful patrons, the CCC was simply trying to put itself in the best possible light, and the average evangelical Christian in Toronto was not particularly well-off. Even granting this, however, the fact remains that the rationalists did not have any influential or wealthy patrons, while the CCC shared anti-atheist views with members of the political establishment, many business leaders, the police, the judiciary, and most of the press.

One segment of the press stands out in relation to social reform and evangelicalism: the Toronto *Globe*. As we have seen in the preceding pages, the *Globe* was invariably hostile to rationalists and outspoken in its defence of evangelical hegemony. The *Globe*'s publisher and president from 1915 to 1936 was William Gladstone Jaffray (1870–1949), who had inherited his controlling share in the paper from his father. Jaffray was a Presbyterian whose "strong fundamentalist convictions" were reflected in every issue: he forbade coverage of horse racing and movie gossip, as well as the advertising of tobacco and recreational alcohol, while encouraging features like weekly sermons and daily Bible verses.[204] Jaffray was a personal friend of Oswald J. Smith, one of the city's leading fundamentalist preachers, and the *Globe* provided much sympathetic coverage of his revivals, as well as other evangelistic work. The *Globe* had also been one of the few Canadian newspapers to forthrightly support William Jennings Bryan and the fundamentalist cause during the Scopes trial in 1925.[205] With Jaffray at its helm, the paper proved to be highly supportive of the CCC, frequently reporting on the group's activities and publishing letters from its secretary, Maud Howe.[206]

MAUD HOWE AND THE CRUSADE AGAINST ATHEISM

It was Maud Margaret Howe (d. 1945) who performed most of the actual work of the CCC over the next fifteen years. As secretary, she organized events, set up new Crusader groups, and wrote pamphlets and innumerable letters to the editor. At the CCC office on Bay Street, she spoke to anyone who dropped by, counselling those who were wrestling with doubt, and attempting to win back people who had lost their faith. She also travelled North America on CCC business. This largely involved networking with other evangelicals, but on a trip to Winnipeg she also met with Marshall Gauvin and attended one of his meetings in an effort to win him back from atheism.[207]

Although she had powerful patrons and allies, Howe was not particularly wealthy or highly placed in society. She was born in Liverpool, attended Manchester Ladies' College, and immigrated to Toronto in 1922 with her husband, Joseph N. Howe. After he decided to seek ordination as an Anglican clergyman and took up studies at Wycliffe College, Maud taught at Havergal College, a Toronto girls' school founded by evangelical Anglicans.[208] When her husband began his ministry, she accompanied him to Saskatchewan and then Prince Edward Island. But this assignment proved very brief; in 1926 the family returned to Toronto, where Joseph died of "sleeping sickness" on 21 October. They had two daughters and two sons.

It was one of those sons who led Howe into her anti-atheist activities. Her first booklet, *A Challenge Answered – Atheism or Christ?*, has this self-composed verse as an epigraph:

My heart, my heart! how fast its beat:
That awful tramp of horses feet –
And the steed – oh! God – deep, deep, blood red:
And my son, my son! is at its head!![209]

The imagery is that of the Book of Revelation's Four Horsemen.[210] Some evangelicals believed the red horse and its warlike rider foretold communism; this may have been the symbolism Howe had in mind.[211] The verse reappeared at the head of a chapter entitled "A Gethsemane Sorrow: Our Sons – Our Daughters." In sections headed "White-Yellow-Red," Howe describes her first-born son's gradual fall from innocence as "the white purity of heaven dim[med] slowly into the yellow tint of earth."[212]

Sometime after her husband died, Howe had sensed that something had gone wrong in her son's life. In flashes, peppered with biblical references and snatches of verse, she recounts her realization, when her son came home from college to visit, that he had become an unbeliever. His comment, "I like Jesus, of course, but I'm not so great on GOD," was the first clue. After she asked him to explain more, the floodgates opened, and he told her his teachers had shown him the truth: "God is a monstrous fable – THERE IS NO GOD." In a blend of rationalist anthropology and Marxist analysis, he laid out his view of the naturalistic development of supernatural religion and its use as a means of social control. Said his shaken mother, "I see, dear – forgive me, but I am just a woman to whom God speaks – I have not understood, perhaps." "Keep your old-world beliefs," he responded. "I love you for them; but we men, we MEN have to *go on* ... I have learnt great things at the College – and I am the MASTER OF MY SOUL."[213] Howe prayed in anguish, "God help us all – Mothers and Fathers whose sons are snatched from our God by treachery and lies."[214]

Howe's crusade on behalf of the CCC was thus a very personal and heartfelt one. These excerpts are typical of her style, which was current in the evangelical discourse of that period. Her warnings about atheism usually included an appeal to a religion of the heart, couched in the language of traditional Victorian gender roles.[215] "Not to weak sentimentality comes the Christ-Call," she wrote, "but to the virile, the pure, the men of vision, the women of the Motherheart."[216] Her appeals were wrapped in emotional, affective language, while rationalists pressed their points with logical argumentation. This may have been the tone each was aiming for, but closer inspection reveals a great deal of emotional moral outrage in the rationalists' presentations, while Howe's rhetoric was paradoxically able to incorporate empirical evidence – quotations from atheist leaders and statistics allegedly demonstrating the worldwide spread of unbelief.[217]

Of course, the CCC's opponents were not impressed with Howe's arguments. In a *Canadian Forum* article entitled "Contemporary Crusades," J.F. White wrote scornfully of Howe's *A Challenge Answered*, "This booklet has the usual emotional qualities of the religious tract, and the only discernible argument running through it is that all education is dangerous."[218] Lita-Rose Betcherman notes that J.S. Woodsworth was baffled by Howe's references to "the 4A's," and herself calls one of Howe's pamphlets "a mumbo-jumbo of cabalistic commentary."[219] Likewise, the historian Ian Angus curtly dismisses the CCC as a pawn of the Canadian ruling class in its struggle against communism.[220]

While the latter argument contains some truth, pigeon-holing the CCC in this way overlooks its roots in popular evangelicalism. To secular leftists (both past and present) Howe may have seemed to be spouting "mumbo-jumbo," but she was communicating in a style that resonated with many religious Canadians. Her rhetoric was derived from the Bible, from emotionally expressive Victorian piety, and from the exhortative and declamatory style developed by evangelical moral crusaders against alcohol, immorality, and other ills. It also drew on the high diction of national peril and purpose deployed during the Great War.[221] At that time the enemy of civilization had been the barbaric and supposedly anti-Christian "Hun"; now the threat was atheism and communism. The rhetoric of the CCC, its guest speakers, and the *Globe* reporters who covered CCC events was usually apocalyptic, warning of the "sordid," "overwhelmingly appalling" spectre of unbelief.[222] Howe frequently alarmed her audiences with very large numbers (of questionable provenance) to make her points. For example, in 1934 she claimed that 17 million atheistic missionaries had been sent around the world by a "communistic-atheistic combine" to secretly lead children astray, and that in Toronto alone, the minds of 13,000 children were being poisoned in this way.[223] Her citations may have been suspect, but these figures had a symbolic power reminiscent of the prophetic numbers used in Daniel or Revelation.

Similarly, to an academic eye, the anti-evolution arguments included in Howe's letters and booklets may have seemed flimsy. They consisted of out-of-context references to scientists who were in fact Darwinists or non-Darwinian evolutionists, as well as quotations from nineteenth-century anti-evolutionists and non-scientists such as the London police commissioner Sir Robert Anderson. Howe also appealed to apocryphal stories regarding the dying Darwin's embrace of evangelicalism.[224] The chief purpose of these stories, however, was not to convert unbelievers. It was to reassure the faithful who saw evolution as a mortal threat that the battle was not lost; and a great many Torontonians fit this description. In 1930 Salem Bland wrote:

> I doubt if there has been any other considerable city in the empire in which hostility to modern science has been so strong and aggressively persistent, and particularly to the theory, in one form or another universally accepted by modern science – the theory of evolution. Not, I imagine, outside some of the southern states of the union could be found any English-speaking city of one hundred thousand or more where the doctrine of evolution would be so fiercely attacked from prominent pulpits and even by newspapers. A fire that has long since gone to ashes in other cities like Toronto still burns fiercely in certain sections here. It is matter for regret that a considerable number of Christian folk in this city still feel that there is a life and death struggle between Christianity and evolution, and that if evolution triumphs the Bible and Christianity are discredited.[225]

However much Bland deplored the fact, this resistance to evolution and other aspects of modern thought made Toronto a fruitful and supportive locale for the Christian Crusade's work. When the CCC brought in conservatives like Charles Marston (a British businessman/archaeologist who sought to debunk higher biblical criticism), they were given a warm welcome and often garnered front-page headlines.[226]

Despite the CCC's frequent anti-communist rhetoric, Howe repeatedly insisted that hers was not a political crusade. The opening paragraph of *A Challenge Answered* stated emphatically: "This book has NO POLITICAL SIGNIFICANCE."[227] The enemy, Howe argued, was atheism as an attitude and as an organized creed. In *Will Atheism Dominate the World?* (1931) she reiterated that the Canadian Christian Crusade Against Atheism was "in no sense a political party" but was "a missionary society out to combat atheism." References to communism and the persecution of Christians in Soviet Russia were nevertheless unavoidable. Howe offered this distinction: "Communism as a political issue is outside [CCC] territory, but a communism that makes atheism one of the bulwarks of its belief brings the need for gravest warning against any cult propagating blasphemy and open denial of the living God in the person of our Lord and Saviour Jesus Christ."[228] We may reasonably doubt Howe's claims to political neutrality, but the fact that she felt the need to make this distinction at all is significant. She wished at least to be perceived as a defender of Christianity, not simply as a pawn of the political status quo. And her pamphlets, letters, and presentations give evidence that she would attack atheism regardless of its political connections. The American Association for the Advancement of Atheism (4A), founded by the libertarian and white-supremacist Charles Lee Smith, came in for almost as much criticism as did communist atheism. The ultimate enemy was not Moscow; it was the devil, who was behind all these forms of unbelief.

By 1933 the CCC had spun off several related groups, most notably the Nurses' Christian Fellowship and the Teachers' Christian Fellowship.[229] The fact that the organization focused its effort on what were at the time predominantly female professions is telling. Articles on the CCC would sometimes appear in the "News of Women's Organizations" section of the *Globe*, and Howe would occasionally send anti-atheist letters to the paper's "Homemaker" page.[230] To draw an analogy with Howe's own family life: if older men (her husband) were unable to defend Christianity, and younger men (her son) were rejecting the faith, then God must be calling women like her to stand up for Christ. This pattern is consistent with the idea, discussed in chapter 3, that women were the mainstay of British and Canadian Christianity, and that religious leaders responded to losses among men by redoubling their efforts among women.[231]

The CCC changed its name in 1934 to the *International* Christian Crusade so as to emphasize its connections with evangelicals in other countries. For its tenth annual conference, in 1938, the Crusaders brought in Dan Gilbert, a youthful evangelist from California, who warned that "communism, atheism, and immorality [were] running rampant in our colleges and universities."[232] Although patrons had died and press coverage dwindled by the late 1930s, the ICC remained active. It even survived Maud Howe's death in 1945. Her daughter, Margaret Gwendolyn Smith, took over as the ICC's general secretary for the next forty-four years.[233] In 1947 the group hosted Dr John S. Bain, an anti-evolution speaker, and it seems to have continued publishing pamphlets attacking evolution and secular humanism in the following decades.[234]

Looking back at the CCC's period of greatest activity, 1929 to 1938, we can make a few generalizations. Anglicans were the most influential group within it, but the endeavour as a whole was an ecumenical Protestant one, similar to many other mission and service groups organized by Canadian evangelicals. It married elite concerns with those of middle-class people like Maud Howe through a shared desire to defend conservative evangelical morality and propriety in Toronto's public life. It focused heavily on women, especially homemakers, teachers, and nurses, as defenders of these religious values. The influence of the CCC and its allies illustrates how steeply the playing field was tilted against unbelievers in Toronto, and it also reveals something about Canadian Christianity.

Historians of Canadian evangelicalism have often stressed its difference from the American tradition, particularly after the emergence of fundamentalism. Canadian evangelicals remained largely within mainstream churches, as opposed to the much larger proportion of American fundamentalists who, viewing themselves as outsiders, left to form breakaway denominations and alternative institutions. The few exceptions such as the fiery Baptist preacher T.T. Shields were very much in the minority. These dissimilarities do much to explain the differing religious trajectories the two countries have taken in the past century.

The reasons this distinction emerged in the first place have been explained elsewhere in terms of cultural or denominational differences.[235] In the context of interwar Toronto we might be able to detect another, rather more pragmatic rationale. In this period Toronto's conservative evangelicals were still very well connected. Most insiders and power brokers were Anglo-Protestant Christians, and evangelical opinions still held great sway over Toronto and Ontario more broadly. There were some troublesome signs of change, to be sure, but nothing that warranted breaking away or going into exile. In other words, why should Canadian evangelicals have acted like angry outsiders, when they were still clearly insiders?[236]

CONCLUSION

The intensity of anti-atheist and anti-communist feeling in the Toronto press seems to have decreased somewhat through the later 1930s, no doubt thanks to the changes in the political scene, the rise of fascism, and the changing fortunes of the Communist Party of Canada. Some observers seem to have grown tired of the endless panics about Reds and atheists. In 1937 J.V. McAree, a writer for the new *Globe & Mail*, wrote a witty column arguing that the overheated rhetoric needed to stop.

> We suggest that whether a man is an atheist or a Methodist is a private matter between him and God. Is it necessary to say that an atheist may be a man of the most scrupulous honor, the most abounding kindliness, and the most useful citizen in a community? Atheism does not indicate a body of principles. It suggests merely an inability to believe certain things, and a man is at perfect liberty to believe anything he likes. He is at no handicap in a civilized community because of his disbelief. If atheism is a world evil it is nothing new. In the past it has been attacked by missionaries; and we think that this remains the only decent way. We doubt if Christ would approve of Christian propaganda carried on by bombs.[237]

These sentiments would never have been printed in the *Globe*. The most direct enabling factor in their publication now was that in 1936 the pious W.G. Jaffray had sold his paper to the wealthy owners of the *Mail & Empire*, who then merged the papers to create the *Globe &*

Mail. The new management was less concerned with enforcing evangelical standards than Jaffray had been.[238] We should also take into account the effects of generational change. As our examination of the Canadian Christian Crusade has revealed, some of the most prominent and vocal defenders of the status quo, like Judge Coatsworth, Canon Hague, and Chief School Inspector Moshier, had by the mid-1930s either died or retired. Toronto's political scene was gradually changing, as evidenced by the election of CCF activist James Simpson as mayor in 1935. Many Torontonians doubtless still hated or feared atheists, but by 1937 the boundaries of public debate had shifted from those of 1927, when Sterry was in the limelight.

What broader patterns do interwar Toronto's struggles over unbelief reveal? The fact that the Rationalist Society of Canada was formed within a year of the Winnipeg Rationalist Society demonstrates that unbelief was finding a foothold in the Canadian public consciousness in the mid-1920s. The RSC provided a different model of organization than Gauvin's group. Bert Leavens was certainly the central figure of the society, but he shared responsibilities with Williams Styles and actively sought out other speakers. This was due in part to their different personalities and organizational models (Gauvin was trying to make a living from lecturing) and also to a difference in social context. Although Winnipeg was in some ways more tolerant of unbelief, Toronto provided rationalists with a greater variety of friends and sympathizers.

The pull towards engagement with the broader left proved irresistible for both groups, and contributed to the dissolution of both, albeit in different ways. Given Gauvin's interest in socialism, it is interesting that he did not follow Leavens's path into the CCF, but that probably had as much to do with the more radical sympathies of his audience as with his own politics. The presence in the RSC of female socialists like Jean Laing and of Lionel Cross, a Black freethinker who was also active in anti-racist efforts, hints at the appeal of rationalism to diverse groups; alliances could be constructed around unbelief. Yet, as with the Winnipeg society, most of the group's support seems to have come from white working-class men. The Toronto society's leadership also seems to have been of roughly the same generation as Gauvin's group, if slightly younger.

The RSC encountered fierce opposition in part because of how aggressive it was in spreading its message. Sterry personally handed his newspaper to some of the province's most powerful figures and paid a heavy price. Members of the RSC did not limit their exposure to indoor venues as Gauvin did, but struggled to maintain a public presence on the streets. But the fact is that they lost more often than they won, and potential allies (like the editor of *The Varsity*) also faced reprisals. One might argue that each loss further helped spread the rationalist message, but the depth of opposition reveals that conservative Christianity still held a great deal of power in Toronto. The elites of that Anglo-Protestant citadel saw themselves as guarding the ramparts against corruption from Russia, Germany, the United States, and at times even Britain. The makeup of the Canadian Christian Crusade shows that those who led the charge against atheism were well-connected evangelicals, many of them elderly representatives of an earlier generation of elite social reformers. They had struggled to make Toronto a moral city, and they were not about to let a pack of "mongrel curs" undercut the foundation of that morality. They would use state power in defence of this local Christendom, as prominent Christians had done for centuries.

While Toronto may have been the leading anglophone Canadian city in the interwar years, it was not the largest metropolis in the nation. That distinction was held for many years by Montreal. What was the status of unbelief in that city? As we shall see, a militant tradition of religious skepticism existed among some francophone residents, but the opposition they faced made the RSC's travails seem mild by comparison.

6

"Je suis un athée fieffé"

Militant Unbelief in Interwar Montreal

"I remember the Université du Prolétariat [i.e., Université ouvrière] and the Association Humanitaire in east central Montreal where hundreds of pipesmoking workers would gather to hear the most violent denunciations of the Church and the capitalist class. When you went up the stairs to the hall, you had to pass a huge picture of Jesus Christ with a knife in his hand dripping from the blood of the worker he was stabbing. And thousands of French-Canadian workers tipped their hats to that picture."[1]

This recollection of 1930s Montreal by radical union organizer Kent Rowley contrasts strikingly with the popular view that francophone Quebec in the interwar period was a monolithic stronghold for conservatism and Roman Catholicism. In this chapter I examine the activities of militant unbelievers who were involved in the organizations Rowley mentions. I make the case that the decision of the communist Université ouvrière (UO) to prioritize anti-religious activism made sense in a deeply Catholic culture in which religion was the lynchpin. This stance made the UO comparable to left-leaning rationalist societies in other Canadian cities. It was a working-class organization run by one charismatic activist, with a handful of regular speakers, which was dedicated to attacking the Church. These attacks prompted state persecution and unofficial violence that was unparalleled in other provinces.

In a society where Catholicism and French-Canadian ethnic identity were virtually synonymous, unbelief could be seen as a betrayal of one's heritage and homeland. Many Canadiens believed it was their divine mission to spread Catholic Christianity throughout North

America. Even those who doubted this narrative considered the church the chief bulwark of French-Canadian cultural survival in the face of British oppression, a position called clerical nationalism. There was little room for explicit unbelief to flourish in a society in which the Church virtually controlled education, health care, and other social institutions. Church power was not only ubiquitous across the province, in rural areas, and in cities but it also reached deep into society, through the pulpit, fraternal societies, unions, libraries, and a host of other organizations.[2] Church and state reinforced one another in a local, Roman Catholic version of Christendom.[3]

The Catholic Church first became the guarantor of French-Canadian *survivance* in the nineteenth century, after more explicitly political avenues were closed off. When the nationalist Patriote movement was crushed by the British authorities in 1838, the way was opened for a conservative cultural nationalism to take shape. That it did was thanks in large part to Ignace Bourget, then bishop of Montreal, who worked unceasingly to strengthen the Church's position in the province. He brought in many new priests from France, encouraged popular lay devotion, and greatly expanded such church-controlled social institutions as schools and hospitals. He also helped introduce Quebec to ultramontanism, the doctrine of papal supremacy that denied the principle of separation of church and state. The clerical hierarchy reached a tacit understanding with the British government that it would be left free to develop its own institutions as long as it supported the British-appointed authorities. These changes bound French-Canadian identity, language, and culture tightly to Catholicism.[4]

Despite the predominance of the Catholic Church for much of Quebec's history, its power was never absolute. It is important to remember that clerical nationalism, even during its century of greatest power (from roughly the 1850s to the 1950s) never went unchallenged. As in other Catholic societies like France, Spain, or Italy, opposition to organized religion frequently took the form of anticlericalism. Anticlerical activists were not necessarily atheists or religious skeptics (some were, while others considered themselves Christians) but they were united by their opposition to the church's influence on the state and its control of society. Articulate, open anticlericalism among French-Canadians dates back at least as far as 1776.

THE ROOTS OF ANTICLERICALISM IN QUEBEC

It was in 1776 that Fleury Mesplet (1734–1794), a French printer and publisher, arrived in Quebec by way of the fledgling United States.[5] His two papers, the short-lived *Gazette littéraire* and the more successful *Montreal Gazette*, were edited by the Voltairean lawyer Valentin Jautard, who helped Mesplet spread Enlightenment thought to their readers. In its later years the *Gazette* became more explicitly anticlerical, giving voice to skeptical correspondents and excerpts from the *philosophes*. The paper sought social reform, campaigning for a reduction in the number of religious holidays on the grounds that they promoted idleness and poverty. It also argued in favour of theatrical performances, which were frowned on by the Church. Mesplet printed sarcastic letters mocking arrogant local monks who lived lives of selfish luxury. One correspondent described seeing a cleric "large of girth and loud of voice" preaching on the virtue of self-denial. The letter ended with the lines, "I do believe that you despise Our Lord divine, and only love your fatness, lard and wine."[6] Mesplet celebrated the French Revolution, hoping that Quebec society too would eventually be reshaped along rational lines. His attitudes were at times deemed seditious, however, and he spent several years in prison.

Although Mesplet died in 1794, the anticlerical Enlightenment tradition in Quebec lived on. The wealthy seigneur and politician Joseph Papineau, for example, quietly gave up his religion around 1810 after immersing himself in Enlightenment ideas, although he returned to the faith on his deathbed.[7] His son, Patriote leader Louis-Joseph Papineau, also became a deist who rejected all revealed religion, even while he continued to view the Church as an important protector of French-Canadian identity.[8]

Anticlericalism was given an institutional home with the founding of the *Institut canadien* in Montreal in 1844 and the formation of the liberal *Parti rouge* in 1847. The *Institut* offered competition to church-sponsored education, hosting lectures on diverse topics and making available a library collection that included anticlerical and deistic volumes. Joseph Doutre, a lawyer and journalist who had publicly declared himself an agnostic, became a leader of the institute's radical wing, which did not hesitate from sparring with Church authorities. Bishop Ignace Bourget successfully pressured some members to leave the organization in the late 1850s and condemned it again in 1869. Some stubborn members, like co-founder Joseph Guibord, refused to leave and were excommunicated.

When Guibord died later that year, his widow attempted to have him buried in a Catholic cemetery despite Church opposition. She pursued the matter legally and sparked a five-year battle that went all the way to the British Empire's highest court, the Privy Council, which ruled in her favour in 1874. Attempts to bury Guibord were nevertheless rebuffed by angry mobs, and it was only in late 1875 that he was laid to rest in a concrete-reinforced grave, accompanied by a combined force of over a thousand soldiers and policemen. Bishop Bourget responded by almost immediately deconsecrating the grave and declaring: "There rests a rebel who has been buried by force of arms."[9] Meanwhile, under church pressure, the *Institut* was fading; it stopped hosting lectures in 1879 and the library shut down in 1880. The *Rouges* were sidelined by the Reform Party and worn down by constant opposition from ultramontanists. The remnants of the party dropped their anticlericalism and became moderate Liberals. Throughout the nineteenth century and in the early years of the twentieth, resistance to Church control was commonly found among these radical and reformist liberals, who were sometimes quiet adherents of Freemasonry. The liberal tradition in Quebec would go on to produce notable anticlerical journalists and politicians like Louis-Antoine Dessaulles (1818–1895), Godfroy Langlois (1866–1928), and Télesphore-Damien Bouchard (1881–1962).[10]

Anglo-American–style freethought was also present in the province in the nineteenth century, but mainly among anglophones. In the middle years of the century Robert Chamblet Adams, a sailor, was introduced to religious skepticism by reading Paine's *The Age of Reason*. After settling in Montreal and becoming a businessman in the mining sector, he organized the Montreal Pioneer Freethought Club in 1880. Adams was also an amateur poet and composed verses on the themes of freethought. His "Pithy Creed of Rationalism" read:

Jehovah ranks with Jupiter;
The Bible's Hebrew literature;
Confucius, Jesus both were men
A future lies beyond our ken.
A miracle do not expect
Seek nature's cause for each effect.

From man have come all gods and creeds
Your only saviour is your deeds.[11]

Adams also tried his hand at writing new moral maxims such as "Thou shalt give women equal rights with men" to replace the Ten Commandments. He was active in the club's broader secularist umbrella organization, the Canadian Secular Union, until his death in 1892.[12]

As we see, traditions of anticlericalism and unbelief had a long history in Quebec. However, professed unbelievers in the province were a tiny minority, constituting the smallest percentage of all the provinces. The 1921 census reported 27 agnostics, 40 atheists, 111 freethinkers, and 979 respondents with no religion in all of Quebec – a grand total of 1,157 (0.05 per cent) out of a population of over 2.3 million. By contrast, at least 2 million (86 per cent) were Roman Catholics.[13] In 1931 those reporting no religion were 1,621 (again just 0.05 per cent) out of a total of 2.8 million.[14] As of 1941, the Quebec population was still 86 per cent Catholic. The social strength of Catholicism, coupled with the bond between cultural and religious nationalism, was the force that maintained the marginal status of unbelief among francophones.[15]

Throughout the interwar period, as a conservative clerical nationalism increased in influence, the pressure to conform grew even more. Furthermore, despite supposedly secularizing trends like urbanization and industrialization, popular piety increased in intensity during these years.[16] Between 1901 and 1931, the number of clergymen and those dedicated to religious communities grew from 8,612 to 25,332. This meant that, whereas in 1901 there had been one clergyman or "religious" for every 166 Catholics, by 1931 there was one for every 97. Most religious were not cloistered but worked in various roles in society. The Church thus had a massive presence not just in the parishes but also in schools, hospitals, and other social institutions. One historian has written that this presence was so overwhelming that it "could almost be called a monopoly."[17]

Unbelief was usually surreptitious. In 1964 the famous editor and politician André Laurendeau vividly recalled an incident from the 1940s when he was campaigning for the provincial *Bloc populaire canadien*. He found himself in a small town with nowhere to stay when a local churchwarden offered to put him up for the night. After they had been chatting and drinking for a few hours, the warden suddenly confessed to being an unbeliever. He had lost his faith years before but, given the social power of Catholicism in Quebec, had been forced to keep it secret. "I think there are people who are born atheists," he said. "There must be a lot of them in the province. But everyone lives in his own hole. Like rats!"[18]

Laurendeau was troubled by the man's plight. He had been obliged to "piece together his own philosophy, but in the worst possible circumstances – without ever expressing it openly." "He gave me the impression of a man buried alive," Laurendeau lamented. "Alcohol helped a little to dull the pain of his spoiled life. The man must have possessed considerable vigour just to be able to keep up appearances when he was such a mess inside. Watching him I had a sense of terrible loss, of an impoverishment of himself and the society he lived in, of a stupid and useless sacrifice. And I wondered how many 'rats' like him there were in our French-Canadian society, each buried in his own separate hole."[19] Laurendeau was particularly struck by the churchwarden's situation because he himself had struggled with religious doubt throughout the interwar period. By the mid-1940s he finally admitted to himself that a "shameful agnosticism" had won: "there is nothing left, it's over." Given his life in the public eye and his involvement with progressive Catholic politics, however, he kept his lack of faith quite private, divulging it only to a few.[20]

ALBERT SAINT-MARTIN AND THE UNIVERSITÉ OUVRIÈRE

Despite such pressures to secrecy in interwar Quebec, a few vocal unbelievers worked hard to spread their views. But they paid heavily for their heterodoxy. I focus here on Albert Saint-Martin and Gaston Pilon, independent communists living in Montreal, who very publicly rejected Christianity and suffered significant persecution as a result.[21] The main vehicle for their views was an organization founded by Saint-Martin, the Université ouvrière (UO), or Labour University. Notwithstanding linguistic and cultural differences, organized unbelief in Montreal was strikingly similar to movements in Toronto and Winnipeg. Its participants were mainly brought together by one hardworking and charismatic individual. As in the other cities, new institutions for unbelievers came into being in the 1925–26 period. Working-class audiences would gather, mainly on Sundays, to hear the featured unbeliever or guest speaker; the lectures were most often of an anti-religious character, interspersed with addresses on other controversial topics. The UO, for all its distinctiveness, fits within the pattern that we have discerned in urban Canada with the Winnipeg Rationalist Society and Toronto's Rationalist Society of Canada (RSC).

Albert Frédéric Saint-Martin was, by the interwar period, a veteran activist. Born in 1865, he had been heavily involved in liberal, labour, and socialist politics since the turn of the century. One of his early causes was Esperanto, the artificial language which its proponents hoped would help overcome petty national hatreds and bring humanity together. As a young man Saint-Martin attended the same Esperanto club as Télesphore-Damien Bouchard, and the two became friends. Bouchard would go on to a long career in mainstream politics as a progressive liberal, while Saint-Martin moved from liberalism to socialism; but early on the two moved in similar intellectual circles, where freethought and anticlericalism were not uncommon. The young Bouchard had older friends who were staunch atheists.[22] Similarly, Saint-Martin had given up on Catholicism by 1893 when his second child was born; when asked to state his faith, he declared that he had "no religion."[23]

A skilled organizer and orator, Saint-Martin was involved with the Quebec wings of the Socialist Party of Canada, the Social Democratic Party of Canada, the Parti ouvrier, Montreal's (anglophone) Labour College, and, for a short time, the Communist Party of Canada.[24] He did all this while maintaining a day job as a court stenographer and clerk. In 1906 he organized and led the first May Day parade in Montreal, which consisted of several hundred people. Anticlerical sentiments were clearly present in the movement even then; when the parade passed Laval University, some marchers stopped and shouted "A bas la calotte!" – "Down with the clergy!"[25] During the First World War Saint-Martin was also active in anti-conscription struggles.[26]

Saint-Martin was never shy about speaking out against the Church. In a 1920 speech delivered at a socialist meeting he described capitalists as "Bluemen," the clergy as "Blackmen," and workers as "Redmen." Condemning workers for their complacency, he said: "As long as they can eat three meals a day, sleep and have a job, they are satisfied, while the Bluemen and Blackmen have all the luxury, and do not work, and yet the Redmen do not dare to revolt, because the Blackmen have told them that if they do revolt they must pay for their sins when they die." Saint-Martin described members of the clergy as tools of capitalists,

Figure 6.1 Albert Saint-Martin, 1905

and pointed to the recent revolution in Russia, where, he said, the workers had triumphed because they were not afraid of being punished in the afterlife.[27]

In 1923 Saint-Martin asked the Comintern to allow the Quebec arm of the Communist Party to become an autonomous national organization. It refused and the Party expelled the obstinate activist, later accusing him of "extreme petty-bourgeois nationalism" and "national nihilism."[28] Thus it was that in 1925 Saint-Martin formed his own organization, the Université ouvrière, the core mission of which was educating and enlightening workers along socialist lines.[29] This aim was carried out primarily through lectures, conferences, and debates. Meetings, which took place on Wednesday and Sunday evenings, frequently attracted from three to five hundred people. (According to the police, some lectures brought in up to two thousand audience members.) It only cost five cents to attend lectures; social events, which involved dancing, singing, and games, cost ten cents. Saint-Martin made a special effort to reach out to women. One ad, from 1932, read: "Ladies are welcome at all meetings and come in large numbers."[30] The UO met at 85 rue Craig and 1408 rue Montcalm, halls both located in the same extremely poor downtown working-class neighbourhood, roughly in the St Henri district. (A 1922 study found that the infant mortality rate there exceeded 20 per cent.)[31] The French-Canadian workers living in such neighbourhoods were precisely the audience Saint-Martin was trying to reach. A police informer commented on the poverty of those who attended lectures: "In that room, those in the audience look like true destitute[s], [and] one feels sorry for them, poorly dressed and almost barefoot, and asking each other [for] something to smoke or to eat."[32]

One of the main appeals of the UO was its participatory nature. Talks would be followed by question-and-answer sessions, and those commenting could come up to the podium to deliver their remarks for up to ten minutes.[33] Saint-Martin encouraged members to deliver lectures of their own and helped them develop their public speaking skills. One attendee, a longshoreman, recalled giving a lecture on the problems of Catholic unions, while one of his co-workers spoke on astronomy, complete with pictures. The UO also had a library, open to anyone who paid five cents per loan or bought a lifetime membership for a dollar.[34] Those who attended the UO seem mainly to have been francophones. There does not appear to have been any formal connection between Saint-Martin's organizations and the Jewish or other immigrant radicals who may have shared their anti-religious views. Linguistic and cultural differences divided Montreal's diverse left.

Saint-Martin was highly respected by his supporters. Fluent in both French and English, he was seen as a cultivated and "advanced" man, with easy humour and a sharp wit.[35] One admirer commented that in some ways he was like a priest in his own church. Unlike a priest, however, Saint-Martin would occasionally amuse his audience by challenging God to stop him from making certain gestures, like playing with his pipe or adjusting the furniture on stage.[36]

Saint-Martin's right-hand man was named Gaston Pilon.[37] Pilon had had a difficult childhood. Orphaned at ten, he had abandoned Catholicism by the age of twenty. He experimented with Protestantism and Freemasonry before becoming a communist. Little is known of his early life, although one UO attendee believed Pilon had received a classical education and that he had even been a monk for a time.[38] While this seems unlikely, it is established that Pilon was arrested and charged with sedition in 1919 for giving anti-conscription speeches.[39] He was described by one reporter as having a brush-cut, piercing eyes, and a wild grin.[40] A more hostile writer characterized him as an unattractive figure whose only compelling feature was a deep voice: "With the frame of a porter, a sickle-shaped face, weary features, with two embers deep beneath his eyelids, more than anything this man inspires repulsion. If he grabs his audience it is with vituperation – and that voice! cavernous, somber, spiteful – against everything that opposes the base instincts of the human animal."[41] Pilon's impassioned denunciations of the Church were one of the main draws of the UO.

Two of Saint-Martin's other staunch supporters were the Godin brothers, Abel and Emile, who helped him found L'Association humanitaire (AH) in 1930. There seems to have been a good deal of overlap between the Université ouvrière and the Association humanitaire; to start with, they operated out of the same building.[42] Perhaps the AH can best be described as the UO's activist response to the crisis of the Depression. Both groups made an effort to reach out to workers and the unemployed. An example of their recruiting style can be seen in an anecdote from the early 1930s. A man named Émery Samuel had recently moved to Montreal and, feeling lonely, was "walking the streets on Sunday, looking for someone from his parish, his village, his county, [when] he had come upon the open door of the Association Humanitaire. A voice had called, 'Come fill your pipe and sit and talk,' and his socialist education had begun."[43]

Communist Party activist Stanley Ryerson estimated the total membership of the AH at around four thousand. He described it as an organization of those "who had abjured the Catholic faith."[44] According to Pilon it had over six thousand members. He claimed that its campaign encouraging Catholics to officially renounce their faith spread across the whole province.[45] Samuel recalled attending an AH meeting of some seven hundred people.[46] Along with their anti-Catholic activities, its members engaged in mutual support and passive resistance against what they saw as unjust treatment of those left unemployed by the Great Depression. One of their first goals was to stop the St Vincent de Paul Society from delivering relief funds, arguing that the municipal government should be giving them directly to those in need.[47] Another tactic, employed in late 1933, was for AH members to engage in sit-ins in local unemployment offices. They refused to leave and were hauled away by police. When they were brought to court, Saint-Martin was there to coach them in their replies.[48] The AH would also prevent bailiffs from evicting the unemployed and intervene in the auctions of their possessions.[49]

The way the association blended anti-Catholicism with humanitarian support for the unemployed may seem strange today but it made sense in the context of interwar Quebec, where the Catholic Church was heavily involved in delivering social welfare programs. To reject the system was to reject Catholicism, and vice versa. The administration of such programs by religious authorities could be quite judgmental and arbitrary. One Montreal priest, for example, would distribute relief vouchers at his church on Friday nights after the Mass. Families who were absent would have to wait until the following Friday. It is easy to see how such an approach could provoke resentment.[50]

Like the AH, the UO encouraged its members and visitors to formally renounce their faith; it seems that the campaigns of the two organizations were very similar. Pilon would often invite his audience to write up declarations of apostasy, which were then sent to the Archdiocese of Montreal.[51] In September 1932 a letter to the editor of *Le Devoir* complained that the archdiocese had received over two hundred letters of apostasy in the past two years, and most were sent from the Université ouvrière. They were almost always signed by the same witnesses, likely UO stalwarts.[52] Meanwhile, members of the AH were issued identification cards that stated their name, occupation, marital status, date of birth, and the fact that they did not belong to any religious sect.[53] Thus both the AH and the UO kept the question of belief front and centre. A text that was frequently used in UO circles was *Les douze preuves de l'inexistence de Dieu* by the French anarchist Sébastien Faure. It seems to have been Saint-Martin's favourite anti-religious material; he sold it at meetings and on several occasions gave a lecture based on its arguments.[54]

The UO had numerous opponents; some of these were on the left. The Communist Party in Quebec frequently criticized Saint-Martin, the UO, and the AH for ineffectiveness and lack of militancy.[55] What is more, the core of the French-speaking Communist Party was made up of people who had left Saint-Martin's groups. In 1927 a number of UO members, led by the organization's president, Évariste Dubé, quit the UO to join the official Communist Party.[56] Others, like

Émery Samuel and Paul Delisle, left soon afterward because they viewed "the association's anti-clerical activities [as] a dead end."[57] This was perhaps the communists' most regular criticism of the UO and AH. When Henri Gagnon, later an influential communist, first became interested in politics, he asked a veteran leftist by the name of Leboeuf to introduce him to the local activists. Leboeuf took him to the Association humanitaire, but Gagnon was disappointed. His first impression of the AH was of a group of atheists lounging about making declarations such as "Let Him come down to earth and we'll take care of him."[58] He recalled: "I ended up attending an anticlerical conference, where the clergy was denounced as the carrier of the seven deadly sins and all the crimes of capitalism. Expressing my disappointment to Mr. Leboeuf, I told him that this kind of organization led nowhere. From my point of view anticlericalism is not a solution to economic problems."[59] After that disappointing experience Leboeuf introduced him to the official Communist Party instead.

Meanwhile the well-documented campaign of Quebec's Catholic Church against all forms of communism persisted.[60] The 1920s and '30s saw the Church attempting to get ordinary Catholics to become more educated and active in defence of their religion. This movement was typically led by the clergy but encouraged as much lay participation as possible. It often blended a clerical nationalist defence of Quebec as a Catholic outpost with ideas borrowed from Social Catholicism as developed in Europe. Social Catholicism, inspired by papal encyclicals like *Rerum Novarum* and *Quadragesimo Anno*, offered an orthodox approach to industrialized modernity – an alternative to liberal capitalism on the one hand and communism on the other. In Quebec this movement was fairly successful, leading to the development of Catholic Action groups, youth organizations, and Catholic unions across the province. Sometimes the goal was to encourage a deepening of devotion.[61] Other times it was to directly confront the enemies of Catholic propriety. For example, in February 1926 parishioners of L'Assomption de Notre Dame in the small town of Baie des Sables formed an organization aimed at quashing blasphemy, Le ligue contre le blasphème. They even wrote to the federal Department of Justice asking for permission to print and post notices warning passers-by that they could be prosecuted for blasphemy.[62] In the 1930s lay associations joined with journalists, politicians, and the clergy in a fierce campaign to defend the Catholic Church from communism, socialism, and the left in general.[63]

One of these was the Association catholique de la Jeunesse canadienne-française (ACJC), originally founded in 1904 and backed by the prominent Abbé Lionel Groulx. It promoted a nationalist agenda and encouraged young Catholics to become active in defence of their faith.[64] The 1930s saw the formation of a series of specialized Catholic youth groups that rivalled the ACJC and were designed for specific constituencies such as the Jeunesse agricole catholique, the Jeunesse indépendante catholique, and the Jeunesse ouvrière catholique.[65] A third category was mainly for adults – the École sociale populaire (ESP) was run by Jesuits under the leadership of Rev. Joseph Papin Archambault. Founded in 1911, it started out promoting reconciliation between labour and management through Social Catholicism, but after 1929 it turned sharply towards an anti-communist mission.[66] Fearing the potential of communist ideology to seduce French-Canadians into abandoning their faith, these groups were ready to combat the threat in the public sphere. Saint-Martin's organizations, while not related to the Communist Party proper, were high-profile and attracted a good deal of attention from such church-related groups. In June 1931, for instance, we find the ESP's Archambault trying to have Saint-Martin dismissed from his position as a stenographer on the grounds that he was a communist.[67]

Later that same year a delegation of Catholic youth from the ACJC visited the UO in an effort to get to know their enemy. In their report describing their impressions, the youth grudgingly complimented the "ringleaders," Saint-Martin and Pilon, for their hard work and self-sacrificing attitude. The ACJC representatives (sometimes known as *acéjistes*) confirmed that Faure's *Douze preuves de l'inexistence de Dieu*, among other works, was frequently distributed:[68] "To give you an idea of what is said of God, a gentleman and two young ladies slyly slip you different tracts of Sébastian Faure, 'Twelve Proofs of the Non-existence of God,' one by Bossi, 'Jesus Christ Never Existed ...' To demonstrate that the Church is merely a diabolical institution and that the priests are only dark and despotic policemen, they flaunt the brochure by Elisée Reclus entitled 'Anarchy and the Church,' that of Jean Nost [i.e., Most] 'The Religious Plague,' those of Gerrold, Sébastian Faure, and others of the same ilk."[69]

The listed texts shed light on the strong European anticlerical tradition to which the UO belonged. Among the works distributed in their meetings, in addition to *Twelve Proofs* by Faure (1858–1942) originally published in 1908,[70] was a work by Emilio Bossi (1870–1920), an anticlerical Italian lawyer and journalist known also by the pseudonymous anagram Milesbo. His *Gesù Cristo non è mai esistito* (*Jesus Christ Never Existed*), originally published in 1900, became quite popular in radical circles and was reissued a number of times.[71] Jean Nost, the author listed for *La Peste Religieuse,* was actually Johann Most, a German journalist and politician involved first in socialist and then anarchist politics – an advocate of terrorist action and a "militant atheist with the zeal of a religious fanatic." His *Die Gottespest* was published in 1887 and translated as *The Deistic Pestilence and Religious Plague of Man.*[72] Élisée Reclus (1830–1905) was a French geographer and anarchist. His *L'Anarchie et l'Église,* which advocated unrelenting struggle against religion because it was the defender of power and authority, was published in 1900.[73] The UO distributed other pamphlets, of course, on anarchism and socialism, as well as works on free love and feminism, such as Faure's *Aux Femmes.*[74] While not explicitly anti-theological, these works were considered dangerous by the *acéjistes* because they contradicted Catholic teaching on family life, the role of women, and the proper ordering of society.

Catholic youth feared the damage anti-religious pamphlets could do to the faith of uneducated French-Canadians: "If these different people have only received an elementary education, they will, ninety per cent of the time, be taken in by the sophisms which are spread across each page, and inevitably the gates of doubt about the existence of God will be forced open."[75] Like the critics of Sterry's *Christian Inquirer*, the *acéjistes* fretted not only about anti-religious arguments but also about their effect on naïve or unwary Christians.

What is more, the young Catholics were surprised by how often the UO speakers discussed religious topics. It seemed that every lecture would touch on God at one point, and a high proportion were focused entirely on attacking religion.[76] In one speech, Saint-Martin boldly reasserted his atheism: "Je suis un athée fieffé ... I shout it out to you, I will tell you again, gentlemen, I am an atheist through and through!"[77] He argued that Christ was an invention of Saul of Tarsus, who created the myth in order to combat the communism of his day. Saint-Martin even advised his audience to stop using blasphemous utterances, because they referred to a God who did not in fact exist. He also spoke out against the language of "natural laws," because such language implied the existence of a divine legislator.[78]

The speakers of the UO railed against Catholicism in particular. Pilon lashed out at the Pope for making pronouncements on economic matters, which were none of his concern. Saint-Martin called priests "a bunch of snivellers," with skin as smooth as snakes.[79] If members of the powerful Sulpician order did not want to work, he declared, they should be shot.[80] Pilon for his part denounced confessionals as the greatest police system ever invented to discover people's secrets.[81] A different speaker, Despatie, called the confessional "a nest of vices," from which people came out knowing more about sin than when they went in.[82] Another Catholic sacrament that came under fire was marriage. Despatie argued that marriage was simply a natural union and asked why the church arrogated to itself the right to interfere. Mlle M. Ouimet, one of the UO's regular feminist speakers, called marriage nothing but "la prostitution légale."[83]

The *acéjistes* found that the UO lectures spent much more time criticizing the church than they did the government; some in Saint-Martin's circle seemed to expect the state and capitalism simply to fade away in the face of communism. The young people felt that it was because the Church defined itself as the main protector of the stability of society that the communists prioritized their anticlerical stance.[84]

Of course, it is not surprising that a group of Catholic youth would focus on the anti-religious content of the UO message. But, as we have seen above, Saint-Martin's opponents on the left frequently made the same point. The historian Andrée Lévesque has examined the surviving transcripts of lectures from the later years of the UO (starting in 1932) and comments: "Few dealt directly with communism, and a large number were anti-clerical harangues denouncing the power and wealth of the church or Roman Catholic dogmas such as the Immaculate Conception."[85] In a piece looking back at interwar Montreal, Communist Party secretary Stanley Ryerson was highly dismissive of Saint-Martin, describing him as an "anti-clerical socialist": "French-Canadian communists in Montreal were critical of this anti-clerical trend. To Saint-Martin's anti-religious diatribes (lectures on the 'Immaculate Conception' and the like), they counterposed proposals for united action in support of ... the unemployed; to which Saint-Martin's rejoinder was to advocate at most a Ghandi-like [sic] policy of passive resistance."[86] Immediately after this criticism, however, Ryerson admitted that "even among the militant francophone radicals ... the trace of an earlier ex-Catholic aversion to the *robes noires* remained."[87] He described riding as the passenger of the communist Roméo Duval, who startled him by suddenly swerving and speeding towards a priest who was crossing the street. The clergyman just barely leaped to safety. Shocked, Ryerson asked Duval why he had done that. The driver replied "off-handedly" that he always did it when he got the chance; he couldn't help himself. Ryerson's pairing of these anecdotes belies his assertion that orthodox communists always avoided the anticlerical extremes of the heretical Saint-Martin.[88]

Nonetheless, the Communist Party in Quebec was typically careful to avoid focusing too much on religion. This was in part thanks to a Marxist emphasis on improving material conditions, rather than engaging in intellectual debates. But it also had a strategic purpose, particularly during the Popular Front period from 1935 to 1939. As one communist recalled: "At first we were anticlerical. Subsequently, we became more realistic. By being anticlerical, we could not consider organizing French Canadians, bringing them to socialism ... This was Saint-Martin's mistake, which did much more harm than good. Where would we find our allies in the Province of Quebec if it were not among Catholics?"[89] For orthodox communists, Saint-Martin became the prime example of how *not* to approach religion.

As historian Marcel Fournier points out, however, Saint-Martin may have had his own strategic rationale. It was entirely normal for newly radicalized French-Canadians to have a strong interest in questions of belief and unbelief. Some had been gradually drifting away from religious practice for reasons that included parental indifference. But many who were newly affiliated with the UO and the Communist Party came from intensely religious backgrounds and were wrestling with the implications of religion for politics and vice versa. Henri Gagnon recounts his personal experience: "Materialism, the primacy of matter in this world, not the next, was a big thing for me, having wanted to be a missionary at twelve years old. It breaks everything. It is a weird impression. This occurred over a period of months. Even then I would ask myself if the Little Jesus idea was true."[90] For many others, the chief barrier to involvement in radical activities was the Church's condemnation of socialism. New leftists had to deal with interventions by local clergy, emotional recriminations from family members, and personal feelings of guilt.[91] Thus it is quite understandable that Saint-Martin and the UO spent so much time on the issue.

The UO communists did not limit themselves to the safety of their own buildings; they would sometimes intervene in public spaces as well. In November 1930 a group of young UO members heckled a meeting of the Canadian Alliance for the Women's Vote in Quebec.[92] In response, the alliance invited Abbé Aimé Boileau to give a speech against Bolshevism. Hearing of this, the young communists returned, accompanied by Émile Godin, then secretary of the UO. They listened more or less quietly while Boileau attacked Russian communism,[93] but in the question period Godin asked what qualified Boileau to address the topic. After a sharp exchange Godin tried to give a longer speech, with noisy approval from his comrades, but he was drowned out by hand-clapping from the largely female audience. When a musical performance began, the communists gave up trying to speak and sat down to enjoy it.[94]

CATHOLICISM STRIKES BACK

Opponents of the Université ouvrière could be considerably more belligerent. On 25 October 1930, a group of Université de Montréal students broke into the UO. They smashed furniture, tore up books, and threw the debris into a bonfire in the street. Saint-Martin complained to the vice-rector, who demanded proof of the damage, witnesses, and a written complaint before taking action.[95] Even then, the university disclaimed any responsibility for the conduct of its students.[96] Saint-Martin sued the city, alleging that the police had stood idly by while private property was being destroyed. The case was dismissed. Saint-Martin appealed, but lost a second time.[97] After years of legal wrangling, however, he took the case to the Supreme Court and won a partial victory; in November 1935 he was awarded $1,500 in damages (despite asking for $5,500).[98]

Another episode occurred in April 1931, when fifty members of the Jeunesse ouvrière catholique (sometimes called *jocistes*) led by an activist named Latrémouille, got into a shouting match with the communists at a meeting of the UO.[99] "Vive le Christ-Roi! Vive Jésus-Ouvrier!" they yelled. A reporter for *Le Devoir* wrote that it was wonderful to see these young workers making their "professions of faith"! Some of the *jocistes* accused the communists of blaspheming God only because they were unemployed and told them they would do better to pray for a job. Others used more colloquial metaphors: "Ah, you don't believe in God? Can you fit inside the cooking pot you have at home? No. It seems that the idea of God can no more fit inside your head than God can in the pot!"[100]

The intruders then pulled down the big red flag and trampled it underfoot. A brawl ensued, the police intervened, and those in charge – one of the Godin brothers and an activist named Lacombe – demanded the youths' arrest. In the midst of the chaos Latrémouille declared that, despite the communists' hatred, the Catholics were there because they loved them and wished them happiness. At this, another aggressive shouting match broke out; this time the police settled it by striking at the communists with their batons until blood flowed. The reporter for *Le Devoir* proudly counted this as "une seconde victoire." The Catholics were taken to the station but the police decided there was insufficient evidence to charge them.[101] And there would be more disruptions.[102]

Only a few days later, a letter-writing campaign began in the pages of *Le Devoir*, demanding that the activities of the UO be shut down. The federal government's crackdown on the Communist Party of Canada in August 1931 no doubt made people wonder why the UO was not also repressed. In August 1932 a man affiliated with the École sociale populaire, Jean Faubert, wrote to *Le Devoir* to give his explanation: "because the Labour University, while a little bit communist, is mainly anti-religious."[103] Faubert expounded this idea further: "There's no doubt that it's the Labour University's attacks against religion that enable it to continue to exist and spread its anti-social doctrines, and even to expand by opening branches as it did last winter on Montcalm Street. If its teachers, in order to overthrow society, first defame religion, then they will have free rein; but if they only attack capitalism, civic authority, government, they'll be locked up. The university is primarily anti-religious. In all its assemblies, in all its conferences, it is the religious question that dominates."[104] The UO's campaign against religion was in fact a cynical strategy, Faubert believed. Saint-Martin's communists knew that criticism of the government would be punished, while criticism of the Church would not. Faubert's letter was followed by a series of others from activists of the ESP, arguing much the same point and calling for the closure of the UO.[105] Local authorities were so concerned about the Université that, starting in 1932, they sent stenographers to record every major speech given there.[106]

In the fall of 1932 Saint-Martin organized Spartakus, a cooperative printing house, as well a journal of the same name.[107] *Forum*, another magazine put out by Spartakus, published contributions from UO supporters, sometimes on anticlerical themes. One contributor, signing himself S. Clave, that is "esclave" or "slave," wrote that religion was the art of exploiting the credulity, fear, hope, and ignorance of others.[108] Saint-Martin wrote most of the material in *Spartakus* itself, and sent copies to judges, members of Parliament and other public figures.[109] He had 19,000 copies printed (11,000 in French and the remainder in English).[110] One article was published as a twenty-four-page pamphlet entitled *Sandwiches à la shouashe*.[111] Unfortunately this endeavour would give the government reason to formally prosecute him.

Saint-Martin constructed a parody of Catholic charity: it was shameful; it was morally and psychologically degrading.[112] "Ensoutanés," clergymen, were thieves. Priests were "paid-organizers" (Saint-Martin used the English phrase) who climbed the ranks and were rewarded extravagantly on the basis of how much money they could raise.[113] The communist argued that churches were designed to mesmerize and dazzle congregations. The dim lighting in the nave contrasted with bright sanctuary lights, the compelling organ music, the dramatic clerical garments, the ritual movements and gestures, repeated again year after year – all these elements were psychologically devised to enthrall the faithful and hypnotize them into emptying their pockets.

Once the clergy had the money, Saint-Martin hypothesized, they would spend most of it on themselves and dole out just a tiny amount to those in need. He imagined the unemployed who asked for charity being forced to their knees with their arms crossed, to give thanks to God for the gifts given them. When their arms got tired they were forced to hold them behind their backs. Then, for the cruel enjoyment ("a truly sadistic theocracy") of dominating the oppressed, sandwiches were placed in front of each on a chair, right where people put their "posteriors."[114]

To complete the humiliation of eating off a chair where people placed their buttocks, the poor were forced to eat the sandwiches with no hands: "Then, without using their hands to touch this precious sandwich of charity, the unfortunates must nibble, grabbing the two pieces of bread with just their lips, tongue and teeth, as best they can, and, then to waste nothing – well, they voluntarily lick the seat of the chair." Meanwhile fat monks watched gleefully, their paunches shaking as their braying laughter echoed down the street. They were cheerful in their utter triumph over the poor, blinded masses. The rule of the whitewashed tombs (pure on the outside, but full of death and decay) had come to pass.[115] The Church assassinated mankind using the diabolical invention of Saul of Tarsus (alias St Paul), Charity. This scam of charity filled the coffers of the clergymen to overflowing.[116] "All crime has a motive," Saint-Martin continued. "That of charitable institutions is clear: it is to make money and to generate a profit from the difference between the fabulous sums they receive from all the dupes, including our legislators, and the insignificant pittance they give to the needy."[117]

For his articles in *Spartakus*, and in particular the sections excerpted in the *Sandwiches* pamphlet, Saint-Martin was charged with blasphemous libel in January 1933.[118] In March, Montreal's Église Saint-Jacques was burned down, and suspicion fell on Raoul Paquette and his wife. When the couple was detained, Raoul was found to be carrying an ID card issued by the Association humanitaire. The case against them does not seem to have led to a trial, but the issue was soon raised in Quebec's National Assembly. Maurice Duplessis, then the leader of the Opposition, implied that it was some of Saint-Martin's communists who were to blame. When he asked Premier Taschereau what he intended to do about the UO's subversive activities,[119] the premier responded by announcing that a new law would be forthcoming. Indeed, the following month the minister of labour introduced legislation aimed at closing the UO. Since the Université was registered as a library, the new law closed all libraries established under the "Loi des bibliothèques et des instituts d'artisans," and required them to make fresh applications for charters. Approval for the UO would not be granted.[120]

Saint-Martin used his considerable experience with the legal system to protect himself and his organization. After the law changed, he simply re-registered the UO, this time as a business association.[121] Meanwhile, by filing different writs, he tried to get the blasphemous libel case dismissed or reviewed on various technicalities.[122] Once the case was underway, Saint-Martin was also charged with seditious libel, and the two cases continued simultaneously.[123] Then the seditious libel case was put on hold as Saint-Martin was sent to be examined for signs of insanity. The communist responded by filing a writ of *habeas corpus* on himself; this was denied.[124] Less than two weeks later Saint-Martin was deemed sane and released on bail.[125]

In September 1933, with his court cases still pending, Saint-Martin faced fresh opposition, this time from fascists. The fascist movement in Quebec, inspired by the governments of Italy and Germany, came into the open in 1933. Two rival leaders emerged: the writer and newspaper editor Adrien Arcand, and J. Anaclet Chalifoux, leader of the Fédération des clubs ouvriers. This latter group donned brown shirts, like the Nazi SA, and caught the city's attention with a massive Easter parade to St Joseph's Oratory. It was a clear statement of their twin fascist and Catholic sympathies.[126]

At around the same time, Saint-Martin had become interested in the ideas of Technocracy that were briefly popular in the United States in the early 1930s. Technocrats envisioned a world run by objective social and economic engineers, in which money would be replaced by units of energy.[127] He formed what he called the Technocracy Education Conference at a new location on rue Saint-Zotique. It seems in practice to have been substantially similar to the UO, and the new name may have been an attempt to deflect hostility from the "communist" nature of his other organizations. At a meeting on 22 September 1933, Pilon and another speaker reportedly gave anti-Catholic talks at one of Saint-Martin's gatherings (he kept the Montcalm and Craig locations alongside Saint-Zotique).

Elsewhere in the city, Italian Catholics were gathering for a special religious feast, in the presence of a papal delegate. The Catholics claimed that Saint-Martin and his followers had come out to insult them during a solemn religious procession. In retaliation a coalition of Italian-Canadian fascists and Chalifoux's French-Canadian brownshirts stormed into the Saint-Zotique location, disrupted the meeting being held there, and "wrecked the premises." Once again the fascists posed as defenders of Catholicism. In writing to Chalifoux to defend himself, Saint-Martin insisted that he had not come out to insult the procession; nor had the ensuing meeting been anti-religious in nature. The authorities, well aware what had happened, were unsympathetic. The commanding officer of the RCMP in Quebec commented: "It is obvious that any radical who attacks the church in this province is asking for trouble."[128]

When the blasphemous libel case finally came to trial, the central question was Saint-Martin's attitude to religion. Since he had parodied the Catholic liturgy, the crown attorney summoned witnesses who would "elucidate the importance of the *Benedicite* and the sermon as essential parts of a religious service."[129] Saint-Martin claimed that his *Spartakus* articles had made no reference to "gods or dogma." His ridicule had been directed "at men of flesh and blood," who he believed were unfairly profiting from the administration of direct relief. He had not attacked charity or religion as such, but the hypocrites and Pharisees who used such concepts as a cloak. His enemies were the "temple thieves of 1933."[130] His reference to Saul's invention of Christianity was explained as a criticism of Saul "the infidel," not St Paul after his conversion to Christianity. He then quoted legal precedent which stated that blasphemy against Judaism or other non-Christian religions was not a crime. Presumably since Saul of Tarsus had been a devout Jew, the criticisms contained in *Spartakus* were not blasphemies. The communist then undermined himself somewhat by stating that "he could not in his conscience permit the libelling of the Jewish or Mahommetan or other deities."[131]

Saint-Martin also quoted experts who stated that "dignified discourse by learned men" did not count as blasphemy. He argued that he had tried hard to make himself a learned man. He had written books, directed the Université ouvrière, and taught Esperanto. He was learned but he was not an academic, because he was "one of the people." His articles were likewise "for the consumption of the people."[132] He made this case calmly but at the end of his arguments he offered up an emotional plea: "I come before the magistrate as a child comes before his papa. I tell him frankly what my intentions were. If he decides that my intentions were guided by malice, calculated rather to wound than to solace the feelings of my fellow men, then he will punish. But if he does sentence me, I shall not regard it as a punishment. I shall say 'Papa did not understand his child's intentions.'" With this, Saint-Martin sat down. The reporter noticed tears in his eyes.[133]

Before a decision was reached in the case, Saint-Martin came under fire from a new direction. The fascist raid on the Saint-Zotique hall showed that at least some of his enemies were willing to use violence against him. Scuffles between his supporters and aggressive opponents became commonplace. This culminated in a brutal assault on Saint-Martin, now in his late sixties. In the evening of 1 October 1933, a gang of club-wielding assailants attacked him on his way to a meeting at the Saint-Zotique location, beating him about the head and shoulders and knocking him down. When police intervened the attackers fled. The activist tried to go about his business but quickly collapsed. He was taken to hospital and received ten stitches to close the head wounds that had been inflicted. Soon afterward, Émile Godin was also attacked and beaten, likewise ending up in hospital.[134] The timing of the violence suggests Chalifoux's fascists were to blame, but the identity of the assailants was never determined.

Since Saint-Martin needed at least two weeks to recover, Judge Lacroix's decision on the blasphemy charges was postponed.[135] Eventually, on 13 November 1933, the verdict was delivered with extensive commentary. Lacroix explained that he had interpreted Article 198 to mean that attacks on *any* religious subjects were blasphemous, provided they were made in bad faith and with offensive language.[136] He felt it necessary to point to an English precedent in which attacks on Christianity, the Bible, sacred persons or objects all counted as blasphemous libel. The judge went on to cite an analysis of the 1927 Sterry case by E.J. Murphy, who had been the prosecutor in that earlier trial. Murphy had argued:

Destroy or discredit or weaken the sense of religion in a people and you remove the best guarantee of government, undermine the force of law and open the way to all sorts of lawlessness and abuse. Government is founded on law and law in its last analysis rests on religion. Where is the security for property, for reputation, for life, if the sense of religious obligation desert the oaths which are the instruments of investigation in Courts of Justice? All tends to shake the fabric of society which is built on Christian ideas. Governments are fully justified in prosecuting the blasphemer or him who would destroy religion and thereby make room for anarchy, by breeding and fostering mischief.

Lacroix agreed with Murphy's opinion. The activities of men like Sterry and Saint-Martin were a threat, not just to individuals but to the fabric of the nation. Saint-Martin's writings were specifically aimed at "un grand nombre de nos amis" ("many of our friends"), that is, local Quebec judges, lawyers, and politicians at all levels, who, in the judge's view, were doing their best to help the suffering population with food and shelter.[137]

Lacroix further asserted that Saint-Martin could have argued his case in a respectful manner, "d'une manière digne et honnête." Moreover, he had chosen a bad time to spread his insults. At a time of suffering and unrest the poor of Montreal needed peace and tranquility, not further agitation. Saint-Martin was deluded, said Lacroix: "Evidently in regard to our clergy and our religious institution, the accused appears to be very misinformed, because the truth accepted by everyone of good faith is that without these religious bodies, faith, morality, charity and honesty, the social conscience of which I speak would have been discarded long ago." It was religion that ensured that society had a conscience, insisted the judge: Saint-Martin's criticisms of religion had been "coarse, hurtful, repugnant and of a kind that wounds the religious sentiments not only of our province but of our country."[138] As an older man with much learning and life experience, Saint-Martin could not plead ignorance of the consequences of his actions: he had not considered the disastrous effects of his irreverent words on the young, the weak, and the ignorant.[139] And, in sum, he could not argue that his arguments had been made in good faith.

Thus the judge claimed he had no choice but to find Saint-Martin guilty. However, he still took pity on him. Saint-Martin's few days in prison for his seditious libel case had been detrimental to his health, which was already precarious because of his injuries. Thus Lacroix imposed a fine of one hundred dollars, which if not paid would default to three months in prison; and two bonds of five hundred dollars, to ensure that Saint-Martin kept the peace (or be liable to an additional three months in prison).[140] Having found a way (at least temporarily) to silence the aged communist, the courts dropped the charges of seditious libel.[141]

THE PERSECUTION OF PILON

The authorities nevertheless continued to crack down on the UO. With Saint-Martin sidelined, its leadership fell to Pilon. A month after Saint-Martin's conviction, on 13 December 1933, Pilon gave a talk on the history of the popes.[142] As usual, a city stenographer was present to record his words. On 18 December, Pilon was in turn arraigned for blasphemous libel.[143] The transcript of his talk, which would be used as evidence in the case, gives us a sense of Pilon's speaking style and his approach to religious topics.[144]

After greeting the audience (about three hundred people) and making a few introductory remarks, Pilon moved to the topic at hand. He referred to his audience as "Mesdames et Messieurs" but spoke fairly casually: "My friends, you have been taught that the popes were all saints, good fellows, infallible men," he said, but his plan was to thoroughly refute that view.[145] He would, he said, make his way through the entire history of the popes, using well-established sources, which he proceeded to list – fourteen works in all – texts by Catholics, Protestants, and atheists, including the four-volume *Histoire du Christianisme et de la Societé Chrétienne, The Concise*

Dictionary of Religious Knowledge, Joseph McCabe's six-volume *The True Story of the Roman Catholic Church,* and entries from the *Encyclopedia Britannica.*[146]

Pilon listed all the popes from the Apostle Peter forward, with the dates they ruled, pointing out contradictions, the popes who ruled for very short periods, and those who were particularly notorious (the list of names and dates filled six legal-sized pages). Most people in Quebec, especially priests, he said, were very poorly educated on papal history. But communists had the strength, energy, and perseverance to unearth the truth of history, and that was what he intended to deliver.

And deliver he did. The list of scandals, sins, crimes and indiscretions of the popes – both mundane and controversial – was meaty indeed: according to Pilon, the early Pope Victor I had been arrested for theft, and been dependent upon Emperor Commodus's mistress for his influence; Pope Sixtus I had invented private confession to save aristocrats from having to confess their sexual sins before entire congregations;[147] early medieval popes had harems and used concubines to bribe or reward men of influence; some popes sent out gangs of thugs to waylay pilgrims to Rome and added the stolen wealth to the papal coffers.

Despite his invocation of textual authority, however, many of Pilon's claims were vague, poorly sourced, or derived from popular legend. He blended well-attested historical facts with generalizations, half-remembered details, and anticlerical mythology. Included, for instance, was the apocryphal story of Pope Joan, with the tale of a bottomless chair used to ensure that future popes had male genitalia. Pilon's talk was more designed to shock and titillate than to maintain historical accuracy. But this is not to say that he was simply making everything up; his account of Peter Damian's vicious 1064 rant against clerical wives, in which women were referred to as whores, pigs, and worse, was factual.[148] He also went into great detail on the well-documented misdeeds of Renaissance popes. The Catholic confessional, he accused, was like a brothel where priests took advantage of women; he even said the Vatican ran actual brothels where prostitutes practised a parody of Catholicism. These more controversial sexual accusations, along with his claims about popes robbing pilgrims, were presented as the most egregious charges against him at his trial.

Before the case came to trial, Pilon faced another challenge. A local Franciscan brother, Rev. Archange Godbout (1886–1960), having dedicated himself to fighting the influence of communism in Montreal, challenged Pilon to a debate. The two clashed before an overflowing audience in a local school on a bitterly cold night in mid-January 1934.[149] Godbout's opening defence of the existence of God earned a fiery counterattack from Pilon, but the Franciscan's closing response received much applause.[150]

In the audience, however, was a well-known journalist with anti-clerical leanings. Olivar Asselin couldn't believe that a respected man of the cloth would stoop so low as to debate a communist; he accused Godbout of lending Pilon credibility that he did not deserve; worse than that, he charged that Godbout was abetting Pilon in a criminal activity! A few weeks later Asselin wrote: "Society, the State, and the home are wholly based on belief in the existence of God. As in all Christian countries, atheism in Canada remains a natural right but on the condition that there not be any propaganda that is likely to offend the beliefs of the majority of the population. Publicly professed atheism, with the goal of propaganda, let alone provocation, has always been held contrary to public order." Therefore, the journalist argued, what Pilon deserved for his atheist propaganda was not a cordial debate but prosecution under Article 16 of the Criminal Code. He even mocked *acéjistes* and other young Catholics for not being manly enough to deal with Pilon informally, even though it would be ten against one – the implication being that Pilon, like Saint-Martin, should be given a severe beating.[151]

Godbout's response? "Defend the basis of religion? Why bother? Don't we have police?"[152] The problem, he continued, was that the law against blasphemy only covered the insult, not the underlying criticism of Catholicism, which was the real problem. Moreover, legal efforts to silence the UO activists had had very little effect. Despite having their charter revoked and their leader being found guilty of libel, they continued to spread their doctrines. Godbout also disdained Asselin's suggestion that young Catholics resort to violence; that would only provoke disorder – not to mention that the idea was anti-evangelical and anti-social.[153]

On 23 January 1934 Pilon was arraigned again, this time for a talk of the week earlier.[154] He was accused of having "cast vile slurs upon the name of the Holy Virgin," as well as for offenses such as blaspheming against the Holy Ghost and calling convents brothels. Pilon's first blasphemy charge finally came to trial in June 1934. Oddly, he was tried by an anglophone jury, having refused the Crown's offer to put together a francophone one. (Perhaps Pilon hoped anglophones would be less defensive of Catholicism.) The trial was short, and Pilon carried out his own defence. The only witness called was a police stenographer, Wilhelmina Lapointe, who read from her transcription of his speech on the popes. In an effort to establish that the speech had been actually welcomed by the listeners, he asked her to verify that he had chosen his theme in response to audience demand. He also asked her if anyone had been offended or insulted at the event, and argued to the jury at that he was not guilty because he had not intended any insult. He respected priests and ministers of any religion as humans, but saw the Church as "a political and economic organization." Like Saint-Martin he argued that he had not condemned Christianity itself, but rather its earthly representatives: "I have not attacked religion. I have not insulted God. I have criticized the officials of a certain organization which every citizen has a right to do." Despite his efforts, Pilon was found guilty on 15 June 1934. He was given a one-year sentence, the maximum allowable penalty, and sent to Bordeaux Prison to do hard labour. He also had to put up a thousand-dollar bond on condition of "keeping the peace," or be liable for another year in prison.[155]

After the judgment, Saint-Martin approached the communist-affiliated Canadian Labour Defence League to ask their help in appealing Pilon's case. According to an RCMP informant, the CLDL agreed, planning to launch a drive for "complete freedom of speech and against the persecution for anti-clerical views."[156] But this was not to be. After a few months, Pilon no longer wanted their help, nor Saint-Martin's for that matter.

Earlier that year Saint-Martin had mockingly announced that the local Franciscans had been praying for Pilon's conversion. This was a good thing, he said, because it would make clear just what such prayers were worth: nothing. But Catholic journalists were quick to quote his words back to him when Pilon did in fact publicly convert.[157] It began in mid-August 1934 with letters written to Archange Godbout, Bishop Alphonse Deschamps, and Archbishop Georges Gauthier. To Godbout, Pilon wrote: "I now understand that only the doctrines of the Roman Church can restore peace on our planet, and they alone can prevent the great and small from devouring one another. Christ on the cross told the thief after he repented that he would be in the kingdom of heaven with Him. Like the thief I want to earn the pardon of the Saviour of mankind."[158] Pilon's conversion was quite a coup for Godbout and attracted much attention. In late September 1934, a "dense" crowd filled the parish hall, where Pilon's public statement of faith was read aloud (Pilon himself was still in prison). Not everyone present was entirely convinced of his sincerity. Godbout had to field some "ridiculous" questions, which he did in good humour.[159]

Pilon compared himself to figures such as Frédéric Ozanam, Ernest Psichari, Giovanni Papini, and Paul Verlaine, who had converted or returned to Catholicism. One irreverent paper, Gilbert Larue's *L'Autorité*, mocked Pilon for being pretentious, saying he was "modestly" comparing himself with Henri Rochefort, Mussolini, and even Paul on the road to Damascus![160] In expressing his desire to dedicate his new life to defending Catholicism from the communist menace, Pilon positioned himself as the person best acquainted with the enemy. He denounced his former comrades as thieves and charlatans who were taking advantage of the poor and suffering workers.

An account of Pilon's conversion accompanied by some of his letters from prison was compiled and published by Godbout's organization under the title *Gaston Pilon*.[161] This was followed by a pamphlet by Pilon himself, attacking communism with the fervour of his earlier assaults on Catholicism.[162] When he was released from prison he began to give anti-communist talks.[163] With the help of Godbout and his organizations, the Apostolat populaire, Pilon started the Association humanitaire catholique, a religious version of the AH.[164] Some observers were not impressed. An editorial in *Le Canada* asserted that Pilon was vulgar, a loose cannon, a madman; his ramblings, his absurd accusations were aimed wildly at all kinds of targets, and his unjustifiably crude language was bringing shame on the clergymen who supported him. It may be that the techniques that had successfully captured and entertained working-class audiences at the UO were less acceptable in his new, more respectable milieu.[165]

In 1934 Saint-Martin was again targeted with a charge of blasphemous libel for an article in *Spartakus*, as well as charged for oral blasphemy and a few other offences. He pleaded not guilty to all charges. For some reason the police chief for Montreal recommended clemency and Premier Taschereau decided to abandon the oral blasphemy charge. Saint-Martin was once again convicted of blasphemous libel but was only fined $25 and $66.70 in costs.[166] Nevertheless he seems to have gradually retreated from activism. In 1935 the UO changed its name to the Bibliothèque de l'université du prolétariat but before long it ceased to exist.[167] By 1936 or 1937 Saint-Martin's Association humanitaire also seems to have dwindled away.

Montreal anarchist Paul Faure commented that in these years Saint-Martin seemed weary and discouraged.[168] He appeared to be intimidated by the new Padlock Act introduced by Premier Duplessis in 1937 to combat communist propaganda.[169] Nor could he still count on his lieutenants: Pilon had converted; Dubé and others had joined the Communist Party; Émile Godin had been injured; and his brother Abel died in June 1938.[170] Saint-Martin himself retreated from confrontational politics. Nevertheless, he did not fully retire. In 1939 he put out a booklet entitled *Frankenstein ou consommateurs*, which argued that consumers needed to be protected from large corporations. He also made enquiries about registering a new organization, but the authorities stalled so long that he gave up the idea.[171] After surviving for another decade, he died in 1947 at the age of eighty-three, while shovelling snow.[172]

TAKING STOCK

How should we understand Albert Saint-Martin and his followers in the broader Canadian context? Were they freethinking communists or communistic freethinkers? The content of their program fell somewhere between that of the OBU Forum and the Rationalist Societies in Winnipeg and Toronto. Despite criticism from both the "orthodox" communists and the Catholics of Montreal, they continued hammering away at the religious beliefs of their contemporaries. If they had so desired they could have moved on to less provocative subject matter. The fact that they did not suggests that irreligion was personally important to them and likely popular with their audience. We can recall that Gauvin's audiences were always largest and most enthusiastic when he was attacking religion.

Saint-Martin and Pilon called themselves communists, but the Communist Party of Canada rejected this identity as a fraud. In some ways Saint-Martin represented an earlier, more eclectic version of socialism that was ill at ease with the strict Marxism of the Third International. Historian Mathieu Houle-Courcelles has pointed to the many anarchist influences upon the OU and the fact that some anarchists found a home there, although he acknowledges that Saint-Martin was not a strict anarchist either.[173]

Perhaps we should not be hasty to categorize these men too precisely. After Pilon's conversion to Catholicism, *La Vie ouvrière,* the organ of the official Communist Party, downplayed the importance of the event. Pilon was never a real communist, it declared, but merely an anticlerical activist; true communists did not waste their time attacking religion. Pilon replied to this idea derisively, insisting that communism, particularly in Soviet Russia, was unavoidably antireligious.[174] The truth may have fallen somewhere in between. Pilon did spend a lot of time on topics that were traditionally anticlerical or atheistic; he spent more time combatting religion than the communists felt comfortable with. But he also linked his denunciations with positive claims drawn from socialist thought.

On 6 June 1934, for instance, just before his trial, Pilon had written about the fundamental struggle between exploitation and communism: "Yes, the Church, religion, the gods must disappear, to be replaced by the materialist technique, that is to say, scientific communism, for the happiness of all mankind."[175] Here Pilon positioned himself between orthodox communists and the anticlerical tradition. It was not just a question of right or wrong beliefs; any substantial change had to be linked to material conditions. Nevertheless, religion was a formidable obstacle in the struggle for a fair society, one that had to be dismantled by constant criticism.

Perhaps what we can say is that Saint-Martin and Pilon were in some sense both freethinkers and communists. If a francophone Montrealer was looking for forthright criticism of religion, the Université ouvrière was the place to go. Like Gauvin and Leavens in their cities, Saint-Martin and Pilon combined a negative critique of religion with positive ideals drawn from socialism, although the proportions differed according to time and place. The freethinking tradition they drew on was different from the Anglo-American one found in Winnipeg and Toronto and was influenced mainly by anticlericals and anarchists from Catholic Europe. It is interesting, however, that Pilon, in condemning the popes, drew in part from a book by Joseph McCabe, the British freethinker who had visited both the Winnipeg and Toronto rationalists.[176] Much of the subject matter was similar across regions: critiques of Christianity as immoral and exploitative were common, often supplemented by historical exposés and biblical criticism.

One major difference is that the UO seems to have given less attention to discussions of the liberating power of science. Despite the fact that the Catholic Church was at best wary of the theory of evolution, we do not hear of any debates on evolution taking place under the auspices of the Université.[177] Saint-Martin saw religion as irrational, as did the anglophone rationalists, but he stressed above all the oppressive nature of church power; the clergy kept people poor and ignorant, and worked as henchmen of the wealthy to stave off unrest and revolution. Economic and political radicalism went hand in hand with unbelief. People like Bert Leavens from Toronto and the OBU's R.B. Russell in Winnipeg would have been quite comfortable with this formulation, while William Styles and Marshall Gauvin may have found it too politically extreme for their liking.

The official repression faced by Saint-Martin and Pilon in Montreal was in some ways comparable to that experienced by the Toronto rationalists. The fact that Judge Lacroix cited the Sterry case in his own decision is telling. One interesting difference between Protestant and Catholic cities, however, is that, while Sterry was prosecuted for criticizing God and the Bible, Saint-Martin and Pilon were both convicted for attacking the Church. Nevertheless, unbelievers in both settings were caught in a wave of anti-leftist repression in the early 1930s. Anyone who threatened the already shaky status quo was suspect. The fact that Saint-Martin and Pilon were organizing the unemployed and condemning official relief efforts as inadequate only made them a greater threat in the eyes of authorities.

Is it possible that the UO and the AH attracted so much hostility just because of their communist ideology rather than their antireligious activities? A parallel case from the same time suggests otherwise. In the 1930s Paul Faure, the French-born anarchist who sometimes associated with Saint-Martin, tried to offer help to a prisoner by the name of J.-S.-A. Gaudry. Gaudry was a militant freethinker, apparently not associated with any organization, although he seems to have received literature for unbelievers from France. When, in 1930, he circulated a violently anticlerical pamphlet, he was thrown in jail for forty-three days of "preventative detention." He accused the police of beating him brutally, knocking out teeth and injuring his ribs. Though he was eventually released, he seems to have been in regular trouble with the law.

In 1938 Faure wrote that Gaudry was again in prison, this time held indefinitely for observation because he was thought to be criminally insane. The anarchist's opinion was that Gaudry was perfectly sane, but that his strong hatred for clergymen led him to act in socially unacceptable ways. In the early 1930s Faure had tried to help the freethinker, but eventually gave up in despair, because in Quebec, "The clergy is king and master."[178] Gaudry's fate suggests that Saint-Martin and

Pilon's militant irreligion would have brought them grief even if they had not been self-proclaimed communists.

Similarly, Toronto rationalists had been targeted in the battle over free speech in the early 1930s, despite the fact that they did not at the time espouse an explicit political position. What the Montreal group had to face that Torontonians did not was unofficial violence, mobilized in part by elements of the Catholic Church. Mobs smashed up their meeting halls and their library and, in Saint-Martin's case, inflicted serious personal harm. Another difference is that after 1934 official repression waned in Toronto, whereas in Montreal it only increased. The new premier, Maurice Duplessis, was even more hostile to communism than Godbout, his predecessor, had been, and his close connections with the Church spelled trouble for unbelievers.

The local Christendom of Roman Catholic Quebec defended itself vigorously in these years. Duplessis's imposition of the Padlock Law made any kind of radical activity very risky. Saint-Martin's advancing age also made pushing onward more difficult. Given the conservative Catholic rule of Duplessis throughout the 1940s and '50s, outspoken unbelievers in the mould of Saint-Martin and Pilon had to retreat into their personal hidey-holes, like the rats Laurendeau's churchwarden spoke of. While there were exceptions, such as the anticlerical *Refus global* manifesto of 1948, most secret unbelievers would have to wait for two decades, when the Quiet Revolution would break many of Quebec's traditional taboos and move the province from being perhaps the most religiously observant in Canada to one of the least.[179]

7

Unbelief on the Coasts

Unbelief was also active in centres beyond Montreal, Toronto, and Winnipeg in the interwar years, although its traces are much sparser. One way we can listen for the voices of unbelievers is to examine public controversies that concern Christianity. Controversial topics open a space for unbelievers to speak up and register their categorical opposition to religion. In this way we can get a sense of their activities and their place in local society. This chapter looks at two such controversies, on opposite sides of the country, to see what they reveal about unbelief in these locations. The first took place in 1920s British Columbia around faith healing; the second related to the teaching of evolution in Nova Scotia public schools in the 1930s. We shall see that the westernmost province was more open to unbelief than any other Canadian locale. Nova Scotia, on the other hand, was relatively conservative; its unbelievers seem to have kept their criticism of religion restrained. I argue, however, that in both provinces a moderate version of Christianity was still the mainstream position of elites and the press in the face of religious conflict. Unbelievers remained marginal.

BRITISH COLUMBIA

From the time of its earliest European settlement, British Columbia has always been somewhat remarkable in its religious patterns. It shares unusually low rates of church attendance and membership with the northwestern US states of Washington and Oregon, but even in that context its levels of outright atheism and agnosticism are exceptional.[1] Records of this pattern extend back to at least 1901.

In the provincial census of that year, 1.5 per cent of the population declared themselves either as atheists or of "no religion." This may seem a very small percentage, but across Canada only 0.16 per cent of the population fell into these categories. This means that 30 per cent of Canada's census-defined unbelievers lived in a province that made up only 3 per cent of its total population.[2]

Of course, refusing to attend church or to identify oneself as part of a religious denomination is not the same thing as being part of a social movement opposing religion. One BC clergyman made this point by distinguishing between "a good deal of theoretical infidelity" and "a great deal of practical infidelity" in the province. Nor were all "theoretical" infidels necessarily militant activists. One Presbyterian missionary did, nonetheless, note the existence of "positive and aggressive infidelity" in BC.[3] The region had more than its share of militant freethinkers such as Robert Lowery and William McAdam, irreverent journalists who published newspapers in the Kootenays around the turn of the twentieth century. They openly derided Christianity for being immoral and irrational.[4]

As noted in our introduction, a fair number of pre-war socialists were forthright in denouncing religion. The Socialist Party of Canada, based in BC, espoused a militantly atheistic Marxism in the pages of the *Western Clarion* newspaper. British Columbian hard-rock miners in particular were involved in this irreligious subculture. The anarcho-syndicalist Industrial Workers of the World (the "Wobblies"), were active in BC and were also frequently critical of the churches. Other workers of a more "labourite" inclination drew upon Paine and Ingersoll to criticize Christianity as oppressive.[5]

Contemporary witnesses suggested a few explanations for BC's relative lack of piety. The most common one was that many new immigrants came to the province simply to get rich quickly, not to settle down or become part of a community. Related to this was the fact that the large majority of the white population consisted of men (70 per cent in 1911), especially young, single men, who were usually part of a rough-and-tumble working-class culture.[6] At a time when Christianity was strongly identified with feminine virtues and civilized behaviour, not to mention sexual self-restraint and temperance, missionaries made little progress among these young men. In this view, BC atheists were generally not "cultured despisers" of religion like middle-class rationalists, but were more likely hard-drinking, thoughtless scofflaws.

Lynne Marks acknowledges that this stereotype holds some truth, especially in areas with large numbers of transient American workers. But she also notes that women and married men were both more likely to reject Christianity than their counterparts in the rest of Canada.[7] One reason for this, she argues, is that migrants who had moved away from their extended families and long-time religious communities may have felt more comfortable about openly confessing their disbelief. The fact that churches and clergymen were few and far between also made a difference. Furthermore, she suggests that in a province with a large minority of Indigenous and Asian residents, whiteness and white supremacy became more of a marker of insider status and privilege than religion, enabling it to be safely discarded by some whites.[8] She also notes that patterns of religiosity varied by region within the province; miners on Vancouver Island tended to be conservative and more likely to declare as religious than miners in the Kootenays, for instance.[9]

In the interwar period, perhaps thanks to the influx of female settlers, BC seems to have become a little more religious; but it still differed from the rest of Canada. As Marks explains: "After increasing between 1901 and 1911, the percentage of British Columbians who defined themselves as atheists/agnostics or as having no religion declined to 1901 levels in 1921 [1.5 per cent] and fell a bit farther in 1931 [1.1 per cent], although remaining significantly higher than in the rest of Canada. In absolute numbers, the irreligious population remained stable between 1911 and 1931."[10]

This was the social context in which the first controversy of our account took place. In 1923 a travelling evangelist, Charles S. Price, came to Vancouver to start a revival. Local churches were quite supportive until it became evident that Price was not only preaching but also conducting highly popular faith-healing services. At this point a segment of the clergy, led by Rev. A.E. Cooke, a Congregationalist, withdrew its support, arguing that modern Christians no longer believed in that type of divine intervention. In their eyes God achieved healing through natural law and the medical profession. Many churches continued to back Price, however, and the city was divided by the debate. The dissenters assembled a committee of clergymen, doctors, university professors and a lawyer to investigate the purported healings. When its report came out almost a year later, claiming to have debunked most of the cases in question, the controversy erupted anew.

The episode has been documented in depth by historians James Opp and Robert Burkinshaw in their respective books, *The Lord for the Body* and *Pilgrims in Lotus Land*.[11] Their accounts show that the debates around faith healing took place largely in a Christian context. Liberal Protestants and some evangelicals took issue with Price's Pentecostal practices but did not quarrel with his end goal of Christian revival. Although many of Price's critics used theories of hypnosis and autosuggestion to explain away supposed healings, their responses did not extend to attacking religion as such.

The controversy did, however, give an opening for local unbelievers to speak out. One of their most strident voices was that of A. McKay Jordan, self-proclaimed president of an organization called the Canadian Secular Society (CSS).[12] In prominent advertisements taken out in local newspapers during the Price scandal, Jordan slammed religion wholesale: "The savage spends his life propitiating unseen forces. The modern scientist works for the benefit of Humanity. The savage mind is a slave to superstition. The scientific mind is strong and free in its love of Truth. Faith and belief are survivals of savage superstition – they are unproductive of good. Science is the voice by which Nature reveals her secrets."[13] Another ad proclaimed: "Science is the only power that can restore to health!" Many sufferers found themselves in a "forest of doubt" because their faith had failed them. Where faith could at best give only hope, science offered certainty.[14] One full-page ad – "FAITH! The Enemy to Progress and the Friend to Imposture" – promised to explain how the public were "humbugged and exploited," and debunked faith healing as "an advertising stunt" aimed at bolstering a dying belief in "untenable nonsense" and extracting money from "a duped and deluded public."[15]

Day after day Jordan poured rationalist rhetoric into his ads to discredit faith healing and scorn faith itself. But he had an ulterior motive. He was a self-styled "energician," who claimed to be able to heal any disease with a special scientific method he himself had invented. Life, in his view, ran on electricity, which entered the body via the eyes. Disease was caused by eye malformations and nervous system disorders that caused one to have too much or too little of this electricity. Purporting to be an expert in such disorders, he urged sufferers to consult him instead. Furthermore, he used anti-religious rhetoric to characterize most mainstream medicine as mere superstition or deliberate deception. In particular he singled out vaccination as harmful "faith-based" nonsense, and also targeted "drugging" and "medication" as nothing but lucrative scams.[16]

Unsurprisingly, Jordan found himself in trouble with medical and legal authorities on several occasions. In 1902 he was fined for "practicing surgery without being properly qualified" and in the 1920s ran afoul of new optometry laws.[17] Was he simply a con artist who used the language of scientific rationalism to fleece unsuspecting victims? There may be some truth to that interpretation, but the situation was a bit more complex. As noted, Jordan was indeed associated with a genuine freethought group, the Canadian Secular Society (CSS), which he seems to have organized himself. And for a few months it held meetings on typical rationalist topics, and enlisted the aid of Dr W.J. Curry, nicknamed the "Red Dentist," who had given freethought lectures before. In April and May of 1923 Curry spoke on evolution under the auspices of the CSS.[18]

In his role as CSS president, Jordan challenged Rev. A.E. Cooke (the opponent of faith healing mentioned above) for having given a sermon that had called unbelievers the most dangerous residents of Vancouver. Jordan accused Cooke of libelling and misrepresenting the non-religious, and invited him to explain to CSS members why, as he had claimed, they were "lower in the social scale than the bootlegger, the dope peddler, or the white slaver." He promised Cooke a cordial hearing at the Secular Society's next meeting and invited him to bring friends, up to and including his whole congregation.[19] Rather surprisingly, Cooke responded favourably, and told Jordan that he would be "very happy indeed to accept [the] courteous invitation," but he did ask for a postponement since he found himself quite busy in the next few weeks.[20] In this he was being entirely honest; Cooke was the Vancouver chair for the council of churches supporting Price's revival. Within a few days he would, as noted above, resign this position, denounce faith healing, and set loose a firestorm of controversy.

It is unclear whether Cooke ever actually appeared before the CSS, but this anecdote shows that Jordan did consider himself a secularist activist, albeit one who condemned modern medicine and promoted his own brand of (pseudo)science. His claim to be an "energician" with unique insight into disease may seem outlandish and unbecoming of a rationalist, but it appeared at a time and place when extraordinary claims were not uncommon. Jordan's ads appeared alongside newspaper articles describing Anglican Archbishop Frederick Du Vurnet's experiments in telepathy, not to mention extensive coverage of Price's faith healing.[21] Jordan's views remind us that those who rejected one type of societal authority, in this case the Christian religion, were sometimes inclined to reject other types, such as the scientific authority of the medical profession, as well. Jordan's intervention in the Price controversy illustrates the presence of an outspoken minority of unbelievers who would not hesitate to go beyond the bounds of polite discourse and express a wide-ranging critique of religion as a whole.

While Jordan's CSS only lasted a few months, its main speaker, W.J. Curry, had a longer track record as a secularist activist in Vancouver. Born in Nova Scotia in 1866, William Jameson Curry migrated to British Columbia sometime in the 1890s and established himself as a pioneering dentist. Over his career he was nicknamed "the tooth carpenter" and later "the Red Dentist."[22] As the latter name suggests, Curry was highly active in leftist politics.[23] In the first few years of the twentieth century he was part of the Socialist Party of Canada, but after he was expelled around 1910 he joined the rival Social Democratic Party of Canada. In the 1920s he moved to the Federated Labor Party, which then merged with the Canadian Labor Party (CLP). He ran for office (unsuccessfully) under the CLP banner in 1925, in the Vancouver North riding.[24] From there he moved to the Independent Labor Party (socialist), and finally to the Co-operative Commonwealth Federation (CCF) in the 1930s. Although he occasionally spoke out in defence of the Communist Party of Canada, he seems never to have joined it. In public pronouncements, however, he was very sympathetic to the Soviet Union.[25]

From about 1920 to 1927 Curry gave widely advertised antireligious lectures, typically using standard rationalist arguments but also blending in a Marxist interpretation of the economic basis and role of religion; biblical stories, he said, were immoral and religion itself mere primitive superstition, a failed attempt to understand the natural laws of the universe.[26] He also drew on Herbert Spencer and Grant Allen's explanations of religion as initiating with the imaginary ghosts of great chiefs and esteemed ancestors.[27] He argued that religion was dying but was kept artificially alive in the scientific age because it was the opium used by the ruling elites to pacify the working class.[28]

The dentist repeatedly spoke on the classical rationalist narrative of the "warfare of science and religion," invoking the "martyrs of science" such as Hypatia, Bruno, and Galileo.[29] His stance as a *socialist* rationalist came through, however, in "Communal versus Imperial Christianity," a lecture in which he laid out his case that "primitive Christianity was a move on the part of the oppressed classes of Judea to throw off the yoke of imperial Rome, and establish a religious communism." He argued that Paul, a patriotic Roman citizen, had

Figure 7.1 William J. Curry, 1925

perverted the radical message of compassion and solidarity spread by Jesus and the original apostles into an oppressive theological system, and promoted the subjection of women and slaves; that Constantine had then used it to prop up the Roman Empire and it had been an imperial institution ever since.[30]

Scientific topics were also among Curry's favourites. Like Gauvin and McCabe, he usually framed his work of popularizing science for working-class audiences in Promethean terms. About his lectures on the history of evolution, the editor of the *B.C. Federationist* enthused: "Little wonder that these great facts of life are kept from the common people! That it is 'forbidden fruit' held by the gods."[31] He brought the narrative up to the Ice Age and concluded with a quasi-Marxist lesson: "The same laws of life still prevail, and a social economic ice age for the human family is coming. In Russia it has already come ... The age for the big stomach and small brain, and also the strong back and weak head is passing. Let it go."[32] He would also draw on modern astronomy to explain the magnitude of outer space and the birth and death of impersonal worlds. The rationalist moral was that the scale of the universe revealed by science rendered Christian notions of humanity's centrality absurd.

In 1922 Curry backed evolution in a series of debates on "Creation vs. Evolution" against a local Baptist, Dr A.I. Brown. The debates were moderated by the brothers Robert and Lyle Telford, both doctors. (Lyle Telford would go on to become a successful CCF politician.)[33] Curry did not limit himself to attacking Christianity; in 1926 he took the negative side in a debate on the question "Has Astrology a Scientific Basis?"[34] He also spoke out against spiritualism on a number of occasions.[35]

As we have seen in earlier chapters, those on the left could condemn explicit atheism as an impediment to organizing workers. On occasion Curry was criticized by other leftists for turning workers away from socialism by attacking religion.[36] When he described secular socialism as a purer form of religion and morality than Christianity, on the other hand, some secularists condemned him for yielding to Christian superstition by using the language of religion in a positive way.[37]

In the 1930s Curry spoke much less on anti-religious themes than in the early and mid-1920s. In November 1932 he revived his critique of religion when discussing "Why Soviets Oppose Religion,"[38] but otherwise, from the mid-1930s forward, in response to the crisis of the Great Depression, he seems to have put his energies into political organizing and Popular Front activities. Curry's lecturing career straddled the worlds of freethought and socialist politics, a position reminiscent of Gauvin's engagement with the One Big Union and the Popular Front in Winnipeg, or Leavens's involvement with the left in Toronto. Like Leavens, Curry decided radical politics was a greater priority than rationalism, and both men ended up identifying with the CCF.[39]

In addition to Curry and Jordan's Canadian Secular Society, there were other attempts in the province to launch groups for unbelievers, although in the interwar period these were ultimately unsuccessful. The Victoria Rationalist Society, described as a branch of the Rationalist Association of England, began hosting lectures in the autumn of 1924.[40] Advertised topics were psychology, the philosophy of Omar Khayyam, and the theme of "Reason and Authority."[41] Their publicity vanishes after December 1924, however. An equally short-lived group, the Vancouver Humanist Centre, was promoted by a man named H. Stanley Kierstead in the summer and fall of 1935. Kierstead claimed to be a local representative for the International Humanist Society of New York.[42] The Centre presented lectures on Spiritualism and the Oxford Group.[43] By the summer of 1936, however, Kierstead had turned his attention elsewhere and was running a Social Credit study group.[44] Later in 1936 someone else attempted to organize a Vancouver Rationalist Association, but it does not seem to have reached the stage of advertising any events.[45]

British Columbian culture clearly had room for open expression of unbelief. But even those who were less outspoken could influence public opinion. Let us return to the controversy around Price's faith healing. A reporter named Harry Cassidy covered some of Price's services in Vancouver for the *Sun* newspaper. The fact that Cassidy was an unbeliever is revealed in letters exchanged with his fiancée, Beatrice Pearce. To her he was forthright about having lost all belief in the doctrines of the Christian church, and considered himself an agnostic.[46] And his uncertainty extended well beyond religious matters:

> Being unsettled in mind is inevitable ... when we are subjecting all of our ideas and beliefs to searching criticism – when we see religion, orthodox morality, patriotism, criterion of success, orthodox ideas on everything and anything – when we see these things, which have had something of a divine right about them during the greater part of our lives, pricked full of holes, it is not strange that we are unsettled in mind. We have lost absolute standards of right and wrong, of judgment, of evaluation, and we have not yet set up other standards in their place.[47]

Pearce sympathized, but was more ambiguous about her beliefs: "I don't mind admitting that I don't know what is what," she wrote. "I don't know if I believe if there really is a God. I'm not a Pagan – neither am I a Christian."[48]

This background doubtless influenced Cassidy's coverage of the healer's services. He confided that he thought it "pitiful" when he saw the weak and vulnerable "drinking in every word." Revulsion came over him when he reflected on the evangelist's approach. Price was, he said, "doing his work on a big business scale, using quite approved commercial methods, with efficiency as the firm's watchword." As for the alleged healings, Cassidy believed Price was simply using hypnotic techniques to bring temporary psychological relief to those who believed strongly enough. He felt sorry for the afflicted who went to be cured (among them his aunt), and he mused that Price's practices seemed "rather a mockery of everything sacred than anything else." His fellow reporter, James Butterfield of the *Vancouver Province*, was more blunt, calling the service "disgusting and degrading," referring to those who dropped to the ground when Price touched them as "a lot of damn stiffs," and commenting that not a single intelligent-looking person went up to be healed. Cassidy's outright statements were expressed in letters, and Butterfield's jibes were muttered to Cassidy at the press table;[49] nevertheless, their skepticism no doubt influenced their reporting.

The *Sun* took an openly hostile editorial stance to Price (after Cooke and other clergy had withdrawn their support), and the *Province* gave more space to the evangelist's detractors than to his supporters.[50] Despite the cynicism or unbelief of their reporters, both papers couched their critique within a broadly Christian framework. The *Sun* described Price as a "menace" for "corrupting religion," and called for Vancouver to return to a "sane and sensible Christianity."[51] When the *Province* published the report claiming to debunk Price's healings, it also printed an editorial arguing for the compatibility of modern science with true Christianity.[52] Given what Butterfield and Cassidy were saying in private, skeptical sentiments may very well have motivated the editors' opposition to Price. But there were still limits to respectable public discourse on religious matters, and so the newpapers stuck with an official espousal of a liberal Christian stance. This observation is in line with Lynne Marks's finding, mentioned above, that while interwar unbelief remained more prominent in British Columbia than in other provinces, it was not growing, either.[53] Unbelievers like Jordan and Curry were tolerated but they were still not mainstream.

NOVA SCOTIA

The social context for unbelief on Canada's east coast was rather different. According to the 1921 census, out of a population of 523,837, the Maritime province of Nova Scotia had 28 freethinkers, 20 agnostics, 7 atheists, and 555 residents claiming no religion. This contingent of skeptics represents 0.1 per cent of Nova Scotians, quite low in comparison with British Columbia's 1.5 per cent but on a par with

Ontario's 0.1 per cent in that year.[54] The census for 1931 did not give such detailed information, but in that year only 342 residents out of 512,846 said they had no religion, a mere 0.06 per cent.[55] Nevertheless, it would be a mistake to stereotype Nova Scotia with the "inherent conservatism" of the Maritimes.[56] The major Christian churches were firmly and long established in Nova Scotia, with Catholics, Presbyterians, Baptists, Anglicans, and adherents of the United Church all well represented, but this was the case for Eastern Canada more generally. In its religious makeup, the province was certainly more conservative than British Columbia, but not that much different from Ontario or Quebec.

Against that backdrop, let us look at a specific religious controversy in Nova Scotia. As we have seen, theories of biological evolution loomed large in the public consciousness in the interwar period. In the autumn of 1934 a new history textbook, *The Story of Civilization*, was introduced for Grade 11 students.[57] The passing reference to evolution on its opening page was enough to spark outrage among conservative Christians in the province. Accusations of atheism flew thick and fast. But few avowed atheists were to be found. As with the Scopes trial almost a decade earlier, the argument was less about biology than about the status of Christianity, the proper relationship between science and religion, the role of the state in education, and the rights of parents to control their children.[58]

The Story of Civilization was published by the Toronto-based Ryerson Press. The text was an entirely Canadian product; its authors, V.P. Seary and Gilbert Paterson, were Ryerson staff members and the illustrations were provided by C.V. Collins of Toronto's Royal Ontario Museum. This Canadian origin was a main reason for the text's adoption; another was the fact that it was shaped by new ideals of "progressive education" then current.[59] The passage that raised objection read: "We are also told that, just as the clumsy waggons of earlier times have developed into the swift motor cars of to-day, so man has evolved from simpler and lower animal forms, reaching far back into the early life of our world." A footnote was appended: "Many persons do not accept the findings of the scientists concerning man's origin and early history. They accept instead the account of creation given in the Book of Genesis."[60]

The textbook was not particularly radical, but it presented a broadly evolutionary view of human history. The much-discussed footnote seems to have represented the authors' attempt to acknowledge and placate anyone who objected on religious grounds to the idea that humanity had evolved from ape-like origins. The Scopes trial was still a recent memory, and opposition to evolution had become an effective rallying cry for fundamentalists across North America.[61] Regardless, writers and publishers realized that they still needed to tread lightly. Research has shown that Scopes and similar confrontations had a chilling effect on North American textbook publishers, who for the next few decades toned down or avoided discussion of evolution.[62] Seary and Paterson must have believed Canadian teens could handle the topic, but they still approached it with caution.

Public opposition to the book was spearheaded by conservative and fundamentalist clergymen from four Christian denominations: Presbyterians, Baptists, Anglicans, and Roman Catholics. It was a Presbyterian minister who initiated the controversy. Alexander A. Murray of Sydney was a strong-willed individual and no stranger to religious conflict. He had moved to Nova Scotia from the United States in late 1933, and after a few months became the minister of First Presbyterian Church, the largest in Cape Breton.[63] From this prestigious pulpit he denounced the textbook before a congregation of twelve hundred people, calling it "the worst he had ever seen." Murray started a petition directed to the premier. The lessons of the book, it complained, were "contrary to the Bible and the traditions of the Christian church," and it was an "unfair and insidious attempt to foster a pagan philosophy upon our children who have neither the opportunity nor the ability to controvert such false teaching."[64] The petition was reproduced in local newspapers, but Murray did not limit his campaign to print. He travelled from church to church across Nova Scotia, speaking against *The Story of Civilization* and rallying conservative Christians to pressure the government against it.[65]

Over the next few months the petition sparked fierce debate in the province. Reporters made the inevitable comparisons with the Scopes trial.[66] A contingent of Presbyterian ministers, a number of whom had been trained in the United States by the famous American fundamentalist theologian J. Gresham Machen, offered support.[67] They were joined by a sizable group of Baptist ministers.[68] The most outspoken of these was John J. Sidey, the leading fundamentalist Baptist in the Maritimes. He argued that evolution had no scientific basis but was simply an atheistic philosophical position.[69] Sidey's close ally J.W. Hill maintained that modernist unbelievers had conspired with atheists and communists to force anti-evolutionists out of prominent positions in churches, colleges, and universities. These unbelievers, he asserted, had based their entire worldview upon evolution and thus defended it with whatever underhanded tactics they could.[70]

Some Anglican clergy joined the fray.[71] Rev. Edward Morris of St Matthias Anglican Church in Halifax complained about the marginalization of fundamentalism and argued that the time had come when "the ravages of lawlessness, atheism and agnosticism must be halted." He wrote ominously that education leaders who promoted such evils "must be dealt with," and railed that he would not permit the province's colleges and high schools to be made into "nurseries of agnosticism, hypocrisy and atheism."[72] Such Anglicans were joined in their overt opposition to the text by a few Catholic clergy such as Bishop Alexander MacDonald, who derided the case for evolution as "a few fossilized molars and jaw-bones and skulls of uncertain age and provenance, plus imagination and the wish not to believe in the Bible."[73]

Concerned citizens also saw unbelief as the culprit behind the teaching of evolution. One local correspondent invoked rationalist agitators of an earlier era. Lewis P. Tanto wrote to the *Halifax Herald* that the whole textbook affair reminded him of the days "when Bradlaugh and Ingersoll were on the rampage, with such champions as Spurgeon, Beecher and Talmage ... defend[ing] the Holy Writ."[74] H. Percy Blanshard of Ellershouse, a frequent and impassioned writer to the *Halifax Herald*, argued that evolutionists were motivated by malice against religion. The only reason people still talked about these "phantasies" of "unrestrained imagination," he said, was that they were unbelievers. Indeed, a "clan of so-called, or self-called, scientists" were motivated solely by their desire to discredit the Bible. They were "avowed atheists" and "the only thing that was anathema to them was any thought that seemed to harmonize with the Scriptures." They were not simply mistaken, he wrote, but willfully wicked in their theorizing.[75]

Many local Christians were clearly convinced that unbelievers were out to destroy their faith and that of their children.[76] But did the atheists, agnostics, and humanists of Nova Scotia use this opportunity to take a stand and condemn religion? Not exactly. Such opponents did exist, but as the 1931 census suggested, they were few. The major newspapers did not print any broadsides against faith in general, even as advertisements. Most of the pro-textbook articles and letters – and there were many – took the liberal Christian position that open-minded religion could coexist with evolutionary science. The *Halifax Herald*'s final editorial on the textbook controversy, in January 1935, for instance, focused on the coexistence of science and religion. In its view, religion did not call for mental stagnation, and the contributions of science to human well-being had been enormous. The problem lay, rather, in "exalting science and materialism above the spiritual and the moral." Qualities like love, faith, brotherhood, and justice were as real as the laws of physics. Lincoln's abhorrence of slavery had meant more for the United States than the construction of the Union Pacific Railroad. When a materialistic humanity learned that "right is right as surely as acid is acidic," then science and religion could become not rivals but partners, and together could "redeem the race."[77] The *Herald*'s liberal position was similar to that taken by the *Vancouver Province* and the *Vancouver Sun* in the Price faith-healing controversy.

This conciliatory approach was common in contributions from moderate clergymen, teachers, professors, and ordinary Nova Scotians. Rev. E.J. Barrass used his pulpit in Truro's First Baptist Church to propose that science answered the question "How?" while religion concerned itself with "Why?" There need be no antagonism between the two; both could be "friends of man and ... allies of God." True, some interpretations of science were harshly materialistic, but other versions were entirely compatible with faith.[78] Many local United Church ministers, for their part, made a point of defending the textbook and the harmony of science with religion if both were properly understood. Rev. Dr J.S. Thomson of Pine Hill Divinity Hall in Halifax called the controversy "a sham fight on issues that are dead for all intelligent people." A modern interpretation of the process of creation was, he wrote, entirely compatible with the theory of evolution.[79] Donald C. Reid, a high school instructor in Cheverie, took a modernist view in defending the textbook in the *Halifax Herald*. He noted, tongue in cheek, that the very existence of anti-evolutionists gave evidence of humanity's animal ancestry. And he blamed obscurantist clergymen for causing the Dark Ages and for inhibiting the growth of science at every turn. He was not, however, a secularist, and wrote that it was a serious mistake to believe that science and religion needed to be at odds. He saw Christianity as "a progressive historical development still in the making."[80]

When Nova Scotia secularists did speak out, they tended to keep the scope of their criticism narrowly focused. One such was Arthur Wellesley Shatford, a hotel proprietor in his mid-seventies living in

Hubbards Cove; although he did not label himself in his contribution to the controversy, on the 1921 census he had declared himself an agnostic.[81] In his letter to the *Halifax Chronicle*, Shatford quoted a number of scientists on the centrality of evolution to modern biology. He pointed specifically to the theory of recapitulation (whereby the shapes taken by the developing human embryo are said to mimic the stages of evolution) as solid evidence for mankind's animal origins. To those whose objections to Darwinism rose from emotion rather than logic, Shatford quoted the German writer A. Wiessner: "He who finds this theory of the universe comfortless, philosophizes with wishes instead of with knowledge." He ended his letter with sound rationalist advice: cast personal feeling aside, accept only demonstrated scientific facts, and remember that "how we behave here and now is the all-important thing."[82]

A number of other Nova Scotians who took a stance in favour of *The Story of Civilization* similarly made no concessions to religion. They did not attempt to reconcile Christianity and science but made strictly secular arguments. They may well have been unbelievers, but they did not label themselves explicitly and outside evidence is lacking. One such person was eighteen-year-old Virginia Tufts of Wolfville, who sent a fiery letter to the *Herald* to reproach anti-evolutionists.[83] She was surprised, she wrote, at the emergence of "many aboriginal expressions of thought and peculiar slants of opinion that one had thought put away in antediluvian mothballs." Expanding on her point, she added: "The quarrel would seem to be with poor old science – she who provides us with light, and motive power, food and clothing and medicine." Its opponents were like a person who believed the moon was made of green cheese, in the way they closed their minds to all countervailing evidence. They based their arguments solely on the Bible, ignoring the fallible nature of the men who wrote it and overlooking biblical descriptions of the pre-scientific world as ruled by "plague, pestilence and superstition." Did such people really wish to go back to an era when whole families were wiped out by diphtheria, for example? People who believed that what was good enough for their grandfathers was good enough for them should thus return to ox-carts and candle-light.[84]

Although she did not explicitly advocate for atheism, Tufts did not give an inch to religion in her letter; neither did J.L. McDonald of River Hebert. McDonald pointed out the flaws of the "so-called" books of Moses that had been uncovered by modern Bible criticism.

Archaeology and anthropology had discovered human remains that were hundreds of thousands of years old, while the Bible's oldest narratives dated back a few thousand at most. Considering these and other arguments, it would be an injustice to both the author and the public were the textbook to be withdrawn.[85] Similarly secular objections were brought by W.P. Lawrence, a local poet and mill owner from Falmouth. He asserted that the superintendent of education and the Council of Instruction were perfectly capable of performing their duties "without advice from the proletariat." Furthermore, if churches were to decide on the orthodoxy of schoolbooks, which church was to pick the censors? History showed that Christians had never been able to agree among themselves. Lawrence also wondered how literally fundamentalists took the scripture which stated that man was made in God's image. Did they imagine God had an appendix? Anthropomorphism was a big word, he wrote, but he believed it was "a small idea and worthy of very small minds."[86] Overall, however, as noted, most who defended the textbook tried to reconcile Christianity with evolution; this handful of secular letters constituted the exception.

We have seen in other provinces that there was frequently an overlap between socialism and secularism. What was the position of the Nova Scotia left on the textbook? At least two unbelievers who intervened in the debate were local radicals: Charles MacDonald and Roscoe Fillmore. MacDonald, for many years a ship's carpenter, owned a small concrete company. He was also a self-taught artist.[87] He had become a socialist and a skeptic around 1901, after migrating to British Columbia from Scotland. He and Fillmore were neighbours and part of a small circle of leftists and freethinkers in the Annapolis Valley known as the Centreville Socialists.[88] When the Centreville group gathered, they often sang labour and socialist songs set to the tunes of popular religious hymns, in part to confound any RCMP patrols that might be passing by.[89]

MacDonald frequently published small advertisements for his company, Kentville Concrete Products. They often included radical commentary, typically only one or two sentences that involved a socialist theme. In his first ad on the evolution controversy MacDonald wrote that, unlike the college professors who had not bothered to read the textbook, "we have looked it over, and pronounce this the only 'real' history ever in the common schools. One up Science."[90] The next week he argued that education was the best preventive measure against poverty, alcoholism, crime, and war. However, because of this it had been "manipulated and worked over, by the agents of the capitalists – held taboo by press, state and church."[91]

MacDonald followed these with ads promoting history and science in general. One of his more pointed pieces read: "The Darwin theory of evolution has not been discredited, quite the contrary, it is an established fact in the minds of all persons with any pretense to general knowledge. A scientific fact does not become outmoded like a piece of machinery – or change color to match the vagaries of a passing 'Elmer Gantry.'"[92] Perhaps pleased with the effect of this statement, MacDonald repeated this same text the following week. Just after Christmas 1934 he printed an ad implying that Christians had burned the great library of Alexandria, had burned heretics and witches at the stake in the hundreds of thousands, and had opposed shortening the hours of child labour. His solution? "Study – – – EVOLUTION."[93] MacDonald finished off his run of ads intervening in the debate with one arguing that the best proof of human evolution could be found in observing humanity itself. "A hairy man in a tantrum, and an enraged ape beating his chest, certainly show closer relationship than any other animals in nature." So too did the mischievousness of children and young monkeys. One had only to look for the signs to see the truth.[94]

His friend Roscoe Fillmore also weighed in. He was a convinced atheist who had abandoned his Baptist beliefs in his youth after reading Ingersoll, Huxley, and Paine.[95] Fillmore wrote a letter to the *Halifax Chronicle* and followed it up with a column in a labour newspaper, the *Steelworker*. The letter compared the textbook debate to the Scopes trial and pointed out the unsavoury connections between Southern fundamentalists and Ku Klux Klan lynch mobs. The whole country would be laughing at Nova Scotia, he said, if the province let local fundamentalists have their way.[96] Fillmore's column, one of the first he wrote for the *Steelworker*, positioned *The Story of Civilization* as an improvement on older textbooks. To this end Fillmore savaged the "Great Man" approach to history, using a class-based critique: "In the past our children have been taught history that was a pack of lies and jingo ravings. The doings of lecherous and cut-throat kings and lords and ladies who rode on the backs of our forefathers and enslaved them were dished up as history. According to these accounts, the progress of the human family was due to accidents, mistakes, wisdom, virtues and miracles of these beings."[97] The fact that the book discussed biological evolution was a mark in its favour, said Fillmore, but more important was that it presented *social* evolution as a fact.[98] It showed that society was not static and that change was inevitable. He particularly appreciated its even-handed discussion of the Russian Revolution. Concluding that this was the best textbook Nova Scotia schools had ever seen, Fillmore urged workers to use their influence in its favour. He cautioned that they should certainly avoid signing any of the petitions against it that were being circulated by the more retrograde clergy.[99]

While we know that MacDonald and Fillmore were both unbelievers, in their public contributions to the textbook controversy they mostly refrained from taking shots directly at religion itself. Fillmore believed that explicit anti-religious propaganda was generally counter-productive for the socialist movement. In 1911 he had opined that it was best to simply ignore religion. In the Maritimes, he wrote: "Comrades are up against a different sort of worker, a priest-ridden worker. These Comrades have not catered to the church – they have simply ignored its insults and antagonism and have gone on their way pointing out the enslavement of the workers and the cure."[100]

This was not an uncommon position for leftists in Nova Scotia. Cape Breton's popular socialist leader J.B. McLachlan had been a devout Christian as a young man but personal tragedies and his adoption of more radical socialist politics led him to gradually abandon those beliefs. In 1932 he wrote poignantly in the *Nova Scotia Miner*: "We have seen a mine blow up and our comrades brought out in roasted and bloody fragments; we have seen the North End of Halifax swept with a hurricane, leaving the battered and mangled bodies of men, women and children clothed in a winding sheet of ice. We have helplessly watched the girl we loved have her lungs eaten, fade, fail and die. If these forces are guided by intelligent, infinite love, then tell us what malignant hate could do to wring and break our hearts more effectively?"[101] McLachlan had provoked controversy at least once by criticizing a local official's religious views in the *Miner*.[102] But religion was a sensitive topic in the region, and so he was usually careful to avoid stirring up conflict directly. One local supporter, Annie Whitfield, said, "He never said anything against religion; he knew when to hold his tongue." McLachlan was nevertheless frequently attacked by right-wing opponents as a godless menace and had to defend himself against the charge.[103] Another local radical union activist, Alexander MacIntyre (for a time president of the *Maritime Labour Herald*), was noted for never criticizing the churches.[104] Generally, it seems that Nova Scotia's interwar leftists' wished to avoid alienating the religious segments of the working class more than they wished to promote militant atheism.[105] Their caution was surely a survival strategy; charges that communism and socialism were inherently atheistic abounded in the Nova Scotia press in the interwar years.[106]

Thus, while there were local unbelievers willing to defend the textbook and evolution against fundamentalist attack, they were for the most part careful to avoid denouncing religion as a broader category and tended not to openly declare themselves as unbelievers in their commentary. We do not find local versions of A. McKay Jordan or W.J. Curry, even on the left. Nor are there any signs of local rationalist or humanist organizations in existence, let alone seeking to get involved in the debate.

There was, however, a famous unbeliever who did speak up on the textbook debate, although he was not from Nova Scotia. The British evolutionary biologist Julian Huxley landed in Halifax on 11 January 1935 for the first stop in a cross-Canada lecture series on "Science and Society." The grandson of Thomas Henry Huxley, "Darwin's Bulldog," and the militant unbeliever who invented the term "agnostic," Julian was himself a secular humanist. In 1927 he had written *Religion without Revelation*, arguing that a religious sensibility could be divorced from any belief in the supernatural, a viewpoint that has sometimes been termed "religious naturalism." From 1927 onward an Honorary Associate of the Rationalist Press Association, Huxley would later become president of the British Humanist Association.[107]

When asked by reporters about the local controversy around evolution, Huxley replied, incredulously, "You mean there is really serious opposition to it?" He chuckled and continued, "Why, all that was settled in England years ago. It's all taken for granted now. I'm rather surprised to learn that it is still an issue in this country." In England, he continued, "people regard science in a much broader light." They have advanced, he said, "beyond the stage of petty conflict between science and religion."[108] Huxley believed, rather, that the real threat to science came not from fundamentalists but from the modern state. He pointed in particular to Germany "where racial pride and nationalistic pride" were in direct opposition to "scientific and particularly biological teaching."[109] The biologist explained that Germany's sciences were suffering because many leading practitioners had been expelled because of their ethnicity. Huxley's public lecture, delivered a few days later, was on the topic "Science and Social Needs." Science needed to be reoriented, he urged, away from serving industry and the military and towards fulfilling the needs of a suffering humanity.[110]

For Huxley, religious conflict over evolution was passé, a waste of time and energy. This seems to have been the attitude of Nova Scotia's government as well. Despite the premier's assertions that he would look into the matter, the provincial government largely ignored the petitions it received. It kept *The Story of Civilization* in schools for the next two decades, replacing it only in 1953.[111] Given the reaction to the controversy on the part of local journalists, liberal clergymen, teachers, and politicians, we can say that a Christianized version of evolution was well entrenched among Nova Scotia's educated elites. However, opposition to it was also influential in certain elements of society. Many conservative Christians believed atheists were using evolutionary theory to combat faith, although for the most part their main opponents were also Christians, albeit of a moderate or modernist variety.

During this debate, some Nova Scotians sought to champion evolution and science over religion but, in comparison to skeptics like Jordan or Curry in British Columbia's faith-healing controversy, these east-coast unbelievers were more circumspect; rather than assail religion as a whole, they dealt with the issues at hand. Nova Scotia society seems to have had less capacity for open unbelief than the other provinces we have examined, except for Quebec. In both Nova Scotia and British Columbia, a moderate version of Christianity remained the mainstream position in matters of religious controversy. Unbelief existed and would make itself heard when conflict over religion arose, but it was still restricted to the margins.

Interwar British Columbia had atheist speakers like Curry, who lectured directly on anti-religious material in a similar manner to Winnipeg's Gauvin, Toronto's Leavens and Styles, and Montreal's Saint-Martin. Curry seemed to have no difficulty finding interested audiences. British Columbia also featured at least four short-lived attempts at creating a rationalist or humanist society, although it is unclear why these did not take root. It may have been that west coast society's relative openness to unbelief meant unbelievers had less motivation to gather. Why organize against religion when it can easily be avoided? Nova Scotia, by contrast, does not seem to have had regular rationalist speakers, and no attempts appear to have been made to create a secularist society, beyond small left-wing groups like the Centreville Socialists.[112]

Perhaps the relative strength of the churches combined with the absence of a large population centre like Toronto or Montreal meant that a critical mass of unbelievers did not gather in the province. We may recall that Marshall Gauvin grew up in nearby New Brunswick but only became exposed to freethought when he travelled to Boston to visit his siblings. Comparing BC with Nova Scotia underscores the finding that some regions of Canada were more congenial to unbelief than others. That said, there may be more to the story in both coastal provinces than the religious controversies discussed here can reveal. Deeper research on unbelief in these regions during the interwar period would be welcome.

8

Conclusion

Naturally, the beginning of the Second World War did not bring about the end of unbelief in Canada. In July 1940 a soldier at Camp Borden in Ontario wrote to Marshall Gauvin. He had been threatened with discipline if he did not go to church services on Sunday. The soldier, Cecil Wolfe, had refused to attend and planned to go on refusing every week. All the other men at the base had fallen into line. He was uncertain what to do in this situation and asked if Gauvin could offer some advice.[1] This was not an isolated case: in 1943 an RAF airman training in Canada refused to attend a religious service and received military punishment. Britain's National Secular Society (NSS) protested the decision.[2] There were no doubt other unbelieving soldiers who had no Gauvin or NSS to speak up for them.[3]

If these interactions show the continuing existence of unbelief, they also demonstrate the ongoing power of religion in interwar Canada. Insisting on compulsory chapel for soldiers was just one of the many ways that institutional Christianity maintained its hegemony during the war years. In the early 1940s concerns about wartime juvenile delinquency led schools on the Prairies and in Ontario to implement courses of religious instruction. The government of Ontario insisted that no one could possibly object, since the courses stressed widely accepted topics like "the brotherhood of all men under ... one God, charity and the golden rule." Furthermore, parents were permitted to withdraw their children if they chose. The *Canadian Forum* noted that some parents did not want their children to attend and revealed that those who withdrew often faced "mental cruelty" from classmates and teachers.[4]

The attributes of unbelief in Canadian society did gradually evolve in the postwar era, as organized unbelief adopted the language of "humanism" that had begun to emerge in the 1930s. This change was no doubt a reaction to the Cold War, which was widely seen as pitting Christian capitalism against godless communism. "Humanism," by contrast, had less explicitly political implications. The leaders and patrons of these new organizations tended to be academically educated professionals, with influential physicians and psychiatrists such as Marian Noel Sherman, Brock Chisholm, R.K. Mishra, and Henry Morgentaler at the forefront.[5] We are some distance from autodidact lecturers like Marshall Gauvin, Albert Saint-Martin, and Bert Leavens with their working-class congregations.

These contrasts help us understand the nature of interwar belief in its differing manifestations. It developed at a specific historical moment – in an era when a self-taught orator could stand up and give an educational talk to a large and receptive audience that had been brought together in part by a collective working-class identity. The associational lives of Canadian rationalist societies bear some resemblance to the nineteenth-century British secularist clubs described by Edward Royle, which were made up of mechanics and artisans. Organized unbelief was usually embedded in a broader working-class and leftwing culture, from Vancouver's "Red Dentist" and Winnipeg's One Big Union, to Montreal's independent communists and the Centreville Socialists singing radical songs to hymn tunes.

Unbelievers were not, however, part of a national movement. There is no evidence that secularist groups in Montreal, Toronto, Winnipeg, or Vancouver were even aware of each other, let alone in contact.[6] The geographical nature of Canada, an archipelago of communities separated by great distances, led to unbelievers linking up with their American counterparts rather than with each other. There were a few points of contact among Canadians. Illustrating the reach of evangelicalism, the Canadian Christian Crusade's Maud Howe battled Toronto's rationalists, visited Gauvin, and weighed in on the Nova Scotia evolution debate. Meanwhile, on the left, we find activist Rose Henderson meeting up with left-leaning religious skeptics in Vancouver, Toronto, and Montreal at various points in this period. The only equivalent among unbelievers is the British rationalist Joseph McCabe, who toured across the country and connected with Gauvin, Ernest Sterry, and others. McCabe's book on the Catholic Church was even used by Gaston Pilon in one of his anticlerical lectures.

The interwar Canadian political establishment was at best indifferent and at worst actively hostile to unbelievers. Gauvin confined his lectures to downtown theatres and was not persecuted by the state, although he was surveilled by the RCMP in the course of his left-wing Popular Front activities. As we have seen, for Sterry, Pilon, and Saint-Martin, the price of outspoken unbelief was much higher. Conservative elites in Toronto and Montreal used the legal tools at their disposal to punish skeptics severely. Canada was still, by law, a Christian country; elites believed Christendom must remain intact.

There were some within the federal Liberal Party who gestured towards giving unbelievers the rights afforded other Canadians. These included Minister of National Revenue James L. Ilsley, who permitted the *Truth Seeker* magazine to enter Canada in 1938, and Speaker for the House Rodolphe Lemieux, who in 1928 gave J.S. Woodsworth and his allies latitude to state their case against the law of blasphemous libel in the House of Commons. Lemieux declared that Parliament was "the temple of freedom of speech" and "the temple of freedom of thought." Ultimately, however, the Liberal Party was more concerned with maintaining the support of francophone Catholics, and this priority overrode any initiatives on behalf of unbelievers. Mackenzie-King's minister of justice Ernest Lapointe served as the spokesperson for Catholics in both cases mentioned. The active defence of unbelievers was usually left to socialists, communists, and progressive newspapers like the *Toronto Star*.

Unbelievers were themselves politically diverse. Sterry declared himself a Conservative, while Styles seems to have remained largely apolitical. Curry, Leavens, Jean Laing, and William Dennison all joined the democratic socialist Co-operative Commonwealth Federation (CCF). Gauvin experimented with progressive liberalism and varieties of socialism, and in the postwar period became a right-leaning anticommunist. R.B. Russell and Saint-Martin stayed active in their versions of independent Marxism, in contrast to Pilon, who moved from Saint-Martin's side to a conservative version of social Catholicism. In the interwar period Canadian unbelievers generally leaned left, but this tendency could entail liberal individualism, democratic socialism, or revolutionary Marxism. The debate over the political implications of unbelief was of course nothing new and has continued into our own time. The attitudes displayed by Gauvin, Leavens, Laing, Saint-Martin, Curry, Fillmore, and the OBU show that in Canada the freethought and socialist traditions were closer together than elsewhere. Of course, these secularist socialists were too socialist for some and too secular for others, but in their own minds the combination was a logical one.

How did interwar unbelievers fit into the religious milieu? They generally remained a marginal subculture. Modernist and moderate Christian clergymen could be remarkably harsh in their condemnation of unbelievers and of atheists in particular. It seems likely that their taking this stance helped them to protect themselves from accusations, levelled by more conservative Christians, that they themselves were closet atheists. We find Rev. A.E. Cooke in Vancouver calling the non-religious "lower in the social scale than the bootlegger, the dope peddler, or the white slaver," shortly before denouncing faith healing.[7] Rev. J.S. Bonnell of Winnipeg, a modernist, delivered a series of lectures excoriating atheism while also urging open-mindedness to science and general religious tolerance on his congregation. Unbelievers functioned as the Other, the outside referent against which all Christians could define their own credentials, whether those were liberal or conservative, Protestant or Catholic.

For conservative Christians and fundamentalists, of course, unbelievers were anathema, a threat to the Church, the family, and the nation. Historically, fundamentalism has not been considered a major feature of Canadian religious life. That assessment is likely accurate, but this study has reaffirmed that fundamentalism was present in the interwar years. We might also point to the existence of a popular conservative evangelicalism, which was not quite fundamentalist but close enough in its theology and resistance to modern science that it functioned in similar ways. In any case the fundamentalist tendency, as minor as it may have been, aroused enough controversy to provide an opening for unbelievers to get their opposing message out to ordinary Canadians. Clashes between fundamentalism and modernism, especially at the much-publicized Scopes trial, helped bring about a re-emergence of organized unbelief in the mid-1920s.

The experience of unbelievers varied from place to place across the country. In comparison with the other provinces, British Columbia was relatively open to unbelief. In Manitoba the Winnipeg Rationalist Society faced no official opposition and seems to have been tolerated as just another subculture. Nova Scotia did not see any official persecution of unbelief, but local secularists were quite cautious in how they expressed themselves, and the local left faced many accusations of godlessness. In interwar "Toronto the Good" clashes over atheism were fierce, as an evangelical Protestant elite struggled to maintain control. And in Quebec, the hostility of its "mini-Christendom" was intense, with official punishment and unofficial violence forcing outspoken unbelievers to retreat into the shadows.

We have seen that transnational links supported Canadian unbelief. One dominant strain was the British secularist and rationalist tradition. A majority of the Winnipeg Rationalist Society's members were working-class Britons, as was Sterry in Toronto. Unbelievers were not, however, simply a transplanted immigrant community. Curry, Gauvin, Leavens, and Styles were all born in Canada, as were Saint-Martin and Pilon. It is also significant that New Brunswick–born Gauvin had converted to freethought while in Boston and spent much of his early career in the United States. The Toronto rationalists were supported by American figures like Franklin Steiner and Emmanuel Haldeman-Julius. Saint-Martin and Pilon, meanwhile, do not seem to have had any direct links to the United States or Europe, but they deployed literature from the European anarchist and anticlerical traditions. There had also been a previous generation of Canadian freethinkers in the nineteenth century with their own British and American connections. A few representatives of that generation had joined the Rationalist Society of Canada. As with so much else in Canadian culture, popular unbelief was a blend of American, British, European, and local contributions.

Working-class unbelievers faced much more serious consequences for their irreligious utterances than did established authors and academics. As Grace Hunter put it in 1926, "What is merely choleric in the Colonel is blasphemous in the private."[8] This class differentiation was justified in terms of distinguishing between civil and insulting speech. The implicit assumption was that religion guaranteed public order and that aggressive infidelity among the masses would lead to chaos. Scholars and novelists were writing for a more sophisticated audience who could handle religious doubt without harmful social implications, but working-class unbelief was a much more dangerous thing.

The experiences of atheist organizations in the interwar period are relevant today at a time when many unbelievers are seeking to develop secular communities that offer the social benefits of religious congregations, minus the theology. One general lesson is that unbelief cannot be held apart from politics. Those who tried to maintain an apolitical stance found themselves limited to repeating anti-religious talking points and remained in a symbiotic, negative relationship with Christianity. The constructive question, "How should we live our lives in a godless world?" needed to be confronted, and necessarily involved political answers. During the Great Depression, that confrontation unavoidably meant grappling with the dramatic crisis of capitalism and the widespread suffering it caused. Most of the unbelievers we have discussed had some involvement with socialism or the left more broadly. However, active political commitment could also prove divisive, attract outside opposition, or lead to a loss of interest in purely irreligious activities.

The status of religion in twenty-first-century Canada is very different from what it was in the interwar period. Almost a quarter of Canadians now state that they have no religion, and many churches have closed for lack of regular attendance even among nominal adherents. The growing presence of other world religions in Canada also means Christianity is not as hegemonic as it once was. The social presence of the churches has receded in our time as well; traditional Christian assumptions around gender, sexual morality, and human nature have lost sway. And politically, Canada is no longer part of Christendom as it definitely was in the 1920s and '30s. Many beliefs that were highly controversial and marginalized among interwar unbelievers are now commonplace – even common sense – for broad segments of the Canadian population.

The vigour and tenacity of unbelief in interwar Canada speaks to the determination of unbelievers to resist the continued power of Christianity in those decades. Rationalist and anticlerical organizations were one conduit through which ordinary people heard of new ideas from philosophy, science, biblical criticism, and the study of history. Though then still a small minority, activist unbelievers already played a significant role in the gradual spread of skeptical ideas that would one day become mainstream. Despite the changed social context of today, the debates and arguments about religion that interwar Canadians engaged in can seem very familiar. From that perspective, the "New Atheism" of the early twenty-first century seems less a novelty than a revival of a long-standing tradition. Perhaps, wherever and whenever gods are worshipped and religious doctrines are expounded or imposed, some independent thinkers will always argue with, mock, and resist belief.[9] But in some times and places the price of that resistance has been high. Interwar unbelievers demonstrated considerable courage and determination in their struggle to create a godless yet more humane Canada.

Notes

CHAPTER ONE

1 Ernest Sterry, "The Jewish God," *Christian Inquirer*, no. 1, December 1926.
2 "Gauvin is Victor of J.N. Sturk in Debate." *Manitoba Free Press*, 25 February 1929, 9.
3 Salutin, *Kent Rowley*, 12.
4 See, for example, the list of recent books on unbelief compiled by the International Society for Historians of Atheism, Secularism, and Humanism: https://atheismsecularismhumanism.wordpress.com/forthcoming-books (accessed 30 November 2022).
5 Cornellisen, *Religiosity in Canada*.
6 It was possible to be a freethinking Christian who sympathized with secularist aims. Gertrude Richardson was an English suffragist who was heavily involved with the Leicester Secular Society. After moving to Manitoba, she gave up on organized religion without abandoning belief in God. Roberts, *Reconstructed World*.
7 See the Glossary in Melton, *Toward a Reasonable World*; see also the introduction to Flynn, *New Encyclopedia of Unbelief*.
8 One of the scholars who made this point most influentially was Lucien Febvre in *The Problem of Unbelief in the 16th Century*. Febvre argued that the conceptual framework and mental tools employed by contemporary atheism did not exist in the early modern period, and that any person who did hold such beliefs would have been an anomaly, one who would not have been able to communicate his or her ideas to society at large. Febvre's argument was at the time very influential, although in recent years scholars have heavily questioned and qualified his assertions. Nevertheless, his point about the historically conditioned nature of unbelief is an important one. Febvre, *Problem of Unbelief*.

9 *Schwartz, Infidel Feminism*, 23–4.
10 For a discussion of his views, see McLeod, *Religious Crisis*.
11 McLeod and Ustof, *Decline of Christendom*, 1.
12 Ibid., 5.
13 Bowen, *Christians in a Secular World*, 10.
14 McLeod, *World Christianities*, 16–17.
15 *Census of Canada*, 1971, v. 1, part 3, table 9 (Catalogue 92–724).
16 Noll, *What Happened*, 15–16.
17 The francophone story was somewhat different and will be explored in chapter 6. Royle, *Victorian Infidels*; Royle, *Radicals, Secularists and Republicans*; Budd, *Varieties of Unbelief*.
18 Royle, *Victorian Infidels*.
19 Budd, *Varieties of Unbelief*.
20 Ibid., 131.
21 Ibid., 13.
22 Ibid., 94–123.
23 Jacoby, *Freethinkers*.
24 Ibid., 150–3.
25 Ibid., 230.
26 Ibid., 232.
27 Ibid., 263.
28 See Flynn, *New Encyclopedia of Unbelief*, 43–4, 374–6; and Peris, *Storming the Heavens*.
29 See for example Gauvreau and Hubert, "Beyond Church History"; Marshall, "Canadian Historians"; Marshall, *Secularizing the Faith*; Christie and Gauvreau, *Full-Orbed Christianity*; Baum, "Catholicism and Secularization"; McKillop, *Disciplined Intelligence*.
30 One prominent approach was to adopt Hegelian idealist philosophy as a framework under which traditional theology and science could coexist. See McKillop, *Disciplined Intelligence*, chapter 6. Later, modernists within the church began to downplay doctrinal correctness and instead emphasized practical Christian ethics.
31 See, for example, Clarke, "English-Speaking Canada," 225.
32 Quoted in Phillips, *Controversialist*, 145.
33 McKay, *Reasoning Otherwise*, 251–3.
34 Fussell, *Great War*.
35 Vance, *Death So Noble*.
36 Ibid., 71.
37 Keshen, *Propaganda and Censorship*, 181–3. Canadian Methodists were particularly alarmed by reports of card-playing and loose sexual morality.

Marshall, *Secularizing the Faith*, 166–7. See also Marshall, "Khaki Has Become a Sacred Colour," 119, 123.
38 Crerar, *Padres in No Man's Land:* Marshall also discusses the Methodist chaplains and probationers who resigned or quietly abandoned the church. Most did not explain why they left, but one, Pierre van Paassen, wrote that he saw his blood-stained hands as being utterly unworthy of approaching the communion table. Marshall, *Secularizing the Faith*, 173–5, 185.
39 Quoted in Marshall, *Secularizing the Faith*, 182.
40 Crerar, *Padres in No Man's Land*, 390n130. Richard Schweitzer's survey of the British and American armies reveals a more complex situation. Schweitzer argues that while irreverence was widespread, outright atheism or agnosticism was relatively rare. See Schweitzer, *Cross and the Trenches*.
41 Crerar, *Padres in No Man's Land*, 222–7.
42 Marshall, *Secularizing the Faith*, 173. For a slightly different interpretation see Haykin and Cleary, "O God of Battles," 190–1.
43 Marshall, *Secularizing the Faith*, 177–8; Brian Clarke also argues for theological ignorance and disenchantment among veterans: Clarke, "English-Speaking Canada," 340.
44 Crerar, *Padres in No Man's Land*, chapter 8. Marshall also points to the disillusionment resulting from the discrepancy between an over-inflated optimism about a "war to end all wars" and bitter post-war realities. Marshall, *Secularizing the Faith*, chapters 6 and 7.
45 Keshen, *Propaganada and Censorship*, 153–9.
46 Ibid., 22–3. Canadian historians have long pointed out that the Protestant interpretation of the conflict shifted from its being "a just war" to being a crusade as it dragged on and casualties mounted. For recent discussions of this theme, see chapters 1, 4, 5, and 6 in Heath, *Canadian Churches*.
47 Acland, *All Else Is Folly*, 251.
48 Pedley, *Only This*, 99–100, 271.
49 Godwin, *Why Stay We Here*, 74–7.
50 Harrison, *Generals Die in Bed*, 41.
51 Ibid.
52 Coates, "War," 1189.
53 Child, *God's Sparrows*.
54 Ibid. Dan goes on to experience a moment of intense joy as he loses his soul in an all-encompassing "immortal kinship" with eternity, before he wakes and goes to fight in the book's climactic battle. He is able to retain the faith that eludes Dolughoff and Quentin, but it has moved some distance from mainstream Christianity. Marshall notes that the spirituality

and superstitions of many soldiers came to bear little resemblance to orthodox Christianity. Marshall, *Secularizing the Faith*, 173.
55 Haykin and Cleary, "O God of Battles," 186.
56 Quoted in Fletcher, "Canadian Anglicanism and Ethnicity," 145–6.
57 *Sixth Census of Canada, 1921*, vol. 1, *Population* (Ottawa: F.A. Acland, King's Printer, 1924), 572.
58 *Seventh Census of Canada 1931*, vol. 1, *Summary* (Ottawa: J.O. Patenaude, King's Printer, 1936).
59 Bibby, *Unknown Gods*, 4.
60 *Sixth Census of Canada, 1921*, vol. 1, *Population* (Ottawa: F.A. Acland, King's Printer, 1924). This gender gap will be discussed in more detail in chapter 3.
61 For recent work on "no religion" and "nones" in Canada, see Thiessen and Wilkins-Laflamme, *None of the Above*, and Thiessen, *Meaning of Sunday*.
62 *Canada Year Book, 1948–49* (Ottawa: Statistics Canada, Publications Division, 1949), 155; *Canada Year Book, 1957–58* (Ottawa: Statistics Canada, Publications Division, 1958), 137; *Seventh Census of Canada 1931*, vol. 1, *Summary* (Ottawa: J.O. Patenaude, King's Printer, 1936).
63 Clarke and Macdonald, *Leaving Christianity*, 76–9. In 1931 and 1941 "no religion" was the only option for unbelievers.
64 "Rationalist" (letter to the editor), *Regina Leader-Post*, 10 October 1951, 15.
65 Brenner, "Identity as a Determinant."
66 Clarke and Macdonald, *Leaving Christianity*, 164–5; Marks, *Infidels and the Damn Churches*, 22.
67 For examples of this type of moralizing, see Comacchio, *Dominion of Youth*, particularly chapter 6.
68 See Clarke, "English-Speaking Canada," 340. A key emblem of the new consumerism was the home radio set. "By 1931, around one-third of Canadian households, and over one-half in urban Ontario, had a receiving set of some kind." The trend continued throughout the 1930s, despite straitened economic conditions: "By the end of the Depression, the percentage of Canadian households owning a radio had jumped to seventy-five, proof that radio was fast becoming a necessity of life." Rutherford, *Making of the Canadian Media*, 80.
69 Linteau, Durocher and Robert, *Quebec: A History*, 459.
70 Fitzgerald, *This Side of Paradise*, 304.
71 Sutherland, *Monthly Epic*, 125–6.

72 Pitsula, *Keeping Canada British.*
73 Rutherford, *Making of the Canadian Media,* 75. Mary Vipond assesses the 1920s in a similar fashion: "They were years of so many fundamental changes and contradictions. It was a decade of prosperity, yet of great hardship for some; of recovery from war, but of recovery without direction or long-term goals, of a search for the re-establishment of traditional values, but of acceptance of the reality of a new world. Perhaps the most definite statement which can be made about the 1920s is that it was a decade of development, diversity, change and confusion." Mary Vipond, quoted in Betts, "Argument of the Century," 21.
74 McKillop, *Disciplined Intelligence,* 458–60.
75 Wright, *World Mission,* 10, 18.
76 Ibid., 18.
77 In his study of radical politics among pre-war Canadian Jews, Simon Belkin mentions the creation of a Yiddish language *Ratsyonale Shul,* a rationalist school aimed at children. Belkin, *Mouvement ouvrier juif,* 308.
78 Speisman, *Jews of Toronto,* 278–9.
79 See Reiter, *Future Without Hate.* Historians of Judaism and Jewish identity have argued for the existence of a uniquely Jewish secularist tradition. See Biale, *Not in the Heavens.*
80 Miller, *Shingwauk's Vision,* 343–4.
81 For an examination of the complex history of interactions between unbelief and racism, see Alexander, *Race in a Godless World.*
82 For a penetrating study of what actually happened at the trial and its larger religious and political implications, see Larson, *Summer for the Gods,* and Larson, "Scopes Trial in History," 245–64.
83 The term "fundamentalist" is used here in its historical sense to refer to the conservative Protestant movement which arose in the United States and Canada in the first three decades of the twentieth century. It sought to defend what it understood as traditional Christianity against modern thought and got its name from *The Fundamentals,* a series of books by conservative theologians. The term gradually became a pejorative one, but at the time many fundamentalists proudly referred to themselves as such and called their version of Christianity "fundamental." For the social, political, and theological reasons why opposition to the public teaching of evolution quickly became a hallmark of fundamentalism, see Marsden, *Fundamentalism and American Culture.*
84 Immediately after the trial, an enterprising Canadian, Dr Leo Frank, tried to arrange a debate between Darrow and Bryan in Charlottetown. "Still After Bryan," *Halifax Herald,* 25 July 1925, 1.

85 Schmidt, *Village Atheists*, 253–66.
86 Betts, "Argument of the Century."
87 Ibid., 50–1.
88 "Most of the papers supported this sense of [British-Canadian] exceptionalism by reporting the ridicule that was being heaped upon Dayton and the United States by British clergy, scientists and journalists." Ibid., 62. Also, Betts points out that some commentators thought the problem was America's populism: "*The Queens' Quarterly* ... noted that, in England, the controversy over evolution had been settled over two generations ago, but in an 'aristocratic atmosphere.'" "The question passed clean over the head of the wayfaring man," the journal noted approvingly, "leaving him in the mass indifferent to it. He left it to his betters." Ibid., 105.
89 Ibid., 29.
90 Ibid., 124–8.
91 Donnell would go on to debate the British rationalist lecturer Joseph McCabe in 1928.
92 McEwen, *Forge Glows Red*, 96–8.
93 Ibid.
94 Ibid.
95 Degras, *Communist International*, 38–9.
96 For examples of these differing approaches, see Kolasky, *Prophets and Proletarians*, 107–12.
97 Thompson and Seager, *Canada 1922–1939*, 161.
98 See Rifkind, *Comrades & Critics* and Doyle, *Progressive Heritage*, 61–159. Some writers, like Kenneth Leslie and Joe Wallace, combined radical politics with Christian faith. Ibid., 140–2, 147.
99 Betts, *Avant-Garde Canadian Literature*, 86–138.
100 Ibid., 120.
101 Brisson, "International Sources of Supply," 389.
102 Friskney and Gerson, "Writers and the Market," 134; Young, "Macmillan Company of Canada."
103 Sutherland, *Monthly Epic*, 114.
104 Leinwand, *1927: High Tide*, 282–3.
105 Norwood, "Elmer Gantry."
106 Rochester, "Bringing Librarianship to Rural Canada," 383.
107 Russell, *Why I Am Not a Christian*; Freud, *Zukunft einer Illusion*. The English translation came in 1928 from London's Hogarth Press.
108 Russell, *Right to Be Happy*; Lindsey and Evans, *Companionate Marriage*. In contemporary usage "companionate marriage" sometimes refers to

a marriage in which common interests and outlook bring the partners together in friendship as well as romantic love. In the 1920s and '30s, however, the phrase "companionate marriage" was used by both its supporters and its detractors to mean temporary trial marriages, which remained childless using birth control, and which could be ended through divorce if the partners did not find each other satisfactory. See "Companionate Marriage," *Oxford English Dictionary*. See also Simmons, *Making Marriage Modern*.

109 Van Doren, "Why I Am an Unbeliever."
110 Hemingway, "A Clean, Well-Lighted Place."
111 Circular, Department of Customs and Excise, 26 Jan. 1923, no. 244-C, Library and Archives Canada [hereafter LAC]. See also Fraser, "Our Hush-Hush Censorship."
112 They also tapped into concerns about "racial degeneration." Lovecraft was a vehement racist who feared that that "Anglo-Saxon" Americans would be swamped by a tide of depraved foreigners.
113 Lovecraft was a committed atheist and a materialist in his understanding of the natural world. Critical readings of the author have multiplied in recent years, and a volume of his work was published as part of the Library of America series in 2005. For two scholarly works discussing the themes mentioned above, see Joshi, "H.P. Lovecraft," and Campbell, "Cosmic Indifferentism," both in Robillard, *American Supernatural Fiction*. The two stories of inhuman ancestry mentioned are Lovecraft, "Facts Concerning the Late Arthur Jermyn," and Lovecraft, *Shadow Over Innsmouth*.
114 Gershwin, Heyward, and Gershwin, *Porgy and Bess*.
115 The law as it was written at that time is quoted in a letter from W. Stuart Edwards (Assistant to the Deputy Minister of Justice) to Irwin L. Honsberger, Ottawa, 4 November 1921, LAC, RG-13, v. 262, fol. 2106-2125 1921, letter 2116.
116 The Toronto papers do not indicate what happened to the case, which would suggest the charges were dropped. "Police Ban Sign That Boosted Book 'Knocking Religion Higher Than Kite,'" *Toronto Star*, 1 November 1921, 1; "Charge Blasphemy Against Bookseller," *Globe*, 1 November 1921, 9; "Matteo Campanile," *Globe & Mail*, 18 May 1951, 12. The case led Irwin Honsberger, an unbeliever living in Long Branch, Ontario, to send an irate letter to the Ministry of Justice. Honsberger demanded details on federal anti-blasphemy laws because, as he wrote, "I wish to protect myself against the over-zealousness of religionists to protect their Deity." Irwin L. Honsberger to the Deputy

Minister, Department of Justice, 1 November 1921, LAC, RG-13, v. 262, fol. 2106-2125 1921, letter 2115/21. Honsberger was later involved with Toronto's Rationalist Society of Canada; see chapter 5.

117 Memo to the Dept. of Justice from the Post Office Dept., 4 February 1887, R188-39-8-E, vol. 66, 1887-137, LAC.

118 For example, in 1925 the National Council of Women convinced the government to ban a number of risqué American magazines like *Saucy Stories* and *Telling Tales:* Sutherland, *Monthly Epic*, 117. In February 1931 the Head Office of the IODE wrote to the prime minister to complain of the atheistic journal *The American Freeman*, which contained expressions such as "God is the bunk," and "Is God a gambler?" *The American Freeman* was (like the *Debunker*) produced by the American freethinker Emmanuel Haldeman-Julius, whose involvement in Canadian controversies will be further explored in chapter 5. Letter from the Head Office of the Imperial Order of the Daughters of the Empire and Children of the Empire to R.B. Bennett, 12 February 1931. No. 432818, LAC.

119 In 1949 there were 505 books on the list. Fraser, "Our Hush-Hush Censorship." See also Whitaker, "Chameleon on a Changing Background."

120 "Banned Books – 1938," *Quill & Quire*, April 1939, 37.

121 The *Truth Seeker* was challenged by readers as early as 1887, although it was apparently not banned until later: Memo to the Dept. of Justice from the Post Office Dept., 4 February 1887, R188-39-8-E, vol. 66, 1887-137, LAC. For the 1895 date, see Ernest Lapointe to Mackenzie King, 7 June 1938. Mackenzie King correspondence, no. 215260, LAC.

122 "Prohibited Publications," Circular, Dept. of Customs and Excise, Canada, 4 May 1926: no. 498-6, LAC. Joseph Lewis, auhor of *The Tyranny of God*, was a prominent American atheist. Helen Jackson was a popular anti-Catholic writer and speaker who made a living speaking to conservative Protestants about the secret horrors perpetrated by the Catholic Church. See Blee, *Women of the Klan*, 89–91; Jackson, *Convent Cruelties*. It is telling that atheistic material was banned alongside religiously inspired anti-Catholic literature: the renewed ban on the *Truth Seeker* likely resulted from protests by Catholic Canadians.

123 "Canada Remains Liberal," *Truth Seeker*, 15 February 1938, 55. One of the readers who wrote to the government was Marshall J. Gauvin, the subject of chapter 3. Gauvin had also long been a contributor to the journal.

124 "Give Error Equal Liberty with Truth," *Truth Seeker*, 1 March 1938, 68.

125 Lapointe to King, 7 June 1938. No. 215260, Mackenzie King correspondence, LAC.

126 Lapointe to King, 1 July 1938. No. 215268, King correspondence, LAC.
127 Memo from E.A. Pickering to King, 29 July 1938. No. 215270, King correspondence, LAC. See also Betcherman, *Ernest Lapointe*, 243.
128 "Catholic Intolerance Rules Canadians," *Truth Seeker*, 15 September 1938, 276.

CHAPTER TWO

1 McKillop, "Apostle of Reason," 53.
2 Gray, "Canadian Anti-Christ," 140.
3 McFarlane ad, *Manitoba Free Press*, 2 March 1929, 8; "Gauvin is Victor of J.N. Sturk in Debate." *Manitoba Free Press*, 25 February 1929, 9; "Debate with Sturk." Box 18, Fol. 26, Gauvin fonds, University of Manitoba Archives; McKillop, "Apostle of Reason."
4 On the morning of the debate Rev. Gordon Burgoyne of Grace United Church gave a sermon on "The Hopelessness of Atheism." Burgoyne ad, *Manitoba Free Press*, 23 February 1929, 20; The following Sunday, Rev. Hugh McFarlane of Home Street United Church devoted his evening service to attacking Gauvin's mosquito line. McFarlane advertisement, *Manitoba Free Press*, 2 March 1929, 8. The modernist Knox United Church took aim at Sturk instead. In the evening after the debate Professor F.W. Kerr condemned "The Sin of Mis-using the Bible," with the by-line: "Are we to go to the Bible to discover the processes of Creation? How Protestants can overcome the heresy of an infallible Book." *Manitoba Free Press*, 23 February 1929, 20.
5 The first lecture drew a "capacity audience" and the second a crowd of 1,700. "Marshall J. Gauvin Speaks at the Playhouse," *OBU Bulletin*, 18 March 1926, 3; and "M.J. Gauvin at O.B.U. Forum: The Proofs of Evolution," *OBU Bulletin*, 25 March 1926, 3.
6 Gray, *Winter Years*, 196–7. The "single tax" is a reference to the economic ideas of Henry George (1839–1897).
7 The visitor was the Canadian historian A.B. McKillop, then a graduate student, who conducted a brief interview with Gauvin. McKillop, "Apostle of Reason," 54.
8 Seibel, "Atheism Succumbs to Doubt," 425.
9 The people who came to hear him will be our focus in the next chapter.
10 Gray, *Roar of the Twenties*, 221–2.
11 Winnipeg's newspapers at the time were the *Manitoba Free Press* (later the *Winnipeg Free Press*) and the *Winnipeg Tribune*.
12 See, for example: "Says Phrenology Has No Science Standing" *Manitoba Free Press*, 5 March 1928, 12; Marshall Gauvin, "Dr. Orlando Miller's

Teachings: Are They Scientific and Worth While?" Box 26, Fol. 38. Gauvin fonds.; "Gauvin Wins Over Fersen in Debate Before Large Crowd," *Manitoba Free Press*, 27 November 1930, 12. Fersen still has a following today. See "Baron Eugene Alexandrovich Fersen," at https://www.scienceofbeing.com/eugene-fersen (accessed 1 December 2022).

13 Marshall Gauvin, Lecture, "Is a College Education Worth While?" Unsurprisingly, Gauvin believed the answer was "no." Neither he nor the vast majority of his regular audience had a university education. Box 21, Fol. 21, Gauvin fonds.

14 Gray, "Canadian Anti-Christ," 139; McKillop, "Apostle of Reason," 55–6.

15 Gray, "Canadian Anti-Christ," 140.

16 In sixteenth- and seventeenth-century English, the word "humanist" referred to any scholar of the humanities. In the late eighteenth century the word "humanism" was retroactively applied to that Renaissance movement, which was interested in rediscovering and propagating ancient Greek and Roman thought and ideals. In the nineteenth century "humanism" came to be applied to anyone who was actively interested in humanity's welfare, as in the modern usage of "humanitarianism" or "humanitarian feeling." As noted above, it was mainly in the twentieth century that it was adopted by Unitarians and secularists: the former tended to mean "religious humanism" while the latter implied "secular humanism," that is, a worldview in which humanity was the measure of all things and the supernatural was excluded. See the entries "Humanism" and "Humanist" in the *Oxford English Dictionary*. See also the entry "Humanism" in Flynn, *New Encyclopedia of Unbelief*, 402–5.

17 Wilson, *Genesis of a Humanist Manifesto*. The year 1933 also saw the publication of British thinker John A. Hobson's book *Rationalism and Humanism*.

18 Gauvin correspondence, 10 June 1938, Charles Frances Potter to Marshall Gauvin. Box 9, Fol. 11, Gauvin fonds.

19 Airhart, *Church with the Soul*, 114–15.

20 See the lectures "How the Saracens Saved the World's Sanity," "Islam: The Religion of the Mohammedans," and "Mohammedanism: The Arabian Improvement on Catholicism." Box 12, Folders 16-18; "Buddhism: The Protestantism of the East," Box 12, Fol. 8; "Confucianism: The Religion of Enlightened China." Box 12, Fol. 10, Gauvin fonds.

21 Recommendations: Letter from Miss Jean Pazarem, 26 August 1929. Box 9, Fol. 11. Funeral addresses: "An Address, delivered by Marshall J. Gauvin, Lecturer for the Winnipeg Humanist Society, at the Funeral of Mrs. Rhoda Ellen Read, Wife of John W. Read, at her home, 800 Simcoe

Street, Winnipeg, Manitoba, December 14th, 1934." Box 27, Fol. 22. Or "Outline used at Mr. Dalman's funer[al], May 20th, 1936." Box 27, Fol. 39, Gauvin fonds.
22 Craig had been sentenced to eighteen months but, likely thanks to public outcry, was released after fewer than five. Resolution and correspondence in the "W.A. Craig file," Box 7, Fol. 20, as well as Gauvin's "The Craig Case and the Grave-Like Silence of the Churches," Lecture notes, Box 22, Fol. 4, Gauvin fonds. See also "Says parole should be granted Craig," *Manitoba Free Press*, 14 January 1929, 6.
23 *OBU Bulletin*, 4 March 1926, 7.
24 Carpenter, *Revive Us Again*.
25 Hindmarsh, "Winnipeg Fundamentalist Network." Furthermore, Michael Gauvreau and Nancy Christie have argued that conservative, revivalistic Protestantism held great appeal for many of Winnipeg's working people at this time. Gauvreau and Christie, "World of the Common Man."
26 For Riley's political stance see Trollinger, *God's Empire*, 74–82. For studies of the fundamentalist-modernist clash in Canada, see Rawlyk, "A.L. McCrimmon, H.P. Whidden, T.T. Shields," and Rawlyk, *Champions of the Truth*.
27 Szasz, "William B. Riley."
28 McCabe and Riley did end up debating one another three years later, in New York City. "Ideas to Clash in New York," *OBU Bulletin*, 7 February 1929, 3; "McCabe Trounces Riley in New York," *OBU Bulletin*, 14 February 1929, 1.
29 It was the wide-ranging contacts of Sidney Smith, a Winnipeg-based multi-millionaire, that brought fundamentalist celebrities such as Riley to Elim Chapel. Hindmarsh, "Winnipeg Fundamentalist Network," 307–8. Riley was merely the latest in a long line of American evangelists and revivalists who had conducted campaigns in Winnipeg. See Crouse, *Revival in the City*, 106–7, 124–5. For Gauvin's previous attacks on Riley, see Gauvin, *Heart of the Bible*. Riley would appear at a number of events sponsored by Elim Chapel. "Church News," *Manitoba Free Press*, 6 October 1928, 30; "Don't Miss Hearing Dr. W.B. Riley" *Manitoba Free Press*, 8 January 1929, 6; "Church News," *Manitoba Free Press*, 3 February 1934, 10. Gauvin retorted with lectures like "Dr. Riley at Elim Chapel: How Much of His Message Was True?" Box 11, Fol. 10, Gauvin fonds.
30 "Report of a Meeting of the Winnipeg Fundamentalist Association held in Macs Theatre at Three O'Clock Sunday January 6th, 1929." Notes made for Gauvin by one of his agents. Box 43, Fol. 30, Gauvin fonds.

31 J.N. Sturk to Marshall Gauvin, 23 January 1928 [i.e., 1929], Box 10, Fol. 9, Gauvin fonds; also "Fundamentalist Proffers Challenge to Rationalists." *Manitoba Free Press*, 26 January 1929, 26.
32 Letters to the Editor, "To Answer Statements Made Against Bible," *Manitoba Free Press*, 2 March 1929, 44.
33 "Sturk Addresses Big Gathering at Walker: Answers Questions Put by Marshall J. Gauvin at Sunday Meeting," *Manitoba Free Press*, 7 March 1929, 9.
34 Foster, *Encyclopedia of the Stone Campbell Movement*.
35 "Dr. David E. Olson to Give Two Addresses," *Manitoba Free Press*, 6 April 1929, 5.
36 "Gauvin-Olson Debates on God and the Bible 1921." Box 38, Fol. 14, Gauvin fonds.
37 "Fundamentalists Issue New Debate Challenge." *Manitoba Free Press*, 20 April 1929, 20.
38 Olson billed himself a "geologist and palaeontologist" in a church page advertisement, *Manitoba Free Press*, 6 April 1929, 8. The longer list comes from a report of a meeting at which Olson spoke, prepared for Gauvin by one of his agents. Olson was quite vague as to the source of his supposed degrees and training. See "David Eugene Olson – The Pride of Fundamentalism," as well as other notes in Box 43, Fol. 37. Gauvin fonds.
39 *Manitoba Free Press*, 4 May 1929, 34; *Manitoba Free Press*, 11 May 1929, 28.
40 "Four Thousand Hear 'Evolution' Debated," *Manitoba Free Press*, 15 October 1930, 1.
41 Russell was interviewed by Douglas Pratt in August 1961. Pratt, "William Ivens, M.A., B.D.," 59. At least three histories of the period have taken Russell's recollections at face value and mention Gauvin as a secularizing influence in its decline: Fast, "Labor Church in Winnipeg"; Gutkin and Gutkin, *Profiles in Dissent*, 86; Naylor, *Fate of Labour Socialism*, 56.
42 Gauvin recalled Ivens as a "money-grubber." Richard Swain, "Rationalism in Winnipeg: The Ideas of Marshall Gauvin," 13 July 1973. Unpublished manuscript. Box 3, Fol. 8. Ed Rea: Research Papers in Manitoba History Collection, UM Archives.
43 I agree with James Naylor's argument that the CCF of the 1930s was primarily a democratic socialist party, as opposed to the social democratic party it became in the 1940s. Naylor, "Not Reform, but the Replacing."
44 Woodsworth's religious views had by this time become quite amorphous, a blend of post-Christian humanism with nature mysticism. See the section "My Religion" in Woodsworth, *Following the Gleam*, 15–19. One of

Woodsworth's biographers argues that by 1921 Woodsworth's thought was "unabashedly secular and rationalist," and that despite a lingering penchant for Christian rhetoric, his outlook was basically that of a "free-thinking deist and humanist." Mills, *Fool for Christ*, 92.

45 All quotations in paragraph from: Marshall Gauvin, "Is Christianity Practicable? Reflections on an Address by Mr. J.S. Woodsworth." 6 November 1938. Box 30, Fol. 5, Gauvin fonds. The following year Gauvin would speak out in defence of the British Empire, defining it as largely beneficent, in his talk "Stop Backing Up: Save the Empire!" The lecture condemned Britain's appeasement of the Axis powers. Marshall Gauvin, "Stop Backing Up: Save the Empire! A New Year's Resolution for Mr. Chamberlain." 1 January 1939. Box 30, Fol. 19, Gauvin fonds. For a history of secularist attitudes to the British Empire, see Corbeil, *Empire and Progress*.

46 For example: "For the Christian religion is founded on Hell ... There can be no Christian religion apart from Hell." Marshall Gauvin, "Jesus Christ the Communist," 3, Box 21, Fol. 3, Gauvin fonds.

47 Laura Schwartz notes this same tendency among nineteenth-century rationalist feminists in England: Schwartz, *Infidel Feminism*, 144.

48 "Is Anglicanism Giving Up Christianity? An Examination of the Recent Report of the Church of England Commission on Church Doctrine," 6 February 1938, 4. Gauvin fonds.

49 Gauvin would at times hedge his bets and say that even if someone named Jesus of Nazareth once existed, he had very little to do with the miracle-worker described in scripture.

50 Even during his most pro-communist phase Gauvin usually qualified the words "Communist" and "Communism," explaining that he meant a broadly socialist approach to economic democracy. For example: "Let me say again that by 'Communism' I do not mean any political party ... By 'Communism' I mean the social achievement under which society as a whole shall own and control for the benefit of society the means of production and distribution; a society in which the welfare of the many will not be subjected to the profit-hunger of the few." Marshall Gauvin, "Has Christ an Alternative to Communism?" 31 March 1937, 1. Box 21, Fol. 6, Gauvin fonds.

51 Marshall Gauvin, "Jesus Christ the Communist." Box 21, Fol. 3, Gauvin fonds.

52 McKay, *Reasoning Otherwise*, 253.

53 Naturally this did not apply to fundamentalist preachers, who rejected the higher criticism. Marshall Gauvin, "An Appeal for Truth in Religious

Teaching." Box 11 Fol. 2. Gauvin fonds; "Marshall J. Gauvin Speaks at the Playhouse." *OBU Bulletin,* 18 March 1926, 3.

54 McKay, *Reasoning Otherwise,* 239.
55 Marshall Gauvin, "The Clergy of the United Church against Marshall J. Gauvin." Box 7, Fol. 12; "The Pulpit and the Truth – The story of clerical intolerance re our advertising." Box 7, Fol 13, Gauvin fonds.
56 Gray, "Canadian Anti-Christ," 141.
57 Marshall Gauvin, "The Clergy of the United Church against Marshall J. Gauvin." Box 7, Fol. 12, Gauvin fonds.
58 Marshall Gauvin, draft version of "An Open Letter to Rev. Prof. F.W. Kerr, Minister of Knox Church, Winnipeg, Man." [1931], Box 7, Fol. 11, Gauvin fonds. Rationalists and freethinkers had a long history of considering their beliefs to be a purified form of religion. See Schmidt, *Church of Saint Thomas Paine.*
59 It was Gauvin's wife, Bertha, who did most of the actual transcription. Notes and correspondence relating to the church page ad controversy, Box 7, Fol. 11–18, Gauvin fonds.
60 Newspaper clipping from Gauvin's file. *Manitoba Free Press Evening Bulletin*, Monday, 3 May 1926. No page number. Box 1, Fol. 27, Gauvin fonds.
61 In these sermons Kerr and Bonnell were following the lead of modernist spokesmen like American Presbyterian Harry Emerson Fosdick, known for his famous 1922 sermon "Shall the Fundamentalists Win?"
62 "If Jesus Returned Today," 27 October 1929. Box 43 Fol. 1; "Science the Ally of Religion," Box 43, Fol. 7. Gauvin fonds. Both are notes of the sermons by Gauvin's agents. On the final page of the first sermon the note-taker wrote approvingly: "To say that the refined, cultured 'old ladies' of both sexes resented some of his rather blunt statements is to put it mildly. There we[re] several occasions when you could cut the air with a knife."
63 *Manitoba Free Press,* 6 April 1929, 6.
64 Marshall Gauvin, [Letter to the editor, *Winnipeg Tribune*], 19 February 1929. Box 8, Fol. 6. Gauvin fonds.
65 Marshall Gauvin, "Is there a Nemesis of Atheism?" Box 13, Fol. 12. Gauvin fonds.
66 When Bonnell preached on "Evolution and the Problem of Sin," Gauvin responded with a point-by-point rebuttal entitled "The Superstition of Sin." *Manitoba Free Press,* 26 April 1930, 6.
67 Box 7, Fol. 18, Gauvin fonds.
68 Marshall Gauvin, "An Open Letter to Rev. Prof. F.W. Kerr." [Winnipeg: Marshall Gauvin, 1931] Box 38, Fol. 20, Gauvin fonds.

69 "Program of Lectures for January 1933." Box 7, Fol. 2. See also the letters to Bonnell in that folder; "Woman's Victory Over the Church," Box 22, Fol. 41, Gauvin fonds.
70 Eddy, *Russia To-Day*. The book had been personally sent by Eddy to Bonnell. Eddy also escorted groups of ministers and laymen, including some Canadians, to visit and observe Soviet Russia. This may be how Bonnell knew him. See Gordon, "Christian Socialist," 141.
71 Marshall Gauvin to J.S. Bonnell, draft letter. Box 7, Fol. 2, Gauvin fonds.
72 "A Humanist Looks at Dr. Bonnell and That Call to Fifth Ave. Church," 13. Undated lecture. Box 26, Fol. 3, Gauvin fonds.
73 See for example his lectures against a Rev. Waite in 1938: Box 13, Fol. 2-3, Gauvin fonds.
74 Even the local Anglican church in Gauvin's neighbourhood, St Margaret's, broadcast its services on CKY once or twice a year between 1922 and 1933. Galston, *Manifest Presence*, 39.
75 Jacoby, *Freethinkers*. Fundamentalists and other conservative Protestants were able to adapt quickly to the new medium and soon dominated the Canadian airwaves. Radio also served to privilege emotional appeals and concise sound bites over lengthy, complex discourses. See Johnston, "Early Trials of Protestant Radio." Gauvin's skills as a debater show that he could be both fiery and pithy, so he may have been able to make the transition, but he does not seem to have made an effort to get onto the radio.
76 The formal content of modernist sermons did also present a challenge. Gauvin was faced with the problem of attacking an ever-evolving opponent. As noted above, he tended to define genuine Christianity as static and fundamentalist; anything else was for him a crypto-atheism. Evidently many of those who went to hear Bonnell or Kerr felt comfortable with some degree of religious change, so even if Gauvin debunked a particular sermon, the following week's sermon might claim fresh insights. Modernism was a moving target.
77 My use of masculine terms here is drawn from Gauvin's own rhetoric.
78 Marshall Gauvin, "Socialism and Religion: Are They Really Antagonists?" Undated. Box 21, Fol. 9, Gauvin fonds.
79 Marshall Gauvin, "Is Anglicanism Giving Up Christianity? An Examination of the Recent Report of the Church of England Commission on Church Doctrine. A Lecture delivered by Marshall J. Gauvin before the Winnipeg Humanist Society at the Dominion Theatre, Winnipeg, Sunday evening, 6 February 1938," 6. Box 29, Fol. 10. Gauvin fonds.
80 Marshall Gauvin, "Tim Buck and the Challenge of the Communist Party" [3 March 1935], 13. Box 21, fol. 10, Gauvin fonds.

81 Marshall Gauvin, "The Need of Liberalism" Undated lecture. Box 20, Fol. 23, Gauvin fonds.
82 Marshall Gauvin, "Free Thought, Free Speech, Free Press," 26 December 1937. Box 20, Fol. 11, as well as a number of other lectures in Box 20, Gauvin fonds.
83 Marshall Gauvin, "The Nazi-Church Struggle in Germany," 18 December 1938. Box 30, Fol. 11, Gauvin fonds.
84 Marshall Gauvin, "The Jew: Is He a Foe or a Friend to Civilization? An Examination of Henry Ford's Campaign Against the Jews: A Gentile View." Box 22, Fol. 24. January 1922; "The Protocols Are Forgeries," Undated lecture. Box 22, Fol. 25, Gauvin fonds.
85 "Gauvin says 'Black Hole' in Jail Not So Black as Painted." *Winnipeg Free Press*, 4 April 1933, 1.
86 "Marshall J. Gauvin Says Ku Klux Klan is Menace to Freedom and Liberty," *Manitoba Free Press*, 5 November 1928, 4; Marshall Gauvin, "The Ku Klux Klan: A Power for Good or a Mischief Maker?" Box 22, Fol. 1; "Is There [a] Superior Race?" Box 22, Fol. 21, "Negroes, Jews and Reason." Box 22, Fol. 22, Gauvin fonds.
87 The ex-judge remained popular with ordinary Winnipeggers and in 1936 was elected by a landslide to the provincial legislature. See Gray, *Winter Years*, 92–5; J.N. Sturk file, Box 10, Fol. 9, Gauvin fonds, UMA; and the following *Manitoba Free Press* articles: "Winnipeg Writers Flayed by Stubbs Before Commission," 31 January 1933, 11; "Stubbs Says He Has No Regrets, even if He Must Quit Bench," 4 February 1933, 22; and "Marshall Gauvin Scores Dismissal of Judge Stubbs," 2 June 1933, 17. See also Stubbs, *Majority of One*.
88 Minutes, Winnipeg Central Labour Council Meeting, 2 March 1926, 2. Microfilm, Archives of Manitoba. In 1928 Gauvin wrote that he had come to Winnipeg "a few weeks after [he] had written to the Secretary of the O.B.U. inquiring as to the prospects offered by Winnipeg for a Rationalist Society." Thus, it is unclear who initiated contact. See Letter Box, "Also a Reply to E. Brooks," *OBU Bulletin*, 16 Feb. 1928, 3. Russell may even have previously been acquainted with the lecturer. When Gauvin was interviewed in 1973, he recalled that he had first met Russell in Moncton and that he was surprised to find him living in Winnipeg. Given the timeframe of Russell's immigration to Canada and the fact that the two had both worked in the railway industry, this is possible, although Russell would not have stayed in Moncton for very long. Richard Swain, "Rationalism in Winnipeg: The Ideas of Marshall Gauvin," 4 July 1973. Unpublished paper. Box 3, Fol. 8. Ed Rea: Research Papers in Manitoba History Collection, UMA.

89 Initial advertisements: *OBU Bulletin*, 11 March 1926; 18 March 1926, and 26 March 1926. Reviews: see for example "M.J. Gauvin Speaks at the Playhouse," *OBU Bulletin*, 18 March 1926, 3, and "M.J. Gauvin at O.B.U. Forum: The Proofs of Evolution," *OBU Bulletin*, 25 March 1926, 3.
90 Campbell, *Canadian Marxists*, 172.
91 Bimba was eventually found guilty of sedition but not of blasphemy. "Bimba Guilty of Sedition," *OBU Bulletin*, 11 March 1926, 1. See also 4 March 1926, 3.
92 Henry Myers. "'Heaven-lit Science' and Religion." *OBU Bulletin*, 29 April 1926, 4.
93 E. Rue, "The Master-Class Viewpoint of Evolution: A Sore Point with the Bosses," *OBU Bulletin*, 13 May 1926.
94 See for example Joseph McCabe, "The Social Factor in Evolution," *OBU Bulletin*, 30 September 1926, 5.
95 Ideas of universal evolution, stretching from atoms to cells, species and societies and then to the cosmos itself, were often drawn from the work of the highly influential philosopher Herbert Spencer. McKay, *Reasoning Otherwise*, 32–6.
96 The *Bulletin* did contain the rare defence of Christianity (or at least the teachings of Jesus the man) and it regularly printed advertisements for the Labor Church. (See for example the letter entitled "Jesus and the O.B.U.," *OBU Bulletin*, 12 July 1928, 3.) Nevertheless, condemnation of religion for being irredeemably oppressive and irrational was a major feature of OBU discourse up until at least 1929.
97 "Who Said the O.B.U. Does Not Function?" *OBU Bulletin*, 26 January 1928, 4.
98 Jordan, *Survival*, 226–7.
99 Minutes of One Big Union Joint Executive Board Meeting, 2 April 1927, 3. Microfilm, from collection "Russell, R.B., Material on Unions and Winnipeg Strike 1891-c1970," MG10 A14-2, Archives of Manitoba.
100 Minutes of One Big Union Joint Executive Board Meeting, 12 April 1927, 1. Microfilm, Archives of Manitoba.
101 The issue that was raised initially was the cost of printing Joseph McCabe's articles in the *Bulletin* (fifty dollars per month) but this developed into "a very lengthy discussion" about the prevalence of anti-religious articles more generally. Minutes of One Big Union Joint Executive Board Meeting, 29 October 1927, 1. Microfilm, Archives of Manitoba.
102 Minutes of One Big Union Joint Executive Board Meeting, 17 December 1927, 1. Microfilm, Archives of Manitoba.

103 Marshall Gauvin, "Labor's Reward: A Message of Hope for All Workers," 27 November, 1927. Box 21, Fol. 22, Gauvin fonds.
104 The first paragraph of the organization's statement of purpose, the "Preamble of the One Big Union," began: "Modern industrial society is divided into two classes, those who possess and do not produce, and those who produce and do not possess. Alongside this main division all other classifications fade into insignificance. Between these two classes a continual struggle takes place."
105 Letter Box, "Criticizes Gauvin's Lecture," *OBU Bulletin*, 1 December 1927, 3.
106 Letter Box, "Gauvin Replies to D. McA," *OBU Bulletin*, 8 December 1927, 3.
107 The first speaker was "Comrade Rose," the second "Comrade Davy." Minutes of the Winnipeg Central Labour Council Meeting, 6 December 1927, 2–3. Microfilm, Archives of Manitoba.
108 Rob Roy, "The Shoemaker to His Last," *OBU Bulletin*, 15 December 1927, 2.
109 "The Doctrine of Free Will," *OBU Bulletin*, 15 December 1927, 4.
110 Letter Box, "Gauvin Replies," *OBU Bulletin*, 22 December 1927, 3.
111 Minutes of the Winnipeg Central Labor Council, 27 Dec. 1927, 5. Microfilm, Archives of Manitoba.
112 "Absolute Justice: A Reply to Mr. Gauvin," *OBU Bulletin*, 29 December 1927, 4.
113 Letter Box, "To the Editor," *OBU Bulletin*, 12 January 1928, 3.
114 Eric Brooks, "The Irrational Rationalist," *OBU Bulletin*, 8 February 1928, 7.
115 Marshall Gauvin, Letter Box, "Also a reply to E. Brooks," *OBU Bulletin*, 16 February 1928, 3.
116 F. Roberts, "Morality of Social Evolution: A Reply to Mr. Gauvin at the Garric,." *OBU Bulletin*, 10 January 1929, 2.
117 Marshall Gauvin, "Morality of Social Evolution: A Reply to Mr. F. Roberts," *OBU Bulletin*, 24 January 1929, 3.
118 F. Roberts, "Mr. Gauvin on Morals and Socialism: Utopias Made to Order," *OBU Bulletin*, 31 January 1929, 3.
119 Marshall Gauvin, "Mr. Roberts as an Authority on Morals and Socialism." *OBU Bulletin*, 14 February 1929, 3.
120 In the course of arguing that capitalism was not the cause of war, Gauvin had claimed that Great Britain had legitimately been defending its subjects from German aggression in the Great War; most of his respondents condemned this line of reasoning. Letter Box, from "J.W.C."

OBU Bulletin, 21 February 1929, 3.; Letter Box, "To Mr. Gauvin" from "Worker," *OBU Bulletin*, 28 February 1929, 3; "Mr. Gauvin's Cheap Sale" from "K.M.," *OBU Bulletin*, 28 February 1929, 5; Rob Roy, "Mr. Gauvin and Socialism," *OBU Bulletin*, 21 February 1929, 1–2.

121 Frank Roberts, "Mr. Gauvin Repudiates the Class Struggle." *OBU Bulletin*, 28 February 1929, 2.

122 Lestor became editor in mid-1928, taking over from T.E. Moore, who was let go because he was not a staunch Marxist. The OBU's conflict with Gauvin began around the same time and may have been the result of a changing of the guard within the organization, as a more rigorous Marxism gained influence over its leaders. Charles Lestor, "Lestor's Corner," *OBU Bulletin*, 28 February 1929, 3. See Charles Lestor, "Lestor's Corner," *OBU Bulletin*, 12 July 1928, 3.; "Lestor's Corner," *OBU Bulletin*, 15 November 1928, 3.

123 It is unclear if the "Dr." was a typographical error, a term of respect, or a snide joke on the *Bulletin*'s part.

124 Marshall Gauvin, "Dr. Gauvin Still Repudiates the Class Struggle," *OBU Bulletin*, 7 March 1929, 2.

125 Letter Box, from "J.C.," *OBU Bulletin*, 7 March 1929, 3. The OBU had, after all, sponsored Joseph McCabe's cross-Canada tour in 1928, at significant expense.

126 Minutes, Central Labor Council Meeting, 21 March 1929, 2.

127 Minutes of the Winnipeg Central Labour Council Meeting, 21 March 1929, 3. Microfilm. Archives of Manitoba.

128 The minutes read: "Comrade Keegan then asked if we had received an answer from Gauvin in connection with the controversy which we had with him through the *Bulletin*, and Comrade Lestor explained what had happened in this connection." Minutes of the Winnipeg Central Labour Council Meeting, 16 April 1929, 4. Microfilm, Archives of Manitoba.

129 Presumably this was a secular Christmas party.

130 R.B. Russell to Marshall Gauvin, 9 December 1931; Gauvin to Russell, 16 December 1931. Box 9, Fol. 13, Gauvin fonds.

131 "Lestor's Corner," *OBU Bulletin*, 4 December 1930, 3.

132 Ibid., 26 January 1933, 3.

133 Though they kept a close and usually respectful watch on developments in Soviet Russia, the Marxists of the One Big Union loathed the Canadian Communist Party.

134 Marshall Gauvin, "The Russian Revolution," 14 October 1917. Box 25, Fol. 7, Gauvin fonds.

135 Notes by Gauvin. Box 25, Fol. 8, Gauvin fonds.

136 Marshall Gauvin, "Russia in Revolution." [1930]. Box 25, Fol. 9, Gauvin fonds.
137 As we have seen, he gave lectures such as "Jesus Christ the Communist." In 1934, as well, he had intended to use Sherwood Eddy's book to speak on the inevitability of world revolution.
138 The Popular Front was announced by the Comintern in August 1935. John Manley suggests that the Canadian party had begun some moves in that direction in the previous two years. See Manley, "Communists Love Canada!"
139 Marshall Gauvin, "Tim Buck and the Challenge of the Communist Party" [3 March 1935], 1, 4. Box 21, Fol. 10. Gauvin fonds. J.H. Gray refers to Gauvin defending Buck but then criticizing Stalin in his 1935 piece: Gray, "Canadian Anti-Christ," 140–1.
140 "Inquiring Into Riots," *Saskatoon Star-Phoenix,* 5 July 1935, 14.
141 "Only 300 Left City Stadium Before Riots," *Regina Leader-Post,* 6 July 1935, 11.
142 "Winnipeg Section of League Against War and Fascism," Kealey and Whitaker, RCMP *Security Bulletins, 1936,* 418.
143 "6" [Entry from November 1936] *R.C.M.P. Bulletins, 1936,* 489; [Entry from June 1937]: Kealey and Whitaker, *R.C.M.P. Security Bulletins, 1937,* 253.
144 "Campaign in Aid of Spanish Loyalists," Kealey and Whitaker, RCMP *Bulletins, 1937,* 308–9.
145 "The New Russian Constitution," 13 December 1936, Box 25, Fol. 10; "Russia: Humanity's Living Christ" Box 25, Fol. 11; "How the Russians Like Living in Russia," 23 April 1939, Box 25, Fol. 12. For the "Church and the Communist Challenge" series, see Box 21, Fol. 2–6, Gauvin fonds.
146 Marshall Gauvin. "Finland, the Finns and Russia." Box 31, No. 6, Gauvin fonds.
147 "Memorial Meeting for Dr. N. Bethune," *Winnipeg Tribune,* 14 December 1939; "Communists Rebuked at Memorial Meeting (Winnipeg)," RCMP *Intelligence Bulletin,* 2 January 1940, in Kealey and Whitaker, RCMP *Security Bulletins, 1939–1941,* 104.
148 Marshall Gauvin, "Just What Has Happened in Russia," [14 January 1940]. Box 25, Fol. 13, Gauvin fonds.
149 Ibid.
150 Marshall Gauvin, "Russia in Chains," undated lecture notes. Box 25, Fol. 14, Gauvin fonds. His statement reminds us of his strong reliance on books in gathering information for his lectures.

151 "Conversation Between Marshall J. Gauvin and Brian McKillop," 9 October 1969, 28, UMA.
152 Marshall Gauvin, Handwritten autobiographical notes, undated. Box 1, Fol. 3, Gauvin fonds.
153 Ibid.
154 "The Challenge of Communism—IV," undated article. Box 21, Fol. 1, Gauvin fonds.
155 "Conversation Between Marshall J. Gauvin and Brian McKillop," 23.
156 Alexander, 210–11. Smith was also the founder of the American Association for the Advancement of Atheism.
157 Gauvin's correspondence with Smith, including a lengthy letter attacking his racism, can be found in Box 10, Fol. 3–6, Gauvin fonds.
158 Noticing the similarities, the literary critic Terry Eagleton has humorously referred to the New Atheists as the "Richard Dawkins school of nineteenth-century rationalism." Eagleton, introduction to *The Gospels*, xxv.
159 Charles Lestor, "Lestor's Corner," *OBU Bulletin*, 26 January 1933, 3.

CHAPTER THREE

1 *Sixth Census of Canada, 1921*, vol. 1, Population (Ottawa: F.A. Acland, King's Printer, 1924), 573.
2 *Seventh Census of Canada, 1931*, vol. 2, Population by Areas (Ottawa: J.O. Patenaude, King's Printer, 1933), 509.
3 This informal survey was reported to the OBU Central Labor Council by a "Comrade Rose." Minutes of the Winnipeg Central Labour Council Meeting, 6 December 1927, 2–3. Microfilm, Archives of Manitoba. The name C.S. Rose appears in Gauvin's membership lists, so it is possible Rose observed this firsthand.
4 Minutes of the Winnipeg Central Labour Council Meeting, 6 December 1927, 2–3. Microfilm, Archives of Manioba.
5 Eric Brooks, "The Irrational Rationalist," *OBU Bulletin*, 8 February 1928, 7.
6 Letter from Gauvin to R.B. Russell, unsent, Box 9, Fol. 13. Gauvin fonds.
7 Gray, "Canadian Anti-Christ," 138. Gray's reference to the editors of liberal newspapers was likely aimed at someone specific, since he began working at the Winnipeg Free Press in 1935. During the church page ad controversy discussed in the previous chapter, Gauvin talked to a newspaper editor, who, according to Gray, asserted that only old women cared about church page ads. Gray, "Canadian Anti-Christ," 141. In his

autobiographical history of the Depression, *The Winter Years*, Gray also mentioned that Edward Hamilton Macklin, the manager and president of the Free Press, "hated preachers."

8   Gray, *Roar of the Twenties*, 349. Gray also appears in Gauvin's membership lists.

9   "Conversation Between Marshall J. Gauvin and Brian McKillop," 9 October 1969, 14. Box 1, Fol. 10. Ed Rea: Winnipeg Labour History Interview Collection, UMA.

10 Membership and mailing lists: Box 36, Folders 1–3. Correspondence: Boxes 6–10. Box 7, Fol. 11, Gauvin fonds, UMA.

11 I included all the unique names that appear on the lists, while eliminating obvious duplicates. Names from correspondence have been included when the writers indicated that they had attended at least one lecture or expressed strong support for Gauvin's work. Most of the letters consulted came from the 1926–40 period, although a few later ones were included because the author reminisced about attending lectures. Significantly, a number of correspondents who mentioned being regular attenders do not show up on any of Gauvin's lists, indicating the piecemeal nature of his record-keeping. Given that these sources come from different years, the resulting composite list should be seen as an approximation of Gauvin's support over the years he lectured in Winnipeg, and not a clear representation of the audience at any one moment in time.

12 A degree of caution is required in interpretation, as some of these government sources were created significantly earlier than Gauvin's lists. Facts such as marital status or profession are going to be more transitory than others such as gender, date of birth, or ethnicity. Rationalists with relatively common names (such as C. Simpson or Fred Smith) have generally been much harder to match with government sources.

13 The type of information found for each person occasionally differs, due to errors, uncertainties, and omissions in the government records.

14 A few individuals from Gauvin's lists, like Judge Lewis St. George Stubbs or the successful businessman Nathan Portnoy, were prominent enough that they have been written about in secondary sources like corporate websites or biographical dictionaries.

15 Some may have died before Gauvin's list-making began, or perhaps their social status kept them from his meetings. Others perhaps lived too far away from Winnipeg or may have found religion in the intervening years. Finally, some simply may have been averse to joining groups.

16 Gauvin frequently recorded only the first initial and last name of supporters.

17 We might ask what effect discounting the non-gendered names has on our estimates. Are A. Young, H. White, and W. Bates more likely to be male or female? It should be remembered that it is more difficult to identify women, who usually changed their last name in marriage, in sources that are one to two decades apart. More information was also discovered about men because women did not appear in the Canadian Expeditionary Force attestation papers (save for the occasional nurse). These two details suggest that it has been easier to identify men and that more women remain unidentified. On the other hand, given that "male" was usually viewed as the default public gender in this era, and that many women on the list are simply identified by their husband's name with a "Mrs." attached, such non-gendered names would seem more likely to be male. Nevertheless, some of the women identified on the 1916 census appear on Gauvin's lists with only their initials. R. Bogoch of 97 Aikens Street appears on a mailing list and as a donor. According to the 1916 census that address was occupied by Rose Bogoch and her husband, Jacob. Thus there is no easy way to allocate the non-gendered names without prejudicing the result.
18 *Sixth Census of Canada, 1921*, vol. 1, *Population* (Ottawa: F.A. Acland, King's Printer, 1924).
19 Many railway workers lived in Transcona; today it is a suburb of the city. Gauvin mailing list: Box 36, fol. 3.
20 Anyone born after the 1926 census would be omitted, and any men too young to appear in the CEF records would have been less likely to show up.
21 It should also be noted that not all the people who appear in this sample were still alive in 1935. Harvey H. Hamilton, a barrister who corresponded with Gauvin about seating arrangements at the lectures (and whose wife, Charlotte, was a dues-paying member) died in 1930 at the age of sixty-two. The same is true of people appearing on the wider list. In June 1935 John Zeemel, a thirty-two-year-old lineman for Winnipeg Hydro, was electrocuted and thrown off a hydro pole, dying from his injuries a few days later. The funeral took place at a funeral home, not in a church, though it is unclear if Gauvin officiated there. He did conduct the funeral of James Lavery, when the latter died in october 1934 at age fifty-six, and performed a memorial service for Rhoda Ellen Read in December of that same year. Hamilton: Note in Gauvin's membership list. Zeemel: "60,000 Volt Shock Hurls City Lineman 40 Feet to Ground," *Winnipeg Free Press*, 5 June 1935, 1; "Deaths," *Winnipeg Free Press*, 13 June 1935, 18; Lavery: *Winnipeg Free Press*, 27 October 1934, page number illegible. Rhoda Ellen Read was sixty-four when she died. A small

memorial booklet was produced containing her picture and the talk that Gauvin delivered at her home. Box 27, fol. 22, Gauvin fonds. For an interesting look at secularist funeral rituals, see Schmidt, *Church of Saint Thomas Paine*.

22 Letter from Gauvin to R.B. Russell, unsent, Box 9, fol. 13. Gauvin fonds.
23 The one exception might be Gauvin's daughter, Madeline. The record is unclear but it does seem that Gauvin's wife was present on occasion and so it is possible that Madeline was as well.
24 Such rituals for children had existed in nineteenth-century British secularism. Royle notes that Charles Watts (who later lived in Toronto) created a "form for the Naming of Infants in 1868." Royle, *Radicals, Secularists and Republicans*, 136.
25 Those from other European countries came from Sweden, Iceland, Finland, the Netherlands, Denmark, Austria, Italy, Poland, Romania, and Ukraine. The British colonies represented were South Africa, Australia, India, Jamaica, and the Turks & Caicos Islands.
26 Statistics Canada, Table A2-14, Population of Canada, by province, census dates, 1851 to 1976. Available at: http://www.statcan.gc.ca/pub/11-516-x/sectiona/A2_14-eng.csv (a downloadable spreadsheet; accessed 30 November 2022).
27 Canada, *Canada Year Book 1932*, Dominion Bureau of Statistics, General Statistics Branch, 103.
28 Those with European backgrounds were of Austrian, Danish, Finnish, French, Italian, Polish, Russian, Swedish, Swiss, and Ukrainian descent.
29 Most of Winnipeg's Black Canadians at that time were men working as railway porters, along with their families. See Mathieu, *North of the Color Line*.
30 "Marshall J. Gauvin Says Ku Klux Klan is Menace to Freedom and Liberty," *Manitoba Free Press*, 5 November 1928. 4. Marshal Gauvin. "The Ku Klux Klan: A Power for Good or a Mischief Maker?" Box 22, Fol. 1; "Is There [a] Superior Race?" Box 22, Fol. 21, "Negroes, Jews and Reason." Box 22, Fol. 22, Gauvin fonds.
31 To get a sense of their ethnicities, I compared distinctive surnames of Gauvin supporters not in the census with unrelated people who were. In the case of sixty surnames mentioned, the vast majority of other people with the same last name were Jewish.
32 Gray, *Winter Years*, 127; Gray, *Roar of the Twenties*, 233–6.
33 At the time, Winnipeg proper only included a few of the neighbourhoods that it does today. Many of Gauvin's supporters came from nearby areas that were then considered separate towns, like St James, St Boniface,

or Transcona. Correspondents writing from these towns to Gauvin would include its name in the return address, while those in the core of Winnipeg would simply write their street address followed by "City."

34 Both David and Louise show up in Gauvin's lists, although David was a paying member (who donated over thirty dollars) and Louise was not.
35 Such men were far from their families' influence, and single men were always less likely to be churchgoers than married men. Marks, *Infidels and the Damn Churches*, 38–9.
36 In 1916 they were listed as agnostics, while in 1921 the enumerator recorded their religion as "None."
37 On the Labour Church, which was organized by William Ivens and supported by J.S. Woodsworth, see chapter 2; and Fast, "Labor Church."
38 The "Non-conformists," "Undenominationals," and "Protestants" have been included under "other Protestant." On "non-" or "un-" denominationalism in Winnipeg, see Hindmarsh, "Winnipeg Fundamentalist Network," 305, 316–17.
39 Nation-wide, in 1921 Anglicans and Presbyterians each made up 16 per cent of the Canadian population, Methodists following at 13 per cent. *Canada Year Book, 1948–49*, 55.
40 Bramadat and Seljak, "Charting the New Terrain," 18–25.
41 See Grant, *Profusion of Spires*, 231–2; Bramadat and Seljak, "Charting the New Terrain," 9–11.
42 Clarke, "English-Speaking Canada," 276.
43 The Winnipeg Unitarian Church became, in the 1960s and '70s, a home for many religious skeptics.
44 See clippings in Box 38, Fol. 33, for letters to the editor from people who had heard Gauvin lecture but who opposed him. See also Gray, "Canadian Anti-Christ," 141.
45 Gray, *Roar of the Twenties*, 219–20.
46 The medical professionals and the lawyers could also be considered business owners, but they have been excluded from that category for the sake of clarity.
47 It may seem strange today to speculate on the religious significance of railways, but in the nineteenth century, at least, it was not uncommon for Canadians and Americans to see railways as a form of providential technology. In this view, the rails helped fulfill God's plan of spreading Christian civilization across North America. On a more abstract level, railroads, telegraphs, and other cutting-edge, world-altering technology were integral components in humanity's God-ordained mastery of nature. Technological progress helped bring the world closer to the Christian

millennium. See den Otter, *Philosophy of Railways*, 25–7. For ideas of providential technology in nineteenth-century America, see Howe, *What Hath God Wrought*.

48 Campbell, *Canadian Marxists*, 127.
49 Ibid., 169.
50 Ibid., 209.
51 Indeed, Gauvin delivered his first talk on rationalism to an audience of his fellow railway employees in Moncton.
52 Melanson and Boughton: Correspondence with Gauvin. Strachan: e-mail correspondence with her granddaughter, Mary Strachan Scriver. It is unclear how long or when precisely Strachan was a teacher.
53 According to her obituary, Gillingham trained several generations of bank managers. *Winnipeg Free Press*, 2005 obituary: http://passages.winnipegfreepress.com/passage-details/id-91947/name-Edna_Gillingham (accessed 30 November 2022).
54 Letter from Pazareno to Gauvin, dated August 1929, Box 9, Fol. 11, Gauvin fonds.
55 Perth's website, "History," http://perths.ca/about (accessed 30 November 2022).
56 Max Freed [obituary] Available at http://passages.winnipegfreepress.com/passage-details/id-170881 (accessed 30 November 2022).
57 These statistics are summarized in *Schwartz, Infidel Feminism*, 11–12.
58 With a few exceptions, such as Nathan Portnoy, Joe S. Sigurdur, and Magnus Thorarinson.
59 Dixon, plagued by ill health and domestic tragedy, had retired from politics in 1923 and worked as an insurance agent until his death in 1931. Gutkin and Gutkin, *Profiles in Dissent*, 48–50.
60 Unsent letter from Gauvin to Mr. F.J. Dixon, 27 December 1928. Box 8, Fol. 1, Gauvin fonds.
61 Sawula is described in chapter 4 of Krawchuk, *Interned Without Cause*. He appeared as a speaker alongside Gauvin at a rally protesting Nazi Germany's invasion of Czechoslovakia in 1938, and was involved in the movement for solidarity with Loyalist Spain as Gauvin was. RCMP reports reprinted in Kealey and Whitaker, *RCMP Security Bulletins, 1937*, 318; and *1938*, 289.
62 Letter from Nils-Erik Johnson to Gauvin, Box 9, Fol. 1, Gauvin fonds; "Delay in Putting Single Men Back on Relief." *Manitoba Free Press*, 12 November 1932, 10.
63 "Dr R.J. Yeo is elected South Centre C.C.F. Head," *Manitoba Free Press*, 10 January 1935, 4. "Blondahl Elected Debate Union Head," *Winnipeg*

Free Press, 17 May 1939, 2. See also "Memorable Manitobans: Robert John Yeo (1885-1951)," available at: http://www.mhs.mb.ca/docs/people/yeo_rj.shtml (accessed 30 November 2022).
64 Campbell, *Canadian Marxists*, 173.
65 Stubbs, *Majority of One*, 149–51.
66 "Conversation Between Marshall J. Gauvin and Brian McKillop," 9 October 1969, 14. Box 1, Fol. 10. Ed Rea: Winnipeg Labour History Interview Collection, UMA.
67 Royle, *Infidel Tradition*, 121.
68 Letter, 31 December 1928, Box 10, Fol. 1, Gauvin fonds.
69 I am indebted to Craig Heron for suggesting this point. Edward Royle makes a similar argument about nineteenth-century British secularism and quotes movement leader G.W. Foote, who in 1896 recalled, "Unless you went to the dram-shop or the gospel-shop, it was 'Bradlaugh or nothing' on a Sunday evening." Royle, *Radicals, Secularists and Republicans*, 330.
70 Note the similarity to controversies over pew rents in some churches.
71 For a discussion of this dynamic in British Columbia, see Marks, *Infidels and the Damn Churches*. For the situation in England, see Schwartz, *Infidel Feminism*, 15–21, 41–4. For the American scene, see Braude, "Forum: Female Experience," and Braude, "Women's History."
72 Opp, *Lord for the Body*, 205–6; Owen, *Darkened Room*; McCann, *Vanguard of the New Age*.
73 Brown, *Death of Christian Britain*.
74 Brown, *Religion and the Demographic Revolution*.
75 "Winnipeg had always been a city in ferment with the ideas wayfaring strangers dropped off, from the single tax [i.e., the ideas of Henry George] to British Israelism. In so cosmopolitan a community, everybody belonged to some minority and the differences in both thought-processes and conviction made Winnipeg's minorities volubly aggressive." Gray, *Winter Years*, 196–7.
76 Nineteenth-century British secularists had also used music to attract and entertain audiences. Royle notes that in one instance "when Alice Bradlaugh played the piano before the morning lecture at the Hall of Science in 1869, this was welcomed as a relief from 'the cold logic, or hard facts, of the lectures.'" Royle, *Radicals, Secularists and Republicans*, 137.
77 On the "Marxist masculinity" envisioned and performed by the OBU's organizers, see McCallum, "Modern Weapon for Modern Man."
78 Gauvin was taking up a common theme among rationalist and freethinkers, which stood in opposition to an influential argument put forth by evangelicals, that Christianity had done much to protect, uplift,

and honour women. This argument was an important part of the evangelical discourse surrounding women's role in upholding holy domesticity and Christian nurture. One of the most pungent critiques of this viewpoint by a freethinker was Elizabeth Cady Stanton's two-part work *The Woman's Bible* (1895–1898). For the evangelical view, see Clarke, "English-Speaking Canada," 288–90; and Cook, "Beyond the Congregation."

CHAPTER FOUR

1 "Canada Finds Editor Guilty of Blasphemy," *Miami Daily News and Metropolis*, 16 March 1927, 19.
2 "Calls Upon Pastor for Public Debate," *Toronto Star*, 19 January 1927, 9.
3 "Scandalous:" "References to Deity Called Blasphemous, Sterry is Committed," *Toronto Star*, 25 January 1927, 1. "Death blow": "Sterry Guilty Is the Verdict of the Jury," *Evening Telegram*, 15 March 1927.
4 The handful of other blasphemous libel trials in Canada all took place in Quebec, and most involved the Catholic Church being criticized by Protestants. Jeremy Patrick, "Not Dead, Just Sleeping," 220–8.
5 Some contemporary newspapers refer to it as the *Inquirer*, and others as the *Enquirer*. Sterry used the former spelling.
6 The paper offered a subscription for "12 parts complete" but just below that it also referred to "this series of 10 numbers." *Christian Inquirer*, December 1926. The only surviving version is an "Approval Copy," so Sterry may have corrected this discrepancy in his final edition.
7 *Christian Inquirer*, December 1926.
8 This piece recalls an often-quoted passage from a 1995 book by militant atheist Richard Dawkins, which begins: "During the minute that it takes me to compose this sentence, thousands of animals are being eaten alive, many others are running for their lives, whimpering with fear, others are slowly being devoured from within by rasping parasites, thousands of all kinds are dying of starvation, thirst, and disease." Dawkins, *River Out of Eden*, 132.
9 *Christian Inquirer*, December 1926.
10 Sterry's paper indicated that it would discuss Osler's thoughts on immortality and Smith's critique of the Bible. An influential physician, Osler had in 1904 delivered the Ingersoll Lecture at Harvard, later published as *Science and Immortality*. While he argued that belief in immortality had been an important asset in human history, he insisted that science knew nothing of a future life. Goldwin Smith was a British academic residing in Canada who valued religion as a bulwark against

disorder but frequently worried that modern thought had discredited Christianity. See Cook, *Regenerators*, 26–40. Sterry also offered for sale the printed copy of a debate between British rationalist Joseph McCabe and the Canadian-born creationist George McCready Price. Price's views would prove to have a immense influence on the creationist movement in the latter half of the twentieth century. See Numbers, *Creationists*, 72–101.

11 Ernest Sterry, "The Jewish God," *Christian Inquirer*, no. 1 (December 1926).
12 "Why He Doesn't Believe in 'The God of the Jews,'" *Toronto Star*, 15 March 1927, 3; "Learned to Be Atheist at His Mother's Knee."
13 Newton's first name was Aaron; he would eventually pay Sterry's bail.
14 "Arrest Atheist Editor Charge of Publishing a Blasphemous Libel." *Toronto Star*, 11 January 1927.
15 "The Information and Complaint of Inspector D. McKinney of the City of Toronto," 7 January 1927, Rex v. Ernest V. Sterry, County of York, General Sessions of the Peace, Archives of Ontario. The indictment also cited a few other lines Sterry had written: "Read your Bible if you have not done it before, and you will find in it hundreds of passages relative to the Divine Being, which any moral and honest man would be ashamed to have appended to his character."
16 Jeremy Patrick, "Canadian Blasphemy Law"; Susan Lewthwaite, "Ethelbert Lionel Cross." Both articles have their strengths and were valuable resources in the preparation of this chapter; but they also have limitations. Lewthwaite's outline of the trial, although effective, is relatively short and focuses primarily on Cross. Patrick's article is longer and includes a section dedicated to the Sterry trial, but it contains oversights; for example, it calls Ernest Sterry "Eugene," and mistakenly indicates that Sterry was ultimately deported back to England. More important, while it notes parallels with the Scopes trial and includes some press reaction, it generally lacks a broader social context and thus positions the trial as a puzzling aberration in the history of Canadian jurisprudence. In this chapter and the next I situate the trial in the context of Toronto's conservative evangelical hegemony and in the wider interwar resurgence of unbelief. I thank Dr Lewthwaite for generously sharing with me her extensive research material regarding Cross, Sterry, and the RSC in general. That sharing provided sources that were previously inaccessible, revealed material I had overlooked, and helped correct some misunderstandings I had conceived in my own research up to that point.

17 "Blasphemous Libel is Charged Against Editor of Pamphlet," *Globe*, 11 January 1927; "Arrest Atheist Editor Charge of Publishing a Blasphemous Libel"; "Editor Charged with Libelling Holy Scriptures," *Ottawa Citizen*, 11 January 1927, 1; "Toronto Editor Facing Charges of Blasphemy," *Ottawa Journal*, 11 January 1927, 1; "Commit Toronto Editor on Charge of Blasphemy," *Manitoba Free Press*, 26 January 1927, 2.

18 "Canadian Editor Charged with Blasphemy," *The Times* (London, UK), 12 January 1927, 12; "Suggest Darrow Aid Alleged Blasphemer," *New York Times*, 13 January 1927, 25; "Arrest Toronto Editor for his Gibes at Bible," *Chicago Tribune*, 12 January 1927, 2; "Blasphemy Charged to New Editor," *Los Angeles Times*, 12 January 1927, 1.

19 "Atheist," *Time* 9, no. 4 (24 January 1927), 18.

20 These articles included, among others: "Libelled Bible," *The Hutchinson News* (Kansas), 27 January 1927, 2; "Athiest!" [sic] *The Huntington Herald* (Indiana), 5; "Libelled Bible," *Ogden Standard-Examiner*, 23 January 1927, 3; "Libel on Scriptures Results in Arrest," *Portsmouth Daily Times* (Ohio), 12 January 1927; "Libelled Bible," *Santa Cruz News* (California), 24 January 1927, 9; "Atheist," *Springfield Daily News* (Missouri), 19 January 1927, 1.

21 "Learned to Be Atheist at His Mother's Knee," "Arrest Atheist Editor."

22 Rex *v.* Ernest V. Sterry, County of York, General Sessions of the Peace, March 1927, Archives of Ontario.

23 "Remand on Blasphemy Charge, Sterry Also Accused of Theft," *Evening Telegram*, 11 January 1927, 1. British rationalists of this era saw New Zealand as a welcome destination because two active freethinkers, Robert Stout and John Ballance, were elected as premier in 1884 and 1891 respectively. Corbeil, *Empire and Progress*, 132–3.

24 Ellen Maude Sterry's maiden name is found on an Ontario marriage certificate for her daughter, Mercia Gwendolyn Sterry, dated 17 August 1920. Interestingly, both Mercia (a typist) and her new husband, Frank Winton (an assistant manager) listed their religion as Anglican on the certificate. Source: Ancestry.com and Genealogical Research Library, Brampton, Ontario, Canada, *Ontario, Canada, Marriages, 1801–1928* (online database, Provo, UT: Ancestry.com Operations, 2010).

25 The family appears on a passenger list for the *Corinthian*, dated 1909. Their religion is given as Church of England. Sterry's profession is listed as "Farming" and "Storekeeper," and his intended profession is given as "Farming, etc." Ellen Maude Sterry was born in 1876. Source: Ancestry.com. *Canadian Passenger Lists, 1865–1935* (online database, Provo, UT: Ancestry.com Operations, 2010).

26 "Blasphemous Libel Is Charged Against Editor of Pamphlet."
27 "Says Darrow's Help Promised to Sterry," *Toronto Star*, 14 January 1927.
28 Application dated 10 May 1926, Rationalist Society of Canada incorporation file, Ontario Corporation Number TC37014, Ontario Ministry of Government Services, Registration Division, Companies and Personal Property Security Branch.
29 "Says Darrow's Help Promised to Sterry."
30 "Learned to Be Atheist at His Mother's Knee"; Lewthwaite, "Ethelbert Lionel Cross," 50–3.
31 "Sterry is Sentenced to Four Months' Term; Conviction on Theft Charge Also Carries Six-Months' Indeterminate," *Toronto Star*, 1 February 1927, 31.
32 "Sterry Conviction Upheld, Court Considers Language an Insult to Christianity," *Toronto Star*, 4 May 1927, 1–2.
33 For example: ads, *Toronto Star*, 19 March 1927, 27 and 22 March 1927, 22.
34 "Sterry Will Be Defended by Darrow: Colored Barrister Could Only Accept Ontario Counsel as Junior," *Evening Telegram*, 14 January 1927, 1. The thinly veiled subtext of the article, which stressed the fact that "Mr. Cross is a colored barrister," was that Cross was being too stubborn and assertive for a Black man; it implied that he should have been grateful that a prominent white lawyer was willing to take on the case.
35 "Says Offer Meant Betrayal of Client," *Toronto Star*, 15 January 1927, 15.
36 "Communists to Fight for Free Speech," *Winnipeg Tribune*, 13 January 1927. MacDonald also pointed out the contradiction inherent in the fact that "literature of the British Rationalist society can be purchased in book stores in the city" which contains "stronger statements" than Sterry had published in his paper.
37 "Would Send Darrow to Aid Blasphemy Case," *Evening Telegram*, 12 January 1927, 6.
38 "Says Darrow's Help Promised to Sterry," *Toronto Star*, 14 January 1927, 5. On 13 June the *Telegram* also reported that in Detroit a "flourishing" group of rationalists were organizing a Toronto Defence Fund and were aiming to collect $10,000 from freethinkers across the United States. "Defence Fund for Sterry Being Launched in U.S.A.," *Evening Telegram*, 13 January 1927, 1.
39 "May Ask for Darrow but Only as Junior," *Toronto Star*, 24 January 1927, 3.
40 "Darrow Not Coming," *Toronto Star*, 12 March 1927, 3.
41 "Provincial Officials Would Cancel Charter of Rationalists," *Evening Telegram*, 11 January 1927, 1.

42 The law as it was written in the 1920s is quoted in a letter from W. Stuart Edwards (assistant to the Deputy Minister of Justice) to Irwin L. Honsberger, Ottawa, 4 November 1921, LAC, RG-13, v. 262, fol. 2106-2125 1921, letter 2116.
43 "Blasphemy Charged Against Editor of 'Christian Inquirer,'" *Evening Telegram*, 11 January 1927, 18. This understanding of the law dated back to the famous Coleridge decision in 1883. See Patrick, "Not Dead, Just Sleeping," 199–200.
44 Patrick, "Canadian Blasphemy Law," 134; "Blasphemous Libel is Charged Against Editor of Pamphlet."
45 "References to Deity Called Blasphemous, Sterry is Committed," *Toronto Star*, 25 January 1927, 1. Lewthwaite makes the same point about subjectivity: Lewthwaite, "Ethelbert Lionel Cross," 57–8.
46 "Blasphemy Case Listed," *Toronto Star*, 2 March 1927, 3.
47 Correspondence quoted in Patrick, "Canadian Blasphemy Law," 138–9. The memo from Price to Bayly, his deputy, is dated 12 January 1927; the letter from Bayly to Armour 13 January; Armour's response, also 13 January. Bayly's report to Price is dated 29 January, and Price's final opinion 10 February.
48 "May Ask for Darrow but only as Junior: Rabbi Prevented by Daughter's Illness from Addressing Rationalist Meeting," *Toronto Star*, 24 January 1927. Ferdinand M. Isserman, "A Religious Teacher's View of Blasphemy," *Canadian Jewish Review*, 4 February 1927; 1, 13, and 11 February 1927, 11, 19.
49 Ibid., 4 February 1927, 13.
50 Ibid., 11 February 1927, 11, 19.
51 "Canada Finds Editor Guilty of Blasphemy."
52 Nathan M. Waldo was of Jewish descent; his father was a rabbi. In 1928 Waldo fled to the United States because he was wanted for jury-tampering. The case in question revolved around his brother-in-law, Dr Benjamin Cohen, who was charged with performing an illegal operation, likely an abortion. See "No Further Arrests in the Jury Scandal," *Toronto Star*, 1 June 1928, 1; and Lewthwaite, "Ethelbert Lionel Cross," 77n60.
53 "Sterry Puts Up a Fight Disputing Allegation of Blasphemous Libel," *Toronto Star*, 14 March 1927, 1; "Why He Doesn't Believe in 'The God of the Jews,'" *Toronto Star*, 15 March 1927, 3.
54 Ibid.
55 "References to Deity Called Blasphemous, Sterry is Committed." McKinney pointed out, accurately, that the *Inquirer* mentioned public schools as one possible location for distribution: "Didn't Intend Libel of

God, Says Cross," *Evening Telegram*, 14 March 1927, 26; *Christian Inquirer*, no. 1, 1.
56 "Sterry Puts Up a Fight Disputing Allegation of Blasphemous Libel," "Why He Doesn't Believe in 'The God of the Jews.'"
57 "References to Deity Called Blasphemous, Sterry is Committed."
58 In one sense Sterry was being honest, since he had indeed entitled the piece "The Jewish God." Nevertheless, his later identification of Baptists as the "deluded superstitionists" in question made it hard for him to claim he was only attacking Jewish ideas of God. It seems he was hoping to enlist popular Christian anti-Judaism and perhaps even antisemitism in defence of his critique. This sort of rhetoric, while not common, dated back several generations among British freethinkers. *The Oracle of Reason*, one of the earliest freethought publications, began calling the Bible "the Jew-book" in 1842, and soon began referring to the God of the Bible as the "Jew-god." See "The 'Jew-Book,'" *Oracle of Reason* no. 4, 25 (1842) and M.Q.R., [Malthus Questell Ryall], "Anatomy of Heterodoxies," *Oracle of Reason*, no. 11, 94 (1842). More ominously, a blending of rationalist criticism of Christianity with antisemitism became a hallmark of the ideology propounded by influential Nazis like Martin Bormann and Joseph Goebbels. See for example "Bormann's Circular on the Relationship of National Socialism and Christianity," reproduced in Conway, *Nazi Persecution*, 383–6.
59 No doubt the Jewish Waldo was keenly aware of the different conceptions of God which the Christian authorities were attempting to elide.
60 "Sterry Puts Up a Fight Disputing Allegation of Blasphemous Libel," "Why He Doesn't Believe in 'The God of the Jews.'"
61 Gibson had said, "Such teaching would deal a death blow to the state as a Christian state, would blot out the name of God, of Jesus Christ and everything that is sacred and dear to a Christian people." "Atheistic Society is a Menace to City, Says Dr. Gibson." *Evening Telegram*, 11 January 1927, 18.
62 "Sterry Guilty is the Verdict of the Jury," *Evening Telegram*, 15 March, 1927, 1. Gibson had said, "I do not believe in restricting free speech, but when it descends to indecency and vulgarity and attacks the very foundation of the nation as in this case, it is a different thing." "Atheistic Society is a Menace to City, Says Dr. Gibson." *Evening Telegram*, 11 January 1927, 18.
63 "Sterry Guilty is the Verdict of the Jury."
64 "Find Sterry Guilty of Blasphemous Libel," *Toronto Star*, 15 March 1927, 1.

65 "Blasphemous Libel: The King *v.* Ernest Sterry," *Canadian Bar Review*, May 1927, 365.
66 "Find Sterry Guilty of Blasphemous Libel," *Toronto Star*, 15 March 1927, 1.
67 "Canada Finds Editor Guilty of Blasphemy."
68 Were they religious Jews interested in the case because of Sterry's derogatory comments about "the God of the Jews?" Were they secular supporters of Jewish descent? Or were they a mixture of both groups, concerned that the case might lead to the prosecution of other non-Christians? The reporter did not elaborate.
69 The *Evening Telegram* gleefully reported that "Ernest V. Sterry may carry on his crusade of atheism in England if he wants to," but "he can't carry on any longer in Canada." "60 Days for Sterry; Then Deportation," *Evening Telegram*, 16 March 1927, 8. "Sixty Days for Editor, Deportation to Follow, Sentence Upon Sterry," *Toronto Star*, 16 March 1927, 1; "To Do 60 Days in Jail and To Be Deported, Sentence on Sterry," *Globe,* 17 March 1927, 13.
70 "May Deport Sterry," *Toronto Star*, 16 March 1927, 9.
71 The verdict drew much attention in the socialist Finnish-Canadian newspaper, *Vapaus*. See for example "Sterry haivattu syylliseksi jumalan pilkkaamiseen," *Vapaus*, 16 March 1927, 1; "Jumalanpilkkaaja saanut tuomion," *Vapaus*, 18 March 1927, 1; "Huomioita ja huomautuksia," *Vapaus*, 25 March 1927, 2. It was also discussed at length in the centrist Finnish-Canadian paper *Canadan Uutiset*: "Jumalanpilkka ei ole sallittu Canadassa," *Canadan Uutiset*, 21 April 1927. Oddly, neither Sterry's arrest nor conviction was mentioned in the official organ of the United Church, the *New Outlook*.
72 "Sterry Guilty of Blasphemy," *Ottawa Citizen*, 15 March 1927, 1; "Jail and Deportation for Blasphemous Libeller," *Ottawa Citizen,* 16 March 1927, 1; "Sterry Guilty: Charged with Blasphemy, He Gets Term in Prison," *Ottawa Journal*, 16 March 1927; "The Blasphemy Law," *Ottawa Journal* 28 March 1927, 6.
73 "Extremists Would Stop Prosecutions for Blasphemy," *Ottawa Citizen*, 15 March 1927, 1; "A Courageous Stand," *Ottawa Citizen*, 23 March 1927, 18. The stand referred to was that of Rev. Cameron, a Baptist who condemned the prosecution.
74 "The Blasphemy Decision," *Manitoba Free Press*, 30 March, 1927, 13.
75 "The Blasphemy Law," reprinted in the *Ottawa Journal*, 28 March 1927, 6.
76 The *Common Round*'s views are reported in "A New Vancouver Weekly," *Winnipeg Tribune*, 30 March 1927, 4. As we shall see in chapter 7, Butterfield was something of a skeptic.

77 Marshall Gauvin, "God, the Bible and Blasphemy," Box 22, Fol. 3, Marshall Gauvin fonds, UMA.
78 "Jehovah, Jupiter, Baal," *Time* 9, no. 13 (28 March 1927), 30.
79 Arthur Brisbane, "Today," *New Castle News* (Pennsylvania), 18 March 1927, 4.
80 Arthur Brisbane, "The World and the Mud Puddles: Stokes was Conservative," *New Castle News* (Pennsylvania), 6 April 1927, 4.
81 "Libeling God in Canada," *Literary Digest* 93, no. 2 (9 April 1927), 30, cited in Jeremy Patrick, "Canadian Blasphemy Law in Context."
82 "Handling of Sterry Case is Criticized in U.S. Press, Too Much Dignity Given It." *Toronto Star*, 2 April 1927, 1.
83 The letter as printed read: "I have read with interest the comments of our cousins across the way on the Sterry case which you published in Saturday's issue. I find them very significant. When people think that a man who blasphemes God ought to be left at liberty to go on doing so without any attempt at restraining him it is a sure sign that their faith is feeble and their sense of reverence greatly impaired." "Voice of the People: American Comment and Its Significance," *Toronto Star*, 6 April 1927, 6.
84 One interesting example can be found in an angry letter to the editor printed in the *Ottawa Citizen*. Alrued Brown of Pembroke condemned the prosecution and the blasphemous libel law in strong terms. He wrote: "In the intellectual world, Toronto has earned a place alongside that of Dayton, Tenn., and Ontario now ranks with Tennessee. Are there no Liberal members of the House of Commons to protest such a position?" As a matter of fact, no Liberal members did; only J.S. Woodsworth and his allies on the left protested. "The Conviction of Sterry," *Ottawa Citizen*, 1 April 1927, 13.
85 Grace H. Hunter, "The Legal Status of Christianity in Ontario: Court Decisions that Remind One of Tennessee and the Scopes Trial," *Saturday Night*, 13 February 1926, 5.
86 "Says Blasphemy Law Should Be Repealed."
87 E. George Smith, "Blasphemous Libel Law May Now Be Abolished," *Globe*, 5 April 1927, 5; "Member Would Abolish Blasphemous Libel Law," *Toronto Star*, 30 January 1928, 5; Patrick, 150–6.
88 "Would Abolish Prosecutions for Ecclesiastical Crimes," *Evening Telegram*, 15 March, 1927, 8; "Sterry is Cause of a Bill Before British Commons," *Toronto Star*, 17 March, 1927, 1. This was not the first time Lansbury had tried to do away with blasphemy legislation. See "The Existence of Blasphemy," *Literary Guide* 6, no. 360, 101.

89 "'Elmer Gantry' Constitutes a Problem for the Police," *Toronto Star*, 28 March 1927, 4.
90 "Says Blasphemy Law Should Be Repealed," *Toronto Star*, 26 March 1927. Cameron's stand provoked one of the *Globe*'s readers to ask angrily if he also supported freedom of speech for truly extreme groups like Mormons or House of David sectarians. Worse yet, "if some lewd and coarse child of liberty ... should pour out a volley of oaths upon the ears of a company of children just let loose from school," would Cameron still defend him? Quo Vadis, letter to the editor, *Globe,* 30 March 1927, 4.
91 "Emma Much Shocked by Assault on Liberty," *Toronto Star*, 19 March 1927, 3; "Miss Goldman Berates City for Cowardice," *Toronto Star,* 21 March 1927.
92 From Sterry's indictment file, 25 January 1927, Rex *v.* Ernest V. Sterry, County of York, General Sessions of the Peace, March 1927, Archives of Ontario. Newton, a British immigrant who worked in the building trade, told reporters that he had been an atheist since he was a boy, and that it was Fox's Book of Martyrs that had "set him against religion." "Remand on Blasphemy Charge, Sterry Also Accused of Theft." Newton also seems to have gone by "Andy"; see "U.S. Is Controlling Centre of Toronto's Rationalism." As noted above, Newton was the only person besides Lionel Cross to advertise in *The Christian Inquirer*. Someone of that name was active in Toronto municipal politics in the late 1930s and was probably involved with the local left; the name appears in contemporary election reporting along with Jean Laing, Joe Salsberg, Tim Buck, Stewart Smith, Rose Henderson, and other notables. The candidate's profession is listed as "contractor." See list of candidates in 1936 municipal election: [Untitled], *Globe & Mail*, 28 November 1936, 18; "Candidates for Alderman," *Globe & Mail*, 22 December 1938, 7.
93 Letter to the editor, E. Lionel Cross, "In Fairness to the Rationalist Society," *Toronto Star,* 22 March 1927, 6.
94 Ads asking for donations, 1927 *Toronto Star*: 19 March, 27; 21 March, 35; 22 March, 22; 23 March, 23.
95 The *Star* lists Chief Justices Latchford, Orde, Riddell, and Middleton, but does not name the fifth judge.
96 "Sterry Conviction Upheld, Court Considers Language an Insult to Christianity," *Toronto Star*, 4 May 1927, 1–2; "Appeal by E.V. Sterry is Dismissed by Court," *Globe,* 5 May 1927.
97 F.J. Moore, "The Blasphemy Law," *Canadian Forum* 7, no. 81 (June 1927), 265.

98 "Cross Sees Sterry in the Reformatory," *Toronto Star*, 28 September 1927, 3.
99 As noted in chapter 2, Woodsworth's religious views were by this point mostly humanistic, though with a Christian tinge.
100 McNaught, *Prophet in Politics*, 135–6.
101 Woodsworth, James Shaver fonds, MG 27 III C7, vol. 5, "Blasphemy," n.d., 1928, LAC.
102 Later in the debate, Conservative MP William G. Ernst rose to point out that a standard work on Canadian law, *Crankshaw's Criminal Code*, did in fact clarify what was meant by blasphemous libel. He quoted, in part: "A blasphemous libel consists in the publication of any profane words vilifying or ridiculing God, Jesus Christ, the Holy Ghost, the Old or New Testament or Christianity in general, with intent to shock and insult believers, or to pervert or mislead the ignorant and unwary." The section in question went on to distinguish between publications that used offensive language and which treated sacred subjects with abuse and "levity," as opposed to the "honest and temperate" expression of religious opinions. *House of Commons Debates*, vol. 1, 1928 (10 February 1928), 367.
103 *Debates*, 362.
104 Ibid., 364.
105 As Jeremy Patrick points out, an internal memo to the minister had advised him of this flaw and suggested a better wording for Woodsworth's bill. Rather than pass the information on, however, Lapointe seems to have saved it for use in scuttling Woodsworth's legislation. Patrick, "Canadian Blasphemy Law," 153.
106 *Debates*, 364.
107 He was previously mayor of Toronto from 1910–12. See the Parliament of Canada website, "The Hon. George Reginald Geary, P.C., K.C., O.B.E., M.C." https://lop.parl.ca/sites/ParlInfo/default/en_CA/People/Profile?personId=9480 (accessed 30 November 2022).
108 "Commons Defeats Proposed Revision in Blasphemy Law," *Globe*, 11 February 1928, 3.
109 Ibid.
110 *Debates*, 365.
111 Ibid., 366.
112 Ibid.
113 Ibid., 367.
114 Ibid.

115 Ibid.; "Commons Defeats Proposed Revision in Blasphemy Law," *Globe*, 11 February 1928. George Lansbury's bill met the same fate in Britain. See Nash, *Blasphemy in the Christian World*, 179.
116 "Commons Defeats Proposed Revision in Blasphemy Law," *Globe*, 11 February 1928.
117 "Mr. Woodsworth on Blasphemy," *Montreal Gazette*, 6 April 1927, 12.
118 "Differ on Irwin's Criticism of Old Testament Jehovah," *Toronto Star*, 17 April 1927, 3.
119 Ibid. The other clergymen asked to comment, Rabbi Isserman and Rev. E. Crossley Hunter (a United Church minister and sometime correspondent of Marshall Gauvin) regretted Irwin's brash language but supported his basic contention that God's moral character evolved throughout the Bible.
120 W.G. MacKendrick, "Control This Blasphemy," *Globe*, 21 April 1928, 4. G.B. Oliver, a frequent critic of modernism in the *Globe*, made much the same point, writing: "Some little time ago in this city the editor of an obscure rationalist paper was sentenced to six months' imprisonment for statements of a similar trend, but couched in terms moderate in character as compared with those made by the learned professor, who does not scruple to denounce Almighty God, the Author and Preserver of his very existence, as a liar and the approver of lying in others, and as guilty of moral turpitude." Oliver went on to say that his suggestion was not vindictive; rather, the description Judge Coatsworth had given of blasphemy applied precisely, in fact, "with additional force" to Irwin's comments. G.B. Oliver, "Professor Irwin and Blasphemy," *Globe*, 19 April 1928, 4. MacKendrick was also backed by H.W. Clarke, who opined that Irwin's unpunished blasphemy was a sign of the End Times. H.W. Clarke, "Protest Against Modernism," *Globe*, 27 April 1928, 4.
121 Irwin eventually wrote letters to the *Globe* and the *Star* arguing that his remarks about God's dishonesty had been taken out of context: W.A. Irwin, "Professor Irwin Explains," *Globe*, 3 May 1928. On Irwin's other provocations, see Moir, *History of Biblical Studies*, 62–3.
122 "McCabe Meeting Ends in Disorder," *Globe*, 15 October 1928.
123 "Communist Leader to Run for Board," *Toronto Star*, 9 February 1929, 23.
124 "Ghosts Suspected Among Penn Relics," *Toronto Star*, 10 February 1930, 1; Ad, *Toronto Star*, 24 November 1933, 36; Ad, *Toronto Star*, 19 February 1938, 32.
125 "Misery Caused Poor People by Callous System – Duncan," *Toronto Star*, 26 August 1941, 2.

CHAPTER FIVE

1 "Say Police Encouraged Heckler's Disturbance," *Toronto Star*, 7 May 1929, 3.
2 E. Lionel Cross, "Voice of the People: Rationalists' Meetings," *Toronto Star*, 3 August 1929, 4.
3 Royle, *Radicals, Secularists and Republicans*, 81.
4 Cook, *Regenerators*, 58.
5 Ibid., 53.
6 See Hawke, *Underwood-Marples Debate*.
7 Cook, *Regenerators*, 52.
8 The situation may have been similar to that in England and the United States, where an older generation of secularists was dying off or retiring. Schmidt, *Village Atheists*, 251–2; Royle, *Radicals, Secularists and Republicans*, 328–34.
9 *Sixth Census of Canada, 1921*, vol. 1, Population (Ottawa: F.A. Acland, King's Printer, 1924) 573. *Seventh Census of Canada, 1931*, vol. 2, Population by Areas (Ottawa: J.O. Patenaude, King's Printer, 1933), 509.
10 Rationalist Society letterhead would later state that the group was "organized Sep. 1st 1925." Letter from B.E. Leavens to F.V. Johns, 1 January 1938, included in Rationalist Society of Canada incorporation file, Ontario Corporation Number TC37014, Ontario Ministry of Government Services, Registration Division, Companies and Personal Property Security Branch. Records for the Rationalist Society of Canada (RSC) are sparse compared to those of the Winnipeg Rationalist Society. No archival collection for the group appears to have survived, aside from their legal incorporation papers and one pamphlet. For the most part information about them is drawn from Toronto's newspapers. Fortunately for the researcher, the members of the RSC found themselves at the centre of several highly publicized controversies, and they were very diligent about advertising their lectures. All of this generated a significant record in local papers. As mentioned in the previous chapter, a broad variety of material was also obtained thanks to Dr Susan Lewthwaite, who generously shared the results of her own preliminary but extensive research on the RSC.
11 Keeping in mind that this statement was a compromise version intended to camouflage the rationalists, there are a few interesting details to note. The idea of finding one's place in the "Body Social" is likely drawn from the thought of Herbert Spencer, who argued that society could be viewed as one enormous organism. "Natural Law" is a concept with an enormously complex pedigree, but in this context it was probably

intended to contrast with a morality based on supernatural laws or commands. Mentioning "this Great Canada of ours" was no doubt intended to express patriotism in the face of opponents who would try to dismiss the rationalists as foreign agitators.

12 RSC incorporation file, application dated 10 May 1926.
13 "Provincial Officials Would Cancel Charter of Rationalists," *Toronto Evening Telegram*, 11 January 1927, 1; RSC incorporation file; "Learned to Be Atheist at His Mother's Knee," *Toronto Star*, 12 January 1927, 34; "Arrest Atheist Editor Charge of Publishing a Blasphemous Libel," 11 January 1927, *Toronto Star*, 1.
14 It is tempting to speculate that a visit from Joseph McCabe precipitated the formation of the Toronto group, as it did in Winnipeg. McCabe's visit to Winnipeg in 1926, however, was not part of a Canadian tour but rather an extension of his American trip. He seems to have travelled up from Minneapolis, and then returned to the United States and moved on to the West Coast. The *Globe* and the *Toronto Star* make no mention of him stopping in Toronto in 1926, and neither does his biography. Cooke, *Rebel to His Last Breath*, 50–2. Advertising for his Winnipeg appearance also claims it to be his first appearance in Canada: Ad, *Manitoba Free Press*, 9 January 1926, 19.
15 Schmidt, *Village Atheists*, 253–66.
16 "Says Atheism Covers Canada," *Halifax Evening Mail*, 25 May 1926, 7.
17 "Hooting at the Sun," *Globe*, 12 June 1926, 18. This fear was likely inspired by the 4A's campaigns among college youth. Schmidt, *Village Atheists*, 254–5.
18 E. Lionel Cross, "The Rationalists," *Globe*, 17 June 1926, 4.
19 "Blasphemous Libel is Charged Against Editor of Pamphlet," *Globe*, 11 January 1927.
20 Canadian Expeditionary Force (161st Huron Battalion) attestation papers, 6 April 1916. Styles seems to have originally spelled his name as Stiles. The 1911 census lists his birthdate as September 1892, while his attestation papers from 1916 have it as April 1894. Other details however, especially the place of residence, suggest this was the same person.
21 "Learned to Be Atheist at His Mother's Knee"; "May Ask for Darrow but Only as Junior," *Toronto Star*, 24 January 1927, 3; "Bible is Ridiculed by Rationalists," *Toronto Star*, 17 January 1927, 7; "Deaths," *Globe & Mail*, 1 July 1955, 26.
22 "Bible is Ridiculed by Rationalists." Leavens's marriage certificate, from 1911, lists his religion as "Disciples of Christ." Archives of Ontario, Series MS932_153, Reel 153.

23 "Learned to Be Atheist at His Mother's Knee"; "May Ask for Darrow but Only as Junior"; "Bible is Ridiculed by Rationalists"; "Deaths," *Globe & Mail*, 23 December 1953, 20; Mrs Leavens was first Vice President in 1931: "Return of Information and Particulars as of December 31, 1931," dated 16 October 1931. RSC incorporation papers. Jack Leavens's first appearance: Ad, *Toronto Star*, 29 December 1934.
24 Letter to the editor: Robert S. Potter, "Atheists versus evangelists," *Toronto Star*, 20 July 1931.
25 Ads, *Toronto Star*, 2 October 1926; 9 October 1926; 16 October 1926; Styles's talk on schools was a rebuttal of statements by the Toronto-based moralistic writer and cartoonist J.W. Bengough. An evangelical, Bengough had been sparring with unbelievers for many years: see Cook, *Regenerators*, 129–32.
26 Ad, *Toronto Star*, 23 October 1926.
27 McLaren and McLaren, *Bedroom and the State*.
28 Edwards, "Behind the North Gate."
29 Steiner's article was reprinted in "U.S. Is Controlling Centre of Toronto's Rationalism," *Evening Telegram*, 13 January 1927.
30 Birks's profession is found on an affidavit included among the RSC's incorporation papers. On Florence Custance see Angus, *Canadian Bolsheviks*, 79–80; Sangster, *Dreams of Equality*, 28–30, 33–5; for some of Custance's writing, see "Organizing the Women's Labor League (1924)," Socialist History Project, available at http://www.socialisthistory.ca/Docs/Leninist/WLL-Custance_24.htm (accessed 1 December 2022). The Women's Labor League was associated with the Workers' Party, a front organization of the Communist Party, which dissolved in 1924.
31 "U.S. is Controlling Centre of Toronto's Rationalism."
32 Ad, *Toronto Star*, 8 January 1927.
33 Readers will remember that prosecutor E.J. Murphy borrowed words from this sermon during the Sterry trial. Gibson also made the prescient observation that Canada was "a Christian nation and founded on Christian principles, where God is recognized in our courts of Justice," and then went on to criticize the lecture Styles had given the previous week, "Godly Women of the Bible." This would suggest there had been at least one Christian informant in the audience. "Atheistic Society is a Menace to City, Says Dr. Gibson," *Evening Telegram*, 11 January 1927, 18.
34 "Called Upon Pastor for Public Debate," *Toronto Star*, 19 January 1927, 9.
35 Ad, *Toronto Star*, 12 February 1927, 10. On Brown, who had been tried for heresy in 1925, see Mayr, "Red Bishop."
36 Ads, *Toronto Star*, 5 and 12 March 1927.

37 Ad, *Toronto Star*, 15 January 1927
38 Ad, *Toronto Star*, 15 October 1927.
39 "The Five Gospels of Rationalism" was delivered by Leavens twice in 1927 and recycled in 1929 and 1933. Ads, *Toronto Star*, 12 February 1927, 10 December 1927, 5 January 1929, and 25 March 1933. Similarly, Styles spoke on "Great Infidels" at least twice: Ads, *Toronto Star*, 24 March 1928, and 8 December 1928. (In 1928 Styles began calling himself "Iconoclast" or "The Toronto Iconoclast" in advertisements: Ad, *Toronto Star*, 4 February 1928.) "The Evolution of the Idea of God" was delivered by Leavens: Ad, *Toronto Star*, 20 March 1927. Lionel Cross delivered five lectures with intriguing titles such as "The Rationalistic View of Life," "The Female of the Species and Satan," "Capital Punishment," and the above-mentioned "Religion and the Sex Question." His final talk for the RSC came on 3 November 1929, on the topic "The Jesuit Enigma." Ads, *Toronto Star*, 4 December 1926, 7 January 1928; 29 December 1928; 9 February 1929; 3 November 1929. Mr B. Millar, a Torontonian, spoke on "The Conflict Between Science & Religion," and "Evolution vs. Direct Creation." Ads, *Toronto Star*, 9 March and 30 March 1929.
40 For example, Leavens debated E.L. Laur of Woodbridge on the usefulness of Christ's teaching to modern society, and Mr. A. Wakefield of London, England, on the resolution: "That the doctrines of Jesus are superior to the doctrines of Robert G. Ingersoll." Ads, *Toronto Star*, 9 April and 16 April 1927. Lionel Cross took the affirmative position in a debate with James Birks, a fellow rationalist, on the question "Does Materialism Explain the Universe?" Ad, *Toronto Star*, 21 January 1928.
41 Styles challenged F.C. Ward-Whate over the content of one of his sermons, and Leavens did the same with a Baptist minister, Dr Brown of Annette St Baptist Church: Ads, *Toronto Star*, 12 November 1927 and 3 March 1928.
42 Ad, *Toronto Star*, 26 January 1929; Styles attacked them again a year later in a talk entitled "The Whence and Why of the Present Crusade Against Atheism." Ad, *Toronto Star*, 24 January 1930.
43 Ad, *Toronto Star*, 11 February 1928. Leavens also seems to have reached out to other religious minorities. He spoke to Toronto's Theosophical Lodge on "Karma, the Reign of Law," on 8 May 1928. Ad, *Toronto Star*, 5 May 1928, 25. On Toronto's theosophists, who competed with the rationalists to provide an alternative to Christianity for local seekers, see McCann, *Vanguard of the New Age*.
44 Ad, *Toronto Star*, 4 October, 1930.
45 Ads, *Toronto Star*, 15 February 1930 and 15 March 1930.

46 Ads, *Toronto Star*, 5, 12, and 19 November 1927. Topics included "The First Cause Argument," "The Power of Thought," and "The Mechanistic Structure of the Universe." Attendance on Wednesdays may not have been as great as expected because a later ad clarified that "everyone [is] welcome to these meetings." After November the Wednesday night meetings cease to be mentioned, so it seems they were not a success. It is also possible they continued to be attended by a regular core of supporters who did not need advertising.
47 Ads, *Toronto Star*, 3, 9, 16, and 30 November 1929. One suggested topic for discussion was "Would an atheistic culture destroy idealism?"
48 Ad, *Toronto Star*, 16 November 1929.
49 Ad, *Toronto Star*, 12 April 1930.
50 Ad, *Toronto Star*, 19 April 1930.
51 For more detail on McCabe, see chapter 2.
52 Ad, *One Big Union Bulletin*, 6 September 1928, 2; Ad, *Toronto Star*, 13 October 1928.
53 "Dr. Inkster Declines Debate on Evolution," *Toronto Star*, 13 October 1928.
54 "McCabe Meeting Ends in Disorder: Speaker Described as Exponent of Evolution Draws Vigorous Protests," *Globe*, 15 October 1928, 14.
55 For more on Riley, see chapter 2.
56 On Smith, see Kee, *Revivalists*, 53–95, and Elliott, "Knowing No Borders."
57 R.E. Knowles, "Evolution Debate Proves Joke in Sunday Clothes," *Toronto Star*, 20 October 1928, 2.
58 "Evolution Theory Suffers Defeat as Audience Votes," *Globe*, 20 October 1928.
59 Ibid.
60 The Observer [Salem Bland], "Drawing Nearer to Peace," *Toronto Star*, 9 April 1930, 6. Regarding Salem Bland's identity as The Observer, see Allen, "Bland, Salem Goldworth." The prolific journalist (and Canada's chief censor during the Second World War) Wilfrid Eggleston, who wrote under the pseudonym Altair, was also in attendance. He took note of the audience's makeup: "The hall was full of fundamentalists who looked on the debate as a sort of modern conflict between God and the devil, and who burst out into a paean of rejoicing, "Praise God from whom all blessings flow" when a vote taken at the end of the end of the meeting showed that evolution had met defeat in the vigorous attack by Dr. Riley." Altair [Wilfrid Eggleston], "Chiefly Concerning Joseph McCabe ..." *Lethbridge Herald*, 3 November 1928, 6.
61 Letter to the editor, J. Macintosh, "Mr. Knowles and Evolution," *Toronto Star*, 25 October 1928, 6.

62 It was held at the National Painter's Hall. Ad, *Toronto Star*, 27 October 1928.
63 This lecture was at the Occident Hall. Ad, *Toronto Star*, 3 November 1928.
64 Sterry spoke at the Occident, while Leavens was at the Victoria Theatre. Ads, *Toronto Star*, 10 November 1928.
65 *Encyclopedia of Cleveland History*, s.v. "Brickner, Barrett Robert," http://ech.case.edu/cgi/article.pl?id=BBR1 (accessed 1 December 2022); "U.S. Atheist Scoffs at Sacred Teaching in City of Churches," *Globe*, 21 November 1930, 1–2.
66 The Observer [Salem Bland], "A Notable Debate," *Toronto Star*, 22 November 1930, 6. See also R.E. Knowles, "Darrow-Brickner Debate Was a Duel of Intellects," *Toronto Star*, 21 November 1930, 1, 38.
67 *The Globe*, "The Brickner-Darrow Debate," 28 November 1930; "Outlook of the Church," 29 November 1930; "Logic and Faith" 17 December 1930, 4.
68 "Note and comment," *Toronto Star*, 22 November 1930, 6.
69 Ads, *Toronto Star*, 15 November 1930 and 28 March 1931. Henderson would give a similarly formatted lecture to the Theosophical Society of Toronto in 1934, entitled "Ibsen – the Man and His Message." Ad, *Toronto Star*, 13 January 1934. Henderson was herself associated with the Quakers at this time. See Campbell, *Rose Henderson*.
70 Ad, *Toronto Star*, 11 April, 5 December 1931.
71 Leavens is listed as secretary-treasurer. Mrs B.E. Leavens is 1st vice president, Irwin L. Honsberger is 2nd VP, and the directors are listed as Mr. Bishop and Harry Green. "Return of Information and Particulars as of December 31, 1931," dated 16 October 1931. RSC incorporation papers.
72 During the RSC's fallow period, something mysterious appeared in the spaces where they would normally advertise. On 16 January 1932, tucked away on the *Toronto Star* church page, readers encountered a small box containing a few words. "HUMANISM," it said. "STUDY IT." And below, as if in explanation, "A Rational Religion, No Miracles." This terse statement was accompanied by no date, place or speaker. Almost a month later on 13 February, in the same space, an ad declared "HUMANISM: Humanity longs for a sensible religion, yearns, groans. Facts, not fables, wanted to-day. Thinkers arise, ministers, educated people, be honest, fearless, progressive. No more humbug." One explanation for these ads is that Leavens was unable to hold a regular schedule of lectures without Styles, but still wished to remind Torontonians who looked at the church page that there was a secular

alternative. We may also recall that Gauvin changed the name of his society from Rationalist to Humanist in 1935 and that the term was becoming more prominent among unbelievers in the interwar years. However, when the RSC reconvened in the fall of 1932 it retained the word "rationalist" in its name. Ads, *Toronto Star*, 16 January, and 13 February 1932.

73 Ad, *Toronto Star*, 31 October 1931. "Issendrath" here seems to have been a misspelling of "Eisendrath."
74 Ads, *Toronto Star*, 19 December 1931, and 6 February 1932.
75 Ad, *Toronto Star*, 22 October 1932.
76 "Bible is Ridiculed by Rationalists," *Toronto Star*, 17 January 1927, 7.
77 Arch, "Old Rationalism."
78 Royle, *Victorian Infidels*, 267–85.
79 Arch's article appeared in the context of a split between left- and right-wing rationalists in the British Rationalist Press Association. Hobson, *Unbelief in Interwar Literary Culture*, 154–6.
80 Ingersoll spoke on "Anarchism, Socialism, or Liberty." Ad, *Toronto Star*, 29 October 1932; Hall spoke on "On the Inside Looking Out (An Exposé of Prison Conditions)." Ad, *Toronto Star*, 26 November 1932. Scarlett: Ad, *Toronto Star*, 6 April 1935. On his career as an organizer see *Encyclopedia of Saskatchewan*, s.v. "Scarlett, Sam (d. 1941)," viewed 1 December 2022, https://esask.uregina.ca/entry/scarlett_sam_d_1941.jsp.
81 Ad, *Toronto Star*, 18 November 1933.
82 Listings appear for Ernest Walker, Ernest T. Walker and Ernest J. Walker, but given frequent typos which appear in RSC ads, these are all likely the same man. The symposium was a discussion between a theosophist (Felix Belcher), a Christian (H. Lindsay), and a rationalist, namely Walker. It took place under Rationalist auspices on 8 April 1934 and seems to have been based on a similar event organized by the Toronto Theosophical Society on 17 December 1933. That one featured Walker, Belcher, and Mr A.B. Davies (a frequent opponent of Leavens) as the Christian. Ads, *Toronto Star*, 16 December 1933, and 7 April 1934.
83 Ads, *Toronto Star*, 5 November 1932, 4 March 1933, 21 March 1936. Laing also spoke on topics like "Fascism and the Churches" and "Myths in Our Civilization." Ads, *Toronto Star*, 2 February 1935, 13 April 1935. For Laing's background as a trade unionist and her socialist-feminist work, see Sangster, *Dreams of Equality*, 111–13, 143, 218; and Campbell, *Rose Henderson*, 329n44. In 1937 Rose Henderson would die in Laing's arms at a political meeting, as a result of a cerebral hemorrhage. Campbell, *Rose Henderson*, 268.

84 Ads, *Toronto Star*, 29 September, and 27 October 1934.
85 "Return of Information and Particulars as of March 31, 1933," in Attorney General, Regina, SK: Re Rationalist Society of Canada Inc., RG 4-32, Attorney General Central Registry Criminal and Civil Files, Archives of Ontario.
86 Dennison had in the 1920s been a member of the United Farmers of Ontario. By the time he was associated with the RSC he was also a supporter of the CCF, serving on the provincial council, and would be elected as a MPP in the provincial legislature from 1943–45 and 1948–51. These were the same periods that Bert Leavens, also affiliated with the CCF, would be an MPP. Dennison was also active in the anti-fascist movement in Toronto. See Campbell (2010), 327–8n28; James Lorimer, "The Mutation of William Dennison," *Globe & Mail*, 10 January 1972, 7; and Bradburn, "Historicist: The Dennison School"; on Dennison's anti-fascist activities see Betcherman, *Swastika and the Maple Leaf*, 122–3.
87 Insects: Ad, *Toronto Star*, 31 December 1932; Ingersoll: Ad, *Toronto Star*, 28 January 1933.
88 "Dennison: a funny kind of socialist," *Globe & Mail*, 15 February 1966, 5. The reference was to a routine meeting where Dennison rebuffed an over-zealous colleague who wished to both sing the anthem and pray.
89 In the RSC's ad Thomas Cruden was listed "a leader in the CCF movement," and as the president of the Socialist Party of Ontario. He spoke on "Canada, the Land of Opportunity," probably with a certain amount of sarcasm. Ad, *Toronto Star*, 18 March 1933. Teskey spoke on "Social Reforms in Health." Ad, *Toronto Star*, 21 April 1933, 26. On Teskey's activism see Nicolaas van Rijn, "York Doctor Luke Teskey Defended Poor in Depression," *Toronto Star*, 26 October 1990, A9. Arthur H. Williams is listed as H.A. Williams in one advertisement but can be identified by his affiliation with the East York Workers' Association. Williams served as a reeve in East York township and later ran for the CCF. His lectures were entitled "What For?" and "Christianity: Practical or Theoretical?" Ads, *Toronto Star*, 2 December 1933, 24, and 22 February 1936. See also Campbell, *Rose Henderson*, 246.
90 Letter to the editor: Pat Kennedy, "Hot Shot for C.C.F.," *Globe*, 2 May 1935. Attacks on the CCF as being anti-Christian communists would intensify over time. See Boyko, *Into the Hurricane*, 106–16. One might hope that J.T. Morley's *Secular Socialists: The CCF/NDP in Ontario, A Biography* would have something to say about the influence rationalists had on the party, but in fact Morley uses the word "secular"

in a sociological sense to mean "worldly," not "nonreligious." Leavens is mentioned, but only in passing. Morley, *Secular Socialists*, 178.
91   Ad, *Toronto Star*, 6 April 1935.
92   Cecil-Smith commanded the Canadians who fought in the Spanish Civil War and was one of the writers of the influential communist play *Eight Men Speak*. Ad, *Toronto Star*, 11 January 1936; Wentzell, *Not for King or Country*.
93   Campbell, *Rose Henderson*, 169.
94   MacDonald: Ad, *Toronto Star*, 13 January 1934. Moriarty also spoke on "Labor, Nationalism and Religion," and asked "Socialism, What Does it Mean?" Ads, *Toronto Star*, 7 January 1933, 6 May 1933, 27 January 1934.
95   Billed as a "prominent socialist," Bruce was an associate of Rose Henderson and a politically active member of the Plumbers' and Steamfitters' Union. Ad, *Toronto Star*, 18 February 1933; Campbell, *Rose Henderson*, 183–4, 210. Sullivan, who spoke on "Politics and Religion," was a union activist who would in the 1940s become president of the Canadian Seaman's Union and secretary-treasurer of the Trades and Labor Congress. Ad, *Toronto Star*, 29 April 1933. See also Dillon O'Leary, "Pat Sullivan in Quebec; Plans Labor Comeback," *Globe & Mail*, 15 April 1947, 1; and Kaplan, *Everything That Floats*. An official of the Socialist Party of Canada, William C. Currey, spoke twice to the RSC, on "Socialism & Religion" and "Evolution: Fact or Fable?" Ad, *Toronto Star*, 9 March 1935. For Currey's involvement in the SPC, see the Appendix to Newell, *Impossibilists*. William C. Currey should not be confused with William J. Curry of Vancouver, whom we shall meet in chapter 7.
96   Edwards, "Behind the North Gate." Ad, *Toronto Star*, October 28, 1933, 24; Withrow, *Shackling the Transgressor*.
97   Ads, *Toronto Star*, 17 and 24 September 1932.
98   Ads, *Toronto Star*, 16 September 1933; 28 April 1934.
99   Ad, *Toronto Star*, 17 December 1932. On another occasion Leavens also debated a spiritualist on whether spiritualism was superior to rationalism. Ad, *Toronto Star* 19 November 1932.
100 Aside from lectures, in this period the RSC also put out a four-page pamphlet entitled *Faith or Fact? The Case for Rationalism*. Buttressed with extensive quotations from Ingersoll, Luther Burbank, Mark Twain, Benjamin Franklin, Thomas Huxley, Charles Darwin, and others, the pamphlet promoted a purely rational and secular approach to life. It declared that superstitions were "barnacles on the ship of progress"

and "Science is the only lever capable of elevating mankind." It went on to urge Torontonians to join the society. A life membership could be had for $10.00, or members could pay $1.00 for their first year and then 25 cents for each following month.

101 Ad, *Toronto Star*, 8 October 1932.
102 Stanley Lloyd, Darius Hogan, William Dennison, and Amber Robinson spoke. Ad, *Toronto Star*, 28 January 1933. Robinson's first name is found in the RSC's incorporation file.
103 Ad, *Toronto Star*, 30 December 1933. She would return in March 1935 to speak on "Man, The Pilgrim." Ad, *Toronto Star*, 2 March, 1935. The other three women were Laing, Henderson, and Custance.
104 Ad, *Toronto Star*, 29 December 1934.
105 Ad, *Toronto Star*, 15 October 1934.
106 Ad, *Toronto Star*, 16 March 1935.
107 "11. Toronto Prepares for 'May Day.'" In Kealey and Whitaker, *RCMP Security Bulletins 1936*, 150.
108 On the registration forms he listed his profession as "cabinet-maker," the same trade that had appeared on the RSC's incorporation papers nine years before. The election took place on 14 October 1935.
109 Ad, *Toronto Star*, 2 November 1935.
110 Ad, *Toronto Star*, 29 March 1935.
111 Letter from B.E. Leavens to F.V. Johns, dated 1 January 1938, RSC incorporation file. It also seems that in 1934 and 1935 the society neglected to file Annual Returns with the appropriate department. Letter regarding the RSC from F.V. Johns, Assistant Provincial Secretary to T.C. Davis, Saskatchewan Attorney General, dated 9 March 1936 in Attorney General, Regina, SK: Re Rationalist Society of Canada Inc., RG 4-32, Attorney General Central Registry Criminal and Civil Files, Archives of Ontario.
112 Rationalist street speakers were still active in Toronto in the summer of 1936. Bert Whyte, a communist who began "soapboxing" in that year, remembered the "fierce competition" provided by the Rationalists at the corner of Queen and Spadina. He recalled one telling veterans, "You fought for King and Country and what did you get? A little round service button—and the King kept the Country!" But "they were good fellows" and so an arrangement was made to share the corner, with "one hour for each." Whyte, *Champagne and Meatballs*, 146.
113 For glimpses of Leavens's CCF activities see Naylor, *Fate of Labour Socialism*, 198–201, 244, 260–1 and Horowitz, *Canadian Labour in Politics*, 65, 146–50.

114 Toronto city directories for 1940–49 list Leavens's different roles in the CCF.
115 "Bertram Elijah Leavens," Legislative Assembly of Ontario website. Available at https://www.ola.org/en/members/all/bertram-elijah-leavens (accessed on 1 December 2022). As noted above, these were the same terms that William Dennison served as an MPP.
116 "Deaths," *Globe & Mail*, 23 December 1953, 20.
117 Ad, *Toronto Star*, 19 November 1938, 9.
118 "Deaths," *Globe & Mail*, 1 July 1955, 26.
119 The Klan claimed the man was Black, though he himself said he was of Indigenous descent. They were targeting him because he was romantically involved with a white woman. Backhouse, *Colour-Coded: A Legal History*, 176–224.
120 "At Osgoode Hall," *Globe & Mail*, 15 January 1937; Lewthwaite 68.
121 Backhouse, "Gender and Race"; Lewthwaite "Ethelbert Lionel Cross," 68.
122 On 1 May 1928.
123 See Ryan, *Eight Men Speak*.
124 Betcherman, *Little Band*; Angus, *Canadian Bolsheviks*; Horn, "Free Speech Within the Law," 27–48.
125 Smith: quoted in Betcherman, *Little Band*, 64; J.S. Woodsworth, "Will the 'The Ward' Save Toronto?" *Canadian Forum* 7, no. 77, 137–8.
126 "Say Police Encouraged Heckler's Disturbance," *Toronto Star*, 7 May 1929, 3.
127 E. Lionel Cross, "Voice of the People: Rationalists' Meetings," *Toronto Star*, 3 August 1929, 4.
128 "Mayor Insists Police Must be Disciplined," *Toronto Star*, 14 August 1929, 1; Betcherman, *Little Band*, 62–8.
129 "Crowd on Street Near Massey Hall Dispersed by Police: Throng on Roadway and Sidewalks Obstructs Traffic: Atheists Hold Meeting," *Globe,* 19 August 1929 (City News Section, 1).
130 "Crowd on Street Near Massey Hall Dispersed by Police"; "'Is It to be Bolshevism or Constitutional Government?' Coatsworth Asks"; "Exaggerated Stories on Reds, Distortion of Report Alleged"; "Communism Spells Murder, Pillage, Merciless Tyranny, Says Shields, and Would Eliminate Civilization"; *Globe,* 19 August 1929 (City News Section, 1).
131 "Mayor Does Not Favour Permits for Meetings," *Toronto Star*, 2 October 1929, 8.
132 Ibid.
133 Ibid.

134 "Chief Draper Gives Public Notice He Will Not Permit 'Red' Meeting Called for Today in Queen's Park," *Globe*, 12 October 1929. The "Canadian Atheist Society" seems to have been a mistaken or deliberately provocative reference to the Rationalist Society of Canada.
135 "High Priests of Atheism Train Guns on the Globe," *Globe*, 16 February 1931, 1.
136 Notably, Haldeman-Julius's publications gave a platform to Joseph McCabe and made possible the latter's fame in North America.
137 "Keep This Trash Out," *Globe*, 29 January 1931, 4; "Brampton Pastor Raps Kansas Editor for Atheistic Sheet," *Globe*, 9 February 1931.
138 See chapter 2, n123.
139 "Keep This Trash Out."
140 Ibid.
141 "'Free Speechers' Backed by U.S. High Priest of Atheism," *Globe*, 4 February 1931, 1.
142 Ibid.
143 "High Priests of Atheism Train Guns on the Globe: Denver and Chicago Join in Campaign to Aid 'Free Speech,'" *Globe*, 16 February 1931, 1.
144 "The 'Free Speech' Crowd," *Globe*, 13 February 1931, 4; "'Free Speechers' Backed by U.S. High Priest of Atheism." I have been unable to locate a copy of the "Canadian Free Speech Edition."
145 "U.S. Is Controlling Centre of Toronto's Rationalism," *Evening Telegram*, 13 January 1927.
146 For a nuanced examination of the roots of this anti-American mythology in Ontario, see Errington, *The Lion, the Eagle*.
147 "Called Upon Pastor for Public Debate"; "Says Offer Meant Betrayal of Client," *Toronto Star*, 15 January 1927, 15. See also Lewthwaite, "Ethelbert Lionel Cross," 58.
148 "Learned to Be Atheist at His Mother's Knee"; for the relationship between secularism and the British Empire, see Corbeil, *Empire and Progress*.
149 "Native-Born Canadians: Leaders of Rationalist Society Resent Being Called Foreigners," *Toronto Star*, 20 January 1927, 4; "Learned to Be Atheist at His Mother's Knee"; "May Ask for Darrow but Only as Junior."
150 It seems likely that Lionel Cross's racialized status had something to do with Ward-Whate's "mongrel curs" remark.
151 Of course, Sterry was certainly not the only Briton to whom this harsh logic applied, as Barbara Roberts documented in her book *Whence They Came: Deportation from Canada 1900-1935*. British authorities frequently complained of Canada's policies in this regard.
152 "New Police Rule Hits Labor Group," *Toronto Star*, 27 June 1932, 7.

153 "Police Break Up Rationalist Meets," *Toronto Star,* 11 July 1932, 7, "Police Disperse Meetings of Rationalist Society," *Globe,* 11 July 1932, 9.
154 "Stewart is Against Atheist Preachers," *Globe,* 5 August 1932, 10.
155 "Ask Courts to Enjoin Police Interference," *Toronto Star,* 29 August 1932, 1; Inspector Douglas Marshall was notorious for his hatred of leftists and his violent approach to clearing the streets. See Betcherman, *Little Band,* 133–5.
156 "Halt Street Meet Case," *Toronto Star,* 24 October 1932, 2.
157 "Protest Police Action," *Toronto Star,* 20 June 1933.
158 "Rationalist Rallies Barred in Division 2," *Toronto Star,* 17 July 1933.
159 "Meeting Moves On," *Toronto Star,* 28 May 1934.
160 "Judge Coatsworth Retires From Police Board," *Globe,* 31 December 1931, 1.
161 Betcherman, *Little Band,* 214–15.
162 For a more in-depth discussion of the letter and the reaction, both public and official see Horn, *Academic Freedom,* 89–91; and McKillop, *Matters of Mind,* 382–6.
163 McCullough, Knowles, and Mulock, all quoted in "The Intellectual Capital of Canada," *Canadian Forum* 11, no. 126, 212.
164 Horn, 89–91. Cody, a clergyman, was the unofficial leader of Canada's evangelical Anglicans and a patron of the Canadian Christian Crusade Against Atheism, as discussed below.
165 The identification of religion with emotional, unreliable women and of irreligion with rational men was a very common theme among unbelievers in this and earlier periods.
166 James Jeans was an English physicist who wrote on science for a popular audience.
167 Allan's editorial was quoted in its entirety in "Toronto 'Varsity' in Hot Water Again – Atheism is Nucleus of Present Trouble," *Gateway,* 5 March 1931, 1.
168 In her history of the connection of the Canadian academy with Protestant Christianity, Catherine Gidney finds that in the 1920s and '30s universities were seen as explicitly religious institutions. It was part of their mission to uphold Christian views and values among the student population. Thus, to accuse a university of promoting atheism was to accuse it of betraying a religious nation's trust. See Gidney, *Long Eclipse,* 3–47. Despite public concern over the morals and beliefs of interwar undergraduates, A.B. McKillop finds that Ontario's students were fairly moderate, at least in comparison with their American counterparts at the time. "They were neither morally out of control nor in revolt against a meaningless past,"

but they were occasionally resentful of heavy-handed authority and paternalism. See McKillop, *Matters of Mind*, 405–20.
169 "Atheistic Editorial 'Absurd, Incorrect,' Declare Graduates," *Globe*, 26 February 1931; see also McKillop, *Matters of Mind*, 385.
170 "Varsity Suspended – Premier Lets Caput Act," *Globe*, 28 February 1931; Masters, *Henry John Cody*, 173–4; on Allan being fired, see Livesay, *Right Hand Left Hand*, 22, 123; and McKillop, *Matters of Mind*, 385.
171 "Nixon to Demand Inquiry into Varsity Charges," *Globe*, 27 February 1931, 1.
172 "Varsity Suspended – Premier Lets Caput Act."
173 "Atheism Takes Its Toll," *Globe*, 18 March 1931, 4. The paper did not mention that Spencer lived to the age of eighty-three, and despite health problems continued to work productively until his final illness. Nor did it address the fact that he was not strictly speaking an atheist.
174 "Facing U.S. Barrier, Queen's Principal Tarries in Tunnel," *Globe*, 6 March 1931, 1.
175 Quoted in McKillop, *Matters of Mind*, 385.
176 The University of Toronto remained particularly vulnerable to these suspicions. Ibid., 362–401.
177 Throughout the 1930s the *Globe* kept up a steady series of prominently placed articles updating Torontonians on the twists and turns of Moscow's anti-religious policies. See for example "Anti-religious war upheld in message from Russian head," *Globe*, 26 February 1930, 2; "Russian Faithful Object of Attack by Atheist Reds," *Globe*, 6 April 1931, 3; "'Godless' is Boast of Soviets," *Globe*, 8 February 1936, 1. Already in 1930 Felix Walter had referred to this in the *Canadian Forum* as "bolshephobia," and complained: "The press campaign is the worst. For years now certain newspapers in this country have made a regular practice of prejudicing their readers against the Russian Experiment." Felix Walter, "Bolshephobia," *Canadian Forum* 11, no. 121 (October 1930), 9–11.
178 Grant, *Profusion of Spires*; Westfall, *Two Worlds*.
179 Ad for College St Baptist Church, *Toronto Star*, 14 March 1931, 29.
180 "Playing With Fire," *Globe*, 10 October 1928, 4.
181 J.F. White, "Police Dictatorship," *Canadian Forum* 11, no. 125 (February 1931), 167–8.
182 It was sometimes called the Canadian Christian Crusade Against Atheism. Howe, *Will Atheism Dominate*.
183 "Christian Crusaders Organize to Battle Evils of Communism," *Globe*, 6 December 1928, 15.

184 Knauss wrote some articles for William Bell Riley in the early 1930s. See Carpenter, *Revive Us Again*, 282. She also wrote books such as *The Rising Tide: A Novel Dealing with the Spread of Bolshevism and Atheism Throughout America*.
185 "Noted Crusader Comes to Toronto," *Globe*, 19 January 1929, 20.
186 The others listed were T.R. Porritt of Victoria, BC, D.D. Moshier, Dr E. Ralph Hooper, and A.H. Cuttle. I have included brief biographical information here on these and a few others mentioned in the main text. I was unable to find information on T.R. Porritt. William H. Adamson (1858–1941), the president of an insurance company, was active in support of a great many evangelical organizations, including the Shantymen's Christian Association, the Sudan Interior Mission, and the Canadian Keswick Conference. "W.H. Adamson Passes, Aged 83," *Globe & Mail*, 12 September 1941, 20. John J. Gartshore (1850–1933) was the president of a railway equipment company, but he was known more for five decades of work spent guiding the Toronto YMCA. He was involved in other evangelical organizations, such as the Toronto Bible College, and was a longtime Sunday school superintendent at St George's United Church. David D. Moshier (1861–1934) was the Chief Inspector of Toronto's schools and a member of the United Church. "David D. Moshier Dies at Age of 74," *Globe*, 12 March 1935, 12. Dr E. Ralph Hooper (1871–1950) had been a medical missionary to Ethiopia, before becoming dean of an evangelical Bible institute in London, Ontario. He was for a time physician to Ethiopian Emperor Haile Selassie. "Dr. E. Ralph Hooper, Missionary Became Dean of Bible Institute," *Globe & Mail*, 15 June 1950, 8. Arthur Haight Cuttle (d. 1959) was a mainstay of the Anglican Church Army and was particularly active in fundraising. "Deaths: Cuttle, Arthur Haight," *Globe & Mail*, 23 March 1959, 37.
187 "Another Conservative Patriot," *Globe*, 12 July 1930, 4.
188 "A Valiant Crusader Gone," *Globe*, 5 September 1931, 4; "Henry O'Brien, K.C., Prominent Citizen, Goes to His Reward," *Globe*, 4 September 1931, 1. "Fundamental" was in this context a direct reference to fundamentalism.
189 "Robert D. Richardson: Business Leader Public Spirited," *Globe*, 15 January 1946, 4; Goldsborough, "Memorable Manitobans: Robert Dennis Richardson."
190 For examples of the causes in which she was involved: "News of Women's Organizations," *Globe*, 23 May 1929, 18; "Nursing Mission has Fine Record," *Globe*, 18 May 1932, 14. I have been unable to locate her obituary or much in the way of personal detail about her.

191 Among his many accomplishments, Blake had helped found Havergal College, the elite girls' school where Maud Howe had taught. He was an ally of H.J. Cody and had been the prime mover in the construction of the "cathedral" of evangelical Anglicanism, St Paul's on Bloor St. Blackwell, "Blake, Samuel Hume."
192 Gibson, "Aikins, Sir James Albert Manning."
193 J.F. White, "Police Dictatorship," *Canadian Forum* 11, no. 125, 171.
194 "Jurist Dean of Toronto Passes Away," *Globe*, 12 May 1943, 4.
195 Katerberg, *Modernity and the Dilemma*, 181–209.
196 "Mrs. Fleming Paid Tribute for Service," *Globe & Mail*, 16 November 1937, 4; "A Noblewoman Gone," *Globe & Mail*, 16 November 1937, 6. Her birthdate can be found in the 1921 Canadian census.
197 Comeau, "Fleming, Robert John." On Fleming's style of evangelical reformism, see Van Die, "Protestants, the Liberal State."
198 "Rev. Dr. John G. Inkster: Veteran Minister of Wide Interests Dies of Injuries," *Globe & Mail*, 20 December 1946, 4.
199 "Dr. Inkster Declines Debate on Evolution," *Toronto Star* 13 October 1928. "Rationalists' View of Second Coming is Hopeless One," *Globe*, 7 July 1930, 12.
200 Katerberg, *Modernity and the Dilemma*, 37–63.
201 When O'Brien died, his duties as treasurer were taken over by his wife and William H. Adamson. This information can be found on the letterhead of Howe's letter to Marshall Gauvin, dated 11 November 1932. Marshall Gauvin fonds, Box 8, Fol. 8.
202 The Anglican priest who had called the rationalists "mongrel curs," Franklin Charles Ward-Whate, was of a similar vintage; he was born in 1864 and died in 1935. An age could not be determined for Maud Howe, since obituaries of the time rarely printed women's ages, and she was not in the country for the 1921 census.
203 Dochuk, "Redeeming the City," and Van Die, Protestants, the Liberal State."
204 "President of the *Globe* for 22 Years," *Globe & Mail*, 29 December 1949, 1–2.
205 Betts, "Argument of the Century," 67.
206 "Morning Monopoly," *Time* 28, no. 22 (30 November 1936), 58; Kee, *Revivalists*, 89.
207 She later wrote him a polite letter thanking him for his hospitality. Letter from Howe to Gauvin on CCC letterhead, dated 11 November 1932. Marshall Gauvin fonds, Box 8, Fol. 8, UMA.
208 "Mrs. Maud M. Howe, Headed Crusade Against Atheism," *Globe & Mail*, January 29, 1945, 7. Havergal was co-founded by Samuel H. Blake.

209 Howe, *Challenge Answered*, title page.
210 Rev. 6:4. There are also echoes of the blood-covered steeds in Revelation chapter 14, where a great river of blood comes up "even unto the horse bridles." Rev. 14:19–20, KJV.
211 See for example an ad from the American evangelist Robert L. Boothby: "4 Mysterious Horses Traveling Through the Earth! What Is Coming? Is the Pale Horse Hitlerism? Is the Red Horse Communism? Is the Black Horse Fascism? Is the White Horse Democracy?" Ad, *Washington Post*, 6 December 1942, L4.
212 Howe, *Challenge Answered*, 61–4.
213 Ibid., 65–7. This may be a reference to William Ernest Henley's poem "Invictus," which concludes with the lines "I am the master of my fate, I am the captain of my soul."
214 Ibid., 68.
215 Of course, unbelievers also trafficked in gendered language, as her son's references to being a rational man attest.
216 Ibid., 5.
217 This is not to say Howe's vastly inflated statistics were accurate. For an interesting argument that unbelief often emerges as a powerful emotion before it becomes a formal intellectual belief, see Ryrie, *Unbelievers*.
218 J.F. White, "Contemporary Crusades," *Canadian Forum* 10, no. 16 (May 1930), 279–80.
219 Betcherman, *Little Band*, 23. As noted above, the "four A's" referred to the American Association for the Advancement of Atheism, founded in 1925 by Charles Lee Smith.
220 Angus, *Canadian Bolsheviks*, 237.
221 On the High Diction of war see Vance, *Death So Noble*, 1996.
222 "Missionary Warns Against Atheism and "Red" Menace," *Globe*, 8 May 1929.
223 "Toronto Children Taught Atheism," *Globe*, 9 May 1934, 5.
224 On these sorts of anti-evolution proof-texts, see Numbers, *Creationists*, 52. For the "Lady Hope" story about Darwin's conversion, see Caudill, *Darwinian Myths*.
225 The Observer [i.e., Salem Bland], "Drawing Nearer to Peace," *Toronto Star*, 9 April 1930, 6.
226 "Toronto-Sized Cities Unearthed in Cradle of Man," *Globe*, 8 May 1935, 1.
227 Howe, *Challenge Answered*, ii; see also "Not in Politics," *Globe*, 4 February 1929, 18.
228 Howe, *Will Atheism Dominate?*

229 "Outlook of the Church: Christian Crusade Closes Stirring Convention," *Globe & Mail*, 10 June 1933, 13; "Responsibilities of Nurses Stressed by Noted Doctor," *Globe*, 14 September 1932, 11.
230 "News of Women's Organizations," *Globe*, 15 January 1931, 14; "The Homemaker," *Globe*, 28 August 1929, 19.
231 See Brown, *Death of Christian Britain*.
232 "Atheism Laid to Communism," *Globe & Mail*, 22 April 1938, 5.
233 "Deaths: Smith, Gwen," *Globe & Mail*, 11 September 1989, E16.
234 Ad, *Globe & Mail*, 17 May 1947, 13.
235 See for example Mark Noll's discussion of the difference and the historiography surrounding it in Noll, "Canadian Evangelicalism." In the context of the CCC, see Katerberg's discussion of H.J. Cody and Dyson Hague. Hague wrote three of the "Fundamentals" booklets that gave the American fundamentalist movement its name, but Katerberg is careful to point out the differences between Hague's polemical conservative evangelicalism and the anti-intellectual, separatist style common to American fundamentalism. Katerberg, *Modernity and the Dilemma*, 2001.
236 For a similar argument, see Clarke, "English-Speaking Canada," 345.
237 J.V. McAree, "'Circle-Bar Fourth Column,'" *Globe & Mail*, 6 October 1937, 12. McAree had previously worked for the conservative Tory paper, the *Mail & Empire*. Judging from its reaction to the Scopes Trial the *Mail & Empire* may have been more sympathetic to modernism in religion than the *Globe* had been. See Betts 84–5.
238 The new owners, William Henry Wright and C. George McCullagh, were quick to rescind Jaffray's restrictions on tobacco advertising and racing news. "Morning Monopoly," *Time* 28, no. 22 (30 November 1936), 58.

CHAPTER SIX

1 Salutin, *Kent Rowley*, 12. I have not found any reproduction of this image, but when police visited the Université ouvrière in 1934 they "took notes on the anti-religious, political and indecent caricatures decorating the walls." Lévesque, "Red Scares and Repression," 305.
2 Dickinson and Young, *Short History of Quebec*, 244–5; Perin, "French-Speaking Canada," 226.
3 McLeod, "World Christianities," 16–17.
4 Lacombe, "French Canada," 135.
5 De Lagrave, *Voltaire's Man in America*.
6 Ibid., 247.
7 Chabot, "Papineau, Joseph."

8 Ouellet, "Papineau, Louis-Joseph," see also Ouellet, *Louis Joseph Papineau*. In his book on atheism in Quebec, Claude M.J. Braun offers a series of short biographies of great unbelievers in the province's history. Papineau is the first, followed by other notable figures like Éva Circé-Côté, Félix d'Hérelle, Marius Barbeau, Norman Bethune, and Marian Dale Scott. Braun, *Québec athée*; Circé-Côté is notable as a writer and feminist active in the interwar years who moved in anticlerical circles and had freethinking tendencies. See Lévesque, *Freethinker*; MacLean, "Parrots, Picnics and Psychic Phenomena."
9 Perin, "French-Speaking Canada," 224–5; Rioux, "Guibord, Joseph." The *Rouges*, meanwhile, were sidelined by the Reform Party, and worn down by constant pressure from ultramontanists. The remnants of the party dropped their anticlericalism and became moderate Laurier Liberals. See Dickinson and Young, *Short History of Quebec*, 185–93.
10 Lamonde, *Louise-Antoine Dessaulles*; Dutil, *Devil's Advocate*; Guttman, *Devil from Saint-Hyacinthe*. Examinations of the liberal tradition in Quebec have been a part of a larger historiographical debate over the distinctiveness of the province's history. See Rudin, "Revisionism."
11 Quoted in Ramsay Cook's *Regenerators*, in which he is called Robert Chambliss Adams: Cook, *Regenerators*, 58–62.
12 Flynn, *New Encyclopedia*, 21; *Constitution and By-laws*.
13 Such numbers probably conceal the extent to which unbelief existed in the province, but they do demonstrate that very few people were willing to openly identify themselves as unbelievers. *Sixth Census of Canada, 1921*, vol. 1, *Population* (Ottawa: F.A. Acland, King's Printer, 1924), 573.
14 *Seventh Census of Canada 1931*, vol. 2, Population by Areas (Ottawa: J.O. Patenaude, King's Printer, 1933), 509.
15 Dickinson and Young, *Short History of Quebec*, 242.
16 Perin, "French-Speaking Canada," 234–6.
17 Linteau, Durocher and Robert, *Quebec: A History*, 454–5.
18 Horton, *André Laurendeau*, 123–4.
19 Ibid.
20 Ibid., 137–8. Ramsay Cook argues that the churchwarden did not exist but was a fictionalized version of Laurendeau himself. See Cook, *Watching Quebec*, 138.
21 Few primary sources on Saint-Martin and Pilon exist that have not already been discussed by other historians. Thus, this chapter focuses less on unearthing new material than on examining the UO's brand of unbelief and placing it in a wider Canadian context. I also compare the response of the state in Quebec to that in locations like Toronto.

22 Guttman, *Devil from Saint-Hyacinthe*, 81.
23 Fournier, *Communisme et anticommunisme*, 21. Moreover, the unconventional names Saint-Martin gave his children signalled his unusual opinions. For example, one daughter was named Hedwiedge Donalda. McKay, *Reasoning Otherwise*, 180.
24 One interesting overlap with the Rationalist Society of Canada is that Saint-Martin once shared a stage with Rose Henderson, who would go on to speak to the RSC in the later 1920s. "Radicals Back Winnipeg Strike," *Montreal Gazette*, 28 May 1919, 4.
25 Literally "Down with the clergyman's skullcap." "Socialists Parade," *Montreal Gazette*, 2 May 1906, 12.
26 "Do Not Register, Socialists Advise," *Montreal Gazette*, 28 May 1917, 7.
27 "A Thrifty Revolutionist," Kealey and Whitaker, RCMP *Security Bulletins, 1919–1929*, 137.
28 Lévesque, "Weakest Link," 2. See also Lévesque, "Red Scares and Repression," 292.
29 Labour colleges and working-class education dated back to the early 19th-century mechanics' institutes but were particularly widespread in the 1920s and '30s. The OBU Forum, discussed in chapter 2, was one example. See also Altenbaugh, *Education for Struggle*.
30 "A toutes ces réunions les dames sont invitées et s'y rendent en grand nombre." Of course, this mention of women may also have been meant to attract men. Ad reproduced in Houle-Courcelles, *Sur les traces*, 171.
31 Copp, *Anatomy of Poverty*, 95.
32 Quoted in Lévesque, "Red Scares and Repression," 295. She also provides the original French: "À cette salle ceux qui « y assistent ont l'air de véritables miséreux et font pitié mal habillés et presque pieds-nu [sic] et se demandent entre eux de quoi fumer et manger." Ibid., 317n20.
33 Ibid., 295.
34 Fournier, *Communisme et anticommunisme*, 21.
35 In his public talks he would at times address crowds in both languages. "Defied the Police," *Montreal Gazette*, 19 September 1908, 9.
36 Fournier, *Communisme et anticommunisme*, 21.
37 According to court documents Pilon sometimes used the alias "Albert."
38 Ibid., 20.
39 "Montreal Orator on Sedition Charge," *Quebec Telegraph*, 22 May 1919, 1.
40 "Le récit de la conversion de Gaston Pilon fait par le Rév. Père Archange." *La Patrie*, 26 September 1934, 3.
41 Rollieu, *Gaston Pilon*, 1–2. "Charpenté en porte-faix, la figure taillée à la serpe, les traits fatigués, avec deux tisons enfoncés sous les paupières,

cet homme inspire plutôt la répulsion. S'il empoigne son auditoire, c'est vitupère – et de quelle voix! caverneuse, sombre, fielleuse – contre tout ce qui s'oppose aux bas instincts de la bête humaine."

42 Larivière, *Albert Saint-Martin*, 143; Fournier, *Communisme et anticommunisme*, 68.
43 Weisbord, *Strangest Dream*, 20.
44 MacLeod, Park, and Ryerson, *Bethune*, 141.
45 Rollieu, *Gaston Pilon*, 12.
46 Weisbord, *Strangest Dream*, 15.
47 The government did turn to direct relief in 1933. The struggle over relief extended far beyond Saint-Martin's agitations. Linteau, *Quebec Since 1930*, 55–6; Dagenais, *Pouvoirs et des hommes*, chap. 3; and Copp, "Montreal's Municipal Government," 112–29.
48 "Resisters Found Guilty on Charge," *Montreal Gazette*, 20 January 1934, 5.
49 Houle-Courcelles, *Sur les traces*, 156.
50 Linteau, *Quebec Since 1930*, 55.
51 Fournier, *Communisme et anticommunisme*, 21.
52 Joseph Alix, "L'Université ouvrière," *Le Devoir*, 6 September 1932, 2, quoted in Larivière, *Albert Saint-Martin*, 150.
53 Ibid., 151.
54 Houle-Courcelles, *Sur les traces*, 142–3; Fournier, *Communisme et anticommunisme*, 20.
55 See for example "Saint-Martin trompe la classe ouvrière," *Vie ouvrière*, November 1933, 5.
56 Fournier, *Communisme et anticommunisme*, 22; Lévesque, "Weakest Link," 10.
57 Weisbord, *Strangest Dream*, 15.
58 Ibid., 45.
59 "Il me fut donné d'entendre une conférence anticléricale, où le clergé était dénoncé comme porteur des sept péchés capitaux et de tous les crimes, du capitalisme. Faisant part de ma déception à M. Leboeuf, je lui dis que ce genre d'organisation ne conduisait nulle part. De mon point de vue l'anticléricalisme n'est pas une solution pour des problèmes d'ordre économique." Gagnon, *Militants socialistes du Québec*, 53.
60 One history of Quebec refers to this opposition as "a virtual crusade against communist influence." Linteau, *Quebec Since 1930*, 62.
61 Perin, "French-Speaking Canada," 234.
62 They were told they did not need permission to do so. Letter, Department of Justice, 15 February 1926. R188-39-8-E, no. 1926-264, LAC.

Jeremy Patrick has discussed *La ligue* and points out that the notice they intended to post did not actually mention the law of blasphemous libel. Instead it cites Articles 238-F and 239, which forbid "vagabonds" and "libertines" disturbing the law in public places. It is unclear if the league was trying to keep unbelievers from airing their views, or if they were simply trying to keep unruly drunks from cursing. Patrick, "Canadian Blasphemy Law," 157–8.

63 Fournier, *Communisme et anticommunisme*, 23–9, Lévesque, "Red Scares and Repression," 294–9; Hamelin and Gagnon, *Histoire du catholicisme québécois*, 373–83.

64 Perin, "French-Speaking Canada," 254; Linteau, Durocher, and Robert, *Quebec: A History*, 456.

65 Ibid 253; Gauvreau, *Catholic Origins*, 17. For the rivalry and differences between the ACJC and the JOC, JIC, etc., see Behiels, *Prelude to Quebec's Quiet Revolution*, 44–5; Linteau, Durocher, and Robert, *Quebec: A History*, 456; Linteau, *Quebec Since 1930*, 63.

66 Gossage and Little, *Illustrated History of Quebec*, 203.

67 Hamelin and Gagnon, *Histoire du catholicisme québécois*, 379.

68 Manseau, "Etre digne de l'Esto Vir."

69 "Manifestez-vous l'idée de connaître ce qu'on dit de Dieu, un monsieur et deux demoiselles vous glissent habilement les différents tracts de Sébastian Faure: 'Douze preuves de l'inexistence de Dieu,' celui de Bossi, 'Jésus-Christ n'a jamais existé ...' S'agit-il de vous montrer que l'Église n'est qu'une institution diabolique et que les prêtres ne sont que les noirs gendarmes du despotisme, on vous vante la brochure d'Élisée Reclus intitulée 'L'Anarchie et l'Église,' celle de Jean Nost, 'La Peste Religieuse,' celles de Gerrold, Sébastien Faure et autres de même acabit." Lafleur, *Université ouvrière*, 8.

70 The earliest edition still in existence appears to be from 1914: Faure, *Douze preuves*.

71 Bossi, *Gesù Cristo*.

72 Most, *Gottespest*; Trautmann, *Voice of Terror*, 6.

73 Guyou and Reclus, "L'Anarchie et l'Église."

74 Lafleur, *Université ouvrière*, 8.

75 "Si ces diverses personnes n'ont reçu qu'une instruction élémentaire, elles seront quatre-vingt-dix fois sur cent prises au panneau par les sophismes qui y sont étalés à chaque page et seront forcément portés à nier l'existence de Dieu ou à en douter." Ibid.

76 "Mais la lutte qu'on y mène revêt plutôt la caractère d'une lutte anticléricale. Sur six conférences auxquelles nous avons assisté, un

rapportait les incidents de voyage d'une américaine en Russie, un autre traitait du conflit sino-japonais, quatre traitaient de religion. Vous voyez par ces chiffres que, chez eux, c'est la lutte anticléricale qui prime tout." Ibid., 10.
77 "Je vous le crie, je vous le dis encore un fois, messieurs, je suis un athée fieffé."
78 Lafleur, *Université ouvrière*, 9.
79 "Les prêtres ne sont que des tas de râleux à mains blanches et à peau lisse qui rappelle celle des serpents." Ibid.
80 "Les maudits Sulpiciens, nous les fusillerons, s'ils ne veulent pas travailler." Ibid., 10.
81 "Le confessionnal est le plus grand système policier jamais inventé pour découvrir le secret des hommes." Ibid.
82 "Le confessionnal est un nid de vices. Beaucoup de gens qui ne connaissaient pas le mal avant d'y entrer le connaissaient lorqu'ils en sont sortis." Ibid.
83 Ibid.
84 Ibid., 8–10.
85 Lévesque, "Red Scares and Repression," 295.
86 MacLeod, Park, and Ryerson, *Bethune*, 141.
87 The "black robes" were the Catholic clergy of all varieties.
88 Ibid., 142.
89 "Au début, nous étions anticléricaux. Par la suite, nous sommes devenus plus réalistes. En étant anticléricaux, nous ne pouvions pas penser organiser les Canadiens français, les amener au socialisme … Ça a été l'erreur de Saint-Martin, qui faisait ainsi plus de mal que de bien. Où allions-nous trouver nos alliés dans la Province de Québec si ce n'était chez les catholiques?" Quoted in Fournier, *Communisme et anticommunisme*, 29.
90 Weisbord, *Strangest Dream*, 45.
91 Fournier, *Communisme et anticommunisme*, 27–9.
92 It is unclear what provoked this intervention. The UO members may have viewed the alliance as a bourgeois organization.
93 In 1927 Boileau founded a young workers' group in Montreal which later evolved into the *Jeunesse ouvrière catholique*. Linteau, Durocher, and Robert, *Quebec: A History*, 456.
94 "Priest is Heckled by Communists," *Montreal Gazette*, 4 December 1930, 12.
95 "Les communistes portent une plainte," *Le Devoir*, 27 October 1930, 3.
96 Larivière, *Albert Saint-Martin*, 143–4.

97 "Reversal Sought in Court Decision," *Montreal Gazette*, 22 October 1934, 7; "Court of Appeals Reducing Arrears," *Montreal Gazette*, 29 November 1934, 3.
98 "Albert Saint-Martin à la cour Supérieure," *Le Canada*, 8 October 1935; "Le cité de Montréal paiera Saint-Martin," *Le Canada*, 30 November 1935.
99 Hamelin and Gagnon, *Histoire du catholicisme québécois*, 429.
100 "Ah, vous ne croyez pas en Dieu? La marmite que vous avez chez vous, pouvez-vous entrer dedans? Non. Il semble bien que l'idée de Dieu ne peut pas plus entrer dans votre tête que Dieu dans le marmite." "Un raid chez les communistes," *Le Devoir*, 27 April 1931, 3.
101 Ibid.
102 In May 1932, for example, members of the ACJC noisily interrupted a meeting. Larivière, *Albert Saint-Martin*, 148–9.
103 "C'est parce que l'Université ouvrière tout en étant un peu communiste, est surtout antireligieuse." Ibid., 149.
104 "Ce sont les attaques de l'Université ouvrière contre la religion qui, il n'y a pas de doute, lui permettent non seulement de continuer d'exister et de répandre ses doctrines antisociales, mais même de se dévelloper en ouvrant des succursales comme elle l'a fait l'hiver dernier, rue Montcalm. Que ses prédicants, pour bouleverser la société, insultent d'abord la religion, ils auront le champ libre; mais, s'ils ne s'attaquent qu'au capitalisme, à l'autorité civile, au gouvernement, on les bouclera. L'Université ouvrière est avant tout antireligieuse. Dans toutes ses assemblées, dans toutes les conférences, c'est la question religieuse qui prédomine." Jean Faubert, "Pourquoi on ne la ferme pas?" *Le Devoir*, 23 August 1932, 2: quoted in Larivière, *Albert Saint-Martin*, 149.
105 Larivière, *Albert Saint-Martin*, 149–50.
106 "Stenographers in Clashes as Bedard Defends Himself," *Montreal Gazette*, 3 March, 1932, 7; Lévesque, "Red Scares and Repression," 295.
107 Larivière, *Albert Saint-Martin*, 143, 150–1.
108 «La religion est l'art d'exploiter la crédulité, la crainte, l'espoir et l'ignorance de ses semblables." R. *v.* St. Martin (1933), 40 R. de Jur. 411 (Que. Sess. Ct.) 28.1–2.
109 Note the similarities to Sterry's distribution of the *Christian Inquirer*. "Disclaims Attack on Things Divine," *Montreal Gazette*, 6 September 1933, 3.
110 Houle-Courcelles, *Sur les traces*, 161.
111 Saint-Martin, *Sandwiches "à la shouashe."*
112 "L'opprobe de l'odieuse, de l'infâme, de l'ignoble charité." R. *v.* St. Martin (1933), 40 R. de Jur. 411 (Que. Sess. Ct.) 16.2.

113 A "véritable sadique théocratique," Ibid., 18.2–3; "précisément où l'on pose le postérieur des gens."
114 "Puis, défense de toucher des mains au précieux sandwich de la charité; il faut que les malheureux grignotent de leur mieux, saisissant rien qu'avec leur lèvres, la langue et le bout des dents, comme ils peuvent, des deux morceaux de pain, et, pour ne rien perdre; eh, bien, ils lèchent volontairement le fond de la chaise." Ibid., 22.7.
115 The reference is to Matthew 23:27; in the KJV the tombs are called "whited sepulchres."
116 R. v. St. Martin (1933), 40 R. de Jur. 411 (Que. Sess. Ct.) 22.8–10.
117 "Tout crime a un mobile: celui des institutions de charité est évident: c'est pour fin de lucre et de profit se composant de la différance entre les sommes fabuleuses qu'elles reçoivent de tous les gogos, y compris nos législateurs et l'insignifiante pitance qu'elles donnent aux nécessiteux." Ibid., 24.8.
118 Larivière, *Albert Saint-Martin*, 151.
119 Ibid., 152.
120 Ibid.; "Les Universités "Ouvrières" à Montréal: une loi provincial," *La Patrie*, 29 March 1933.
121 "Labour University is Reincarnated," *Montreal Gazette*, 8 May 1933.
122 "Trial for St. Martin," *Montreal Gazette*, 10 May 1933, 4; "Albert St. Martin Will Face Trial," *Montreal Gazette*, 15 September 1933, 6.
123 "To Face Two Charges," *Montreal Gazette*, 3 June 1933, 14.
124 "Albert St. Martin Case is Postponed," *Montreal Gazette*, 30 June 1933, 7.
125 "Albert St. Martin is Adjudged Sane," *Montreal Gazette*, 21 July 1933, 4.
126 Betcherman, *Swastika and the Maple Leaf*, 36.
127 On technocracy, see Akin, *Technocracy*. For some contemporary Canadian reactions to technocracy, see Wayne W. Parrish, "What is Technocracy," *New Outlook*, November 1932, 13–18; Colin McKay, "Labour and the Technocrats," *Canadian Unionist*, February 1933, 149, 156–7; George Soule, "Technocracy: Good Medicine or A Bedtime Story?" *OBU Bulletin*, 5 January 1933, 4, 5.
128 "Ancient Zealot is Still at his Post," *Montreal Gazette*, 30 September 1933, 7; an RCMP informant who was present when the fascists arrived claimed he'd had to "flee for his life." "The Riot at St. Martin's Hall," an entry from October 1933, Kealey and Whitaker, *RCMP Security Bulletins: The Depression Years, Part I*, 41.
129 "'Spartakus' Case," *Montreal Gazette*, 27 September 1933, 4.
130 "Les voleurs du temple de 1933." Larivière, *Albert Saint-Martin*, 157. The reference is to Matthew 21:13, in which Jesus drives moneychangers

out of the temple and tells them they have turned the house of prayer into a den of thieves.

131 "Disclaims Attack on Things Divine."
132 Ibid.
133 Ibid.
134 Larivière, *Albert Saint-Martin*, 158.
135 Ibid., 158–9.
136 R. v. St. Martin (1933), 40 R. de Jur. 411 (Que. Sess. Ct.) 9.1.
137 "Albert St. Martin Declared Guilty," *Montreal Gazette*, 14 November 1933, 7.
138 "Evidemment en ce qui concerne notre clergé et nos institutions religieuses, l'accusé semble bien mal renseigné, car la vérité admise par tout le monde de bonne foi, c'est que sans ces corps religieux, la foi, la moralité, la charité et l'honnêteté, je pourrais dire la conscience sociale auraient fait naufrage depuis longtemps." "Grossières, blessantes, répugnantes et d'une nature à blesser les sentiments religieux du peuple chrétien qui habite non seulement notre province mais notre pays." R. v. St. Martin (1933), 40 R. de Jur. 411 (Que. Sess. Ct.), 67.1.
139 Ibid., 68.5.
140 Ibid.,"Albert St. Martin Declared Guilty," *Montreal Gazette*, 14 November 1933, 7.
141 Larivière, *Albert Saint-Martin*, 159.
142 "Pilon trouvé coupable de libelle blasphématoire," *Le Devoir*, 15 June 1934, 3.
143 "Charged With Libel," *Montreal Gazette*, 19 December 1933, 3.
144 Gaston Pilon, "L'Histoire des Papes" (speech, Université ouvrière, Montreal, 13 December 1933) Transcribed by Wilhelmina Lapointe, included in the court documents: R. v. Pilon (15 June 1934) Montreal 15958 (Que. Sess. Ct.), available from the Bibliothèque et Archives nationales du Québec in Montreal.
145 "Mes amis on vous à enseigné que les papes étaient tous des saints, de bons garçons, des hommes infaillibles," Ibid.
146 Matter, *Histoire du Christianisme*; Jackson, *Concise Dictionary*; McCabe, *True Story*. Note the similarities to Gauvin's reliance on textual authority.
147 The dates Pilon gives for Sixtus are almost a thousand years too late; it is unclear if he was confusing him with Pope Callixtus II or if the stenographer made a mistake at some point.
148 See Karras, *Unmarriages*, 120–1.
149 "Franciscains et Communistes s'affrontent rue Montcalm," *Le Devoir*, 14 January 1934, 3.
150 Rollieu, *Gaston Pilon*, 4.

151 "Même en l'absence de tout texte explicite, la société, l'État, chez nous, reposent tout entiers sur la croyance à l'existence de Dieu. Comme dans tous les pays chrétiens, l'athéisme au Canada reste de droit naturel, mais à condition de ne faire l'objet d'aucune propagande, surtout qui soit de nature à heurter les convictions de la majorité de la population. L'athéisme professé publiquement, dans un but de propagande, à plus forte raison de provocation, a toujours été tenu pour contraire à l'ordre public." Quoted in Rollieu, *Gaston Pilon*, 2–3. Asselin may have meant this statement sarcastically.

152 "Défendre les bases de la religion! Mais, à quoi bon? N'avons-nous pas les gendarmes?" Ibid., 3.

153 Ibid., 4.

154 Oddly enough, in February 1934, when Saint-Martin was at the preliminary enquiry for one of Pilon's cases, he was himself arrested on new charges of seditious libel and for inciting violence. "Albert St. Martin Faces Two Counts," *Montreal Gazette*, 7 February 1934, 3.

155 "Pilon trouvé coupable de libelle blasphématoire," *Le Devoir*, 15 June 1934, 3; "Papal Criticism Ruled Blasphemy," *Montreal Gazette*, 16 June 1934, 17; Court records: R. *v.* Pilon (15 June 1934), Montreal 15958 (Que. Sess. Ct.); nothing appears to have come of the second blasphemy charge that had been levelled at Pilon. It is likely it was originally pressed only because the authorities were unsure whether attacks on popes constituted blasphemous libel. If the first charge had not led to a conviction, Pilon's remarks on the Virgin Mary and the Holy Spirit would have provided a more clear-cut case.

156 [Entry 22] July 1934, Kealey and Whitaker, RCMP *Security Bulletins: The Depression Years, Part I*, 165.

157 "Le récit de la conversion de Gaston Pilon fait par le Rév. Père Archange." *La Patrie*, 26 September 1934, 3; Rollieu, *Gaston Pilon*, 1.

158 "Je crois comprendre maintenant que seules les doctrines de l'Église romaine peuvent rétablir la paix sur notre planète et que seules elles peuvent empêcher les grands et les petits de se dévorer les uns les autres. Le Christ sur la croix disait au larron, après son repentir, qu'il serait dans le royaume des cieux avec lui. Comme le larron je veux mériter le pardon du Sauveur des hommes." Ibid., 5.

159 Ibid.

160 Henri Rochefort was a French radical who allied himself with the right in later life, though he remained an unbeliever. See Williams, *Henri Rochefort*, 251–78. Mussolini was personally anticlerical but for political reasons made his peace with the Roman Catholic Church; *L'Autorité* was a liberal newspaper with anticlerical leanings.

161 Rollieu, *Gaston Pilon*.
162 Pilon, *Du Communisme et Catholicisme*.
163 "Gaston Pilon, la star Pola Negri et les communistes," *Le Canada*, 26 November 1937.
164 "Révérend Père Archange Godbout."
165 "Gaston Pilon et le clergé," *Le Canada*, 26 November 1937; See also "L'Association humanitaire se fait anti-catholique," *L'Autorité*, 14 December 1935; "Pour Dieu! Ce qu'on rigole chez les humanitaires!" *L'Autorité*, 21 December 1935; "Comment les humanitaires multiplient leurs sottises," *L'Autorité*, 28 December 1935.
166 Lévesque, "Red Scares and Repression," 304.
167 Larivière, *Albert Saint-Martin*, 159.
168 Houle-Courcelles, *Sur les traces*, 173.
169 Any building used to disseminate radical ideas could be summarily shut down by the Attorney General for one year. Gossage and Little, *Illustrated History of Quebec*, 206.
170 Comeau and Bernard, *Droit de se taire*, 487.
171 Larivière, *Albert Saint-Martin*, 159.
172 Ibid., 160. In the decades to come Saint-Martin would serve as an inspiration for a new generation of Quebec leftists. A radical publishing house, the *Éditions coopératives Albert Saint-Martin*, was founded in Montreal in 1975 and put out important historical work on the history of Quebec's left, including Larivière's biography of Saint-Martin himself.
173 Houle-Courcelles, *Sur les traces*, 140–6, 155–6.
174 Rollieu, *Gaston Pilon*, 7.
175 "Une lutte terrible entre le régime d'exploitation et le communisme. Oui, l'Église, la religion, les dieux doivent disparaître pour être remplacés par la technique matérielle, c'est-à-dire le communisme scientifique, pour le bonheur de tous les hommes." Ibid., 6.
176 McCabe visited Montreal in 1928, although we do not know if members of the UO went to hear him speak. His presentation was in English. "Optimism Leads to Hope for Art," *Montreal Gazette*, 8 October 1928, 10.
177 Ramsay Cook discussed an interesting clash in early-twentieth-century Quebec between a doctor who wished to prove that evolutionary science was compatible with Catholicism and a bishop who rebuked his philosophical assumptions. Cook, *Watching Quebec*, 142–55.
178 "Le clergé est roi et maître." Houle-Courcelles, *Sur les traces*, 174–6.
179 Gossage and Little, *Illustrated History of Quebec*, 220.

CHAPTER SEVEN

1 Block, *Secular Northwest*; Bramadat, Killen, and Wilkins-Laflamme, *Religion at the Edge*.
2 Marks, *Infidels and the Damn Churches*, 4–6.
3 Ibid., 6, 29.
4 Ibid., 55–9.
5 Ibid., 59–64.
6 Ibid., 8.
7 Ibid., 214–15.
8 Ibid., 67–8.
9 Ibid., 60–2.
10 Ibid., 218.
11 Opp, *Lord for the Body*, 155–95; Burkinshaw, *Pilgrims in Lotus Land*, 101–11.
12 This does not appear to have been related to the earlier Toronto-based Canadian Secular Society.
13 Here we can see the secularist's disdain for "savages," which likely translated into contempt for Indigenous culture. A. McKay Jordan, "Superstition or Humanity?," ad, *Vancouver Sun*, 17 May 1923, 2.
14 A. McKay Jordan, "In a Forest of Doubt," ad, *Vancouver Sun*, 16 May 1923, 2; Same ad in *Vancouver Province*, 17 May 1923, 3.
15 A. McKay Jordan, "Faith!," ad, *Vancouver Sun*, 6 May 1923, 31.
16 Ibid.
17 "Wisdom of Womanhood," *Vancouver World*, 21 January 1902, 8; "Peculiar Surgery," *Daily Colonist*, 22 January 1902, 1; "To Prosecute Jordan Under Optometry Act," *Vancouver Province*, 23 December 1921, 11; "Charge Against Optometrist Dismissed," *Vancouver World*, 10 May 1922, 2; "Dr. Jordan Appeals Against Conviction," *Vancouver World*, 16 February 1924, 7.
18 Ads, *Vancouver World*, 18 April 1923, 9; and 19 April 1923, 9; ad, *Vancouver World*, 16 May 1923, 9.
19 "Dr. Jordan Writes Open Letter to Rev. A.E. Cooke," *Vancouver Sun*, 14 May 1923, 4; also "Sends Challenge to Rev. A.E. Cooke," *Vancouver World*, 9 May 1923, 4.
20 "Rev. A.E. Cooke Accepts Invitation," *Vancouver World*, 14 May 1923, 4; also "What is Your Opinion," *Vancouver Sun*, 15 May 1923, 4. In fact, Cooke's acceptance may not have been all that surprising. He was a liberal Congregationalist who was open to skeptical viewpoints. In a published sermon in June 1923, he made a point of favourably quoting rationalists

and agnostics like Herbert Spencer, Philip Vivian, and Ernest Renan. "What Kind of God Do We Believe In? Pastor's Question," *Vancouver World*, 23 June 1923, 18.

21 See "Two Divines in Limelight," *Vancouver Sun*, 20 May 1923, 1; see also Klassen, "Radio Mind." The *Vancouver Sun*, where Jordan published his full-page ads, also contained lengthy articles on the claims of Canadian spiritualists, about evidence for the existence of Atlantis, and on other extraordinary topics. See "Carnarvon and King Tutankhamen Meet in the Spirit World," *Vancouver Sun*, 11 May 1923, 3; and "The Riddle of Civilization," *Vancouver Sun*, 19 May 1923, 4. In this context Jordan's claims did not seem so outlandish.

22 Steeves, *Compassionate Rebel*, 30.

23 Aside from his activities with socialist parties, he and his wife, Anna Evelyn Curry, were involved with the Women's International League for Peace and Freedom throughout the 1920s. "Peace League Hears Interesting Address," *Vancouver Daily World* (5 March 1923), 7; "Women's League Hears Paper on Peace Events," *Province* (Vancouver) 15 January 1929, 9. In 1925 Curry attended the third annual Summer School of Social Science, a political retreat organized by the theosophical socialist Jack Logie, held under the auspices of the Federated Labor Party at Summerland, BC. He spoke on "The Evolution of Man" and on "The Poets of Revolt." Leftist figures like Rose Henderson and E.T. Kingsley also spoke. "Summer School of Social Science," *Canadian Farmer-Labor Advocate*, 23 July 1925, 5; W.J. Curry, "The Summerland Summer School," *Canadian Labor Advocate*, 28 August 1925, 8; Wagar, "Theosophical Socialists," 39.

24 W.J. Curry, "Campaign Manifesto: Capitalism in Decay, Labor Must Assume Control," *Canadian Labor Advocate*, 16 October 1925, 1; "How Labor Fared," *Canadian Labor Advocate*, 30 October 1925, 1.

25 W.J. Curry, "The Truth About Russia," *Canadian Labor Advocate*, 26 February 1926, 8.

26 "Bible Morality Subject," ad, *Vancouver Daily World*, 31 January 1924, 9.

27 "Dr. Curry's Lectures," *B.C. Federationist*, 20 October 1922, 4; "Spencer's Ghost Theory," *Province* (Vancouver), 12 October 1922, 24.

28 "Studies in Evolution Begin," *B.C. Federationist*, 11 November 1921, 4.

29 "Announcements," *Province* (Vancouver), 21 November 1921, 24; "Dr. Curry's Lectures: 'The Martyrs of Science,'" *B.C. Federationist*, 3 November 1922, 4.

30 "Dr. Curry and Christianity," *B.C. Federationist*, 27 October 1922, 3; "Christianity and the Class Struggle," *B.C. Federationist*, 15 February 1924, 4.
31 "Lessons in Evolution Given by Dr. Curry in Vancouver," *B.C. Federationist*, 25 February 1921.
32 Ibid. Another lecture on the evolution of humanity was given at a Unitarian church. Ad, *Province* (Vancouver), 25 February 1922, 28.
33 "Creation vs. Evolution," *Vancouver Sun*, 3 February 1922, 14; Ad, *Province* (Vancouver), 19 February 1922, 1.
34 Ada Muir, editor of "The Torch Monthly," took the affirmative side. The debate was held at a Unitarian church. "The Free Forum," ad, *Vancouver Sun*, 18 December 1926, 8.
35 Ad, *Vancouver Daily World*, 9 November 1922, 9; Ad, *Vancouver Daily World*, 1 November 1923, 9.
36 "Attacks on Religion" (letter), *B.C. Federationist*, 22 April 1918, 6.
37 "Religion and Morals" (letter), *B.C. Federationist*, 9 January 1920, 7. For the history of secularists describing secularism as a form of religion, see Schmidt, *Church of Saint Thomas Paine*.
38 "Why Soviets Oppose Religion – Forum," *Vancouver Sun*, 19 November 1932, 18.
39 Curry died in Vancouver in 1953 at the age of eighty-seven.
40 "Victoria Gains Another Society," *Times Colonist* (Victoria, BC), 17 October 1924, 9.
41 "Rationalists Hold Meeting," *Times Colonist* (Victoria, BC), 21 October 1924, 2. "Quite a Large Number Gathered," *Victoria Daily Times*, 11 November 1924, 5; "Rationalist Society," *Victoria Daily Times*, 2 December 1924, 11.
42 "Humanism vs. Communism" (letter), *Vancouver Sun*, 25 July 1935, 4.
43 Ad, *Vancouver Sun*, 21 September 1935, 17; ad, *Vancouver Sun*, 28 September 1935, 18.
44 "Social Credit Study Group," *Vancouver News-Herald*, 4 August 1936, 12.
45 Bob Bouchette, "Lend Me Your Years: The Call to Rationalism – Reason Over All?," *Vancouver Sun*, 13 October 1936, 6.
46 Cassidy and Pearce, *Papers of Harry Cassidy*, 345, 405, 463–4.
47 Ibid., 4.
48 Ibid., 172–3, 213, 389.
49 Ibid., 238-240. Beatrice Pearce, Cassidy's fiancée, saw Price in action at a different service. She was equally skeptical. Ibid., 233.

50 "No Religious War in Vancouver," *Vancouver Sun*, 16 May 1923, 4. "Hypnotic Suggestion Used by Dr. Price in Meetings Here: This is Conclusion of Committee of Enquiry," *Daily Province*, 22 December 1923, 28; "Minority Case is Set Forth," *Daily Province*, 22 December 1923, 2.
51 "No Religious War in Vancouver."
52 "Spirit of Worship," *Vancouver Province*, 22 December 1923, 6.
53 Marks, *Infidels and the Damn Churches*, 218.
54 *Sixth Census of Canada, 1921*, vol. 1, *Population* (Ottawa: F.A. Acland, King's Printer, 1924), 572–3.
55 *Seventh Census of Canada 1931*, vol. 1, *Summary* (Ottawa: J.O. Patenaude, King's Printer, 1936).
56 Forbes, *Challenging the Regional Stereotype*.
57 "Protest Over School Text-Book Spreading," *Halifax Herald*, 7 November 1934, 1; Seary and Paterson, *Story of Civilization*.
58 Thanks are due to Robin Bates for permitting me to read his unpublished paper, "'Bewildering and Contradictory Speculations': Canadian Protestant Culture and Evolution, 1914–1934, With a Case Study," which discusses the textbook controversy and provided a helpful starting point for my own research. That paper was submitted to Dr Ian McKay on 21 April 2003. A note about terminology: the word "creationist" was rarely used at the time, if at all. It implies a unified position that did not exist until later in the twentieth century. Thus, the term "anti-evolutionist" will be used instead.
59 "Defends New School Text-Book," *Halifax Herald*, 8 November 1934, 4.; Patterson, "Society and Education."
60 Seary and Paterson, *Story of Civilization*, 1. The footnote seems to have been designed to stave off controversy. Another detail that hints in that direction is the caption given under a picture of Darwin. "In the background is the house at Downe, where the great scientist lived after 1842, not far from the village church in which for many years he regularly read the lessons." The emphasis on Darwin as a faithful Christian seems designed to deflect religious criticism. Ibid., 173. On the opposite page, however, the authors described *The Origin of Species*, not the Bible, as the "book which has probably had a greater influence on the trend of human thought than any other single contribution to knowledge." Ibid., 172.
61 See Betts, "Argument of the Century."
62 Giordano, *Twentieth-Century Textbook Wars*, 117–18; Larson, *Summer for the Gods*, 230–1.
63 Later in 1935 First Presbyterian would acrimoniously split. Murray organized one faction into a new congregation, Westminster Church.

He was outspoken in his opinions and would continue to be what one historian calls "a disruptive presence" in the denomination through the late 1940s. MacLeod, *W. Stanford Reid*, 104–5.

64 "Petition Against School Text Book," *Halifax Herald*, 6 November 1934, 3.
65 "North Sydney Presbyterians Score Book," *Halifax Herald*, 16 November 1934, 1. "Meeting Asks Removal of School Book," *Halifax Herald*, 23 November 1934, 3; "School Text by Boulardarie Group," *Halifax Chronicle*, 26 December 1934, 3.
66 "Evolution Theory is Under Fire," *Halifax Chronicle*, 6 November 1934, 1–2.
67 "Varied Views Given by Scores in School Textbook Controversy," *Halifax Herald*, 13 December 1934, 15; "Pictou Meeting Joins in Textbook Protest," *Halifax Chronicle*, 16 November 1934, 1; "U.S. Fundamentalist Seen in N.S. Unrest," *Toronto Star*, 14 December 1934, 7; "Cleric Has Faith in Lunenburg's Teachers," *Halifax Chronicle*, 27 November 1934, 1–2.
68 "Tear Page from Book is Advice of Cleric," 24 November 1934, *Halifax Chronicle*, 1; "Baptist Convention is Critical of Teachings," *Halifax Herald*, 23 November 1934, 3; "Would Replace Debated Text," *Halifax Herald*, 1 December 1934, 3; "Preacher Regrets Theory Advanced," *Halifax Herald*, 21 November 1934, 3; "Oppose Book," *Halifax Chronicle*, 27 November 1934, 2; "Preacher Flays Evolution Theory," *Halifax Chronicle*, 19 November 1934, 2.
69 Rawlyk, *Champions of the Truth*, 39–75; John J. Sidey, Letter to the editor, *Halifax Herald*, 1 December 1934, 6.
70 J.W. Hill, "Evolution," *Halifax Chronicle*, 20 November 1934, 8.
71 "Ask that Text Book be Revised or Withdrawn," *Halifax Chronicle*, 8 December 1934, 3.
72 "Clergy Criticized for Inactivity Over School Books"; "Menace to Empire is Foreseen," *Halifax Chronicle*, 9 November 1934, 1.
73 Alexander MacDonald, "The Case Plainly Stated," *Halifax Chronicle*, 5 January 1935, 10. MacDonald had the support of an internationally renowned scholar. Étienne Gilson, a French philosopher and historian of medieval philosophy, had been living in Canada for seven years, working as the director of the Institute of Medieval Studies at the University of Toronto. Asked about the textbook controversy, Gilson replied: "Evolution is something that looks scientific enough, but it is absolutely impossible to establish. A scientific fact can be shown in a laboratory. But that man comes from a lower animal – how could we prove it? How low is the animal from which we are supposed to come?" "Opinion Divided on Merits of Textbook," *Halifax Chronicle*, 13 November 1934, 1.

74 "Conflicting Attitudes on School Text-Book," *Halifax Herald*, 17 January 1935, 6.
75 H. Percy Blanshard, "School books," *Halifax Herald*, 26 November 1934, 6.
76 One significant fact about education in the province that was never discussed explicitly in the controversy helps make sense of some parental concerns: secondary education had only recently become compulsory for many teens. In 1933 the age at which Nova Scotia's teens were permitted to leave school was raised to sixteen for urban students and fourteen for rural ones. This was part of a nation-wide trend. During the 1920s and '30s most provinces gradually raised the age at which students were allowed to leave school. Most of the Grade 11 students assigned *The Story of Civilization* would have been sixteen, and thus could have left school rather than read it if they were so inclined. It was only in 1946 that a student had to complete the school year even if they turned fourteen or sixteen partway through it. See Oreopoulous, "Canadian Compulsory School Laws," 9.
77 "Science and Religion," *Halifax Herald*, 19 January 1935, 6.
78 "Says Much Noise Made," *Halifax Chronicle*, 17 December 1934, 3.
79 "Terms Text Book Row 'Sham Fight,'" *Halifax Chronicle*, 17 December 1934, 12; "Issue Sham Fight Declares Speaker," *Halifax Herald*, 17 December 1934, 6. A number of local United Church ministers argued that Darwinism specifically was outmoded and that newer interpretations of evolution left more room for God. Rev. Gerald Rogers of Pictou is an example of a minister who took this line. "Gives New Light on Controversy," *Halifax Herald*, 29 November 1934, 2; Gerald Rogers, "Giving Leadership Only," *Halifax Chronicle*, 3 December 1934, 8; "Pictou Minister is Believer in Evolution Theory," *Halifax Chronicle*, 24 November 1934, 4. This was a common viewpoint in the early twentieth century, which historian of science Peter J. Bowler has termed "the eclipse of Darwinism." See Bowler, *Reconciling Science and Religion*.
80 "Varied Views Given by Scores in School Textbook Controversy," *Halifax Herald*, 13 December 1934, 15.
81 On the 1891 census he had called himself a secularist.
82 A.W. Shatford, "How We Behave, What Matters," *Halifax Chronicle*, 26 December 1934, 8. The recapitulation theory of the embryo, while popular at the time, was disproved later in the twentieth century.
83 In the 1921 census Tufts's family was listed as Baptist. Various articles in Halifax newspapers indicate that she was an aspiring poet and occasional book reviewer.
84 "Varied Views Given by Scores in School Textbook Controversy."

85 J.L. McDonald, "That Book," *Halifax Chronicle*, 31 December 1934, 8.
86 W.P. Lawrence, "Falmouth Man Enters Controversy," *Halifax Chronicle*, 27 December 1934, 3. Lawrence's letter had originally been published in the *Hants Journal*, in response to one Gilbert Grossley.
87 Charles Wm. Macdonald.
88 Fillmore, *Maritime Radical*, 153, 160.
89 Ibid., 161.
90 Ad, *Advertiser* (Kentville), 15 November 1934, 5.
91 Ad, *Advertiser* (Kentville), 22 November 1934, 5.
92 Ad, *Advertiser* (Kentville), 13 December 1934, 5; Elmer Gantry was the titular preacher and scoundrel of Sinclair Lewis's 1927 satirical novel.
93 Ad, *Advertiser* (Kentville), 27 December 1934, 7.
94 Ad, *Advertiser* (Kentville), 10 January 1935, 7.
95 Frank and Reilly, "Emergence of the Socialist Movement," 108.
96 Roscoe A. Fillmore, "That Text Book," *Halifax Chronicle*, 19 November 1934, 8.
97 Roscoe A. Fillmore, "A Worker's Notes," *The Steelworker*, 24 November 1934, 5; see also Fillmore, *Maritime Radical*, 174.
98 His position is reminiscent of that of the OBU, as discussed in chapter 2. Biological evolution was seen as a guarantor of social evolution, which in turn implied the eventual triumph of socialism.
99 Roscoe A. Fillmore, "A Worker's Notes," *The Steelworker*, 24 November 1934, 5.
100 Frank & Reilly, "Emergence of the Socialist Movement," 108.
101 McLachlan was referring to the death of his daughter Kate in 1927. Originally from the *Nova Scotia Miner*, 21 December 1932, and quoted in Frank, *J.B. McLachlan*, 440.
102 The official was a Pentecostal. MacEachern, *George MacEachern: An Autobiography*, 95.
103 Frank, *J.B. McLachlan*, 68, 182–3, 214, 420–1.
104 MacIntyre was viewed positively by local priests and was invited to work with the budding cooperative-based Antigonish Movement. Ludlow, *Canny Scot*, 185.
105 Baum, "Social Catholicism in Nova Scotia," 140–1.
106 Earle, "Radicalism in Decline," 47, 57; Ludlow, *Canny Scot*, 134–5.
107 Huxley, *Religion Without Revelation*; "Foresees Science in New Conflict," *Halifax Herald*, 12 January 1935, 2.
108 "Bennett Reforms, Old Stuff Huxley Thinks," *Halifax Chronicle*, 12 January 1935, 1, 8; "Sees Power Balance with Lloyd George," *Toronto Star*, 12 January 1935, 21.

109 "Foresees Science in New Conflict," *Halifax Herald*, 12 January 1935, 2.
110 "Says Human Race Being Destroyed," *Halifax Herald*, 14 January 1935, 12. Huxley would go on to popularize the neo-Darwinian synthesis that was revitalizing the field of evolutionary biology in the interwar years. This new synthesis would put natural selection back on central stage and close off the alternative theories of evolution that reconcilers of science and religion preferred.
111 In November 1934 Premier Macdonald had promised those opposed to the textbook that the Council of Public Instruction would deal with the matter. However, the minutes of the Council for November 1934 through February 1935 contain no mention whatsoever of the controversy. Either the Council considered the topic sensitive enough to keep out of the minutes, or not important enough to talk about. "Book Fight Recalled," *Halifax Chronicle*, 8 November 1934, 1; Council of Public Instruction minutes and other material, 3 November 1934 to 14 February 1935. RG14, vol. 44. Nova Scotia Archives; Fisher, "Be-All and End-All," 137–9.
112 Nor were all members of the Centreville Socialists unbelievers.

CHAPTER EIGHT

1 Cecil Wolfe to Marshall Gauvin, 28 July 1940, Box 10, Fol. 15, Gauvin fonds.
2 Tribe, *100 Years of Freethought*, 114.
3 In an oral history interview conducted after the war, an anonymous Canadian veteran recalled: "So after about five church parades – and the damned things were compulsory –about 10 of us decided to refuse to go any more. We were atheists, we told the hut corporal. He told the sergeant and the sergeant told the lieutenant and so on. So we were excused church parade this Sunday, but it wasn't a case of going back and hitting the sack. We were given special duties." The soldiers were put to work oiling down their barracks, a gruelling task that took much of the day. The men who went to church were taken to the beach afterwards for a swim and a picnic. The message was clear. "Next Sunday when the company lined up for church parade, the sergeant major bellowed out that all those wishing to miss the church parade because of, as he put it, religious dissent, they were to fall out. Not a person moved. Not one man. Last time they had us oiling the hut, and I figured if we tried the atheist stunt again they'd either have us doing the next hut in line or painting the goddamned water tower blazing red." Broadfoot, *Six War Years*, 92–3.

4 Quoted in Keshen, *Saints, Sinners, and Soldiers*, 217. A similar situation in the United States led a humanist mother to sue the local school district, leading eventually to a Supreme Court ruling forbidding religious education in American schools. See McCollum, *One Woman's Fight*.
5 Sherman was a doctor and ex-missionary who came to atheism in 1945 and became a secular humanist leader in British Columbia. Block, "Ungodly Grandmother." Chisholm, a psychiatrist, was an outspoken humanist, as well as Canada's first deputy minister of health, and the first director of the World Health Organization. Flynn, *New Encyclopedia of Unbelief*, 174. Mishra and Morgentaler, both physicians, were involved with the creation of the Humanist Association of Canada in 1968 (Mishra first started a humanist group in Montreal in 1954). Melton, *Toward a Reasonable World*, 13–14.
6 Marshall Gauvin spoke on the Sterry trial but did not mention Sterry's involvement with the Rationalist Society of Canada.
7 "Dr. Jordan Writes Open Letter to Rev. A.E. Cooke," *Vancouver Sun*, 14 May 1923, 4; see chapter 7.
8 Grace H. Hunter, "The Legal Status of Christianity in Ontario: Court Decisions that Remind One of Tennessee and the Scopes Trial," *Saturday Night*, 13 February 1926, 5.
9 This is the contention of the classicist Tim Whitmarsh in regard to Greco-Roman atheism. Despite the major differences in the way the ancients thought about religion and divinity in comparison with medieval or modern people, Whitmarsh argues that certain atheist arguments and intuitions have remained consistent over the millennia. Whitmarsh, *Battling the Gods*.

Bibliography

ARCHIVAL SOURCES CONSULTED

Ottawa, Ontario

LIBRARY AND ARCHIVES CANADA
Bennett, R.B. correspondence
Department of Customs and Excise circulars
Department of Justice correspondence
King, Mackenzie correspondence
Post Office Department memos
Woodsworth, James Shaver fonds

Toronto, Ontario

ARCHIVES OF ONTARIO
Attorney General Central Registry Criminal and Civil Files
Ontario Ministry of Government Services, Registration Division, Companies and Personal Property Security Branch. Rationalist Society of Canada incorporation file
R v. Ernest V. Sterry (March 1927) County of York (General Sessions of the Peace)

Winnipeg, Manitoba

UNIVERSITY OF MANITOBA ARCHIVES
Gauvin, Marshall fonds
Rea, Ed fonds: Research Papers in Manitoba History Collection

ARCHIVES OF MANITOBA
Russell, R.B., "Material on Unions and Winnipeg Strike 1891–c1970"

Quebec City, Quebec

BIBLIOTHÈQUE ET ARCHIVES NATIONALES DU QUÉBEC
R. v. St. Martin (1933), 40 R. de Jur. 411 (Que. Sess. Ct.).
R. v. Pilon (15 June 1934), Montreal 15958 (Que. Sess. Ct.).

Halifax, Nova Scotia

NOVA SCOTIA ARCHIVES
Council of Public Instruction minutes

NEWSPAPERS AND MAGAZINES

Advertiser (Kentville, NS)
Autorité (Montreal)
B.C. Federationist
Canada (Montreal)
Canadan Uutiset (Port Arthur, ON)
Canadian Bar Review
Canadian Forum
Canadian Jewish Review
Canadian Farmer-Labor Advocate
Canadian Labor Advocate
Canadian Unionist
Chicago Tribune
Christian Inquirer
Daily Colonist (Victoria)
Devoir (Montreal)
Gateway (University of Alberta)
Globe & Mail
Halifax Chronicle
Halifax Herald
Huntington Herald (Indiana)
Hutchinson News (Kansas)
Kingston Standard (ON)
Lethbridge Herald
Literary Digest
Literary Guide (London, UK)
Los Angeles Times
Man (Toronto)
Manitoba Free Press
Miami Daily News and Metropolis
Montreal Gazette
New Castle News (Pennsylvania)
New Outlook

New York Times
Ogden Standard-Examiner
One Big Union (OBU) Bulletin
Oracle of Reason
Ottawa Citizen
Ottawa Journal
Patrie, La
Portsmouth Daily Times (Ohio)
Presbyterian Record
Province (Vancouver)
Quebec Telegraph
Santa Cruz News (California)
Saskatoon Star-Phoenix
Saturday Night
Springfield Daily News (Missouri)
Time (New York)
Times (London)
Toronto Evening Telegram
Toronto Globe
Toronto Star
Truth Seeker
Vie ouvrière
Washington Post
Winnipeg Free Press
Winnipeg Tribune
Vancouver Daily World
Vancouver Sun
Vapaus (Sudbury, ON)

BOOKS AND ARTICLES

Acland, Peregrine. *All Else Is Folly*. Toronto: McClelland & Stewart, 1929.

Airhart, Phyllis D. *A Church with the Soul of a Nation: Making and Remaking the United Church of Canada*. Montreal and Kingston: McGill-Queen's University Press, 2014.

Akin, William E. *Technocracy and the American Dream: The Technocrat Movement, 1900–1941*. Berkeley: University of California Press, 1977.

Alexander, Nathan. *Race in a Godless World: Atheism, Race, and Civilization, 1850–1914*. Manchester: Manchester University Press, 2019.

Allen, Richard. "Bland, Salem Goldworth." In *Canadian Encyclopedia*. Toronto: Historica Canada, 2013. http://www.thecanadian encyclopedia.ca/en/article/salem-bland.

Altenbaugh, Richard J. *Education for Struggle: The American Labor Colleges of the 1920s and 1930s*. Philadelphia: Temple University Press, 1990.

Angus, Ian. *Canadian Bolsheviks: The Early Years of the Communist Party of Canada*. 2nd ed. Bloomington: Trafford, 2004.

Arch, Robert. "The Old Rationalism and the New." *Rationalist Annual*, 1931.

Backhouse, Constance. *Colour-Coded: A Legal History of Racism in Canada, 1900–1950*. Toronto: University of Toronto Press, 1999.

– "Gender and Race in the Construction of 'Legal Professionalism': Historical Perspectives." The Chief Justice of Ontario's Advisory

Committee on Professionalism, First Colloquia on the Legal Profession, 20 October 2003. https://papers.ssrn.com/sol3/papers.cfm?abstract_id=2273323.

"Baron Eugene Alexandrovich Fersen." Lightbearers World Center, 2020. https://www.scienceofbeing.com/eugene-fersen.

Baum, Gregory. "Catholicism and Secularization in Quebec." In *Rethinking Church, State and Modernity: Canada Between Europe and America*. Edited by David Lyon and Margaret Van Die, 149–65. Toronto: University of Toronto Press, 2000.

– "Social Catholicism in Nova Scotia: The Thirties." In *Religion and Culture in Canada/Religion et Culture au Canada*, edited by Peter Slater, 117–48. Waterloo, ON: Wilfrid Laurier University Press, 1978.

Behiels, Michael D. *Prelude to Quebec's Quiet Revolution: Liberalism Versus Neo-nationalism, 1945–1960*. Montreal and Kingston: McGill-Queen's University Press, 1985.

Belkin, Simon. *Le mouvement ouvrier juif au Canada. 1904–1920*. Sillery: Éditions du septentrion, 1999.

Betcherman, Lita-Rose. *Ernest Lapointe: Mackenzie King's Great Quebec Lieutenant*. Toronto: University of Toronto, 2002.

– *The Little Band: The Clashes Between the Communists and the Political and Legal Establishment in Canada, 1928–1932*. Ottawa: Deneau, 1982.

– *The Swastika and the Maple Leaf: Fascist Movements in Canada in the Thirties*. Toronto: Fitzhenry & Whiteside, 1975.

Betts, Edward G. "The Argument of the Century: The Ontario Press Coverage of the Scopes Trial and the Death of William Jennings Bryan," MA thesis, Queen's University, 1992.

Betts, Gregory. *Avant-Garde Canadian Literature: The Early Manifestations*. Toronto: University of Toronto Press, 2013.

Biale, David. *Not in the Heavens: The Tradition of Jewish Secular Thought*. Princeton: Princeton University Press, 2011.

Bibby, Reginald. *Unknown Gods: The Ongoing Story of Religion in Canada*. Don Mills, ON: Stoddart, 1993.

Blackwell, John D. "Blake, Samuel Hume." In *Dictionary of Canadian Biography*, vol. 14. Toronto and Quebec: University of Toronto/Université Laval, 1998. http://www.biographi.ca/en/bio/blake_samuel_hume_14E.html.

Blee, Kathleen M. *Women of the Klan: Racism and Gender in the 1920s*. Berkeley: University of California Press, 1991.

Block, Tina. *The Secular Northwest: Religion and Irreligion in Everyday Postwar Life*. Vancouver: UBC Press, 2016.

- "Ungodly Grandmother: Marian Sherman and the Social Dimensions of Atheism in Postwar Canada." *Journal of Women's History* 26, no. 4 (Winter 2014), 132–54.
Bossi, Emilio. *Gesù Cristo non è mai esistito*. Milan: Società Editoriale Milanese, 1900.
Bowen, Kurt. *Christians in a Secular World: The Canadian Experience*. Montreal and Kingston: McGill-Queen's University Press, 2004.
Bowler, Peter J. *Reconciling Science and Religion: The Debate in Early-Twentieth-Century Britain*. Chicago: University of Chicago Press, 2001.
Boyko, John. *Into the Hurricane: Attacking Socialism and the CCF*. Winnipeg: J. Gordon Shillingford, 2006.
Bradburn, Jamie. "Historicist: The Dennison School of Speech Correction." *Torontoist*, 2012. http://torontoist.com/2012/01/historicist-the-dennison-school-of-speech-correction.
Bramadat, Paul, and David Seljak, "Charting the New Terrain." In Bramadat and Seljak, *Christianity and Ethnicity*, 3–48.
- eds. *Christianity and Ethnicity in Canada*. Toronto: University of Toronto Press, 2008.
Bramadat, Paul, Patricia O'Connell Killen, and Sarah Wilkins-Laflamme, eds. *Religion at the Edge: Nature, Spirituality, and Secularity in the Pacific Northwest*. Vancouver: UBC Press, 2022.
Braude, Ann. "Forum: Female Experience in American Religion." *Religion and American Culture* 5 (Winter 1995): 1–21.
- "Women's History Is American Religious History." In *Retelling U.S. Religious History*, edited by Thomas A. Tweed, 87–107. Berkeley: University of California Press, 1997.
Braun, Claude M.J. *Québec athée*. Montreal: Michel Brûlé, 2010.
Brenner, Philip S. "Identity as a Determinant of the Overreporting of Church Attendance in Canada." *Journal for the Scientific Study of Religion* 51, no. 2 (2012) 377–85.
Brisson, Frédéric. "International Sources of Supply." In Gerson and Michon, *History of the Book*, 389–93.
Broadfoot, Barry. *Six War Years 1939–1945: Memories of Canadians at Home and Abroad*. Don Mills: PaperJacks, 1974.
Brown, Callum. *The Death of Christian Britain: Understanding Secularisation 1800–2000*, 2nd ed. London: Routledge, 2009.
- *Religion and the Demographic Revolution: Women and Secularisation in Canada, Ireland, UK and USA Since the 1960s*. Woodbridge: Boydell Press, 2012.

Budd, Susan. *Varieties of Unbelief: Atheists and Agnostics in English Society, 1850–1960*. London: Heinemann, 1977.

Burkinshaw, Robert. *Pilgrims in Lotus Land: Conservative Protestantism in British Columbia, 1917–1981*. Montreal and Kingston: McGill-Queen's University Press, 1995.

Campbell, James. "Cosmic Indifferentism in the Fiction of H.P. Lovecraft." In Robillard, *American Supernatural Fiction*, 167–228.

Campbell, J. Peter. *Canadian Marxists and the Search for a Third Way*. Montreal and Kingston: McGill-Queen's University Press, 1999.

– *Rose Henderson: A Woman for the People*. Montreal and Kingston: McGill-Queen's University Press, 2010.

Canada. *Criminal Code*, Section 296 (RSC 1985, c. C-46).

"Canada." In *The Encyclopedia of Unbelief*, edited by Gordon Stein, vol. 1. Amherst, NY: Prometheus Books, 1985.

Carpenter, Joel. *Revive Us Again: The Reawakening of American Fundamentalism*. Oxford: Oxford University Press, 2003.

Cassidy, Harry, and Beatrice Pearce. *The Papers of Harry Cassidy and Beatrice Pearce: The Courtship Years, 1917–1925*. Edited by Keith Walden. Toronto: The Champlain Society, 2009.

Caudill, Edward. *Darwinian Myths: The Legends and Misuses of a Theory*. Knoxville: University of Tennessee Press, 1997.

Chabot, Richard. "Papineau, Joseph." In *Dictionary of Canadian Biography*, vol. 12. Toronto and Quebec: University of Toronto/Université Laval, 1988. http://www.biographi.ca/en/bio.php?id_nbr=3592.

Charles Wm. Macdonald: Seaman, Labourer, Artist, Manufacturer (1874–1967). Halifax: Art Gallery of Nova Scotia, [1980].

Child, Philip. *God's Sparrows*. Toronto: McClelland & Stewart, 1937.

Christie, Nancy, and Michael Gauvreau. *A Full-Orbed Christianity: The Protestant Churches and Social Welfare in Canada, 1900–1940*. Montreal and Kingston: McGill-Queen's University Press, 1996.

Clarke, Brian. "English-Speaking Canada from 1854." In Murphy and Perin, *Concise History of Christianity*, 261–360. Oxford: Oxford University Press, 1996.

Clarke, Brian, and Stuart Macdonald. *Leaving Christianity: Changing Allegiances in Canada*. Montreal and Kingston: McGill-Queen's University Press, 2017.

Coates, Donna, "War." In *Encyclopedia of Literature in Canada*, edited by W.H. New, 1186–96. Toronto: University of Toronto Press, 2002.

Comacchio, Cynthia. *The Dominion of Youth: Adolescence and the Making of Modern Canada, 1920–1950.* Waterloo: Wilfrid Laurier University Press, 2006.

Comeau, Gayle M. "Fleming, Robert John." In *Dictionary of Canadian Biography,* vol. 15. Toronto and Quebec: University of Toronto/Université Laval, 2005. http://www.biographi.ca/en/bio/fleming_robert_john_15E.html.

Comeau, Robert, and Bernard Dionne. *Le droit de se taire: Histoire des communistes au Québec, de la Première Guerre mondiale à la Révolution tranquille.* Montreal: VLB Éditeur, 1989.

Constitution and By-laws of the Montreal Pioneer Freethought Club. Montreal: Montreal Pioneer Freethought Club, 1880.

Conway, J.S. *The Nazi Persecution of the Churches, 1933–1945.* Vancouver: Regent College Publishing, 2001.

Cook, Ramsay. *The Regenerators: Social Criticism in Late Victorian English Canada.* Toronto: University of Toronto Press, 1985.

– *Watching Quebec: Selected Essays.* Montreal and Kingston: McGill-Queen's University Press, 2005.

Cook, Sharon Anne. "Beyond the Congregation: Women and Canadian Evangelicalism Reconsidered." In Rawlyk, *Aspects of the Canadian Evangelical Experience,* 403–16.

Cooke, Bill. *A Rebel to His Last Breath: Joseph McCabe and Rationalism.* Amherst: Prometheus Books, 2001.

Copp, Terry. *The Anatomy of Poverty: The Conditions of the Working Class in Montreal 1897–1929.* Toronto: McClelland & Stewart, 1974.

– "Montreal's Municipal Government and the Crisis of the 1930s." In *The Usable Urban Past: Planning and Politics in the Modern Canadian City.* Edited by Alan F.J. Artibise and Gilbert A. Stelter, 112–29. Toronto: Macmillan, 1979.

Corbeil, Patrick J. *Empire and Progress in the Victorian Secularist Movement: Imagining a Secular World.* London: Palgrave Macmillan, 2022.

Cornellisen, Louis. *Religiosity in Canada and its Evolution from 1985 to 2019.* Ottawa: Statistics Canada, 2021. https://www150.statcan.gc.ca/n1/pub/75-006-x/2021001/article/00010-eng.pdf.

Crerar, Duff. *Padres in No Man's Land: Canadian Chaplains and the Great War.* Montreal and Kingston: McGill-Queen's University, 1995.

Crouse, Eric R. *Revival in the City: The Impact of American Evangelists in Canada, 1884–1914.* Montreal and Kingston: McGill-Queen's University Press, 2005.

Custance, Florence. "Organizing the Women's Labor League (1924)." Socialist History Project. http://www.socialisthistory.ca/Docs/Leninist/WLL-Custance_24.htm.

Dagenais, Michèle. *Des pouvoirs et des hommes: L'Administration muncipale de Montréal, 1900–1950.* Montreal and Kingston: McGill-Queen's University Press, 2000.

Dawkins, Richard. *River Out of Eden: A Darwinian View of Life.* New York: Basic Books, 1995.

Degras, Jane, ed. *The Communist International 1919–1943. Documents,* vol. 2, *1923–1928.* London: Oxford University Press, 1960.

De Lagrave, Jean-Paul. *Voltaire's Man in America.* Translated by Arnold Bennett. Montreal: Robert Davies Multimedia Publishing, 1997.

Den Otter, A.A. *The Philosophy of Railways: The Transcontinental Railway Idea in British North America.* Toronto: University of Toronto Press, 1997.

Dickinson, John A., and Brian Young. *A Short History of Quebec.* 4th ed. Montreal and Kingston: McGill-Queen's University Press, 2008.

Dochuk, Darren. "Redeeming the City: Premillenialism, Piety and the Politics of Reform in Late-Nineteenth Century Toronto." In *Historical Papers 2000,* edited by Bruce L. Guenther, 53–72. Canadian Society of Church History, 2000. http://www.stuartbarnard.com/csch-sche/wp-content/uploads/2013/06/2000-historical-papers-complete.pdf.

Doren, Carl Van. "Why I Am an Unbeliever." *Forum* 76, no. 6 (December 1926), 864–9.

Doyle, James. *Progressive Heritage: The Evolution of a Politically Radical Literary Tradition in Canada.* Waterloo: Wilfrid Laurier University Press, 2002.

Dutil, Patrice. *Devil's Advocate: Godfroy Langlois and the Politics of Liberal Progressivism in Laurier's Quebec.* Montreal: Davies, 1994.

Eagleton, Terry. Introduction to *The Gospels.* London: Verso, 2007.

Earle, Michael. "Radicalism in Decline: Labour and Politics in Industrial Cape Breton, 1930-1950." PhD diss., Dalhousie University, 1990. https://dalspace.library.dal.ca/handle/10222/55122.

Eddy, Sherwood. *Russia To-Day: What Can We Learn from It?* London: George Allen & Unwin, 1934.

Edwards, Frank. "Behind the North Gate: The Prison Story of Dr. Oswald Withrow." *Profile Kingston,* 15 September 2004.

Elliott, David R. "Knowing No Borders: Canadian Contributions to American Fundamentalism." In *Amazing Grace: Evangelicalism in*

Australia, Britain, Canada, and the United States, edited by George A. Rawlyk and Mark A. Noll. Montreal and Kingston: McGill-Queen's University Press, 1994.

Errington, Jane. *The Lion, the Eagle and Upper Canada: A Developing Colonial Ideology.* 2nd ed. Montreal and Kingston: McGill-Queen's University Press, 2012.

Fast, Vera. "The Labor Church in Winnipeg." In *Prairie Spirit: Perspectives on the Heritage of the United Church of Canada in the West*, edited by Dennis L. Butcher et al., 233–49. Winnipeg: University of Manitoba Press, 1985.

Faure, Sébastian. *Douze preuves de l'inexistence de Dieu.* Rambouillet, Seine-et-Oise: La Ruche, 1914.

Febvre, Lucien. *The Problem of Unbelief in the 16th Century: The Religion of Rabelais.* Cambridge, MA: Harvard University Press, 1985.

Fillmore, Nicholas. *Maritime Radical: The Life & Times of Roscoe Fillmore.* Toronto: Between the Lines, 1992.

Fisher, Bruce Hubert. "'The Be-All and End-All of Teaching': Nova Scotia's Provincial Examinations in History, 1893–1972." MEd thesis, St Mary's University, 2000. https://library2.smu.ca/handle/01/22632.

Fitzgerald, F. Scott. *This Side of Paradise.* New York: Scribner, 1920.

Fletcher, Wendy. "Canadian Anglicanism and Ethnicity." In Bramadat and Seljak, *Christianity and Ethnicity in Canada*, 138–67.

Flynn, Tom, ed. *The New Encyclopedia of Unbelief.* Amherst, NY: Prometheus Books, 2007.

Forbes, Ernest R. *Challenging the Regional Stereotype: Essays on the 20th Century Maritimes.* Frederiction: Acadiensis Press, 1989.

Foster, Douglas Allen, et al. *Encyclopedia of the Stone Campbell Movement: Christian Church (Disciples of Christ).* S.v., Crossroads College. Grand Rapids: Wm. B. Eerdmans Publishing, 2004.

Fournier, Marcel. *Communisme et anticommunisme au Québec 1920–1950.* Montreal: Les Éditions coopératives Albert Saint-Martin, 1979.

Frank, David. *J.B. McLachlan: A Biography.* Toronto: J. Lorimer, 1999.

Frank, David, and Nolan Reilly. "The Emergence of the Socialist Movement in the Maritimes, 1899–1916." *Labour / Le Travail* (1979): 85–113.

Fraser, Blair. "Our Hush-Hush Censorship: How Books Are Banned." *Maclean's Magazine*, 15 December 1949, 24–5, 44.

Freud, Sigmund. *Die Zukunft einer Illusion.* Leipzig: Internationaler Psychoanalytischer Verlag, 1927.

Friskney, Janet B., and Carole Gerson. "Writers and the Market for Fiction and Literature." In Gerson and Michon, *History of the Book*, 131–8.

Fussell, Paul. *The Great War and Modern Memory*. New York: Oxford University Press, 1975.

Gagnon, Henri. *Les militants socialistes du Québec d'une époque à l'autre*. Saint-Lambert, QC: Les Éditions Héritage, 1985. http://www.pcq.qc.ca/Dossiers/PCQ/Histoire/LesMilitantsSocialistes.pdf.

Galston, Robert, et al. *A Manifest Presence: 100 Years at St. Margaret's*. Winnipeg: St Margaret's Anglican Church, 2010.

Gauvin, Marshall J. *The Heart of the Bible*. New York: Truth Seeker Company, 1921.

Gauvreau, Michael. *The Catholic Origins of Quebec's Quiet Revolution, 1931–1970*. Montreal and Kingston: McGill-Queen's University Press, 2005.

Gauvreau, Michael, and Nancy Christie. "'The World of the Common Man Is Filled with Religious Fervour': The Labouring People of Winnipeg and the Persistence of Revivalism, 1914–1925." In Rawlyk, *Aspects of the Canadian Evangelical Experience*, 337–50.

Gauvreau, Michael, and Ollivier Hubert. "Beyond Church History: Recent Developments in the History of Religion in Canada." In *The Churches and Social Order in Nineteenth- and Twentieth-Century Canada*, edited by Michael Gauvreau and Ollivier Hubert, 3–45. Montreal and Kingston: McGill-Queen's University Press, 2006.

Gershwin, George, DuBose Heyward, and Ira Gershwin. *Porgy and Bess*. New York: Gershwin Publishing, 1935.

Gerson, Carole, and Jacques Michon, eds. *History of the Book in Canada*, vol. 3, *1918–1980*. Toronto: University of Toronto Press, 2007.

Gibson, Lee. "Aikins, Sir James Albert Manning." In *Dictionary of Canadian Biography*, vol. 15. Toronto and Quebec: University of Toronto/Université Laval, 2005. http://www.biographi.ca/en/bio/aikins_james_albert_manning_15E.html.

Gidney, Catherine. *A Long Eclipse: The Liberal Protestant Establishment and the Canadian University, 1920–1970*. Montreal and Kingston: McGill-Queen's University Press, 2004.

Giordano, Gerard. *Twentieth-Century Textbook Wars: A History of Advocacy and Opposition*. New York: Peter Lang, 2003.

Godwin, George. *Why Stay We Here? Odyssey of a Canadian Officer in France in World War I*. London: Allan, 1930.

Goldsborough, Gordon. "Memorable Manitobans: Robert Dennis Richardson (1854–1946)." Winnipeg: Manitoba Historical Society, 2018. http://www.mhs.mb.ca/docs/people/richardson_rd.shtml.

Gordon, J. King. "A Christian Socialist in the 1930s." In *The Social Gospel in Canada: Papers of the Inter-Disciplinary Conference on the Social Gospel in Canada*, edited by Richard Allen, 122–53. Ottawa: National Museums of Canada, 1975.
Gossage, Peter, and J.I. Little. *An Illustrated History of Quebec*. Oxford: Oxford University Press, 2012.
Grant, John Webster. *A Profusion of Spires: Religion in Nineteenth-Century Ontario*. Toronto: University of Toronto Press, 1988.
Gray, James H. "The Canadian Anti-Christ." *Canadian Forum*, January 1935, 138–41.
– *The Roar of the Twenties*. Toronto: Macmillan of Canada, 1975.
– *The Winter Years: The Depression on the Prairies*. Toronto: Macmillan of Canada, 1966.
Gutkin, Mildred, and Harry Gutkin. *Profiles in Dissent: The Shaping of Radical Thought in the Canadian West*. Edmonton: NeWest Publishers Limited, 1997.
Guttman, Frank Myron. *The Devil from Saint-Hyacinthe: Senator Telesphore-Damien Bouchard, A Tragic Hero*. Bloomington, IN: iUniverse, 2009.
Guyou, Georges, and Élisée Reclus, "L'Anarchie et l'Église." *Le Supplément littéraire des Temps nouveaux* 3 (nos. 19–20), 158–61.
Hamelin, Jean, and Nicole Gagnon. *Histoire du catholicisme québécois: Le XXe siècle, tome 1, 1898–1940*. Montreal: Boréal Express, 1984.
Harrison, Charles Yale. *Generals Die in Bed*. New York: Morrow, 1930.
Hawke, J.T. *The Underwood-Marples Debate*. New York: D.M. Bennett, 1877.
Haykin, Michael A.G., and Ian Hugh Cleary. "'O God of Battles:' The Canadian Baptist Experience of the Great War." In Heath, *Canadian Churches*, 170–95.
Heath, Gordon L., ed. *Canadian Churches and the First World War*. Eugene, OR: Pickwick Publications, 2014.
Hemingway, Ernest. "A Clean, Well-Lighted Place." *Scribner's Magazine*, March 1933, 149–50.
Hindmarsh, D. Bruce. "The Winnipeg Fundamentalist Network, 1910–1940: The Roots of Transdenominational Evangelicalism." In Rawlyk, *Aspects of the Canadian Evangelical Experience*, 304–19.
Hobson, J.A. *Rationalism and Humanism*. London: Watts & Co., 1933.
Hobson, Suzanne. *Unbelief in Interwar Literary Culture: Doubting Moderns*. Oxford: Oxford University Press, 2021.
Horn, Michiel. *Academic Freedom in Canada: A History*. Toronto: University of Toronto Press, 1999.

- "'Free Speech Within the Law': The Letter of the Sixty-Eight Toronto Professors, 1931." *Ontario History* 72, no. 1 (March 1980): 27–48.
Horowitz, Gad. *Canadian Labour in Politics*. Toronto: University of Toronto Press, 1968.
Horton, Donald J. *André Laurendeau: French-Canadian Nationalist, 1912–1968*. Oxford: Oxford University Press, 1992.
Houle-Courcelles, Mathieu. *Sur les traces de l'anarchisme au Québec (1860–1960)*. Montreal: Lux, 2008.
House of Commons Debates. Volume 1, 1928 (10 February 1928).
Howe, Daniel Walker. *What Hath God Wrought: The Transformation of America, 1815–1848*. Oxford: Oxford University Press, 2007.
Howe, Maud. *A Challenge Answered – Atheism or Christ?* Toronto: Maud Howe, 1930.
- *Will Atheism Dominate the World?* Toronto: Maud Howe, 1931.
Huxley, Julian. *Religion Without Revelation*. New York: Harper & Brothers, 1927.
Isitt, Ben. "Elusive Unity: The Canadian Labor Party in British Columbia, 1924–1928." *BC Studies* 163 (Fall 2009): 33–64.
Jackson, Helen. *Convent Cruelties; or My Life in a Convent*. Detroit: H. Jackson, 1919.
Jackson, Samuel Macauley. *The Concise Dictionary of Religious Knowledge and Gazetteer*. New York: Christian Literature Company, 1889.
Jacoby, Susan. *Freethinkers: A History of American Secularism*. New York: Metropolitan Books, 2004.
Johnston, Russell. "The Early Trials of Protestant Radio, 1922–38." *Canadian Historical Review* 75, no. 3 (1994): 376–402.
Jordan, Mary V. *Survival: Labour's Trials and Tribulations in Canada*. Toronto: MacDonald House, 1975.
Joshi, S.T. "H.P. Lovecraft: The Fiction of Materialism." In Robillard, *American Supernatural Fiction*, 141–66.
Kaplan, William. *Everything That Floats: Pat Sullivan, Hal Banks, and the Seamen's Union of Canada*. Toronto: University of Toronto Press, 1987.
Karras, Ruth Mazo. *Unmarriages: Women, Men, and Sexual Unions in the Middle Ages*. Philadelphia: University of Pennsylvania Press, 2012.
Katerberg, William H. *Modernity and the Dilemma of North American Anglican Identities, 1880–1950*. Montreal and Kingston: McGill-Queen's University Press, 2001.
Kealey, Gregory S., and Reg Whitaker, eds. *RCMP Security Bulletins*. St John's: Canadian Committee on Labour History, 1992–99.

Kee, Kevin. *Revivalists: Marketing the Gospel in English Canada, 1884–1957*. Montreal and Kingston: McGill-Queen's University Press, 2006.

Keshen, Jeffrey A. *Propaganda and Censorship During Canada's Great War*. Edmonton: University of Alberta, 1996.

– *Saints, Sinners, and Soldiers: Canada's Second World War*. Vancouver: UBC Press, 2004.

Klassen, Pamela. "Radio Mind: Protestant Experimentalists on the Frontiers of Healing." *Journal of the American Academy of Religion* 75, no. 3 (2007): 651–83.

Knauss, Elizabeth. *The Rising Tide: A Novel Dealing with the Spread of Bolshevism and Atheism Throughout America*. New York: Christian Alliance Publishing Co., 1927.

Kolasky, John, ed. *Prophets and Proletarians: Documents on the History of the Rise and Decline of Ukrainian Communism in Canada*. Edmonton: Canadian Institute of Ukrainian Studies Press, 1990.

Krawchuk, Peter. *Interned Without Cause: The Internment of Canadian Antifascists During World War Two*. Winnipeg: Kobzar Publishing Company, 1985. http://www.socialisthistory.ca/Docs/CPC/WW2/IWC04.htm.

Lacombe, Sylvie. "French Canada: The Rise and Decline of a 'Church-Nation.'" *Quebec Studies* 48 (Fall 2009), 135–58.

Lafleur, Gustave. *L'Université ouvrière et ses dangers*. Montreal: Association catholique de la jeunesse canadienne, [1931].

Lamonde, Yvan. *Louise-Antoine Dessaulles, 1818–1895: un seigneur libéral et anticlerical*. Saint-Laurent: Fides, 1994.

Larivière, Claude. *Albert Saint-Martin, militant d'avant-garde (1865–1947)*. Laval: Éditions Coopératives Albert Saint-Martin, 1979.

Larson, Edward J. "The Scopes Trial in History and Legend." In *When Science and Christianity Meet*, edited by David C. Lindberg and Ronald L. Numbers, 245–64. Chicago: University of Chicago Press, 2003.

– *Summer for the Gods: The Scopes Trial and America's Continuing Debate over Science and Religion*. Cambridge, MA: Harvard University Press, 1997.

Leinwand, Gerald. *1927: High Tide of the 1920s*. New York: Basic Books, 2002.

Lévesque, Andrée. *Freethinker: The Life and Works of Éva Circé Côté*. Translated by Lazer Lederhendler. Toronto: Between the Lines, 2017.

– "Red Scares and Repression in Quebec, 1919–1939." In *Security, Dissent, and the Limits of Toleration in War and Peace, 1914–1939*,

edited by Barry Wright, Eric Tucker, and Susan Binnie, 290–323. Toronto: University of Toronto Press, 2015.
– "The Weakest Link: French-Canadian Communists Before 1940." Robert S. Kenny Lecture, University of Toronto, Thomas Fisher Rare Book Library, May 2008. https://fisher.library.utoronto.ca/events-exhibits/kenny-prize-and-lecture.
Lewis, Joseph. *The Tyranny of God*. New York: Freethought Press Association, 1921.
Lewis, Sinclair. *Elmer Gantry*. New York: Harcourt, Brace, 1927.
Lewthwaite, Susan. "Ethelbert Lionel Cross: Toronto's First Black Lawyer." In *The African Canadian Legal Odyssey: Historical Essays*, edited by Barrington Walker, 50–73. Toronto: University of Toronto Press, 2012.
Lindberg, David C., and Ronald L. Numbers, eds. *When Science and Christianity Meet*. Chicago: University of Chicago Press, 2003.
Lindsey, Ben, and Wainwright Evans. *The Companionate Marriage*. Garden City, NY: Garden City Publishing, 1927.
Linteau, Paul-André, René Durocher, and Jean-Claude Robert. *Quebec: A History, 1867–1929*. Translated by Robert Chodos. Toronto: James Lorimer, 1983.
Linteau, Paul-André, et al. *Quebec Since 1930*. Translated by Robert Chodos and Ellen Garmaise. Toronto: James Lorimer, 1991.
Livesay, Dorothy. *Right Hand Left Hand*. Erin, ON: Press Porcépic, 1977.
Lovecraft, H.P. "Facts Concerning the Late Arthur Jermyn and His Family." *The Wolverine*, no. 9, March 1921.
– *The Shadow Over Innsmouth*. Everett, PA: Visionary Publishing, 1936.
Ludlow, Peter. *The Canny Scot: Archbishop James Morrison of Antigonish*. Montreal and Kingston: McGill-Queen's University Press, 2015.
MacEachern, George. *George MacEachern, an Autobiography: The Story of a Cape Breton Labour Radical*. Edited by David Frank and Donald MacGillivray. Sydney, NS: University College of Cape Breton Press, 1987.
MacLean, Jenne. "Parrots, Picnics and Psychic Phenomena: The Feminism, Nationalism and Social Reform of Éva Circé-Côté in *Le Monde Ouvrier*'s Montreal, 1900–1940." MA thesis, Queen's University, 2000. https://www.collectionscanada.gc.ca/obj/s4/f2/dsk2/ftp03/MQ53008.pdf.
MacLeod, A. Donald. *W. Stanford Reid: An Evangelical Calvinist in the Academy*. Montreal and Kingston: McGill-Queen's University Press, 2004.

MacLeod, Wendell, Libbie Park, and Stanley Ryerson. *Bethune: The Montreal Years*. Toronto: James Lorimer, 1978.

Manley, John. "'Communists Love Canada!': The Communist Party of Canada, the 'People' and the Popular Front, 1933–1939." *Journal of Canadian Studies*, Winter 2002, 59–86.

Manseau, Caroline. "Etre digne de l'Esto Vir. Une exploration de la socialisation religieuse chez les acéjistes (1904–1931)." SCHEC: *Études d'histoire religieuse* 73 (2007), 49–60.

Marks, Lynne. *Infidels and the Damn Churches: Irreligion and Religion in Settler British Columbia*. Vancouver, BC: UBC Press, 2017.

Marsden, George M. *Fundamentalism and American Culture: The Shaping of Twentieth-Century Evangelicalism 1870–1925*. New York: Oxford University Press, 1980.

Marshall, David B. "Canadian Historians, Secularization, and the Problem of the Nineteenth Century." *Historical Studies: Canadian Catholic Historical Association* 60 (1993–94): 57–81.

– "'Khaki Has Become a Sacred Colour:' The Methodist Church and the Sanctification of World War One." In Heath, *Canadian Churches*, 102–32.

– *Secularizing the Faith: Canadian Protestant Clergy and the Crisis of Belief, 1850–1940*. Toronto: University of Toronto Press, 1992.

Masters, Donald Campbell. *Henry John Cody: An Outstanding Life*. Toronto: Dundurn Group, 1995.

Mathieu, Sarah-Jane. *North of the Color Line: Migration and Resistance in Canada, 1870–1955*. Chapel Hill: University of North Carolina Press, 2010.

Matter, M.J. *Histoire du Christianisme et de la Société Chrétienne*. 2nd ed. Paris: Firmin Didot Frères, 1838.

Mayr, Bill. "The Red Bishop." *Kenyon College Alumni Bulletin* 34, no. 1 (Fall 2011).

McCabe, Joseph. *The True Story of the Roman Catholic Church*. Girard, KS: Haldeman-Julius Publications, 1930.

McCallum, Todd. "'A Modern Weapon for Modern Man': Marxist Masculinity and the Social Practices of the One Big Union, 1919-1924." MA thesis, Simon Fraser University, 1995. https://core.ac.uk/download/pdf/56370962.pdf.

McCann, Gillian. *Vanguard of the New Age: The Toronto Theosophical Society, 1891–1945*. Montreal and Kingston: McGill-Queen's University Press, 2012.

McCollum, Vashti Cromwell. *One Woman's Fight*. Madison, WI: Freedom from Religion Foundation, 1993.
McEwen, Tom. *The Forge Glows Red: From Blacksmith to Revolutionary*. Toronto: Progress Books, 1974.
McKay, Colin. "Labour and the Technocrats." *Canadian Unionist* 149 (February 1933), 156–7.
McKay, Ian. *Reasoning Otherwise: Leftists and the People's Enlightenment in Canada, 1890–1920*. Toronto: Between the Lines, 2008.
McKillop, A.B. "Apostle of Reason: Some Notes on the Life of Marshall J. Gauvin." *Proceedings of the First Annual Archives Symposium*, 53–60. Winnipeg: Department of Archives and Special Collections, University of Manitoba, 1979.
– *A Disciplined Intelligence: Critical Inquiry and Canadian Thought in the Victorian Era*. Montreal and Kingston: McGill-Queen's University Press, 2001.
– *Matters of Mind: The University in Ontario, 1791–1951*. Toronto: University of Toronto Press, 1994.
McLaren, Angus and Arlene Tigar McLaren. *The Bedroom and the State: The Changing Practices and Politics of Contraception and Abortion in Canada, 1880–1997*. 2nd ed. Toronto: Oxford University Press Canada, 1997.
McLeod, Hugh. *The Religious Crisis of the 1960s*. Oxford: Oxford University Press, 2007.
– ed. *World Christianities, c.1914–c.2000*. Vol. 9 of *The Cambridge History of Christianity*. Cambridge: Cambridge University Press, 2006.
McLeod, Hugh, and Werner Ustof, eds. *The Decline of Christendom in Western Europe, 1750–2000*. Cambridge: Cambridge University Press, 2003.
McNaught, Kenneth. *A Prophet in Politics: A Biography of J.S. Woodsworth*. Toronto: University of Toronto Press, 1959.
Melton, J. Gordon, and Mark Vandebrake, eds. *Toward a Reasonable World: A History of Unbelief*. Waco: ISR Press, 2014.
Miller, J.R. *Shingwauk's Vision: A History of Native Residential Schools*. Toronto: University of Toronto Press, 1996.
Mills, Allen. *Fool for Christ: The Political Thought of J.S. Woodsworth*. Toronto: University of Toronto Press, 1991.
Moir, John S. *A History of Biblical Studies in Canada: A Sense of Proportion*. Chico, CA: Scholars Press, 1982.
Morley, J.T. *Secular Socialists: The CCF/NDP in Ontario, a Biography*. Montreal and Kingston: McGill-Queen's University Press, 1984.

Most, Johann. *Die Gottespest*. New York: Internationale Bibliothek, 1887.
Murphy, Terrence, and Roberto Perin, eds. *A Concise History of Christianity in Canada*. Oxford: Oxford University Press, 1996.
Nash, David. *Blasphemy in the Christian World: A History*. Oxford: Oxford University Press, 2007.
Naylor, James. *The Fate of Labour Socialism: The Co-operative Commonwealth Federation and the Dream of a Working-Class Future*. Toronto: University of Toronto Press, 2016.
– "'Not Reform, but the Replacing of Capitalism:' The Co-operative Commonwealth Federation in the 1930s." In *Party of Conscience: The CCF, the NDP, and Social Democracy in Canada*, edited by Roberta Lexier, Stephanie D. Bangarth, and Jon Weier, 1–21. Toronto: Between the Lines, 2018.
Newell, Peter E. *The Impossibilists: A Brief Profile of the Socialist Party of Canada*. London: Athena, 2008.
Noll, Mark. "Canadian Evangelicalism: A View from the United States." In Rawlyk, *Aspects of the Canadian Evangelical Experience*, 3–20.
– *What Happened to Christian Canada?* Vancouver: Regent College, 2007.
Norwood, Gilbert. "Elmer Gantry," *Canadian Forum* 7, no. 80 (May 1927), 242–5.
Numbers, Ronald. *The Creationists: From Scientific Creationism to Intelligent Design*. Expanded ed. Cambridge, MA: Harvard University Press, 2006.
Opp, James. *The Lord for the Body: Religion, Medicine, and Protestant Faith Healing in Canada, 1880–1930*. Montreal and Kingston: McGill-Queen's University Press, 2005.
Oreopoulous, Philip. *Canadian Compulsory School Laws and their Impact on Educational Attainment and Future Earnings*. Analytical Studies Branch Research Paper Series (Statistics Canada), no. 251 (May 2005).
Osler, William. *Science and Immortality*. Cambridge, MA: Harvard University Press, 1904.
Ouellet, Fernand. *Louis Joseph Papineau: A Divided Soul*. Ottawa: Canadian Historical Association, 1961.
– "Papineau, Louis-Joseph." In *Dictionary of Canadian Biography*, vol. 10. Toronto and Quebec: University of Toronto/Université Laval, 2017. http://www.biographi.ca/en/bio.php?id_nbr=5203.
Owen, Alex. *The Darkened Room: Women, Power, and Spiritualism in Late Victorian England*. Chicago: University of Chicago Press, 2004.
Parrish, Wayne W. "What is Technocracy?" *New Outlook* (November 1932), 13–18.

Patrick, Jeremy. "Canadian Blasphemy Law in Context: Press, Legislative, and Public Reactions." *Annual Survey of International and Comparative Law*, no. 16 (2010): 129–63.
– "Not Dead, Just Sleeping: Canada's Prohibition on Blasphemous Libel as a Case Study in Obsolete Legislation." *University of British Columbia Law Review* 41, no. 2 (2008): 193–248.
Patterson, Robert S. "Society and Education during the Wars and Their Interlude: 1914–1945." In *Canadian Education: A History*, edited by J. Donald Wilson, Robert M. Stamp, and Louis-Philippe Audet, 360–84. Scarborough: Prentice-Hall of Canada, 1970.
Pedley, James H. *Only This: A War Retrospect*. Ottawa: Graphic Publishers, 1927.
Perin, Roberto. "French-Speaking Canada from 1840." In Murphy and Perin, *Concise History of Christianity*, 190–260.
Peris, Daniel. *Storming the Heavens: The Soviet League of the Militant Godless*. Ithaca, NY: Cornell University Press, 1998.
Phillips, Paul T. *The Controversialist: An Intellectual Life of Goldwin Smith*. Westport, CT: Praeger, 2002.
Pilon, Gaston. *Du Communisme et Catholicisme*. Montreal: L'Apostolat populaire, 1935.
Pitsula, James M. *Keeping Canada British: The Ku Klux Klan in 1920s Saskatchewan*. Vancouver: UBC Press, 2013.
Pratt, Douglas Frederick. "William Ivens, M.A., B.D., and the Winnipeg Labor Church." BA thesis, St Andrew's College, 1962.
Rationalist Society of Canada. *Faith or Fact? The Case for Rationalism*. Toronto: Rationalist Society of Canada, n.d. [1933?].
Rawlyk, George. "A.L. McCrimmon, H.P. Whidden, T.T. Shields, Christian Education, and McMaster University." In *Canadian Baptists and Christian Higher Education*, edited by G.A. Rawlyk, 31–62. Montreal and Kingston: McGill-Queen's University Press, 1988.
– *Champions of the Truth: Fundamentalism, Modernism, and the Maritime Baptists*. Montreal and Kingston: McGill-Queen's University Press, 1990.
Rawlyk, George, ed. *Aspects of the Canadian Evangelical Experience*. Montreal and Kingston: McGill-Queen's University Press, 1997.
Reiter, Ester. *A Future Without Hate or Need: The Promise of the Jewish Left in Canada*. Toronto: Between the Lines, 2016.
"Révérend Père Archange Godbout, 1886–1960." *Au fil des ans: Bulletin de la Société historique de Bellechasse* 5, no. 3 (September 1993). Available at http://www.shbellechasse.com/aufildesans/05_03.pdf.

Rifkind, Candida. *Comrades & Critics: Women, Literature and the Left in 1930s Canada*. Toronto: University of Toronto Press, 2009.

Rioux, Jean-Roch. "Guibord, Joseph." In *Dictionary of Canadian Biography*, vol. 9, Toronto and Quebec: University of Toronto/Université Laval, 1976. http://www.biographi.ca/en/bio.php?id_nbr=4470.

Roberts, Barbara. *A Reconstructed World: A Feminist Biography of Gertrude Richardson*. Montreal and Kingston: McGill-Queen's University Press, 1996.

– *Whence They Came: Deportation from Canada 1900–1935*. Ottawa: University of Ottawa Press, 1988.

Robillard, Douglas. *American Supernatural Fiction: From Edith Wharton to the Weird Tales Writers*. New York: Garland Publishing, 1996.

Rochester, Maxine K. "Bringing Librarianship to Rural Canada in the 1930s: Demonstrations by Carnegie Corporation of New York." *Libraries & Culture* 30, no. 4 (Fall 1995) 366–90.

Rollieu, Jean. *Gaston Pilon*. Montreal: L'Apostolat populaire, 1934.

Royle, Edward, ed. *The Infidel Tradition from Paine to Bradlaugh*. London: Macmillan, 1976.

– *Radicals, Secularists, and Republicans: Popular Freethought in Britain, 1866–1915*. Manchester: Manchester University Press, 1980.

– *Victorian Infidels: The Origins of the British Secularist Movement, 1791–1866*. Lanham, MD: Rowman & Littlefield Publishers, 1974.

Rudin, Ronald. "Revisionism and the Search for a Normal Society: A Critique of Recent Quebec Historical Writing." *Canadian Historical Review* 73, no. 1 (1992): 30–61.

Russell, Bertrand. *Why I Am Not a Christian*. London: Watts, 1927.

Russell, Dora. *The Right to Be Happy*. New York: Harper & Brothers, 1927.

Rutherford, Paul. *The Making of the Canadian Media*. Toronto: McGraw-Hill Ryerson, 1978.

Ryan, Oscar, et al. *Eight Men Speak: A Play*. Ottawa: University of Ottawa Press, 2013.

Ryrie, Alec. *Unbelievers: An Emotional History of Doubt*. Cambridge, MA: Harvard University Press, 2019.

Saint-Martin, Albert. *Sandwiches "à la shouashe."* Montreal: Spartakus, 1932.

Salutin, Rick. *Kent Rowley: The Organizer, a Canadian Union Life*. Toronto: James Lorimer, 1980.

Sangster, Joan. *Dreams of Equality: Women on the Canadian Left, 1920–1950*. Toronto: McClelland & Stewart, 1989.

Schmidt, Leigh Eric. *The Church of Saint Thomas Paine: A Religious History of American Secularism*. Princeton: Princeton University Press, 2021.
– *Village Atheists: How America's Unbelievers Made Their Way in a Godly Nation*. Princeton: Princeton University Press, 2016.
Schwartz, Laura. *Infidel Feminism: Secularism, Religion and Women's Emancipation, England 1830–1914*. Manchester: Manchester University Press, 2012.
Schweitzer, Richard. *The Cross and the Trenches: Religious Faith and Doubt among British and American Great War Soldiers*. Westport, CT: Praeger, 2003.
Seary, V.P., and Gilbert Paterson, *The Story of Civilization*. Toronto and Halifax: Ryerson Press, 1934.
Seibel, George. "Atheism Succumbs to Doubt." *The American Mercury*, December 1932, 424–31.
Simmons, Christina. *Making Marriage Modern: Women's Sexuality from the Progressive Era to World War II*. Oxford: Oxford University Press, 2009.
Soule, George. "Technocracy: Good Medicine or a Bedtime Story?" *OBU Bulletin*, 5 January 1933, 4–5.
Speisman, Stephen A. *The Jews of Toronto: A History to 1937*. Toronto: McClelland & Stewart, 1979.
Steeves, Dorothy G. *The Compassionate Rebel: Ernest Winch and the Growth of Socialism in Western Canada*. Vancouver: J.J. Douglas, 1977.
Stubbs, Lewis St. George. *A Majority of One: The Life and Times of Lewis St. George Stubbs*. Winnipeg: Queenston House, 1983.
Sturk, John N. *Prospectus of the Looting of a Legacy: A Religious Tragedy: The Current Teachings of the United Church of Canada Versus Her Statutory Creed*. Winnipeg: Berean Bible and Tract Depot, [1931?].
Sutherland, Fraser. *The Monthly Epic: A History of Canadian Magazines, 1789–1989*. Markham: Fitzhenry & Whiteside, 1989.
Szasz, Ferenc M. "William B. Riley and the Fight Against Teaching of Evolution in Minnesota." *Minnesota History* 41, no. 5 (Spring 1969), 201–16.
Thiessen, Joel. *The Meaning of Sunday: The Practice of Belief in a Secular Age*. Montreal and Kingston: McGill-Queen's University Press, 2015.
Thiessen, Joel, and Sarah Wilkins-Laflamme. *None of the Above: Nonreligious Identity in the US and Canada*. Regina: University of Regina Press, 2020.

Thompson, John H., and Allen Seager. *Canada 1922–1939: Decades of Discord*. Toronto: McClelland & Stewart, 1985.

Trautmann, Frederic. *The Voice of Terror: A Biography of Johann Most*. Westport, CT: Greenwood Press, 1980.

Tribe, David. *100 Years of Freethought*. London: Elek, 1967.

Trollinger, William Vance, Jr. *God's Empire: William Bell Riley and Midwestern Fundamentalism*. Madison: University of Wisconsin Press, 1990.

Vance, Jonathan F. *Death So Noble: Memory, Meaning, and the First World War*. Vancouver: UBC Press, 1997.

Van Die, Marguerite. "Protestants, the Liberal State, and the Practice of Politics: Revisiting R.J. Fleming and the 1890s Toronto Streetcar Controversy." *Journal of the Canadian Historical Association* (New Series) 24, no. 1, 89–129.

Wagar, Samuel Eldon Charles. "Theosophical Socialists in the 1920s Okanagan: Jack Logie's Social Issues Summer Camps." MA thesis, Simon Fraser University, 2005.

Walker, Barrington, ed. *The African Canadian Legal Odyssey: Historical Essays*. Toronto: University of Toronto Press, 2012.

Weisbord, Merrily. *The Strangest Dream: Canadian Communists, the Spy Trials, and the Cold War*. Toronto: Lester & Orpen Dennys, 1983.

Wentzell, Tyler. *Not for King or Country: Edward Cecil-Smith, the Communist Party of Canada, and the Spanish Civil War*. Toronto: University of Toronto Press, 2020.

Westfall, William. *Two Worlds: The Protestant Culture of Nineteenth-Century Ontario*. Montreal and Kingston: McGill-Queen's University Press, 1989.

Whitaker, Reg. "Chameleon on a Changing Background: The Politics of Censorship in Canada." In *Interpreting Censorship in Canada*, edited by Allan C. Hutchinson and Klaus Peterson, 19–39. Toronto: University of Toronto Press, 1992.

Whitmarsh, Tim. *Battling the Gods: Atheism in the Ancient World*. New York: Knopf, 2015.

Whyte, Bert. *Champagne and Meatballs: Adventures of a Canadian Communist*. Edmonton: AU Press, 2011.

Williams, Roger L. *Henri Rochefort: Prince of the Gutter Press*. New York: Charles Scribner's Sons, 1966.

Wilson, Edwin H. *The Genesis of a Humanist Manifesto*. Amherst, NY: Humanist Press, 1995.

Withrow, Oswald Charles Joseph. *Shackling the Transgressor: An Indictment of the Canadian Penal System.* Toronto: Thomson Nelson & Sons, 1933.

Woodsworth, James Shaver. *Following the Gleam: A Modern Pilgrim's Progress – to Date!* Ottawa: Woodsworth, 1926.

Wright, Robert. *A World Mission: Canadian Protestantism and the Quest for a New International Order, 1919–1939.* Montreal and Kingston: McGill-Queen's University Press, 1991.

Young, David. "The Macmillan Company of Canada in the 1930s." *Journal of Canadian Studies* 30, no. 3 (Fall 1995): 117–33.

Index

4A. *See* American Association for the Advancement of Atheism

Adams, Robert Chamblet, 170–1, 283n11
agnosticism, 5, 10, 19–20, 217
American Association for the Advancement of Atheism, 10, 126, 162, 160
anticlericalism, 16, 168–71, 178
Association humanitaire, 167, 176–78, 186, 194
atheism, 5, 164, 223, 227n8;
  in Canada, 8, 151–3, 209;
  on the left, 27, 59, 206, 217.
  See also New Atheism
autodidacticism, 41, 92–3, 98, 127, 221

Bible, 51, 110, 116–17; higher criticism and, 51, 98, 213; unbelievers' critiques of, 10, 27, 39
biblical criticism. *See* Bible: higher criticism and
Bland, Salem, 133–4, 139, 161–2
blasphemous libel, 31–2, 233n116, 254n4, 263n102; attempted repeal of law, 114, 116–19; prosecution of Pilon, 190, 192–3; prosecution of Saint-Martin, 187–90; prosecution of Sterry, 97, 99–100, 105–11; Sterry's appeal, 115
Bonnell, John S., 53–5, 240n61, 241n70
Bradlaugh, Charles, 9, 119, 253n69
British Columbia: levels of religiosity and unbelief in, 199–201, 208, 218

Canada: as Christian nation, 8, 22, 122, 153; religiosity compared with United States, 8, 148; status of unbelievers in, 221–5
Canadian Christian Crusade (CCC): elite support for, 158; formation of, 154–5; later years, 162–3; membership, 155–7; political alignment of, 162
Canadian Secular Society (Vancouver), 202–4
Cassidy, Harry, 207–8
Catholicism, 18–19, 23, 190–1, 193–4; in Quebec 167–8, 170–1;

provision of social welfare, 177, 285n47; social Catholicism, 178-9
Christian Inquirer, 97-9, 254n6; "the God of the Jews" section, 118-19, 259n58
Christendom, 7-8; in Canada, 122, 225; in Ontario, 153, 166; in Quebec, 168, 198
churches, Canadian, 18-19; in British Columbia, 199-200; in Manitoba, 86-8, 94; in Nova Scotia, 208-9, 210; in Quebec, 167-8, 171
Coatsworth, Emerson, 108-11, 141-2, 144, 150, 156
Communist Party of Canada: approach to religion, 27-8, 182, 196; official persecution of, 141-2, 184, 198; and Popular Front, 68-9, 138, 182; relationship to Université ouvrière, 174, 177-8, 181-2, 193, 195
companionate marriage, 30, 146, 232n108
Cooke, A.E., 201, 203, 293n20
Co-operative Commonwealth Federation (CCF), 49, 92, 138-40, 222, 238n43
Crerar, Duff, 14-15
Cross, E. Lionel, 102-3, 141; campaign against KKK, 140; defence of Sterry, 99, 104-5, 107-11, 114-16, 257n34; as rationalist, 102, 131, 268n39-40, 276n150
Curry, William J., 203, 204-6
customs and excise: blocking skeptical literature, 32-4

Darrow, Clarence, 25-6, 104-5, 134-5
Dawkins, Richard, 3, 247n158, 254n8
deism, 5, 169
Dennison, William, 137-8, 139, 272n86, 272n88
doubt, religious, 14, 153, 158, 172, 180; among the clergy, 23
Draper, Denis (chief constable), 141, 143-4, 146-7, 150, 155

Elmer Gantry. See Lewis, Sinclair
Enlightenment, 5, 9, 169
evangelicalism, 26; in Toronto, 124, 142, 154-8, 160-4; in Winnipeg, 46-7, 237n25, 237n29
evolution, 31, 58-9, 161-2; debates on, 46-8, 132-4, 196, 206; lectures on, 40, 134, 203, 205-6; opposition to teaching of, 58, 209-16. *See also* Scopes trial

faith healing, 201-2
Fillmore, Roscoe, 214-16
First World War, 13-14, 22, 82, 84; attitudes of soldiers, 14-15; attitudes of veterans, 18, 19; books by veterans of, 15-18; chaplains, 14, 16
free speech struggle (Toronto), 124, 141-5
freethought, 5, 10, 39, 41-2, 170-1. *See also* rationalism; secularism
French-Canadians: and anticlericalism, 169-72; and the Catholic Church 22, 23, 167-8, 178-80, 182

fundamentalism, 46, 223, 231n83; in Nova Scotia, 210–11; in Toronto, 155–6, 158, 163–4, 282n235; in Winnipeg, 46–8, 72

Gauvin, Marshall: childhood and teen years, 38–9; conflict over newspaper advertisements, 52–4; conversion to freethought, 39, 42; debates 37–8, 43, 47–8; and fundamentalists, 46–8; later years, 71–2; lecture topics, 42–4, 53–4, 55, 56–7; lecturing style, 42, 55, 88; and modernists, 50–5; move to Winnipeg, 40, 57–8; Popular Front activities, 67–8; and radical Christians, 49–50; relation to communism, 67–71, 73; relation to One Big Union, 57–8, 60–7, 73; views on Marxism, 60, 62–5; views on socialism, 39, 56–7, 71
Globe (Toronto newspaper): editorial stance on unbelief, 143–7, 152, 158, 164–5; support for fundamentalism, 158
Great Depression, 225: in Montreal, 176–7; in Toronto, 137, 141, 145, 150; in Winnipeg, 55, 66–7, 71, 73, 92–3; in Vancouver, 206
Great War. *See* First World War

Haldeman-Julius, Emanuel, 145–7, 234n118, 276n136
Henderson, Rose, 135, 221, 270n69, 271n83, 284n24
Holyoake, George, 9, 137
Howe, Maud, 155, 158–63

humanism, 5, 43–4, 236n16, 270n72; post–Second World War, 220–1
Huxley, Julian, 44, 217–18, 300n110

Ilsley, James, 32–3, 222
Indigenous people, 19, 24–5, 201, 293n13
Ingersoll, Robert G., 10, 39, 72, 124, 139
Institut canadien, 169–70
Isserman, Ferdinand, 107, 113–14, 116–17, 264n119

Jews, 23–4, 81, 87–8, 231n77, 259n58
Jordan, A. McKay, 202–4
Judaism, 18–19, 23–4, 188, 231n79

Kerr, Fredrick William, 53–4, 72, 235n4
King, W.L. Mackenzie, 33, 68, 116
Ku Klux Klan, 22, 57, 81, 140, 215, 275

Labor Church, 49, 86, 238n41
Laing, Jean, 137–8, 139, 165, 271n83
Lapointe, Ernest, 33, 222; on blasphemous libel debate, 116–18, 263n105
Laurendeau, André, 171–2, 283n20
Leavens, Bertram: debates, 131–2, 135–6, 139; early years, 127–8; lecturing, 129, 131, 138–9; political activities, 138–40
Lewis, Sinclair, 30, 114
Liberal Party of Canada, 26, 222

MacDonald, Charles, 214–15
Manitoba: unbelievers in, 40, 74. *See also* Winnipeg Rationalist Society
Marks, Lynne, xv, 85, 201
Marxism: criticism of, 60, 64–5; and unbelief: 12–13, 28, 62–3, 200, 245n122
McCabe, Joseph: in Toronto, 132–4, 157; and *The True Story of the Roman Catholic Church*, 191; in Winnipeg, 40, 46–7, 49, 58–9, 64–5
McKillop, A.B., 23, 70–1, 235n7
McLeod, Hugh, 7–8
Mesplet, Fleury, 169
modernism (theology), 50–1, 53, 120, 223, 241n76
Murphy, E.J., 107–10, 189, 267n33

New Atheism, 3–4, 72, 225, 247n158
Nova Scotia: evolution controversy in, 209–16, 218; unbelievers in, 208–9, 212–16

One Big Union (OBU) (Winnipeg), 40, 57–60; relationship with Gauvin, 60–7

Paine, Thomas, 5, 9–10
Pilon, Gaston, 175–6, 179, 190–2; conversion to Catholicism, 193–4; prosecution of, 193
Price, Charles S., 201–2, 207–8

Quebec: as local Christendom, 167–8; religion in, 167–8, 171; repression of unbelievers in, 171–2, 197–8; unbelief in 168–72, 196–7. *See also* Saint-Martin, Albert; Université ouvrière

radio, 10, 55, 71, 230n68, 241n75
rationalism, 5–6, 9–10, 20, 136; in Vancouver, 204–7. *See also* freethought; Gauvin, Marshall; Rationalist Society of Canada; secularism; Winnipeg Rationalist Society
Rationalist Society of Canada (Toronto): American contacts, 126, 130, 131, 145–8; debates, 131–2; demise, 140; formation and incorporation, 125–7; lecture schedule, 129–30, 131, 134, 135–40; leftward political turn, 136–40; soap-box lecturing, 127, 129, 274n112; street meetings dispersed by police, 143–5, 148–50. *See also* Leavens, Bertram; Styles, William
Riley, William Bell, 46–7, 133, 237n28–9
Ryerson, Stanley, 176, 181–2
Russell, R.B., 40, 49, 57–9, 65–6, 89–90

Saint-Martin, Albert: and anarchism 179–80, 195; anticlerical activities, 175–7, 179–82, 184–6; attacked by fascists, 188; and the Communist Party, 174, 177–8; early years 173–4; later years, 195; political activities 173–5, 177–8, 186–7, 195; prosecution of, 187–90, 194; *Sandwiches à la shouashe* pamphlet, 185–6.

Scopes trial, 25–6, 46, 209–10, 223, 231n82; compared with Sterry trial, 112–13
Second World War, 220
secularism, 5–6, 9, 250n24. *See also* freethought; rationalism
secularization, 7–8, 11–12, 94
Smith, Goldwin, 12, 98, 254n10
socialism: and Albert Saint-Martin, 173–5, 176–8, 182, 195; and Marshall Gauvin, 38–9, 56–71, 73; in Nova Scotia, 214–17; and Rationalist Society of Canada, 135–41; in relation to unbelief, 9–10, 12–13, 216–17, 222, 225; and William Curry, 204–6; and Winnipeg Rationalist Society, 91–2. *See also* Communist Party of Canada; Co-operative Commonwealth Federation (CCF)
Socialist Party of Canada, 12–13, 92, 173, 200, 204
Steiner, Franklin, 130–1, 147–8, 224
Sterry, Ernest V.: appeal in blasphemous libel case, 115; arrest, 99–100; blasphemous libel case and trial, 103–11; and *Christian Inquirer*, 97–9; early life, 100–2; and Joseph McCabe, 132; later years, 121; lecturing, 134; political views, 102; punishment, 111; trial for theft, 103
Story of Civilization, The, 209–10, 215, 218
Stubbs, Lewis St. George, 57
Sturk, John, 37–8, 47–8, 64, 72
Styles, William, 127–8, 135, 139, 145; lecturing, 129, 130–1, 139–40

Toronto: as evangelical stronghold, 142, 144, 154, 166; unbelievers in, 124–5. *See also* Rationalist Society of Canada
Toronto Star, 107, 222
Truth Seeker, 32–3, 39, 71–2, 234nn121–2

unbelief: among Canadian Jews, 23–4; as concept, 5–6; among First Nations, 24–5; among French-Canadian Catholics, 23. *See also* agnosticism; atheism; deism; freethought; humanism; rationalism; secularism
unbelief in literature: American, 30–1; blocked by Canadian customs, 32–3; Canadian, 29
unbelievers: connections between, 224; economic class of, 12, 34, 88–91, 158, 224; gender categories of, 20, 77–8, 94; as outsiders, 31, 148; paranoia about, 21
United States, 8, 30, 224; freethought tradition, 10, 42; reaction to Sterry case, 100, 112–13; as threat to Canada, 8
Université ouvrière, 167, 172–7, 179–81, 182–3, 195–8; attacks on, 183–4, 187; closure of, 194, government persecution of, 184, 186; literature distributed by, 179–80
University of Toronto, 120, 278n176; professors' letter on free speech, 147; *Varsity* editorial, 151–3, 156

Vancouver, 201–8

Watts, Charles, 124, 250n24
Winnipeg: subcultures of, 40. *See also* Winnipeg Rationalist Society
Winnipeg Rationalist Society (later Winnipeg Humanist Society): age of members, 78–9; class makeup of members, 74–6; employment or profession of members, 88–91; ethnic makeup of members, 81–2; gender makeup of members, 77–8; members' country of origin, 80; political affiliations of members, 91–2; relationship to One Big Union, 74–5; religious denominations of members, 82–8
Withrow, Oswald, 129, 138
Woodsworth, James Shaver, 49–50, 238n44; attempt to repeal law of blasphemous libel, 114–20